THE LIFE OF JOHN BRIGHT

JOHN BRIGHT

FROM A PHOTOGRAPH TAKEN OF HIM IN THE ATTITUDE IN WHICH HE USUALLY SPOKE

THE LIFE OF
JOHN BRIGHT

BY

GEORGE MACAULAY TREVELYAN

LATE FELLOW OF TRINITY COLLEGE, CAMBRIDGE

BOSTON AND NEW YORK
HOUGHTON MIFFLIN COMPANY
1925

First Published . . . *May 1913*
Reprinted . . . . . *July 1913*
,, ... *September 1913*
,, ... *September 1913*
,, ... *December 1913*
,, ... *December 1913*
,, ... *September 1914*
New Edition . . . . *May 1925*

Printed in Great Britain by T. and A. Constable Ltd.
at the University Press, Edinburgh

AUTHOR'S PREFACE

The pleasure of writing a biography is dependent on three things: the sympathy of the biographer for his subject; the interest of the new material which he has to handle; and his relations to those who have honoured him by trusting to him the memory they revere. In all three respects I have been most fortunate, and wish to express my gratitude to the family and relations of John Bright, who have smoothed the path for me by forbearance, by encouragement, and by much active help.

To the very many persons who have sent letters of John Bright, or contributed other documents or information, either to Mr. John Albert Bright in former years, or more recently to myself, I offer the most sincere thanks in his name and in my own. They are too numerous for me to make acknowledgments separately to all. But documents printed in the course of the volume will indicate the identity of some at least of these benefactors.

My debt to the author of the *Lives* of Cobden and of Gladstone may be traced on half the pages of this volume.

If in some places I seem to speak with a personal intimacy of events that occurred ten years before I was born, the reader may bear in mind that my father entered the House of Commons in 1865—the last General Election held under the auspices of Palmerston. That was the great Parliament which, after Palmerston's death, rejected the more limited Reform Bill of the year 1866 and passed the larger measure of 1867. My father, from his first entrance into the House of Commons, saw much of Mr. Bright, who treated him with the free kindness of a great man to a young friend and admirer. It is to this source that I owe many reminiscences of those days, too recent as yet to have been completely overtaken by the slow foot of history, but already too far away for the recollections of most of our political veterans.

Chelsea, *April* 1913.

CONTENTS

SOME BOOKS ON JOHN BRIGHT

C. A. Vince. *John Bright* in 'The Victorian Era Series.' 1898.

For aids to a conception of Bright's place in our political evolution, and of the character of his oratory, I am much indebted to Mr. Vince.

G. Barnett Smith. *The Life and Speeches of John Bright, M.P.* 1882.

Barry O'Brien. *John Bright, a Monograph.* 1910.

William Robertson. *Life and Times of Rt. Hon. John Bright.* Rochdale, local: republished by Mr. Fisher Unwin.

J. Travis Mills. *John Bright.* 1893.
A small monograph based on some personal knowledge.

The Speeches of the Rt. Hon. John Bright, Thorold Rogers. 2 vols., 1869.

Public Addresses of John Bright, Thorold Rogers. 1879.

The Public Letters of Rt. Hon. John Bright, H. J. Leech. 1885.

I have benefited much from five volumes of cuttings of Bright's speeches, etc., from 1860 onwards, made by Mr. William Wright, who kindly placed them at my disposal.

'WE feel that Mr. Bright is entitled to a higher eulogy than any that could be due to intellect or any that could be due to success. Of mere success he was indeed a conspicuous example; in intellect he may lay claim to a most distinguished place; but the character of the man lay deeper than his intellect, deeper than his eloquence, deeper than anything that can be described or seen on the surface, and the supreme eulogy which is his due I apprehend to be this, that he elevated political life to a higher elevation, and to a loftier standard, and that he has thereby bequeathed to his country the character of a statesman which can be made the subject not only of admiration, and not only of gratitude, but of reverential contemplation.'

MR. GLADSTONE *in the House of Commons, March* 29, 1889.

INTRODUCTION

How clear-cut is the sturdy image evoked by those two blunt Saxon syllables, 'John Bright!' Once the rallying-cry of the masses seeking enfranchisement—the trump of doom to Whig and Tory in possession—the name in memory has since become the symbol of an honest man in politics, of a strong, kind face framed in venerable white hair. But to no one have the words 'John Bright' ever suggested change or hesitation, sophistry or self-interest. His views of peace and war, of Church and State, of trade and freedom, the same throughout the half-century of his public life, are as limpid and resistant as a block of crystal. If the language in which he set them forth to his countrymen often surpassed the more elaborate orations of his great compeers, it was by reason of a strong simplicity, learnt neither in academies nor senates, but springing direct from man's common experience on earth, and reaching thence straight upwards into the sphere of faultless and noble literature. His voice had a bell-like clearness; in the largest hall he never strained, and scarcely seemed to raise it. The sound of it was music and poetry. He was singular among orators for his absence of gesture: there he stood foursquare, and sometimes half raised his arm. His oncoming was as the surge of the full swollen tide, not of the sea in storm; he awed his listeners by the calm of his passion, a terrible steed restrained by a yet stronger hand. Thus he uttered his plain man's prophecy to his fellow-citizens, bidding them keep the paths of peace and freedom, righteousness and good sense, when statesmen and diplomats led them, as ever, astray.

He flattered no one, great or small, man or woman, in politics or in private life, but always spoke his thought. 'Thou must 'not mind all the fault John finds with thee,' wrote his sister, 'as he makes no scruple to say the *very* worst he can to our 'faces. But in justice to his character, I must say he says 'very little if anything against his friends, or enemies either, 'behind their backs; unless it be touching the aristocracy and 'the clergy, and to these he would be glad to make known his 'opinions concerning them any way opportunity may offer.' So wrote his sister Priscilla to his sister-in-law, Margaret Priestman, in the early 'forties, in the middle of the Corn Law struggle. The words remained true of him till his dying day. Only a deep and tender humanity of disposition could make so strict a truth-teller a tolerable member of society; and John Bright was not only tolerated but loved. Any defect in subtlety or want of understanding of the idiosyncrasies of others was far outweighed by his sympathy with the broad human joys and sorrows, the common weal and woe, the great homely things of love and death, which drew men and women to this most formidable giant of their time with a personal affection, quite alien from mere political gratitude. Though he appeared the simplest man who ever played a part in the annals of our island, the union in him of two rival simplicities renders him, in one sense, a strange, almost mysterious being: for the hard-hitting and implacable champion of truth and right was also a most compassionate lover of his kind. In him were blended the Old Testament and the New, the two indispensable contradictories, that man must learn to reconcile in his breast, or else remain till doomsday the thing he is. By careful search some rudiments of these two opposites can be found in each of us, but in none did they come to such double perfection as in John Bright.

Be the lake waters never so clear, if they are deep enough the eye is lost at length in their darkness. Deep in Bright's heart there lies always something unseen, something reserved and solitary. Although he was a popular hero, and a man so sociable that he never travelled by train but he drew into conversation his chance carriage-companions, though he was always happy and tender and talkative when wife or child or friend were near, and was formidable, not through his silence but through his sayings—yet the presence of an inner life of deep feeling and meditation could be felt as the moving power in all he did. He never tired of the sight of mountain and stream, or of the sound of Milton and the Bible passages. Some, from the heights of a superior culture, have condemned Bright as middle-class in mind and soul, a Philistine interested in cotton and the ballot, in whom the sight of Oxford spires would evoke only some surly comment on the laws excluding dissenters from the privileges of the University. It was, indeed, his one boast, when at length he was drawn an unwilling captive into the Cabinet, that he still 'dwelt among his own people.' But middle-class is not always second-rate: Bright was a

Lancashire man, and he was also a Friend, and the Friends are a spiritual aristocracy. He practised the silence of his sect, and drew thence the strength of his soul, the purity of his heart, and the quality of his speech.

Such a man could not have ruled the country from Downing Street, or led the House of Commons from the Treasury bench. He could not have consented to the compromises demanded of those who wield the power of State. In December 1868, at the age of fifty-seven, he first took office. But it is the previous thirty years of his life, from his first connection with the Anti-Corn Law League to the passing of the second Reform Bill, that constitute the real life of Bright. Save for his friend Cobden, he would afford the unique instance in our history of a member of Parliament in no connection with any official party, exercising an immense influence on the thoughts and hearts of his fellow-countrymen. That personal influence covered the whole range of political action and touched on all the main topics of the day; but the chief incidents of his story are the Corn Law agitation, the Crimean War, the American Civil War, and the winning of the franchise for the working men. In the first of these controversies Bright served under Cobden as his chief lieutenant; during the Crimea he fought at his side as an equal; but the American and the franchise questions were Bright's own, in which Cobden in the one case followed the initiative of his friend, and in the other remained for all practical purposes neutral. Bright won the working classes the vote, by long years of single-handed agitation which concentrated on his head the hatred and scorn of the upper class and of the official world, and the devoted loyalty of the artisans, who for a while regarded him as their sole political champion. At length, after Palmerston's death in 1865, Gladstone in three eventful years reconstituted the Liberal party, no longer as a Whig party but as a party of progress and democracy, sworn to carry Bright's principles into effect, and in the first instance to enfranchise the working classes. Then there followed in rapid succession the Franchise Act of 1867, which Disraeli indeed introduced, but which Bright and Gladstone compelled him to make effective; the disestablishment of the Irish Church; the Irish Land Act; the Ballot Act; and a host of other reforms in that great period of Liberal fruition, which Bright had prepared by thirty years of guerilla warfare carried on from the public platform and the benches below the gangway, in defiance alike of Whigs and of Tories.

The life-task of the great agitator was now fulfilled. He

never took up another cause as his own ; he never again went forth to rouse the land. His personal popularity even with those who had most reviled him when he was in active service, showed that he had in effect retired. He entered the Cabinet and disappeared from the forefront of political life. Seldom, indeed, has any public man, after labouring long years in the wilderness, seen so many of the reforms which he has urged placed upon the Statute Book. Only in the matter of Foreign Policy did he feel, as he showed when he resigned over the bombardment of Alexandria (1882), that his countrymen were still opposed to his views. In his later years he found no great objects to pursue ; and his second illness (1870), nearly coinciding as it did with the commencement of his official career, took away much of his vital force, so that those who heard him in Parliament only during the 'seventies and 'eighties could not realise his former greatness. But never was veteran more loved and honoured : the esteem in which he was held by Liberals made the mere fact of his opposition to the Home Rule Bill a severe blow to the chances of that measure. The last three years of a singularly fortunate political life were saddened for him by the breach with many of his old political friends.

It will, perhaps, be remarked by some readers that this work contains more numerous quotations from speeches than is usual in a political biography. If so, there is reason enough. Not only were Bright's speeches his one form of perfect achievement, but they were his one great political weapon. Not by administration or legislation, not by arguing in the Cabinet or sharing in the counsels of a party, but by his public orations as a private citizen he profoundly modified English politics and the relations and balance of English classes. He himself, when consulted as to a biography, used to put the question aside by saying 'My life is in my speeches.' But after two generations have gone by, not even the greatest speeches can be widely read or completely understood, except with the help of historical comment, and of such reproduction of a great personality as the biographer, by aid of private letters and recollections, can all too feebly accomplish.

LIFE OF JOHN BRIGHT

CHAPTER I

ORIGIN AND SCHOOLDAYS, 1811-27

'Lo, Strength is of the plain root-Virtues born:
Strength shall ye gain by service, prove in scorn,
Train by endurance, by devotion shape.
Strength is not won by miracle or rape.
It is the offspring of the modest years,
The gift of sire to son.'

GEORGE MEREDITH, *France*, 1870.

DURING the revolution that drove James II. from the throne, and legally secured to the Society of Friends, scornfully called 'Quakers,' the toleration with which Penn's royal patron had precariously endowed them, the family of Bright was cultivating a farm two miles to the east of Lyneham in north Wiltshire. How much these country folk heard, and what they thought of the turmoil and treason around them, the riding of horsemen, and the going to and fro of armies not far south of their village, when James's officers deserted at Warminster, and he himself turned back at Salisbury, and William of Orange passed on invincible, this we shall never know. Did the Brights by their farmhouse fire on those November evenings pray for the maintenance of the liberties of England, which their descendants were destined so greatly to enjoy, and in no small measure to enlarge? Whatever they may have thought of the Prince of Orange, he rode on to London about his business and left them to theirs beside the plough.

But the long, quiet, rustic centuries were drawing at length to a close. The impulse of the English folk-wandering, which has, with rapidity increasing up to our own day, everywhere uprooted the peasant families from their ancestral lands, early laid hold of the Brights. In the reigns of William and Anne, various households of Brights near Lyneham are found to be Quakers and connected with the wool industry; and perhaps in consequence of these connections they soon begin to move north to more industrial regions. About the time of the accession of the House of Hanover, Abraham Bright and his wife Martha,[1] Quakers, deserted Lyneham for Foleshill, near Coventry in Warwickshire. The rest of the Brights ere long disappeared from Lyneham, but the site of two of their old homesteads continued to be known in the countryside as 'Bright's Farm' and 'Bright's Orchard.' The 'Farm' has, in our own day, been repurchased by one of the family.

During the greater part of the eighteenth century successive generations of Brights, descendants of Abraham and Martha, sojourned near Coventry, engaging in the woollen trade, and intermarrying, as was then the rule of their sect, with other families of Friends.[2]

The first coming of the Brights to Rochdale in Lancashire took place during the Napoleonic wars, as the outcome of the first connection of the family with cotton. It forms a humble but characteristic incident in the metamorphosis of our society from rural to industrial, of which the economic bases were laid with relentless haste in that hard era of foreign war and domestic oppression, and of which the political consequences appeared in a later age, under the leadership of John Bright. The story of his father's coming to Rochdale has been told in a fragment of Autobiography which John Bright wrote in 1879 for the benefit of his children:

> 'My dear father' [Jacob Bright] 'was born in Coventry in the year 1775. His father and mother were Jacob and Martha Bright. My grandfather was in his later days in bad health and in humble circumstances. My father was sent to Ackworth School' [a Friends' school in Yorkshire] 'when about nine years of age, and remained there about five years.[3] From Ackworth he came to Low Leighton near New Mills in Derbyshire, where he was apprenticed to a Friend, William Holme, who had a small farm, and

[1] Her maiden name was Jacobs. For this reason some have conjectured that a strain of Hebrew blood was introduced by her into the orator's family tree. But there is no evidence or tradition to this effect. Jacobs was a common name among Quaker gentiles, particularly in Ireland.

[2] Whenever in this book 'Friend' is spelt with a capital F it means 'Quaker.' The word 'Quaker' is said to have been first given by Justice Bennett, when George Fox warned him to 'quake at the word of the Lord.' John Bright never used the word 'Quaker,' and disliked it.

[3] He 'remained there' in the most literal sense. His parents were too poor, and journeys too difficult to permit of his returning to Coventry for holidays. When he first saw his parents again after five years' absence he did not at once recognise them, nor they him. This he told his son John.

had a few looms employed in weaving fustians. Here he learnt to weave, and afterwards became familiar with cotton-spinning, being employed at a small place called The Tor, at New Mills, where the business was carried on by John and William Holme, the sons of the master. In the year 1802 these sons removed to Rochdale and built a good mill called then and now the Hanging Road Mill.' [It is said to have been the second cotton mill established in the neighbourhood of Rochdale.] 'My father,' continues John Bright, 'was with them and assisted them in starting the machinery in the mill, and he also afterwards attended the market at Manchester, delivering the produce of the mill with invoices to the different customers.'

In 1809 two Manchester Friends, Roger Merrick and Joseph Flintoff, impressed by Jacob Bright's ability, offered to provide the capital of £6000 in order to set him up in the cotton business. He thereupon left the employment of the Holme brothers, and set up the Bright Mills at Rochdale, on the hill overhanging the town on the north. On the edge of this hill, by the side of a large piece of common land known as Cronkeyshaw, stood a small red-brick house called Greenbank, which he now first rented and occupied. Divided from this dwelling-house only by a courtyard was a derelict worsted mill, with an old-fashioned engine, which he converted into the first cotton mill of the new firm, Jacob Bright & Co.[1] 'It was on Christmas Day in the year 1809 that their steam engine began to work. It was an engine made by Boulton and Watt of Birmingham, its beam was of wood and its arrangements altogether were of a very primitive character.' Jacob Bright's business was cotton-spinning. He received bales of raw cotton by canal or from carriers, span it in his mill, and gave out the warp and weft thus manufactured to handloom weavers, whom he paid by the piece to weave it in the weaving chambers at the top of their own houses. He then sold the fully manufactured article in Manchester or elsewhere. He prospered, and in fourteen years was able to sever the connection of the business with Friends Merrick and Flintoff, after treating them with the generosity which their early kindness to him had deserved.

Jacob Bright's first wife had been the sister of the Holme brothers, but she had died almost at once without children. In July 1809, the year of his setting up the business and

[1] On the site where the school now stands (1913).

moving into Greenbank, he married Martha Wood, a Friend from Bolton. 'My dear mother,' writes John Bright, 'was a delicate woman, but she had an excellent natural capacity, a logical mind, and qualities of head and heart rarely excelled.' There is no exact science of heredity, and nothing is more conjectural than the derivation of a great man's qualities of mind and heart. But it is the tradition of the Bright family that John inherited much from his mother. It is certain that he owed her much for the manner of his upbringing.

'She was only about twenty years of age,' he continues, 'when she married my father, who was then thirty-four. They had eleven children, seven sons and four daughters. The eldest boy was named William. He died when he was only four years old. I was the second child, then about three years old, and became then the eldest of the family.'

John Bright was born at Greenbank 'unto Jacob Bright, cotton spinner, and Martha his wife,' 'on the sixteenth day of the eleventh month, one thousand eight hundred and eleven,' as his 'birth-note' tells us. On the back of the birth-note his mother has written the words, 'John was born about 8 o'clock on 7th day evening.[1] May he indeed love his Creator in the days of his youth, and continue steadfast unto the end.' He was a seven months' child, and for long so delicate that he was wrapt in cotton wool, and his father afterwards told him that he had often carried him about not knowing if he were alive or dead. But he escaped his elder brother's fate, and grew up eventually with a robust and powerful frame.

We are most of us inclined to believe that children in the nursery show the ultimate bent of their life's character; if this is usually so, it is not so always, as the following words prove. They come from a note-book kept by John Bright's mother in the year 1819, when he was already seven or eight years old:

> 'John is a volatile child. He possesses a temper quite opposite to his [deceased] brother William. It is more pliable; he is rather of a timid spirit, which perhaps is in part occasioned by his constitution being rather delicate. . . . I have no wish at all to see my children great or noted characters, neither have I any right to expect that they will be distinguished for any extraordinary talents. But that they may be found filling up their station, however

[1] In Quaker language first month=January, eleventh month=November; first day=Sunday, seventh day=Saturday, and so forth.

humble it may be, with uprightness and integrity, is both at this time and often my humble prayer.'

'I remember little of my younger years,' writes John Bright, 'beyond the unceasing care and tenderness of my parents. With so many young children our house was well filled. Those of us who were old enough to learn were sent to a cottage near the house, where a nursery governess had charge of us and taught us. From the cottage we could see the kitchen window, and when the blind was let down, at noon, we knew that dinner was ready and we were expected to run across the field to join the rest of the family at home.'

Next after this home, in every respect so healthy and so happy, mention must be made of another influence in the formation of his childish ideas, and of that secret bent of character which, more than the ideas of childhood, remains unalterable by subsequent impressions. This was the Friends' Meeting-House in Rochdale. Every First Day, the family trooped down from Greenbank, and sat, an ever-lengthening row of sober little people, on the bare wooden benches opposite the platform, which modest elevation, the nearest likeness permitted among the Friends to chancel or pulpit, was reserved for the 'elders' chosen from the leading members of the congregation. Here the boy joined in the priestless worship, where piety neither was decked in robes and symbols, nor grew clamorous in its Protestantism, but where silence spoke in the heart. Here he grew accustomed to men and women uttering their thoughts under the stress of real emotion, but without gesticulation, without shouting, and without violence of language. The Friends were never numerous in Rochdale, and the building was humble as a village Meeting-House. Outside, but hid by a high brick wall from the view of the street, lay the tiny green with a few stone tablets let flat into the grass, to which after more than seventy years was to be added one like the rest, bearing the name of John Bright.[1]

Early in 1820, when he was eight years old, he began as a day-boy to attend Townhead School at the top of Yorkshire Street, close to the Friends' Meeting-House. The boy was kindly treated at this Rochdale school by the master, William Littlewood, for whom he always retained an affectionate regard; but he was there only for a few months.

[1] See below, last illustration in the book.

The remaining period of his school education, between the ages of ten and fifteen, was spent, except for the holidays, at a distance from home, in a series of Friends' schools in Lancashire and Yorkshire. The first of these was at Penketh, near Warrington, which he began to attend in the summer of 1820, boarding, together with some of his fellow scholars, boys and girls, in the hospitable farm of some Quakers named Davies. 'Behind the house,' he writes, 'was a good garden and orchard, and a vinery where grapes were abundant, and beyond the garden were cornfields, through which we walked daily to the school. We had scripture reading in the family, and I remember how I found a place for some of the New Testament narratives. The vineyard mentioned in the 13th chapter of Luke, I pictured as just like our vineyard; and I fancied I could see the discontented brother of the Prodigal Son returning from the field down the short lane which led from the house to the neighbouring cornfield. These imaginings of my boyhood have remained with me ever since. Our schoolmaster was not well qualified for his office. His temper was not good, and the school was much less pleasant than our home with the kind and generous farmer.'

Next year he was moved to Ackworth, near Pontefract, the large Quaker establishment at which his father had been educated. It was an age of ill-treatment in schools; alas! in all probability no worse in that respect than all previous ages, but rather the first in which reformers were beginning to notice and resent the miseries inflicted on children. Bright did not indeed suffer the 'cruel and disgusting mockery of an education' which little Dick Cobden had just lived through, as his biographer tells us, in a Yorkshire Dotheboys Hall. But even in Quakerdom there was then room for educational amendment. According to Bright's own account the head master at Ackworth was kind and even lovable, but incompetent; the four under masters were kind; but the 'apprentices' (ushers) were raw, inexperienced youths, knowing not what they did, from whom the 'timid and docile boy,' as he still was, according to his own account, 'suffered much annoyance and injustice which seemed almost like persecution.'

> 'On one occasion as I was clinging to the side of the bath and about to come out, shuddering with the intense cold, one of the apprentices, a man for whom in after years I have had much respect, supposing I had not been overhead in the water, thrust me backwards into the bath by pushing

me with a common besom so that my face was miserably scratched and disfigured.

'In those days, now nearly sixty years ago, schools were very different from what they are now. Even this great school, maintained by a religious society in many things in advance of public opinion in gentleness and kindness and justice, was in many respects grievously mismanaged. In the matter of food, it was insufficient in quantity and in quality. In the matter of punishments, it was harsh if not barbarous, and the comforts and health of the children were very inadequately attended to. What I suffered induced my father to make enquiries, and he placed before the committee of management facts to prove that a thorough reform was needed, and from the part he took in regard to this may be dated the commencement of improvements which have been made from that time to the year in which I am now writing (1879). Now the school is good so far as I know in all respects. The masters are better paid. The children are better fed, and their education is more complete.'

Comparing the schools of our day to those of the boyhood of Dickens, Cobden, and Bright, we may boast that the masters and the food are certainly better. If the breed of scholars had proportionately improved we should be doing well. It is not cruel masters or short rations that crush originality of mind and character under our modern system of education, materially so perfect. It is the constant pressure of a stupid public opinion among the boys, moulding them all to one conventional standard. But Bright nowhere in his account of his numerous schools makes any complaint against his Quaker schoolfellows, of whom at Ackworth there were 180 boys and 120 girls.[1]

'I left Ackworth,' he continues, 'at the time of the General Meeting in the summer of 1823, and soon after this I was sent to a school at York kept by William

[1] There is a charming account of a boy's life at Ackworth School by another of its distinguished scholars, William Howitt, in his *Boy's Country-Book*, referring to a period twenty years before John Bright was there. Howitt tells us that the school was 'for all, or any in the [Friends'] society; for rich and poor—all were treated alike there; and the nonsense about rank and money, that got only too soon thrust into children's heads, was never heard there.' He tells a delightful story about an old Quaker, 'an honest worthy man, though exceedingly poor,' who, when the Society paid for his son's schooling at Ackworth, walked seventy miles there with the lad, in order to save the coach-fare which the Society would otherwise have had to pay.

Simpson. It was the first house on the left side as we passed out of Walmgate Bar. The ancient city interested me and we had more of reasonable freedom than at Ackworth. The Meeting at York too was attractive. During the two years I spent at York, I learned more than in any other two years of my school life.'

This school has since moved into new quarters, and is now famous as 'Bootham.' Its only fault, so far as Bright was concerned, was that York lay too low for the health of one who had been from birth rather a weakly child, and had got no good from the semi-starvation of Ackworth. So after two years he was in a fortunate hour sent to yet another Friends' school at Newton-in-Bowland, a village on the upper reaches of the Hodder, deep among moorland hills on the borders of north Lancashire and Yorkshire. There the bracing winds of the Pennines, and the conditions of his life in this secluded valley of the old world, wrought a lasting improvement in his bodily and spiritual equipment for grappling with the new. At Newton-in-Bowland he ceased to be the 'timid and docile boy' and became the heart of oak we know.

'Our master was Francis Wills, an Irishman and a Friend. He was a little man, well informed, of a lively disposition and somewhat hot temper, but kind and generous and anxious to make the boys comfortable. There were about thirty boys in the school, besides six who lived in the village, the sons of villagers. There was a small garden and a humble meeting-house, and near it a little brook ran merrily down towards the river. A short distance above the school was an ancient burial-ground belonging to the Friends, in which were graves, but without tombstones or anything to mark who of past generations had been buried there. Our school studies and tasks were not hard upon us, and we had plenty of liberty for play and amusement. The Hodder afforded us as much fishing as we liked to have, and in it we bathed during the summer, and here I learned to swim as did many others of the boys. We took long walks up the hills among the remains of lead mines that had once been worked, and occasionally we made excursions to Clitheroe and to Whitewell, where we wandered among the woods and visited some small caves in the hillsides which were called Fairy-holes. We had a good deal of birds' nesting.

The year and a half I spent there seemed to make a complete change in me.'

The earliest extant letter of Bright's, in a beautiful round handwriting, almost perfect in its symmetry, is written from this moorland school to his sisters at their school at York. Among other items of news he says:

> 'We got another little brother on the 14th of this month, Father intends to call him Samuel, which I think is a very pretty name. I have got a hawk here, I don't know whether you have ever seen one or not, it is about the size of a crow, has a crooked bill, is savage, and will scarcely eat anything, but birds, mice and raw flesh. I mean to keep it till I go home, and then I shall lodge it in the Parrot cage. I suppose you have been for a long time expecting a letter from me, but I have waited for an opportunity to have one conveyed to you without cost, which I think can be done now, as one of the boys is going home to Bradford and his father going very often to Leeds can take it there and get it forwarded by some one going to York.'

Such were the thrifty thoughts of love before the penny postage removed the tax on family affection.

From the valley of the Hodder he came out at the age of fifteen into the world of men and affairs, with a strong body, and a constitution which was to serve him without any serious catastrophe to his health for another thirty years, carrying him safe through the strain of five years' daily and nightly work in the forefront of the Corn Law agitation, and to break down for the first time only after the misery he suffered during the Crimean War. He had also acquired at Newton-in-Bowland a gift destined to be of yet longer endurance than his health, the love of northern hill scenery, and of its running streams. To wander by these, rod in hand, was till the end of his life an insatiable desire and a constant refuge from worldly cares.

'I left Newton,' he writes, 'on the 16th of February 1827, and at the age of fifteen years and three months my school education terminated. I came home and soon began to be employed in my father's mill, and to take an interest in the business. I had learned some Latin and a little French, with the common branches then taught in such schools as I had been placed in. Reading, writing, arithmetic, grammar and geography

—no mathematics and no science.' A scanty stock! But as we shall see, his real education in literature, history, economics, and politics, was about to begin with himself as master. The schools of his sect had done well for him, for they had preserved the influences of his home. His boyhood had been passed in the atmosphere of the Society of Friends, that intangible but pervading spirit which instils rather than teaches the doctrine of the equality and brotherhood of men and women, of rich and poor; the nothingness of worldly distinctions; and the supreme duty of humane conduct. He had not, like so many pupils of more fashionable places of education, unlearned the lessons of his home, and of his own nature—the independence of opinion, the quick response to the whisper of conscience, the aspirations after a higher life. He may have suffered more than he learnt from some of his masters, but at least he had not been taught, like most young Englishmen, to quail before the public opinion of his schoolfellows, or to put on the air of being ashamed of the things of the mind and heart. Like Wordsworth, he emerged from these simple old country schools not moulded down to the pattern of gentility or of bourgeoisie, and he had therefore still the chance of growing into a great man.

CHAPTER II

HOME LIFE, BUSINESS, AND POLITICS AT ROCHDALE, UP TO THE DEATH OF HIS FIRST WIFE, 1827-41

'There is no class of people in England more determined and more unconquerable, whichever side they take, than are the people of the county from which I come.'—JOHN BRIGHT *in the House of Commons.*

THE life of John Bright, from the end of his schooldays until his death, falls into two periods of unequal length, of which the exact point of division is marked by the death of his first wife. The first part consists of those years (1827 to 1841) when he took an active share in the business of his father's firm, and did no political or public work except in Rochdale and the neighbouring towns. The second part covers the remaining forty-seven years of his life, during which he devoted most of his time and energies to politics at a distance from Rochdale, his native town becoming to him a place of domestic retreat rather than the scene of his labours. The period of his Rochdale activities, the subject of this chapter, is the key to his subsequent career. For in this period he formed all his economic, social and political views, in which half a century of larger experience wrought little change. As the world appeared to him when he looked at it from Rochdale, such, in London, he found it still.

In the second quarter of the nineteenth century, many of the merchant princes and cotton lords of Manchester were already almost as much cut off from social intercourse with the hands whom they employed as were their rivals, the squires, from the agricultural labourers starving in a decent obscurity beyond the park gates. This utter social division between rich and poor, in town and country alike, is still, under much improved economic conditions, a fundamental evil of our own age. And the way in which it formerly exacerbated the acute miseries of the poor in Manchester during the hungry 'thirties and 'forties was described by two keen observers—Engels and Mrs. Gaskell. In his capacity of German philosophic visitor, Engels noted, as specially characteristic of the epoch and of the country, the long lines of brilliant shop-frontage on the main streets of Manchester, through which the middle class passed from their comfortable homes outside to their business premises in the centre, the whole being so planned that the bourgeoisie need never catch sight of the squalid and noisome regions where the workmen lived, and of which the great city in fact mainly consisted. Mrs. Gaskell, the wife of a Unitarian minister, after working for many years at her husband's side in the slums of Manchester, delivered her soul in *Mary Barton.* According to her, the social division of rich and poor in the cotton capital was in itself as great an evil as the difference of wealth that caused it.

> 'At all times,' she wrote,' it is a bewildering thing to the poor weaver to see his employer removing from house to house, each one grander than the last, till he ends in building one more magnificent than all, or sells his mills to buy an estate in the country, while all the time the weaver, who thinks he and his fellows are the real makers of his wealth, is struggling on for bread for his children, through the vicissitudes of lowered wages, short hours, few hands employed, etc.'

The meeting face to face of the masters with the men's deputation, in the sixteenth chapter of *Mary Barton*, shows the gulf between the two worlds down which Mrs. Gaskell bade England look and tremble. Manchester of that day had many merits, and there was as much public spirit and humanity in these merchant princes and cotton lords as in any other class in the kingdom. But the new factory system was beginning to divide them off socially from those whom they employed.[1]

Now, if John Bright had been brought up in Manchester society, thus divided against itself, he might have held with more qualification his characteristic faith in the common interest of employer and employed, which rendered him so

[1] So, too, as regards the Manchester employers and their relations to the weavers, Bamford, the Radical (*Early Days*, chap. xii.), writes: 'But even those days (*circa* 1800), advantageous as they certainly were when compared with the present ones (*circa* 1840), were considered as being greatly altered for the worse since the days that could be spoken of from remembrance. The two classes of workmen and employer were already at too great a distance from each other, and it was a subject of observation that the masters were becoming more and more proud and uplifted each day.'

persuasive a champion of the union of all classes against the rural landlords; he would perhaps have been less puzzled by Lord Ashley's denunciations of the cotton lords; and he might, as a human being, have been imbued with less of that sense of his own oneness with the working men which enabled him to lead them to the winning of the franchise, when Cobden stood aside.

Although Greenbank mill at Rochdale was only ten miles from Manchester, in some respects it was worlds away. In the smaller manufacturing towns of Lancashire and Yorkshire, many masters were still relatively poor, still preserved the simple habits of life and expenditure, and the old way of mixing on more or less intimate terms with their men, that had marked the manufacturers of former generations. When John Bright at the age of fifteen began to 'help in the warehouse,' he was entering a society democratic in its atmosphere and singularly free from social distinctions. The 'cash nexus' was far from being the only bond between his father, Jacob Bright, and the hands in the mill, which stood, as was said above, at the door of his own modest dwelling. Jacob Bright knew each one of his employees, and much about their families. So good a Friend could not fail to take thought, after the manner of his sect, for the human beings with whom he came in daily contact. He was often consulted by his people as to their private affairs, and in their quarrels and difficulties was welcomed as a judge in Israel. He was constantly helping their households in those bad times, out of his private means. When any one married he increased their wages. The children employed in the factory were never allowed to be beaten: the leathern strap, hung up in so many mills in the bad days before the factory acts, had never been seen at Greenbank. He had the children taught out of his own funds, and finally built them a school. 'On winter nights, with a large lantern in his hand, and wrapped up warmly in a thick overcoat, he would stand at his mill gates, giving directions to the respective men to superintend the children on their way home.' He was 'owd Jacob' with his men, many of whom continued through life to call his sons plain 'John' and 'Thomas' when speaking to them. A story, that paints 'owd Jacob' to the life, tells how coming up the hill one day from town he found a neighbour in trouble on the road: a valuable beast of burden belonging to him had met with an accident and had to be killed. The onlookers were thronging round the poor man with expressions of sorrow; to one of the loudest of these Jacob Bright turned and said: 'I'm sorry five pounds. How much art thou sorry?'—and then and there raised a subscription.

In this half-democratic, half-patriarchal society John Bright was now placed during the formative years of early youth. Some of the abler workmen became his companions and friends, from whom he learnt the hot radicalism of that day and district; he heard at first hand bitter memories of 'Peterloo' from those who had gone to attend a meeting and come back from a massacre; he listened to the hopes of the artisans, that they might be admitted as citizens to the franchise. Thus he grew up, seeing some things, at least, with a working man's eyes. Of the various sects that have arisen since the corruption of the early Christians by worldly success, the Society of Friends has most consistently felt and taught the equality and fraternity of all mankind. To the Brights of Rochdale, far removed in temperament as they were from the Jacobins, the doctrine of 'Liberty, Equality, Fraternity' formed a part of their inherent and inbred religion.

In the warehouse with him was one Nicholas Nuttall, who 'took in the work from the mule spinners.' 'Nicholas,' writes his renowned pupil, 'was a great politician of the radical type.' In December 1830, a few weeks before the introduction of the Whig Reform Bill, Nicholas, in common with all Lancashire Radicals, was much excited because their leader, 'Orator Hunt,' who eleven years before had held the meeting that ended in the Peterloo massacre, was candidate at a by-election in the borough of Preston. He had had the temerity to put himself up against the then Whig potentate Edward Stanley, 'the Rupert of debate,'

> 'afterwards Earl of Derby and for many years [leader] of the Tory party, though at the time of this election Stanley was not reckoned among the Tories. His family had long had great influence in Preston, and it was thought a daring step for any one to enter the field against him. In those days elections were held for many days, I think for fourteen days. Day by day I heard from Nicholas the progress of the contest. His interest in it was extraordinary and he communicated to me some of his enthusiasm, and through him I became something of a politician. The son of the great peer was defeated, and Hunt became member for Preston to the great joy of Nicholas and to my entire satisfaction. At that time I knew little of the questions in dispute, but I sympathised with the multitude who supported the Radical candidate.

'In fact, I could not be otherwise than Liberal. My father was Liberal, though we had no elections in our town and there was rarely a contest for the county. I was, as I now am, a member of the Society of Friends. I knew something of their history and of the persecutions they had endured, and of their principles of equality and justice. I knew that I came of the stock of the martyrs, that one of my ancestors, John Gratton of Monyash in Derbyshire, had been in prison for several years because he preferred to worship in the humble meeting-house of his own sect rather than in the church of the law-favoured sect by whom he and his friends were barbarously persecuted. John Gratton's granddaughter was my father's grandmother. He was a man of influence in the part of the country where he lived, and I observed, many years after the time of which I am now writing, in a Parliamentary return for which I moved, that when Nonconformist places of worship were legalised by the Toleration Act, all the meeting-houses of Friends in Derbyshire were registered by and in the name of John Gratton.

'I have said that my father was liberal in his views of political affairs. He took in the *Manchester Guardian*, a weekly Liberal paper. There were no daily papers in Lancashire, and few, if any, in the Kingdom and in London. The *Guardian* was published on Saturday, and on the evening of that day my father read his paper or I read it to him. The Parliamentary reports were very brief, and as I read the scraps of speeches in the House of Commons he would ask me, "What did Joseph Hume say?" Joseph Hume was then, as he was during all his Parliamentary career, distinguished for his Liberal views, and especially for his anxiety to prevent any waste of public money. I have known him intimately in later years when I sat near him in the House of Commons.'

In the following passage Bright tells us something of the order of the day at Greenbank when he first began to help his father in the business:

'Sladen came to our house every morning about half-past five o'clock, for the keys of the mill, and it was my duty to get up and give them to him. In those days there were no lucifer matches, and I have not forgotten the trouble I had to strike a light with the old tinder-box and flint and steel. I had a room over the counting-house which I fitted up for my own use, with a comfortable chair, a desk, and a small cupboard with shelves for a few books. The door into the office was just opposite the furnace of one of the boilers, and the old "steam tenter," Josiah Lee, or "old Siah" as he was commonly called, brought a shovelful of fire from his furnace and carried it into the grate in my room, and thus I had a good fire made in a few minutes. Here I often read a good deal before breakfast and was undisturbed.'

In this way he supplied the gaps of his meagre school education. Besides history and poetry, to which he was devoted throughout life, we find him sending for books of statistics and studying the *Spectator*, a new Radical weekly, which had early espoused anti-Corn Law views.

'The years 1831 and '32 are memorable for the great agitation which produced the Reform Bill. I was too young,' he writes, 'to take much part in it, but I well remember the London papers bringing the news to Rochdale of the great bill as it was first introduced in the House of Commons, and the sensation which it caused throughout the country. Rochdale was not included in the first list of new boroughs, and a public meeting was held in the newsroom to memorialise the government to grant a member to our town.'

The petition met with success, and the Whigs put down Rochdale for enfranchisement along with the other great towns of the industrial north.

In later years he told his vivid recollection of a meeting held during the crisis of the Reform Bill, in the market-place at Rochdale, when young Dr. Kay was the speaker. Bright as an old man recalled the emotion he felt that day in common with thousands of his fellow townsmen, ready ripe for rebellion, when the orator rolled out the magnificent lines of Shelley, which seemed to have been prophetically written for that moment in English history:

'Rise like lions after slumber
In unvanquishable number!
Shake your chains to earth, like dew
Which in sleep had fall'n on you:
Ye are many,—they are few.'[1]

[1] Dr Kay was born at Rochdale, 1804; he has been called, not without reason, 'the founder of the English system of popular education.' He eventually married Janet, the heiress of the Shuttleworths, and became Sir James Kay-

In October 1831 the Bill was lost in the Lords. But the next six months of almost revolutionary agitation caused its second reading to be carried there by a majority of nine, at dawn on the morning of April 14, 1832, after a night of fierce and uncertain conflict. During that night of high debate at Westminster, John Bright, not yet one-and-twenty, was making his first journey to London, wrapped up on the top of the 'Peveril of the Peak' stage coach, the rain pouring down upon him in torrents. As yet no railway ran between Lancashire and the capital. They started from Manchester at eight in the evening of the 13th, and by dint of relays of four always excellent horses, were due to reach London at five next afternoon. At some point on the road, after the wet night was over, one of the passengers

> 'observed something coming towards us, but still in the distance, and we all looked with great interest. We saw horses galloping and carriages coming at a speed which would quickly have left behind our coach if they had been going the same way. By-and-by we found they were chaises with four horses in each chaise, having two or three men inside, and they were throwing out placards from each window. These were express chaises coming from London, bringing the news to all the people of the country—for there were no telegraphs then—of the glorious triumph of popular principles even in the House of Lords. It has always been to me a pleasure to think of the excitement this incident caused among us coach passengers when we found what was the business and message of those gentlemen in the express.' [1]

Less than two months later, after the abortive attempt of the Duke of Wellington to form a Tory Ministry, the people's wishes were fulfilled and they obtained 'the Bill, the whole Bill, and'—as the Radicals soon came to think in more senses than one—'nothing but the Bill.' But at any rate it was a new era, for the blank negation of perpetual privilege was gone, and henceforth the political tools were to him who could use them.

Shuttleworth. His quotation from Shelley did not lose in repetition by Bright, when he afterwards told the story to Mr. E. J. Broadfield. The quotation is from the *Masque of Anarchy,* which had just been posthumously published (1832), though written in 1819, when the news of 'Peterloo' reached Shelley in Italy. Bright himself quoted these lines at the end of his speech to his supporters at Durham after his first election to Parliament in 1843.

[1] *Addresses*, p. 415. Rochdale, September 25, 1877.

In 1830 John Bright suffered his first great sorrow. His mother, a woman of very remarkable character, had become more rather than less intimate with her elder children as they grew up ; and the relation meant most of all, perhaps, to John.

> 'She was,' he writes, 'about 41 years of age. She had had eleven children and was never robust, and now we had the grief to witness a gradual decline. As the summer drew nigh her weakness increased, and we lost all hope of her recovery.' 'It was on the 18th of June that she passed from her family on earth to one of the "many mansions" prepared for such as she was. It was late in the evening, and we stood round her bed as her spirit left her poor wasted form. During that last day, when only partially conscious, she often mentioned my name. Though not her first-born child, I was her eldest living one, and I have a strong feeling that her motherly sympathy with me was even more than usually strong.'

Her death, as he tells us, was a great calamity—'a loss which never could be repaired. From it sprung many troubles and disappointments, which disturbed us in after years.' The father, a good, honest, plain man, with that additional touch of conscientious humaneness which so many of the Friends took from their religion, was neither in intellect nor in personality a match for the leading spirits among his children, as the mother had always been. The six brothers and four sisters who survived their mother[1] formed a large party of high-spirited young people, now left very much to their own guidance. Most of them were clever, and even original, and the girls were all of them handsome, especially Esther, a singularly noble woman, who unfortunately died in 1850 shortly after her marriage to James Vaughan.[2] Priscilla, destined to play a considerable part in her brother's life, had strong powers

[1] Their names in order of age were *John* (twice married), *Sophia* (married T. Ashworth), *Thomas* (married Carolina Coultate), *Priscilla* (married Duncan McLaren), *Benjamin*, *Margaret* (active in the Temperance cause; married Samuel Lucas, editor of the *Morning Star*), *Esther* (married James Vaughan, afterwards Sir James Vaughan, magistrate of Bow Street), *Jacob* (married Ursula Mellor), *Gratton*, *Samuel* (married Selina Gibbs). Of these Gratton and Benjamin died young, and Esther and Sophia shortly after they were married. Many years afterwards John Bright wrote: 'I have lost two sisters soon after marriage. . . . These events so affected me that I never attend a wedding ceremony without a feeling of doubt and sadness.'

[2] One day, many years after, when John Bright was an old man, he was sitting on the lawn when every one else was away except his granddaughter, Esther Clark. She was playing about, and he called her to him, and with his

both of mind and character. Jacob the younger, who was only nine in 1830 when his mother died, was ere long to show that he had all John's fearless and unyielding temper, together with a greater measure of intellectual daring and suppleness—qualities destined to earn him a place of his own in English political life.

Throughout the 'thirties the absorbing passion of these brothers and sisters was neither religion nor business, still less the forbidden dances and pleasures of the world, but politics. Preoccupation with affairs of State was then very uncommon among Friends; many were studiously neutral, many patiently Conservative, and many like old Jacob Bright, were strong but quiet Liberals, neither speculative nor active in such matters. Ever since the death of Penn, the sect had avoided politics as being more beset with worldly snares for the children of light than the common business transactions in which so many of them managed to thrive without endangering their principles.[1] Such seclusion from public life had been natural in former times, when power was monopolised by the landlord class and by the adherents of the State Church, but in the new and more liberal age now dawning, a closer relation to politics was to be expected in people so actively philanthropic as the Quakers. In the Reformed Parliament (1832-33) Joseph Pease, in the plain dress of the Friends, had successfully taken the affirmation and his seat, the first of his sect to sit in the British House of Commons, at least since the seventeenth century. The anti-slavery movement had been helped even by strict Friends, as being non-political; and the fact that the elders had been active in that matter made it easier for the young generation to answer more fully to many of the other calls of good citizenship. As the years went on, and drew John Bright deeper and deeper into a merely political life, these worldly entanglements evoked, as we shall see, much criticism from the older and the more religious members of his society, including

hand on her head spoke to her of the Esther after whom she had been named, telling her that she bore the name of one of the noblest women he had ever known, and that he could have no better wish for the young Esther than that she should grow up with some of the other's beautiful qualities. He was so deeply moved that she crept away awed, as a child is by grown-up feeling.

[1] In 1814 the second ship which sailed from Liverpool to Calcutta, after the abolition of the East India Company's monopoly, was the *Bengal*, owned by Cropper, Benson & Co., and Rathbone, Hodgson & Co. There was fear of attack by the French, and merchant ships in those seas usually carried cannon. The Quaker principles of the owners of the *Bengal* would not allow of real arms on board, but they had wooden cannon placed at the portholes to scare an ignorant enemy. A picture of the ship thus protected is now in possession of Mr. Charles Cropper of Ellergreen.

some who loved him best. But prior to his marriage in 1839 his interest in politics met with no such discouragement, for the family of which he was already the real leader was self-sufficing and saw relatively little of other Friends. The Meeting at Rochdale was neither large nor remarkable, and the Brights of Greenbank were a law unto themselves.

John Bright was a zealous and fairly successful member of the Rochdale Cricket Club until the year 1833. In that year he and a number of his fellow-citizens founded the 'Rochdale Literary and Philosophical Society,' on the model of similar educative and debating institutions then springing up in many northern towns. Its first meeting was presided over by John Bright, aged twenty-one. Thus early had his personal qualities made themselves felt in the arena of his native town. At one of the first meetings he proposed and carried by eighteen votes to four a proposition the truth of which he never afterwards questioned—namely, 'that a limited monarchy is best suited for this country at the present time.' At another meeting the company was unanimous in favour of the then very advanced doctrine that 'Laws for restricting the importation of grain are impolitic.' On other occasions Bright was of opinion that 'the universal education of the people is necessary,' and that 'the moral tendency of public amusements, such as the theatre, circus, etc., is injurious.' In January 1834 he proposed and carried a resolution that Alfred was more entitled than Alexander to the appellation of 'Great,' doubtless overwhelming the Rochdale doctors and tradesmen with stores of historical learning, acquired before breakfast in front of the furnace coals imported for his benefit by 'old Siah.' It was a full and generous life that he had already carved out for himself, and in spite of his being in the mill, it was at this period, on its intellectual side, not wholly unlike the life of a clever undergraduate at a college.

About this time he made the first of many visits to Ireland, in company with a relation who was going there on business. 'What I most remember of our journey was the crowd of beggars that gathered round the coach at every place where we stopped to change horses. Nothing like it could be seen in England,' even in those hard times. In June and July 1833 he made a pleasure tour in Belgium and the lower Rhine, whence he returned 'speaking French with much greater facility.' His letters home, written on the old self-folding paper before the days of envelopes and postage stamps, tell his family how he admired the cathedral at Brussels and the 'beautiful pictures of the old masters, and wondered at the ignorance of the Catholics, exhibited in their supporting about 2000 priests for this Cathedral alone,' the unthrifty rascals, worse than Rochdale with its absentee vicar! He drove out to Waterloo and spent nearly five hours viewing every detail with a guide, till 'a thunder-storm came on which added greatly to the effect'; 'there are plenty of bones scattered over the plain even now, and the land has been so much enriched by the blood and the interment of the slain, that the wheat grows 7 or 8 feet high—as Byron says—

'"How the red rain has made the harvest grow."'

Finally, returning through Holland, where cholera is raging, he gets ill himself, but fortunately it turns out not to be cholera in his case, so the Rochdale Literary and Philosophical is not deprived of its most active member.

He was already zealously engaged in Temperance lecturing [1] in Rochdale and the neighbouring towns, such as Burnley, and had found a staunch ally for this and other causes in his friend, William Roberts. Bright took his early efforts at oratory in the Literary and Philosophical, the Bible meetings and Temperance lectures with the seriousness natural to the great artist he was. His early morning studies, and his perfect familiarity with the Bible and Milton, had not a little to do with the high standard of language which he set before himself from the first. 'If my manner of speaking is good,' he wrote when an old man, 'it may have become so from reading what is good.' And again: 'It is a good thing to use few words and the best words, which are those which are simple and forcible, with no needless use of adjectives, too many of which spoil speaking and writing. To assist in attaining to a practice like this, the reading of good books—I mean well-written books—is helpful, so that the eye and the ear and the mind may become familiar with good language.'

It was natural for one starting with high and somewhat literary ambitions of oratory, and with a nervous fear of breaking down, to make the initial mistake—or adopt the necessary first precaution—of writing out his speeches and committing them to memory. The first person to advise him to alter this method was a Baptist minister, the Rev. John Aldis. Being stationed at Manchester in the year 1832, Aldis was invited

[1] Bright was a teetotaller during his Anti-Corn Law campaigns and for some time afterwards. Later in life he took wine for a short time by doctor's orders, but soon gave it up. None was kept in his house.

over to Rochdale to speak at a Bible Society meeting in the Friends' Meeting-House. He was waiting near by in a tradesman's parlour in Yorkshire Street, when, as he tells us,

> 'a slender modest young gentleman came, who soon surprised me by his intelligence and thoughtfulness. I took his arm on the way to the meeting, and I thought he seemed nervous. I think it was his first public speech, at all events in such connection. It was very eloquent and powerful and carried away the meeting, but it was elaborate and memoriter. On our way back, as I congratulated him, he said that such efforts cost him too dear, and asked me how I spoke so easily. I then took the full advantage of my seniority to set fully my notions, that in his case, as in most, I thought it would be best not to burden the memory too much, but having carefully prepared and committed any portions when special effect was desired, merely to put down other things in the desired order, leaving the wording of them to the moment. Years rolled on. I had entirely forgotten the name of the young Friend, when the Free Trade Bazaar was held in London [1845]. One of those engaged for it—Mr. Barker of Stockport—calling on me, asked if I had called on Mr. Bright. I said I had not been able to attend the meetings and did not personally know him at all. He replied "You must, for I heard him say that you gave him his first lesson in public speaking." I went to a subsequent meeting and recognised the young Friend of 1832.' [1]

Bright did not venture to follow completely the advice given him by Mr. Aldis in 1832, until another four or five years had gone by. For when in 1876 Mr. Aldis' story was brought to his notice, he wrote:

> 'I cannot say that I remember clearly what Mr. Aldis remembers. Mr. Cobden came over to Rochdale at my invitation to attend a meeting on Education in the schoolroom of the Baptist Chapel, West Street; that may have been the occasion on which Mr. Aldis was present.[2] I spoke a carefully prepared speech, full I doubt not of the

[1] *Robertson*, pp. 52-53, the first place where this story was printed.

[2] This visit of Mr. Cobden's occurred in 1836 or 1837 (see *Morley*, i. 189). Mr. Aldis referred to 1832. As late as June 4, 1889, Mr. Aldis 'narrated the facts again' to Mr. John Eastly, who noted that 'his memory and mind are as clear as ever, and it was evidently a meeting prior to that which Mr. Bright named which the conversation had reference to.'

faults of youth and inexperience, and it had cost me so much in preparation and in anxiety that I resolved from that day never to speak another written speech, and I have kept my word.'

We may then, in any case, conclude that before he began his Corn Law campaignings in the 'forties, he had already adopted his lifelong custom of writing out only the heads of his argument, interspersed with an occasional 'key-sentence,' and ending up with the peroration transcribed in full.

Jacob Bright the elder was no hard task-master to his sons. From August 1835 to April 1836 John took a tour in the Mediterranean—analogous to a voyage round the world in our own day. He followed in Byron's tracks, quoting his poetry at every turn, with a zeal which was the literary hall-mark of those who were young when the news came from Missolonghi. He went out by steamer, touching at Lisbon, and journeyed in Greece, Egypt, Palestine, Sicily, and Italy; he moved about the Levant in sailing-vessels, spent altogether more than a month in quarantine, caught the fever at Athens, and finally returned, full of enthusiasm, to entertain his fellow-townspeople with a lecture on his travels. It cannot be said that like Cobden in his almost contemporaneous Eastern tour, Bright formulated any new theories of Turkish misrule or of British Foreign Policy—but he benefited greatly in body and mind. The untravelled but keen-witted family at Greenbank must have devoured his letters home—bulletins on vast sheets of thin foolscap, beautifully written within and without in every available corner, and 'crossed' in the elaborate manner which cheap paper and lower postage rates have since happily driven out of fashion.

From Malta ('9th month, 3, 1835') he writes:

'Hitherto I have read little on the voyage owing chiefly to the depression caused by sickness—have, however, finished the *History of the Ottoman Empire* in 2 vols., also Walter Scott's *Ivanhoe* — the evening on deck till near 12 admiring the setting of the silvery moon, and watching the beautiful sparkling of the phosphorescent appearances of the waves as they dash from the paddles.'

He falls in with

'an Armenian Bishop, a deck passenger! He, poor fellow, knows little of the splendours of an English

Bishopric and dreams seldom of a translation to certain additional thousands per year. He eats little but olives and oil and bread.'

The British Consul at Smyrna is 'a puppy' who draws £500 a year, but will do nothing for his countrymen in their quarantine difficulties.

They begin to go up into the Holy Land from Jaffa. They bivouac within two hours' ride of Jerusalem, and he asks his family to imagine the scene,

> 'under a fine palm tree whose branches spread majestically from the top of the stem'—'two Arabs and a black Nubian bending o'er the fire watching its progress, myself and two or three more puffing away with long Turkish Chibouks (pipes), others lying stretched upon their hay couch, the stars shining with a brilliancy much greater than they ever favor [1] us with in my native land.'

Before dawn they start on again,

> 'passing up the mountains by an excessively rough path. My horse being very good I determined if possible to have the first view of the Holy City, and therefore pushed on as rapidly as possible. At 4 minutes past 6 I reached the summit and beheld the sun just rising over the city. During the ascent we had a prospect perhaps unequalled for beauty. On the sides of the mountains was to be seen almost every variety of color—patches of verdure here and there and a few olive trees of a light green—spots of earth and sand of a reddish color, but in greater abundance than either was seen the bare rock shining like polished marble, and the whole had an appearance of a vast surface of marble.'

As might be expected, the 'trumpery pictures,' 'the mummery of an ignorant priesthood,' and 'the lamentable departure from the simplicity of Christianity,' prevent him from feeling as he would have wished at the Holy Sepulchre. But the Bible scenery gives him unending delight and he returns again and again to the description. 'This is what the Scriptures call the "Hill Country of Judea," very properly too, for hill succeeds hill in almost endless continuation—none immensely high, but yet steep and difficult of ascent; they are

[1] Bright, like his friend Cobden, spelt 'favor,' 'color,' 'labor,' etc., without the 'u,' in American fashion.

notwithstanding well cultivated and very productive, though apparently little more than barren rocks.' He describes the peasants' system of terracing in some detail. 'Along these terraces are planted olive trees; these being set in straight rows the mountains have a very singular and a very beautiful appearance.' But he can still spare a thought for England. 'I am very much vexed about the Corporation Bill, which is foolish enough, you will say, but yet I should much like to see the Lords humbled. *Le jour viendra.*'

After his return from the East, in April 1836, Bright became more active than ever as a local politician. In January 1837, he issued a spirited address 'To the Radical Reformers of the Borough of Rochdale,' calling on them to support against the sitting Tory member the Liberal candidate, Mr. Fenton, who was pledged to Household Suffrage, Ballot, Short Parliaments, abolition of Corn Laws and of Church-rates. At the general election in the summer, resulting from the death of King William IV., Mr. Fenton was elected by 374 votes to 349. The numbers remind us how restricted was the franchise, even in populous and democratic towns, under the provisions of the First Reform Act.

Some time in 1836 or 1837 occurred a trivial incident which proved the beginning of great things. Bright, like other active-minded people within the radius of Manchester influence, had just begun to hear the name of Richard Cobden, not in connection with Free Trade, but as that of a man who, though in a relatively humble position in the commercial world, was already becoming known in the cotton capital as a reformer and a man of ideas. One of the causes he had at heart was popular education, then left by the State to the private benevolence of citizens. John Bright, whose father already made provision for the teaching of the children in his factory,

> 'went over to Manchester to call upon Cobden to ask him if he would be kind enough to come to Rochdale and to speak at an education meeting which was about to be held in the schoolroom of the Baptist Chapel, in West Street of that town. I found him,' said John Bright, recalling the scene after forty years, 'in his office in Mosley Street. I introduced myself to him. I told him what I wanted. His countenance lit up with pleasure to find that there were others that were working in this question, and he, without hesitation, agreed to come. He came and he spoke;

and though he was then so young a speaker, yet the qualities of his speech were such as remained with him so long as he was able to speak at all—clearness, logic, a conversational eloquence, a persuasiveness which it was almost impossible to resist.'[1]

Thus began the most important, and perhaps the most intimate and unclouded friendship in English political history. But five years passed away before its consequences began to be apparent. It was, as we shall see, Cobden who in the autumn of 1841 persuaded Bright to leave Rochdale and become a national agitator, but until that date it is impossible to assign any of Bright's actions or opinions to the direct promptings of his friend rather than to the normal development of his own life and his own thoughts.

Neither Cobden nor Bright were among the seven men who founded the Anti-Corn Law Association at the York Hotel, Manchester, on September 24, 1838. In October, however, the name of John Bright was added to the 'Provisional Committee,' actually a few days before that of Richard Cobden. In January 1839 Jacob Bright, senior, gave £50 to the first of those famous subscription lists which paid for the overthrow of the landed oligarchy, while in the same month his son John was again chosen as a committee-man of the Association, together with some hundred others, all except Bright and half a dozen more being Manchester men. In the following two months this 'Manchester Anti-Corn Law Association' was converted into the 'National Anti-Corn Law League.' Cobden had become its recognised chief from the moment when, in his first public appearance in the cause in December 1838, he persuaded the Manchester Chamber of Commerce to put itself in the forefront of the battle.[2]

Bright was as yet merely one of the most active members of the League in provincial Lancashire. On February 2, 1839, he held an open-air meeting at Rochdale to denounce the Corn Laws. About three thousand working men were present. Bright moved 'that the Corn Laws have had the effect of crippling the commerce and the manufactures of the country,

[1] This was the occasion on which Bright delivered the last of his 'written' speeches. See pp. 26-27 above.

[2] The possibility of such a course had been in Cobden's mind for some time; for in the autumn of 1837, while walking with Ashworth, Cobden had 'stopped suddenly and said with abruptness, "I 'll tell you what we will do; we 'll use the Chamber of Commerce for an agitation to repeal the Corn Law," and had added, "I am determined to put forth my strength for the repeal of these Corn and Provision Laws."' *Ashworth*, p. 25.

have raised up rival manufactories in foreign countries, have been most injurious and oppressive in their operation with the great bulk of our population, and the working classes have been grievously injured by this monopoly of the landed proprietors.' But it turned out that the great majority of the artisans present, though Free Traders, were Chartists first and foremost. They carried the following reasoned amendment :

> 'That it is the opinion of this meeting that though the Corn Law is an injurious tax, yet the present House of Commons, or any other House of Commons constituted on the present suffrage, will never repeal that law so as to be beneficial to the working classes, and this meeting is of opinion that the present Corn Law agitation is made up for the purpose of diverting the minds of the people from the only remedy of all political grievances ; therefore it is necessary that the people must first be in possession of their political rights to effect the repeal of these Corn Laws.'

The meeting broke up with three cheers for the Chartist National Convention, and three groans for the Chamber of Commerce of Manchester.

There was much force and likelihood in the prophecy of the Rochdale workmen that the Corn Laws would not be repealed till the franchise had been extended. The Manchester magnates who went up to London, full of consequence and primed with the irrefutable arguments of their Cobden, were treated with a contumely designed to make them feel their unimportance at Westminster. The landed oligarchy could scarcely have been more contemptuous if they had been a deputation of their own workmen. They were told that they could overthrow the monarchy sooner than repeal the Corn Laws. The House of Commons did not contain two hundred Free Traders ; Whig or Tory, it was a landlords' house only a little less than before the Reform Act of '32. And yet for all that, the workmen of Rochdale were wrong on the point of tactics, as they themselves soon came to see. In seven years the House of Commons was brought round to total repeal ; and the extension of the suffrage eventually came not as a prelude but as a consequence of that great economic revolution. Meanwhile a young Quaker walked back to Greenbank sadly enough, from the fiasco of his first Anti-Corn Law meeting.

But John Bright was not the man to be daunted. He soon made Rochdale enthusiastic in the cause. In January 1840 he started a Rochdale Anti-Corn Law Association principally composed of working men, and by March could boast of a petition 'for a total, immediate repeal of the accursed corn-laws,' with 9700 signatures, 'being signed by almost every male adult of the town.'

In 1836-38 Jacob Bright, senior, built a new cotton mill, about two hundred yards away from Greenbank on the other side of Cronkeyshaw common, on the site over which the Brights' factory buildings have since steadily expanded. The original mill at Greenbank went on until it was closed during the cotton famine caused by the American Civil War, after which it was not thought worth while to reopen such antiquated premises.

Shortly afterwards, when John Bright was engaged to be married, a house was built a little higher up the moor for him to inhabit. He gave it the name of One Ash, in honour of an ash-tree which was a conspicuous feature in the garden, and in memory of his favourite ancestor John Gratton, whose Derbyshire home of long ago had been called Monyash.[1] On the top of the hill overlooking Rochdale, there now stood Greenbank, One Ash, and the new mills, three points of a family triangle with part of the bare Cronkeyshaw common lying between them. So they stood throughout the rest of John Bright's life, and so they stand to-day.

Besides the weekly meeting for worship confined to one particular town or village, the Friends from larger groups and districts attended monthly, quarterly, and yearly meetings, which were great events not only in the spiritual but in the social life of the community. The rule, then strictly observed, that Friends must marry only Friends, bound the Society together—only too closely it may be,—stimulated social intercourse within its borders, and kept alive the desire of the young people and their parents in one town to see something of those in another. Before railways, travelling for pleasure was not common. But Friends often moved about the country on business, when they were always received into other Friends' houses; and they assembled together from distant quarters for the periodical meetings, which were always times of hospitality and good-will.

In the summer of 1838 a general meeting[2] was held at Ack-

[1] See p. 19 above.

[2] A meeting of those concerned with Ackworth School, not the yearly meeting of the whole Society of Friends, which then took place in London.

worth in Yorkshire, in connection with the old school where John Bright had been educated and his father before him. To Ackworth meeting came the Brights out of the west, and out of the north Elizabeth Priestman of Newcastle, taking care of her grandmother Margaret Bragg, a noble old lady, famous in the Quaker world for her religious journeys through England, and the power of the Spirit in her when she preached. Elizabeth was left by herself during the meeting, her grandmother presumably being called up among the elders of the congregation; but seeing two pleasant girls near by, Elizabeth asked if she might sit with them. They proved to be Sophia and Priscilla Bright, and they were so much charmed by their new friend that when the meeting was over, they ran up to their brother John—much in the spirit of two young ladies at a ball in other circles, but in similar circumstances—crying, 'Come here, John, we 've some one who 'll just suit thee.' Many a true word is spoken half in jest. Before the day was over John felt the power of love.

Shortly after this, John and his sisters Priscilla and Esther went on a journey to Scotland; on their way thither they found themselves at Newcastle upon the first day, and went to meeting. After meeting, Priscilla made inquiries about Elizabeth Priestman from a Friend who proved to be her father, Jonathan Priestman. He invited them up to his house, named Summerhill, at the top of Westgate, then outside the town,[1] a house where John Bright was henceforth a frequent and a welcome guest.

> 'Elizabeth Priestman was reared in a home where intellectual activity existed side by side with a strict form of Quakerism; where the utmost refinement of manner was combined with the warmest popular sympathies and where the strongest opinions were urged in the gentlest tones. When brought into contact with such a family, John Bright's bluntness and directness of speech stood out in marked contrast, but his manly honesty and uprightness were at once recognised, and it soon became evident that he would win the prize which he had come to seek. The manufacturing districts were a little-known part of England; it then seemed a long way from Newcastle to

[1] In the fields round Summerhill, now in the heart of Newcastle, grazed a cow that supplied milk to the Priestman family. On one occasion the cow was seized by the authorities, on the refusal of Jonathan Priestman to pay Church-rates. As the distraint took place at the time of a monthly meeting, when the house was full of guests and the milk was wanted, the hospitable Friend was the more incensed.

Rochdale, and North Country Friends felt that a precious possession was about to be carried away. "Who is this young man Bright whom Elizabeth Priestman is going to marry?" one of them asked in anxious tones of a Lancashire Friend. "A very popular young man very much thought of by our working people," are the only words of the answer now remembered.'[1]

On the 27th of the 11th month, 1839, John Bright and Elizabeth Priestman took each other in marriage in the Friends' Meeting-House at Pilgrim Street, Newcastle. For their honeymoon they went to the Lake district, to Hawkshead, the happy village by Esthwaite Water, where Wordsworth's mind had unknowingly secreted such treasures during his schooldays. Chance has preserved for us a picture of the Brights' honeymoon, as it lived in the memory of the survivor, after death had parted them:

'To-day three years ago was just such a day as this as to the outward—all nature wore a smile even through the blight of winter. The air was mild, the sun shone upon the fields. The bells of Hawkshead Church gave out sweet music, as my precious Elizabeth and myself walked leisurely to meeting.'

And again, in 1882, Bright as an old man revisited the scene:

'Drive to Colthouse Meeting-house, where we, my bride and I, attended meeting the first time after our marriage. Drove on to Hawkshead, found the house in which we then dined with the old and venerable John and Margaret Bragg. Nearly 43 years have since passed.'

This lady whom Bright made mistress of One Ash in the last weeks of 1839 was loved by all who knew her. Her brothers and sisters almost worshipped Elizabeth Priestman, and so did her father's servants and workpeople at Newcastle. She was lively and open in disposition, and threw herself into the interests of all her friends. If she had lived she would have played a great part in her husband's life.[2]

[1] *Records of a Quaker Family* (The Richardsons of Cleveland), by Mrs. A. O. Boyce.

[2] I am sorry that there is no portrait of her worthy of reproduction. An oil painting was taken of her after death, but her husband never liked it. More than fifty years after her death an old gentleman spoke of her to her daughter, Mrs. Clark, saying that he remembered her before her marriage, adding, 'I think your mother was always most fully described by the word "angelic."'

Her mother, Rachel Priestman, became very intimate with Bright, and in some measure filled the place of his own lost mother. He was often with his new relations on the Tyne, and they exercised an important influence over him. It was a different influence from that of his brothers and sisters at Greenbank, less political and more religious, for while the Brights were chiefly concerned with the application of religion to conduct, the Priestmans possessed more of the mystic's fervour, though mysticism among Friends is self-possessed and concerned only with the hidden experiences of the soul.

Bright, much as he liked his father-in-law, reckoned his wife's descent from the female side of her family, which had been remarkable for three generations back. Her mother Rachel Priestman, her grandmother Margaret Bragg, who had taken her to Ackworth on that lucky day, and was much loved by John Bright, and her great-grandmother Rachel Wilson, had all been or still were preachers and missionaries, often travelling through England and America to address and encourage Friends. Rachel Priestman was a 'plain Friend,' and kept her love of nice things in very close bounds. Even in those days when most Friends still wore the plain dress, there was a considerable difference in its cut and style, and the shade of the grey or dove or drab. All music and nearly all pictures were forbidden in the Priestman household. But the value set upon sincerity and simplicity encouraged a certain style in the equipment of a house, which saved it from the invading vulgarity of Victorian taste in furniture, while the love of beauty found its outlet in china and linen, and above all in flowers.

We shall see more, in later years after Elizabeth Bright's death, of the long and friendly struggle of the Priestman influence against the Bright nature, in the endeavours of John's mother-in-law to preserve him from politics in order that he might possess and cultivate his own soul.

The year 1840, the one year of unclouded happiness which Bright enjoyed with his young wife at Rochdale before her health began to give way, witnessed his epic battle with the vicar, a theme worthy not only of the comic muse but of a glance from Clio herself; for it reveals the men and the passions of that age in their native colours. To the biographer of Bright its importance lies in the fact that the battle of the Rochdale Church-rates first showed to the world, as well as to an astonished vicar, the stuff there was in one of his parishioners.

In the period immediately following the Revolution of 1688,

when the dissenters were barely a twentieth part of the population, glad to enjoy, under the shelter of the Whig magnates, a precarious and limited toleration, it was not unnatural that all the inhabitants of a parish should from time to time be subjected to a 'rate' for the purposes of the church where nearly all of them worshipped. But after the Wesleyan movement and the rapid growth of all forms of dissent that followed on it, active non-conformists became as numerous, at least in North England, as active Churchmen, and Church-rates became, therefore, a most invidious privilege. In parish after parish trouble arose, growing ever more acute as the nineteenth century wore on. After the passing of the First Reform Bill the dissenters expected that the compulsory rate would immediately be abolished, but the concession was most unwisely delayed until 1868. It was indeed in the competence of a majority of parishioners to refuse the churchwardens' demand to have the rate levied, but even this right was not always allowed by the Church without litigation, and if a majority of one could be secured, and all the due forms had been observed, the rate was by law compulsory on every parishioner.

Jacob Bright, senior, refusing to pay his Church-rate, had his property distrained more than twenty times between 1811 and 1833.[1] His son used to recount these family reminiscences, when pestered in his old age by fashionable ladies besieging him for subscriptions to church bazaars. In 1835 the Church-rate at Rochdale was defeated by a majority, but the wardens proceeded to act in spite of this vote, and distrained illegally on some of the poorest persons in the parish, from one of whom they carried off his Bible.

Five years later the story was told by John Bright to an assemblage of several thousand parishioners, in the presence of the leading partisans of the Church clergy, none of whom could deny its truth.[2] 'They entered,' said Bright, 'the house of an inhabitant of Spotland, poor James Brearley, who was then on his death-bed; the illegal claim upon the poor weaver was fourpence; they seized a looking-glass, but this would not cover the costs, and their ruthless hands then seized his family Bible, and sold it for an illegal rate.' But there were dissenters rich enough to take the case up from court to court until these proceedings were finally condemned as illegal.

[1] For details see *Robertson*, pp. 16-22. It is therefore incorrect to state, as is done in Raines' *Vicars of Rochdale*, ii. 311, that in Vicar Hay's time Church-rates were not collected 'from quakers or from certain individuals known to be peculiarly hostile to the impost.'

[2] At the meeting in the churchyard described p. 39 below.

During this period of injudicious insistence on doubtful rights, the churchmanship of Rochdale was continuously on the wane. The pluralist vicar, Mr. Hay, one of the famous magistrates of the 'Peterloo' massacre, seldom resided in the parish, and left the field of religious work more and more to the dissenters, whom he rated for the benefit of his own emptying church, and who retaliated by speaking of him as 'Peterloo.'[1]

But in March 1840 Hay was succeeded by John Nassau Molesworth, a foeman worthy of Bright's steel. The new vicar was a man of devoted energy, destined to raise the Church life of the town to a high level; but with many admirable virtues he combined a most pugnacious and sometimes tyrannical temper. His quarrels with his bishop, against whom he revived a false charge of drunkenness, showed that his zeal could overflow the narrow bounds of sect. But most of all he loved to enforce the privileges of his Church against her foes. In the first few months of his arrival in Rochdale, Molesworth raised again the question of the Church-rate, and fought it to a finish in one last glorious struggle which convulsed the town as no other event in its recorded history.

A preliminary skirmish occurred on June 17—thus described in John Bright's diary: 'This morning a meeting was held in the Commissioner's Room to address the Queen on her escape from assassination. In the placard the Vicar was announced as chairman, but J. B.' (viz. the diarist) 'compelled an appeal to the meeting which decided against the Vicar, on the ground that he had listened without rebuke to the disgraceful language uttered at a public dinner in the City of Canterbury in 10th month last, disgraceful to all who tamely heard it, and traitorous to the Queen.' Bright was here referring to a Tory banquet held at Canterbury in the previous autumn, which had caused scandal because Mr. Bradshaw, M.P., had there expressed with unwise vehemence the natural resentment of the Tories against Queen Victoria for her partiality to their rivals in the Bedchamber Question.[2] John Bright told his fellow-townsmen that since Mr. Molesworth had been present at this banquet, had heard the offending speech, and had pro-

[1] In an 'Address to the Inhabitants of Rochdale,' 1840, John Bright says: 'In 1795 the Vicar of the Parish was concerned in directing the Soldiers to fire upon the people, when (August 3) two aged men, each having seen 80 years, were shot dead on Rochdale Bridge! In 1819 (August 16) the late Vicar's voice was heard shouting "Onward, Onward!" to the Yeomanry Cavalry as they rode down the people assembled in Manchester to petition Parliament.'

[2] Bradshaw's words (as reported) can be read in the *Annual Register*, 1839, p. 311. The speech made a great scandal, and occasioned a duel between two M.P.'s. But Bradshaw claimed that his words had been misreported.

posed the health of the man who made it, he was therefore not a fit person to take the chair at a meeting complimentary to her Majesty in person. The vicar, however, insisted that the chair was his by right, or at least by previous arrangement with those who had summoned the meeting. An angry scene ensued between the two parties, which ended in the vicar declaring the meeting dissolved, and leaving the room, 'followed by a bevy of parsons and a sprinkling of Tories.'[1] The majority of the assembly remained behind, and, after formally adjourning to an open space, held a mass meeting of two thousand people at which they carried their address, and sent it up to Earl Stanhope for presentation to the Queen. 'The principle maintained in this contest,' concludes the diarist, 'was the right of a public meeting to appoint its chairman, and at the same time a fitting condemnation was passed upon those who become disloyal to their monarch the moment she ceases or refuses to do the bidding of their party.'

To give a complete picture of the attitude of Bright and his fellow-townsmen to the monarchy, it is only fair to quote from his diary of four months before :

> '1840, 2 month, 10. This day the Queen is married ; in Rochdale there is no appearance of rejoicing, and how or why should there be ? The people are discontented, out of employ, short of food ; let the Government repeal the Corn Law, cease to plunder the mass for the aggrandisement of the Aristocracy, and give them education in spite of the Church, and then they may reasonably be asked to feel and to show some pleasure at a royal marriage.'

But the attempted assassination of the young Queen, and the chance of a fair hit at the vicar, had warmed John Bright's loyalty up to bloodheat, even before the Repeal of the Corn Laws.

On July 10 following, the vicar and churchwardens demanded a rate, and refused the proposal that it should be optional. A poll was demanded, and held for five days, resulting in a defeat of the compulsory rate by 4060 votes to 3976. The Church party, instead of accepting the decision, and falling back on an optional rate, called another meeting for July 20, to renew their full demand. This meeting was to be held at the church itself.

[1] The Church account of the affair is that some Liberal magistrates went out also, and that the most respectable inhabitants of Rochdale held a subsequent meeting in the Town Hall—the vicar in the chair—and passed their address to the Queen.

The ancient church of St. Chad, on the brow of the steep hill to the south of Rochdale, is reached from the town below by a long flight of old stone steps, up which on July 20 flocked a clamorous mob of four or five thousand parishioners. When the doors of the church were opened for the meeting, an ugly rush took place to secure standing room inside, hats were crushed and clothes torn, and some determined persons made entry by the rude device of leaping from points of vantage on to the massed heads of their fellow-parishioners and being so carried into the church, as it were in triumph. The scene inside was a welter of rage and tumult that nothing could reduce to order. Finally, since not half the crowd could gain admittance, the proceedings were adjourned to the graveyard outside. This was more convenient ground for a public meeting than most cemeteries, as there are no grass plots and no enclosures to be respected, the whole space being paved with flat stone tombs of the seventeenth and eighteenth centuries. A few of these flat grave-stones are raised two or three feet above the rest, and one of them, still shown to the visitor, served as improvised hustings. Bright, as he wrote in his diary that evening, 'stood on a tombstone with the vicar and his brood of clergymen, and told them more truth than they are accustomed to hear!'

The 'truth' thus defiantly poured forth to a raging mob of friends and foes, was afterwards printed on a broadsheet and widely circulated throughout Lancashire. A passage from this speech may serve to give some idea of Bright's early eloquence, as yet imperfect and unchastened, but breathing the same vigour, simplicity, and idealism that inspired his maturest art:

> 'I hold that to quote scripture in defence of Church-rates is the very height of rashness; the New Testament teems with passages inculcating peace, brotherly love, mutual forbearance, charity, disregard of filthy lucre, and devotedness to the welfare of our fellow-men. In the exaction of Church-rates, in the seizure of the goods of the members of his flock, in the imprisonment of those who refuse to pay, in the harassing process of law and injustice in the Church courts, in the stirring up of strife and bitterness amongst his parishioners—in all this a clergyman violates the precepts he is paid to preach, and affords a mournful proof of the infirmity or the wickedness of human nature. I believe that in these contests for the

iniquitous exactions of the Church, more mischief will be done, and more strife engendered, than will be atoned or compensated for by all the preaching of the clergy of this parish during the rest of their lives. Fellow-townsmen, I look on that old building, that venerable building, for its antiquity gives it a venerable air, with a feeling of pain—I behold it as a witness of ages gone by, as one of the numberless monuments of the piety or zeal of our ancestors, as a connecting link between this and former ages; I could look on it with a feeling of affection, did I not know that it forms the centre of that source of discord with which our neighbourhood has for years been afflicted, and did it not seem the genial bed wherein strife and bitter jarring were perpetually produced to spread their baneful influence over this densely-peopled parish! I would that that venerable fabric were the representative of a really reformed Church—of a Church separated from her foul connexion with the State—of a Church depending upon her own resources, upon the zeal of her people, upon the truthfulness of her principles, and upon the blessing of her Spiritual Head! Then would the Church be really free from her old vices; then would she run a career of brighter and still brightening glory; then would she unite heart and hand with her sister Churches in this kingdom, in the great and glorious work of evangelising the people of this great Empire, and of every clime throughout the world!'

The consequence of this meeting in the graveyard was a second poll of the parishioners, held within less than a month of the first. The clergy were determined to have the recent decision overthrown, cost what it might. The ardours of the contest far exceeded those of a parliamentary election. During the days of the polling many of the factories were closed, as the men could not be kept out of the streets. Red and blue bands paraded and fought; food and drink were to be had for the asking; drunken voters were brought up in wagons, for the possession of which fierce battles took place between the sober. There was wholesale intimidation and corruption on the Church side, and as the polling was open, this turned hundreds of voters. But in violence the anti-rate party were certainly not behindhand, for if the poorer they were the more popular side, and their strength was in the mob. Some companies of the 79th Highlanders were called out with fixed bayonets, to the intense indignation of Bright. The fortunes of the poll varied from day to day. The vicar, unfairly if not illegally, at the last moment prolonged the polling beyond the hours agreed; and he finally announced the result as 6694 in favour of the rate to 6581 against.

But the end was not yet. On January 18, 1841, nine gentlemen were summoned before the magistrates for refusing to pay the rate thus imposed. The court-room and streets round were filled by eager partisans of both sides. 'The informations,' notes Bright in his journal, 'were dismissed on the ground that all the wardens must unite in the proceedings, whereas only one of them had taken out the summons.' After that, it was found impossible to enforce the compulsory Church-rate in Rochdale, and Mr. Molesworth, thus saved from his worse self, was able to begin his real work in life, helping to raise the religious life of a people that can be led but not driven.

Twenty years after these events, while supporting in the House of Commons a Bill to abolish Church-rates, Bright spoke as follows:

> 'I live in a town in which contests about Church-rates have been carried on with a vigour and determination, and, if you like it, with an animosity which has not been surpassed in any other part of the kingdom. . . . What was the result of that struggle? The result was that the Church-rate was for ever entirely abolished in that parish. I have since seen several lists of candidates for the church-wardenship put forth by Churchmen, each of which claimed support upon the ground that they would never consent to the reimposition of a Church-rate; and the parish has been for many years upon this question a model of tranquillity. It would not be enough that it should be a model of tranquillity if the result had followed which the learned gentleman foretold in such dolorous language, that religion would be uncared for, and that the Gospel would no longer be preached to the poor; but I will undertake to say that since that contest that venerable old parish church has had laid out upon it, in repairing and beautifying it, from money subscribed not altogether, but mainly by Churchmen, ten times, aye, twenty times as much as was ever expended upon it during a far longer period of years in which Church-rates were levied.' [1]

[1] My authorities for the above paragraphs on the religious history of Rochdale are Raines' *Vicars of Rochdale*; a small handbook of the same title by the Ven. J. M. Wilson, Canon of Worcester; the *Dict. of Nat. Biog.* on Molesworth; Robertson's and Barnett Smith's lives of Bright; Bright's

In October 1840 a daughter was born to John and Elizabeth Bright, whom they named Helen.[1] A prospect of long family happiness seemed to be opening out before them ; but almost from the date of Helen's birth, her mother showed signs of consumption, and in spite of changes of residence in pursuit of health, which divided her from her busy husband to the constant grief of both, the decline became month after month more rapid.

During the period of his married life, both before and after his wife's decline began, Bright, as his journal shows, visited Manchester at least once a week, going in by the new-fangled 'railway' either on business of the mill or for Corn Law purposes—sometimes dining with Cobden, sometimes attending a committee, or writing an article for the *Anti-Corn Law Circular*. His speaking for the League was still almost entirely confined to Burnley, Bury and the neighbourhood of Rochdale, but Cobden knew how great a help Bright's oratory would be to the cause, if he could take him all over the island as his companion on his now ceaseless missionary journeys. Whether, if Mrs. Bright had lived, Cobden would have persuaded her husband to adopt the nomad habits of an agitator moving from town to town without rest for five years on end, it is impossible to determine. I am inclined to believe that but for his wife's death Bright would have led a happier but a less important and a less public life.

In 1841 Bright took a house for his wife at Leamington, on the doctor's advice.

> 'There is not a period of my life,' he afterwards wrote to his sister-in-law, 'to which I turn with more satisfaction than to that I spent at Leamington. It seems that I could have been well content for ever almost to have cared for that dear sweet being whose very presence made me happy. And she bore her sufferings and the gradual sinking to the grave with such a gentle temper, and could smile upon us as she passed for ever from our sight.'

At length the end came. 'It seemed not like the chamber of death,' he wrote in after years. 'There was nothing fearful in that memorable time—it was more as the gate of Heaven.'

pamphlet *On the late Church Rate Contests, 9th month 1840*; the broadsheet of his speech; his private diary for 1840 (MS.); and an important pamphlet on the Church side, *The Correspondence between the Vicar of Rochdale and John Bright, Esq., M.P. With Introductory Remarks by the Vicar. 1849.*

[1] Now Mrs. W. S. Clark of Street, Somerset.

On the 10th of September he wrote to Cobden:

> 'It has pleased the Almighty to take from me my beloved and cherished companion. She sank peacefully to her rest about one o'clock this day. She had almost no suffering, and death to her had long lost his terrors. Until she became mine, I did not know that mortality ever was the abode of so much that was pure and lovely. Her sainted spirit I cannot doubt is now an inhabitant of that city "where none can say he is sick," and in this deep affliction my heart rejoices in the full assurance that to my precious wife the change is inconceivably glorious.
>
> 'I know thou wilt sympathise with me in this very deep trial, and it is therefore I write to inform thee of it.
>
> 'I hope this may reach thee before thou leaves to-morrow.'

On the 13th Cobden was at Leamington, at his friend's side, bringing with him, as was his custom, not the mere balm of comfortable talk, but a plan to aid the stricken. The story has been told once for all in Bright's own words.[1]

> 'At that time I was at Leamington, and on the day when Mr. Cobden called upon me—for he happened to be there at the time on a visit to some relatives—I was in the depths of grief, I might almost say of despair, for the light and sunshine of my house had been extinguished. All that was left on earth of my young wife, except the memory of a sainted life, and a too brief happiness, was lying still and cold in the chamber above us. Mr. Cobden called upon me as his friend, and addressed me, as you might suppose, with words of condolence. After a time he looked up and said, "There are thousands of houses in England at this moment where wives, mothers, and children are dying of hunger. Now," he said, "when the first paroxysm of your grief is past, I would advise you to come with me, and we will never rest till the Corn Law is repealed." I accepted his invitation. I knew that the description he had given of the homes of thousands was not an exaggerated description. I felt in my conscience that there was a work which somebody must do, and therefore I accepted his invitation, and from that time we never ceased to labour hard on behalf of the resolution

[1] Bright's speech at the unveiling of Cobden's statue. Bradford, July 25, 1877.

which we had made. Now, do not suppose that I wish you to imagine that he and I, when I say "we," were the only persons engaged in this great question. We were not even the first, though afterwards, perhaps, we became the foremost before the public. But there were others before us; and we were joined, not by scores, but by hundreds, and afterwards by thousands, and afterwards by countless multitudes; and afterwards famine itself, against which we had warred, joined us; and a great minister was converted, and minorities became majorities, and finally the barrier was entirely thrown down. And since then, though there has been suffering, and much suffering, in many homes in England, yet no wife and no mother and no little child has been starved to death as the result of a famine made by law.'

Meanwhile, through no fault of Corn Laws, one little child was motherless and one man forlorn.

CHAPTER III

'THE CONDITION OF ENGLAND QUESTION'

'We, your petitioners, dwell in a land whose merchants are noted for their enterprise, whose manufacturers are very skilful, and whose workmen are proverbial for their industry. The land itself is goodly, the soil rich, and the temperature wholesome. It is abundantly furnished with materials of commerce and trade; it has numerous and convenient harbours; in facility of internal communication it exceeds all others. For three-and-twenty years we have enjoyed a profound peace. Yet, with all these elements of national prosperity, and with every disposition and capacity to take advantage of them, we find ourselves overwhelmed with public and private suffering. We are bowed down under a load of taxes; our traders are trembling on the verge of bankruptcy; our workmen are starving; capital brings no profit and labour no remuneration; the home of the artificer is desolate, and the warehouse of the pawnbroker is full; the workhouse is crowded, and the manufactory is deserted. We have looked on every side, we have searched diligently in order to find out the causes of a distress so sore and so long continued. We can discover none in nature or in Providence. Heaven has dealt graciously by the people; but the foolishness of our rulers has made the goodness of God of none effect.'

Chartist Petition to the House of Commons, 1838-39.

At the time of Queen Victoria's accession, a prophecy that the new reign would come to be regarded in the retrospect as a period of domestic peace and plenty, and of progress in the well-being of the people, would have seemed to the then starving millions a mockery of their distress. Yet, in the course of that memorable reign, real wages, that is wages measured by their purchasing power, very nearly doubled, and the Victorian era became a synonym for economic and social progress. John Bright was a living force in the work of elevating the condition and status of the masses. The significance of his life, otherwise than as a series of speeches delivered, derives from 'the condition of England question,' as Carlyle in 1840 dolefully called it, and in particular from those parts of the question with which Bright concerned himself as an agitator—the landlord power, the Corn Laws, and the franchise.

It is a law of human affairs that monopoly of power leads to its abuse. But the evils of the system that concentrated local and central authority in the hands of the landlord class had been kept within bounds and concealed from the eye by much that was gracious, in the period before the French Revolution and the contemporary 'industrial revolution' in England. In a society mainly agricultural like that of the eighteenth century, the country gentlemen would in any case have been the leaders of the nation, even if they had not acquired an almost formal monopoly of power. And in the age of Reynolds and Gibbon our aristocracy was what aristocracies always claim to be but very seldom are, the diligent and successful patrons of art, letters, and intellect. In politics half the oligarchy were engaged in defending the 'liberties of the subject' against King George III. The Whig aristocrats discoursed of Brutus and Hampden, and thought of themselves as the leading citizens of a free country. There was a breath of liberty about the England of Chatham, unlike the hothouse atmosphere of Versailles or the parade-ground where Frederick surveyed his grenadiers.

But these pleasant times and picturesque attitudes passed away before the end of the century. The potentialities of evil latent in the landlord monopoly of power became manifest when the industrial revolution came to its crisis. The inevitable miseries of the period of transition from the old to the new economic order in town and village were enhanced, not only by a twenty years' war with the French Revolution, but by the fact that all power in Britain was in the hands of one class. The country gentlemen, as any other class would have done in similar circumstances, used the power of the State to supervise the economic changes, not a little in their own interest.

It was indeed necessary to enclose much village and common land in order to grow food for the rapidly increasing population of the island, prior to the development of the great sources of food-supply oversea. But the enclosures were effected by the landlord Parliament with but slight consideration for the property of the many and the interests of the poor, as Arthur Young himself confessed. The peasants lost through the Enclosure Acts their ancient right over the land, without receiving any permanent compensation; and this unhappily took place during the very years marked by the destruction of the peasants' village industries owing to the invention of machines, and the consequent transference of manufacture to specialised centres of industry. Thus deprived at once of his two sources of independence, and ruined by war taxes and prices, the villager became the landless hireling of the big tenant-farmer and landlord. If the peasant refused to serve the farmer at starvation wages, he could only move to the town. But there he was equally at the mercy of the manufacturer, in those hard days when there were no effective Factory Acts, and when trade unions were punished as illegal associations. The happy truth that short hours and good wages would produce better work, was still hidden from mankind. One half of the accepted political economy of the day taught the educated classes to believe that self-interest and ruthless competition were the true philanthropy, and that starvation was Nature's discipline for a people who would breed too fast. Such doctrine fell gratefully on the ears of enclosing landlords and sweating manufacturers, who paid scant attention to the other half of the school of wisdom from which they quoted, for as yet they eschewed free trade. They practised all that was harshest in 'the dismal science,' and left all that was good in it unheeded.

This marked retrogression in the physical and moral state of the people, of which, in spite of much subsequent reform, the inherited effects have by no means yet disappeared from our midst, was largely the result of the twenty years' war against the French Revolution. Our national glories were paid for not only by a debt burdening posterity, but by taxation that raised to starvation prices nearly everything men required. At the same time Napoleon cut us off from the wheat supplies of the Continent. The knowledge of what that war had meant to the mass of the people while it lasted, and the legacy of misery and degradation that it left behind, was burnt into the soul of Bright, and reinforced by its modern example the faith of his peace-loving forefathers. His view of the unnecessary character of the war begun in 1793 may be wrong—or it may be right; but his grasp on the fact that war though sometimes sport to the rich is always death to the poor, was to stand England in good stead in coming years.

Economic misery and loss of social independence were accompanied by political reaction. The privileged classes over here would have been more than human if they had not taken alarm at the French Revolution. From Shakespeare's cliff could be descried the shores of a land where the country houses were being sacked by the villagers, where the 'quality' were hiding in garrets or perishing on the scaffold, where hares and pheasants were being knocked on the head like vermin.

The plague-blast of fear and suspicion crossed the Channel, and our rulers ceased to trust the people. The 'loyal Britons' to whom Chatham had appealed, became the 'swinish multitude' of Burke's later philosophy. Politics became hard and brutal. Critics of the existing order of things were persecuted and silenced, everywhere except in the House of Commons, where they were outvoted by six to one.

Up to the beginning of the war against the French Revolution, the country had not felt scarcity, except in years of failure in the crops. In the eighteenth century, England was still a corn-exporting country, and the Corn Laws, which then took the form of bounties on export, aroused no passion either of approval or of criticism. At one period Lord North repealed the bounties, though not in response to any important agitation. Between 1763 and 1792 the price of wheat varied between 34 and 57 shillings a quarter. In the following twenty-three years of rapidly rising population, foreign war and 'industrial revolution,' it varied between 49 and 126 shillings, but this terrible addition to the miseries of the time cannot be attributed to the Corn Laws: the Act of 1804 imposed heavy duties, but only when wheat stood at or below 63 shillings, and it was therefore a dead letter, as the price never fell below 70 shillings during the rest of the war. Napoleon was a better friend to the landlords than any Corn Law could be.

When, however, peace returned, one of the chief benefits which it might have been expected to bring was a fall in the price of corn; and, in fact, the first result of restored trade with the Continent on its release from Napoleon's thraldom, was a fall of wheat from well over 100 to 65 shillings a quarter. It was then that it seemed good to the wisdom of Parliament to set about starving the people by law in real earnest.

Three classes conceived that they had an interest in the Corn Law of 1815 and its successors—the parson, whose tithe varied with the price of corn,[1] the tenant farmer, and the land-

[1] Bright in 1843, speaking at Durham of the attitude of the Church clergy to the Corn Laws, said, 'It is a misfortune that by a law made by the Parliament of the country, this body of men, especially appointed to take charge of the flock, should, instead of being the shepherds, appear to all men's eyes as the shearers; and that their enormous influence should, in almost all the parishes of England, be bound up in the conservation of the most odious enactment which was ever recorded upon the statute-book.' Cobden, a loyal Churchman, wrote to Bright in 1842, 'The Church clergy are almost to a man guilty of causing the present distress by upholding the Corn Law, they having themselves an interest in the high price of bread.'

lord. These classes had for twenty years been enjoying an artificial prosperity from the war prices so injurious to the nation at large. During the first years of the century landlords' rents had doubled in many districts of England, and large tracts of new land had been brought into cultivation. In Scotland it was estimated that rents had risen from two millions in 1795 to over five millions in 1815. But so long as the war lasted, the rise in food prices more than made up to the farmers for the rise in rents. In South England the farmers, who in the previous century had generally done their work side by side with their labourers, and even eaten their meals, and lived on terms of social intercourse with them, now assumed the habits of a separate caste. Many of them were enabled to live a life of ease and moderate luxury, and to imitate the sports and habits of the country gentlemen; while the agricultural labourer declined into an abject condition, losing at one and the same time his rights over the land, his village industries, and the purchasing power of his wage. Before the war ended, the farmers had come to regard comfort and plenty as theirs by right. To the farmer, therefore, as well as to his landlord, the fall of prices on the return of peace seemed a calamity at variance with the laws of nature and Providence. The farmer, instead of agitating against the landlord for a proper reduction of rents, combined with him to demand an improper enhancement of prices.

So Parliament passed the Corn Law of 1815. This famous measure absolutely prohibited the importation of foreign corn until wheat stood at 80 shillings a quarter, and other grain at proportionate rates.[1] The legislature ignored the prosperity enjoyed by British agriculture in the last century under low prices, and the patent misery of the nation under the high prices of the recent war. To maintain rents which had doubled while the people starved, it was determined to perpetuate by law the artificial conditions which the war had created.

Never was any class more supreme in a State than the landlords of Britain in the year of Waterloo, but the outrage which they inflicted on the nation was so cruel that the victim dared to writhe. There had been no political agitation of a formidable character for many years past, but the Corn Bill of March 1815 aroused the middle and lower classes to united action. The Lord Mayor and City magnates set an example, followed in most of the towns of North and South England: meetings

[1] Colonial corn, then a very limited supply, might be introduced when wheat was at 67 shillings.

were held to petition Parliament, usually with the Mayor presiding. The Manchester petition bore 54,000 signatures, including the names of the great commercial houses that reappeared a generation later in the lists of the League. The *Times* newspaper pleaded the cause of the nation against the landlords day after day in its one leading article, and apologised for mentioning the fact that Europe was at that moment being divided up by the Congress at Vienna, because 'in the present agitated state of the public mind, no subject but that of the Corn Laws appears worthy of attention.' A week later the escape of Napoleon from Elba partially distracted the attention of the paper and of the public.

While the middle classes thus expressed themselves in a manner then so unusual, the working classes were roused to the madness of despair. There were riots all over the country. Bakers' shops were plundered ; the houses of unpopular persons were attacked, and had to be defended by the military. Large crowds surrounded the House of Commons to intimidate the supporters of the Corn Bill. Croker was rescued with difficulty, and the Whig, Sir Robert Heron, appeared among his brother members with his coat torn to rags. The House has never been persuaded by such arguments : the hated measure passed by majorities of more than three to one, and became the law of the land. These events, that opened the great question settled in 1846, took place while John Bright, a little fellow of three, was toddling about the house and fields at Greenbank.

Between 1815 and 1838 the middle-class manufacturers, though continuing to be opposed to the Corn Law, let the agitation against it drop, partly because they were not yet whole-hearted Free Traders, and the goods which they themselves manufactured were, until 1824, heavily protected. But the working men, always the first to starve and the last to benefit when prices rose, still gave voice to their implacable hatred of the Corn Law.[1] At 'Peterloo' in 1819 the ragged cotton-spinners who met to demand Parliamentary Reform,

[1] The middle-class founders of the Anti-Corn Law League in the autumn of 1838 declared that they 'could not but regret that the merchants and manufacturers of Manchester should have been so long supine, and praised the poor hand-loom weavers, who had set the example of petitioning for the repeal of the Corn Laws.'—Prentice, *League*, i. 70. The short-lived movement among the manufacturers against the Corn Law in 1815 had been inspired in the minds of all manufacturers save a few by the belief that the Corn Law would raise the price of labour. When the League movement was started in 1838, the manufacturers had changed their standpoint, and neither expected nor wished for a reduction of wages as a result of Free Trade. See Prentice's *Manchester*, pp. 18, 75.

carried a banner with the device 'No Corn Laws,' and if that day the banner went down in blood, its motto was all the dearer to them for that. Whenever, as in 1825, there were even higher prices and worse distress than in other years, the cry to repeal the Corn Laws rose loud, and loudest of all in Lancashire among the working men. In 1827 Colonel Perronet Thompson, one of that fine band of Radical veterans of the Peninsular War, brought out his *Corn Law Catechism*, a model pamphlet which for many years held the first place for popularity in the political literature of the common people. This, too, was the period when Ebenezer Elliott of Sheffield began to write his *Corn Law Rhymes*, which told, certainly not in the language of literary insincerity or of 'middle-class agitation,' what the Corn Law meant to him and to his fellows :

> 'Bread-taxed weaver, all may see
> What that tax hath done for thee,
> And thy children vilely led,
> Singing hymns for shameful bread,
> Till the stones of every street
> Know their little naked feet.'

It was in such language and from such people that John Bright at Rochdale first heard of the Corn Laws. From the beginning to the end of his life he always regarded it as a working man's question, and as a question of simple humanity ; Ebenezer Elliott's lines were always in his heart and often on his lips :

> 'Child, is thy father dead?
> Father is gone!
> Why did they tax his bread?'

—this simple inquiry seemed to him, as to many others in those years of gathering wrath, to admit of no answer that could satisfy.

In 1828 the Waterloo Corn Law was replaced by the famous 'Sliding Scale,' the measure still in operation when Bright began his anti-Corn Law campaigns. By the 'Sliding Scale' wheat was admitted at the trifling duty of one shilling when the price was 73 shillings a quarter, but the duty rose rapidly to a prohibitive standard as the price fell. In practice it was not much better than the Act which it replaced.

The advent of the Whigs brought a large measure of political liberty and abolished many abuses, but made little difference to the Corn Law question. The Reform Bill of 1830-32 passed the unreformed House of Commons, only because it was so ingeniously constructed as to satisfy the middle class for the time being, while still leaving the landlords the strongest power in the State. The enfranchisement of the middle class was incomplete, and the distribution of seats unfairly favoured the landed interest. The *personnel* of the two front benches continued much the same in the 'thirties as it had been in the 'twenties. In spite of a Radical wing of men individually able but collectively impotent, like Joseph Hume, Charles Buller, and the historian Grote, the Whigs were a landlord party only one degree less than the Tories. After five years (1830-35) of beneficent and far-reaching legislation, the Whigs became sterilised. A landlord Parliament of able and liberal-minded men came to the end of its tether as an instrument of reform, just because it was a landlord Parliament. On the great question of the day it was fettered by class interest. It was the work of the Anti-Corn Law League to force the hands of Whig and Tory squires by a monster agitation of all other classes, enfranchised and unenfranchised alike. Apart from its economic results, Cobden's victory was a political and social revolution as great as the First Reform Bill. Only when Honourable Gentlemen had been compelled, very reluctantly, to repeal their own Corn Laws, did the sovereignty of England begin in any effective manner to be transferred from the squires to the middle class. And even then the process was far from complete.[1]

In 1840, the year before Bright's great activities began, the enhancement through the tariff of the price of corn and meat, butter and cheese, hay and oats, was reckoned by a secretary of the Board of Trade at £36,000,000 a year. This sum, he said, although only a part of it went into the Treasury, 'the public are in fact paying as effectually out of their pockets as if it did go to the revenue in the form of direct taxes.' Taking bread alone, he calculated that 'each person consumes on the average a quarter of corn (a year). We can put down at 10 shillings what Protection adds to its natural price.' [2] But this 'average' quarter of corn per head was not consumed by all

[1] 'The Reform Act of 1832,' wrote Bagehot, that acutest of observers, 'did not for many years disclose its real consequences; a writer in 1836 . . . would have been sure to be mistaken in them. A new Constitution does not produce its full effect as long as all its subjects were reared under an old Constitution, as long as its statesmen were trained by that old Constitution.'

[2] Deacon Hume, before the Committee of the House of Commons, July 1840. *Import Duties*, No. 601 (1840).

classes. The wealthier families were fed largely on meat and other foods superior to corn; while the lowest classes, who suffered most from the Corn Law, could not afford bread, but lived on potatoes, turnips, and other inferior foods. There remained a large middle section of the population, the better-off working men and the lower middle orders, to whom bread was the staple diet; these therefore used more than the 'average' quarter of corn per head, and paid much more than the ten shillings a year per head to keep up the landlords' rents. In case of a fair-sized family the tax on bread alone would amount to several pounds a year—a fifth of their income, as Cobden calculated. Meat, still more highly taxed, was placed beyond their means, and it was but seldom that they could afford butter, cheese and sugar.

Not only this bread-eating class, but the potato-fed class below them—the latter including the agricultural labourers at six shillings a week, the alleged 'beneficiaries' of Protection—struggled through from year to year by 'clemming.' 'Clemming,' a word terribly familiar under the Protectionist régime, means 'starving.' The prevalence of the habits of 'clemming' and eating potatoes and turnips, was among the reasons why corn did not always keep up at the price intended by a benevolent legislature. Prices of wheat, in fact, varied with the English harvest. The nation depended year by year on the home harvest instead of on the world harvest, from the steadying effect of which it was cut off by the Corn Laws.

These were the reasons why Bright felt so passionately about the Corn Laws. Once, in November 1843, while addressing a meeting of merchants, bankers, traders and others of Manchester, he said, 'I confess I have more sympathy with the millions of the working classes of Yorkshire and Lancashire than I have with the merchants and manufacturers of England. The latter are able to help themselves, and if they choose to invite upon their necks the hoofs of the landed oligarchy, they deserve the trampling. But the millions who toil, and who for years have been craving to be permitted to toil for their daily food, they have little power or influence over the Government. They are an enormous but a disorganised mass, and for them I have a sympathy, more intense than it is possible for language to describe.'

The 'enormous but disorganised mass' of the wage-earners in town and country would indeed have had no chance of freeing themselves from Protection if they had not had the help of the middle class. But the manufacturers found their trade being ruined by the taxes on food and raw material. One of the aspects of the tariff most resented in Lancashire was its effect upon foreign nations in stimulating competition with English manufactures. Foreign nations, if our laws had permitted them, would have continued to supply us with the food and raw material which they had in greater abundance than ourselves. But when we ourselves stopped that trade, they had nothing else to exchange for our manufactured goods, and were therefore forced to begin manufacturing those very goods for which England was renowned. In the heyday of British Protection, our foreign market ceased to expand. It is a mistake to suppose that our export trade has been always on the increase. Under the Protective system it was stagnant for long years together. The value of the declared exports in the five years succeeding the introduction of the Reform Bill (1830-34) was actually less than what it had been in the five years that succeeded the end of the war (1816-20), although three millions had been added to the population.

Home trade was in an equally bad condition, varying according to the good and bad harvest; the vast majority of the population, after buying food, had not the money to buy other articles. Cobden showed that no agricultural labourer in England spent more than thirty shillings a year in manufactures, if shoes were excepted. Bad as foreign trade was, more goods were exported to Brazil in one year than had been consumed in the same time by the whole agricultural peasantry and their families in England.[1]

With home and foreign trade stagnant, and population increasing by leaps and bounds, there must needs have been terrible suffering, even if such wealth as there was in the island had been well distributed.

The tariff that organised the ruin of the British manufacturer, did not even pretend to give him 'protection.' Huskisson's principal achievements in his budgets of 1824-25 had been a great reduction of the tariffs protecting English-made goods. The landlord M.P.'s were perfectly willing, so long as corn was well taxed, to let him make or mar British industry by an experiment in his Free Trade fad. And so it came about that when the Whigs and Peel succeeded to Huskisson, by far the greater part of the duties were imposed upon food and raw material, which the manufacturers and their workmen required cheap, while only a very small part of the tariff was directed to excluding foreign goods of the kinds

[1] Cobden's speech in House of Commons, March 13, 1845.

which they were producing. In 1840, out of more than twenty millions of revenue raised by Customs, the amount of duties levied on the plea of protection to British manufactures scarcely exceeded a million sterling. Thus, even if the protection of a million had been in the true interest of the manufacturers as a whole, they had to write it off against twenty times that sum collected in duties, chiefly on food and raw material, which were not even intended to benefit them, and most of which were doing them visible and daily injury.[1]

It is not easy to estimate the influence of the economists in the Free Trade movement. In its early and less democratic stages much must be attributed to the sound theorists who persuaded the minds of some of our statesmen. Had it not been for the rude interruption of the French war, Pitt might have realised the complete body of Adam Smith's doctrine in a series of peace budgets, before any one else understood what he was doing.[2] Huskisson, who thirty years later took up Pitt's abandoned task, was also inspired, directly or indirectly, by Adam Smith; and the personal influence of Ricardo in the House of Commons was considerable in the early 'twenties. The remissions of tariff by Huskisson and by Poulett Thomson, the Whig minister who followed slowly in his steps, were made by them in pursuance of a theory which the ordinary Whig or Tory member did not believe because it was still speculative, and had not been tested before his eyes. But the House tolerated experiments from men whose intelligence they respected—provided corn was left untouched. The mere power of academic persuasion would never have broken down the sacred barrier of the Corn Laws; for 'the dismal science' by itself could not call out the fighting forces of politics. The economists based their arguments on a view of human life, which, though true as regards commerce, was only partially true and wholly repulsive in many other relations of man to man. And they did not know how to carry their arguments from the study to the platform.

'The free traders,' Poulett Thomson confessed, 'have never been orators since Mr. Pitt's early days. We hammered away with facts and figures and some arguments; but we could not elevate the subject and excite the feelings of the people.' Indeed to render the valuable results of political

[1] See Select Committee of the House of Commons on Import Duties, 1840, report and evidence.

[2] It has been wittily said by Mr. Herbert Paul that Fox 'thought political economy was a dodge of Pitt's.' And nearly all of his supporters and opponents were equally in the dark.

economy human and popular is not easy, and it is a characteristic trumph of English political genius to have found out the way. In the first years of Queen Victoria's reign, the men born to do it were just beginning to buckle on their armour for a kind of warfare altogether new in history. Cobden and Bright were about to replace Malthus and Ricardo. Books of political economy used, it is said, to begin with the words, 'Suppose a man on an island.' But Cobden's thought began with visible starving Stockport, and having put a girdle round the commercial globe came back with gathered treasures of observation to end at Stockport again; while to Bright Free Trade was a religious passion, sustained by pity and wrath, which he had the gift to communicate in their purest form to thousands of hearers at a time.

But this religious passion was based upon careful and accurate thought. At the end of Bright's diary for 1843 is a short treatise on the Corn Laws in his handwriting, in which he has summed up his philosophy of the question:

> 'Corn Law.
>
> 'Monopoly of the home market given to the proprietors of the British soil, under pretence of public good. Monopoly presupposes some advantage to those who possess it.
>
> 'It gives to them the possession of the market and excludes foreign grown corn in order that in a market insufficiently supplied they may obtain a higher price than their corn is really worth. This higher price can only be obtained by preventing the food market being as abundantly supplied as it would be if the regular laws of commerce were not interfered with. This higher price therefore exists and is procurable only from the existence of scarcity intentionally created by law.
>
> 'This increased value places the food out of the reach of those whose means are most limited, whilst the more wealthy classes are still able to procure as much as they require. The pressure of scarcity comes then upon the poorest portion of the people.
>
> 'In a besieged city the rich and powerful can hold out longest—the poor and defenceless feel famine soonest.
>
> 'This law-made famine is unequal, sparing the rich and crushing the poor.
>
> 'Famine on board a ship at sea would be equally borne by all. Admiral and cabin-boy would share the biscuits,

but as the Corn Law scarcity is created for the especial benefit of one class it is but likely that all the suffering should be averted from that class.

'The scarcity affects various portions of the community in the inverse ratio of their power to endure it. The laborers probably are the only class that feel it in a positive insufficiency of food, and of these the weakest and poorest, whose labor is least valuable and least skilled, bear the greatest intensity of the suffering. Thus *Handloom Weavers*[1] and *Farm Laborers* are always heavy sufferers from scarcity.

'That portion of the population, a portion of whose food is thus withheld, or who are in consequence of the high prices of their usual food driven to articles of a lower quality, are evidently prevented from continuing or becoming consumers or purchasers of manufactured goods, clothing, furniture, hardware, earthenware, etc., and thus the demand for these articles declines so soon as a serious advance in the price of food takes place.

'Not only is the demand for manufactured goods cut off so far as this portion of the people are concerned, but a class, probably quite as numerous, above them in the social scale find it as much as they can do to provide food enough of their usual quality, and are compelled greatly to restrict their purchases of articles of manufacture, and to discontinue the consumption of many of them, and thus also all persons engaged in manufacturing pursuits find their customers impoverished, and the demand for their labor partially or wholly destroyed.'

In the winter of 1841, when Bright on his wife's death took the field in earnest, the political, economic, and social conditions of the country were all rapidly tending to a crisis on the Corn Law question that would sweep everything else aside. The Whigs had at length been beaten out of office in the General Election of the summer. While Cobden and his bereaved friend were making their compact at Leamington, Peel was settling into Downing Street, envied by the world as the leader of the Protectionist party returning victorious from the polls. But to himself and to his few intimates the chief in his hour of triumph appeared rather as a harassed and conscientious man of business, turning over the books of the country and reading there with growing alarm the tale of financial deficit and

[1] For the case of the Handloom Weavers, see p. 59 below.

economic distress, the legacy of high Protection. Meanwhile, in the provinces the stagnation of trade and the bankruptcy of one merchant and manufacturer after another was giving to Cobden's middle-class supporters the energy of despair; and the break-down of the Chartist movement was setting the political working men free to support the Anti-Corn Law League.

The Chartist agitation of 1838-42 was the first organised demand for a new Reform Bill to give votes to the working men. It was the first stage of the franchise movement which Bright conducted so vigorously and wisely through its later stages after 1848 until its triumph in 1867. To those who would rightly understand his life, it is important to observe how the movement previously failed when it had no such leadership.

The early Chartists neither sought nor obtained help from the middle classes; their oratory denounced manufacturers and landlords together as common tyrants of the people. Though the six points of the 'Charter' demanded changes in political machinery alone, the movement of which it became the watchword was social and economic. 'Chartism,' said one of its leaders, 'is a knife and fork question.'[1] It was the awakening of the town artisans, especially in the north, to a class consciousness of their wrongs and of the cruel conditions of life to which they had been reduced in the last fifty years. They, the larger and more miserable of the 'two nations,' described by Disraeli in his *Sybil*, knew by daily bitter experience the facts that we read with a shudder in old blue-books of that time. Their womenfolk and their little children in the coal mines dragged loaded trucks all day along low passages inch-deep in water, going on all fours like horses, with the chains fastened round their half-naked bodies.[2] Above ground, children worked in the fields in overseers' gangs, horribly reminiscent of the slave labour of Roman *latifundia*; and though since the Act of 1833 much had been done for children in factories, women as well as men still worked in them from twelve to sixteen hours a day. Yet as regards both hours and pay, the northern factory hand in the early 'forties was probably better off than most workpeople. The men in the

[1] Stephens. See also the heading to this chapter, p. 45 above.

[2] Children's Employment Commission, First Report, Mines, 1842, throws much light on the violence of the miners in the Chartist riots at Newport, 1839. The conditions of their employment were such as to breed barbarism.

factories were often paid 16s., sometimes 20s. a week, and the women 10s. or 12s. But the hand-loom weaver paid by the piece, struggling in his own home against the competition of the power-loom in the factories, earned not much more on the average than 8s. a week, and Bright described in his Corn Law orations how often in Lancashire he heard the sound of the shuttle going at midnight in the cottage of some hand-loom weaver working for dear bread and life. In the less highly organised trade of South England long hours and small pay were the rule, though rates of course varied greatly according to place, time, and trade. The agricultural labourer was paid from 6s. to 9s. a week. And during the two first years of Chartist agitation, the average annual price of wheat was 64s. and 70s. a quarter.

The hovels where the working people dwelt in the country rivalled for noisomeness the 'courts,' cellars,[1] 'alleys,' and 'wynds,' where the town artisan brought up his diseased and ignorant children to endure their heritage of misery; that in such surroundings the whole working class did not grow up habitual criminals is a credit to human nature. In one Dorsetshire village thirty-six persons dwelt on an average in every house. In the towns the over-crowding was nearly as bad: large families slept habitually in one bed; blankets and furniture were luxuries seldom known. Such was the lot of those in full work, but the chronic stagnation of trade caused terrible unemployment. In 1842, although 128,000 emigrated that year, the number of paupers was 1,429,089, nearly one-tenth of the total population. These were the days when Carlyle saw the workmen sitting 'enchanted' in St. Ives Workhouse, and was inspired by the spectacle to write his *Past and Present.*

Chartism, the claim that the working man should have a vote, was devised as a remedy for these conditions. It was a sign of good augury, for which other classes were not duly thankful, that in the worst hour of their misery and degradation our working men turned their hopes to constitutional and parliamentary methods of relieving their economic distress. It was in part the outcome of the Trade Union movement, which though still in its infancy and struggling hard against persecution[2] from without and mistakes within, was begin-

[1] A fifth of the inhabitants of Liverpool lived in cellars. *Engels*, 36. *Walpole's England*, iv. p. 358, chap. xvii.

[2] The Whig Government in 1834 transported six Dorsetshire labourers for 'administering illegal oaths' in forming a branch of the Grand National Trade Union.

ning to teach self-help and self-respect to the submerged millions.

It is not probable that the Chartist leaders, even if they had acted wisely, could have won the battle for the vote in that generation. Mountains of prejudice, that only the slow detrition of time could reduce, barred off the working man from the franchise. The Whigs liked well that in Reform-time the shadow of the working class should loom up behind them, an ominous ally in reserve, and be referred to in perorations as 'the people,' but Whigs and Tories were alike shocked at the idea of men in rags having direct and normal political power. The connection between a good coat and the right to the franchise seemed an obvious first postulate of civilised society; it was an instinct beyond the assault of argument, outside the proper limits of political controversy. A man in a bad coat—and in those days most working men had shocking bad coats—was still regarded as a possible French Revolutionist, a Jacobin in embryo. The best years of John Bright's life were to be spent in removing this deep-seated prejudice, and he only succeeded when the coats were better. In the early 'forties Bright was otherwise engaged, and the economic distress and agitation of the Corn Law period, which had caused the claim for the franchise to be brought forward by the worst sufferers, made not only the landlords but even the more sympathetic of the middle class anxious as to the uses to which the vote might be put by starving men. Furthermore, the illiteracy of a large part of the working classes made Cobden and many other educationists more anxious to teach them to read than at once to give them the vote. Macaulay, who in the early 'forties was well in advance of his Whig colleagues both as regards the Corn Laws and Factory Legislation, delighted both sides of the House with a philippic against working-class enfranchisement, tainted with the panic conservatism of Burke.[1]

These fears, so far as they were fears of revolution, were beside the mark. The English working men have never been Jacobins. But the Chartist leaders did their very best to give their enemies ground in reason, and succeeded in making these conservative warnings plausible and effective. At a time when the workmen could do nothing politically without some help from the middle orders of society, the Chartist leaders proclaimed a political class war, and threatened a social class war to follow. 'If they will not reform this,' said Stephens at a Chartist mass meeting in 1838, 'they shall have the revolution

[1] *Miscellaneous Works and Speeches.* Speech of May 3, 1842.

they so much dread. We shall destroy their abodes of guilt, which they have reared to violate all law and God's book. If they will not learn to act as law prescribes and God ordains, so that every man shall by his labour find comfortable food and clothing, . . . we have sworn by our God, by heaven, earth, and hell, that we shall wrap in one awful sheet of devouring flame the manufactories of the cotton tyrants and the palaces of those who raised them by rapine and murder.' [1] Such was, too often, their language, and yet they had no economic or social legislation to propose. They offered only the verbiage of vague threats to be carried out either if the vote were refused or else after it had been won. This was scarcely the way to obtain the vote from the enfranchised classes. It repelled even the more advanced middle-class supporters of Reform, and caused Francis Place, the Nestor of the working class, who had himself drawn up the People's Charter with its six points,[2] to despair of the movement which he had helped to initiate.

Place was waiting, as his letters show, for just such a man to lead the working classes as John Bright proved himself in later years. At present he could only mourn over the academic ineffectiveness of Hume and the other Radicals in the House, while the ranting of Stephens and Feargus O'Connor in the country reduced him to despair. The Chartist movement 'made respectable by sincerity, devotion, and even heroism in the rank and file, was disgraced by the fustian of its orators and the political and economic quackery of its pretentious and incompetent leaders, whose jealousies and intrigues finally brought it to nought.' [3]

In 1839, the second year of the movement, a split between the 'Physical Force' Chartists and the peaceful section was the beginning of the end; the abortive rising of the Welsh miners and their attack on the inn at Newport, dispersed by the military, brought things to a crisis. The Government hit back, and in the winter of 1839-40 had most of the Chartist leaders under lock and key. Chartism in 1840 'had become little but an organisation for breaking up public meetings.' The men who a few months back had been the acknowledged leaders of millions, and had hoped in sober earnest to bring the

[1] Gammage's *Chartist Movement*, p. 57. Gammage was himself a Chartist, and his book is a storehouse of information on the whole subject.

[2] Manhood Suffrage, Annual Parliaments, Equal Electoral Districts, Abolition of the Property Qualification for Members, Ballot, Payment of Members. Graham Wallas, *Life of Place*, pp. 359, 367, and *passim* chap. xiii. on Chartism.

[3] Mr. and Mrs. Webb's *History of Trade Unionism*, p. 158.

golden age to earth, suddenly found themselves flung back into complete disappointment and comparative obscurity. Their balked idealism curdled into a quarrelsome bitterness. Their methods in 1840 were thus described by their former ally:[1] 'They go from place to place where Anti-Corn Law lectures are given, they there make a disgraceful broil, which is reported in the *Northern Star* as a *glorious victory*. These 150 men call themselves *the people*, and their impudence and tyranny is without example.'

After the failure of the organised Chartist movement, though Feargus O'Connor and a few other leaders remained Protectionists partly from jealousy of the success of Cobden's League, the great majority of the political working men were free to devote their time and energy to the cause of Free Trade. From 1815 onward the Corn Laws had always been more unpopular with the working class than with any other.[2] But in the autumn of 1838 the high price of wheat, 77 shillings a quarter, had brought the middle-class 'League' into existence at the moment when the Chartist movement was at its prosperous beginning, and this coincidence had for a time estranged the champions of two causes, which were competing for the immediate attention of the public. One section of the Chartists had always, in spite of this inevitable rivalry, remained strong Free Traders. Ebenezer Elliott had said, 'I am for your Charter, but I am not for being starved to death first.' And now that Chartism had collapsed, the working men were certain to fall into line behind the League, if its middle-class organisers did not refuse their support. Of that there was little fear. The two most popular orators of the League, Bright and W. J. Fox, were thoroughgoing democrats. Cobden, indeed, believed that the middle class was the most intelligent part of the community, and would fain have seen it the repository of political power, to hold the balance between the landlords and the wage-earners; but he took a national, not a class view of the Corn Law question, both as to the results that would follow from Free Trade and as to the means and arguments by which the victory was to be won. Neither Cobden, Bright, nor any of the Leaguers looked on the abolition of the Corn Laws as a means of enabling them to pay lower wages, as some of the manufacturers had done in 1815.[3] The Leaguers said, and said truly as the event showed, that Free Trade would raise wages. They aspired to get the support not only of the

[1] *Francis Place*. (G. Wallas, p. 376).
[2] See pp. 50-51 above.
[3] See p. 50 above, note.

working men in town and country but of the manufacturers and of the very farmers themselves; and they succeeded—chiefly because they were convinced, and could give reasons to convince others, that Repeal would benefit every class of the community.

Cobden had no notion of quarrelling with the working men. When in the autumn of 1838 a friend had written to him despairingly of the vagaries of Radicalism and the violences of Chartism, he had replied that he preferred to see ill-directed violence rather than tame acquiescence in evils that had been borne too long, but that for his part he had a better plan to offer. 'I think the scattered elements may yet be rallied round the question of the Corn Laws. It appears to me that a moral and even religious spirit may be infused into that topic, and if agitated in the same manner that the question of slavery has been, it will be irresistible.'[1]

[1] *Morley*, i. 126.

CHAPTER IV

THE BATTLE OF THE CORN LAWS. I. BRIGHT'S ACTIVITY BEFORE HIS ENTRY INTO PARLIAMENT, 1842-43

'If I were the Conservative Party of England I would not for a hundred thousand pounds an hour allow those Corn Laws to continue! . . . Do you count what treasuries of bitter indignation they are laying up for you in every just English heart? Do you know what questions, not as to Corn prices and Sliding-scales alone, they are *forcing* every reflective Englishman to ask himself? . . . When two millions of one's brother-men sit in work-houses, and five millions, as is insolently said, *rejoice in potatoes*, there are various things that must be begun, let them end where they can.'

CARLYLE, *Past and Present*, bk. iii. ch. v.

At the General Election of midsummer 1841 the electors showed that they were weary of the Whigs, and in this at least they reflected the opinion of the unenfranchised millions. The Whigs had borne rule for eleven years—save for those few months round the Christmas of 1834, when Peel had been fetched post-haste from Rome—and they had done nothing during the last half of their long occupation except produce an annual deficit in their finance, and confess that they knew no remedy either for the deficit or for the stagnation of trade that was its cause. The Tories, in 1841, came back from the polls with a large majority. Peel, who had skilfully built up the party fortunes from their abject condition after the Reform Bill, was now supported in office by Stanley's vigour in debate, and Graham's high talents as minister—these two having come over from the Whigs in the interests of Church defence. Mr. Gladstone, a young man of thirty-two, labelled, now somewhat to his own discomfort, with Macaulay's sentence about those 'stern and unbending Tories,' brought his genius to the common stock of the great administration, and learnt to his own astonishment, in the apprenticeship which Peel made him serve in the Board of Trade, that finance and commerce could absorb him no less than poetry and religion.

In the autumn of 1841 nothing seemed less likely than that

the in-coming ministers, before they appealed again to the electors, would make England a Free Trade country. Protection had been one of the Tory cries at the recent electoral contest, because the Whigs in falling had clutched at some feeble Free Trade proposals which aroused the fears of the monopolists while evoking the scorn of the League. The Protectionists had routed the Whigs, but the League itself had lost nothing; several northern towns returned Leaguers in preference to Whigs or Tories; above all, Stockport returned Cobden.

When the new House met in August 1841 to turn out the beaten Whigs, and put Peel on the right side of the Speaker's chair, Cobden showed his mettle in a maiden speech on the Corn Laws which marked the beginning of democracy as a force to be reckoned with in that Chamber. Charles Villiers, who had hitherto borne the burden and heat of the day in Parliament with his annual motion for Repeal, now gave up without jealousy the place that worth and talent must yield to genius. Gladstone at once perceived that 'Cobden will be a worrying man about corn,' but no ministerialist foresaw that the supple, insistent commercial traveller on the back benches opposite had commenced a process of 'worrying' that would drive Graham and Gladstone, and their so solid-seeming chief, to confess themselves the converts of Manchester.

Cobden had come to the House of Commons to teach and not to learn. In the formation of his opinions and his plans he consulted not his brother members, but his friends in the north. And Bright became one of his chief confidants from the moment of that solemn compact at Leamington on September 13.[1] On the 9th of October Cobden wrote the following letter, perhaps the first of the many intimate exchanges of counsel that passed between these two until they were parted by death:

'My dear Bright,—The Parliamentary recess ought to be employed in some well-considered course of systematic agitation. Something *new* is wanting to give a novelty to our proceedings. The League has grown somewhat stale. If any object could be devised for calling a great convention of delegates together, and they could be incensed, and then set to work in their several locations, doing something useful, it would be a good step. But I

[1] See p. 43 above. Up to the time of the death of Bright's wife, Cobden's letters to him still began 'My dear Sir.' After it, they begin 'My dear Bright.'

really am at a loss for a new move. Can you help me to a suggestion?

'Are you ready to devote a portion of the winter to the working up to a head the agitation you have helped to set in motion? I don't see how it can be worked by Lancashire men without you. Pray give me a line of encouragement.'

Thus after an interval of four weeks did Cobden tactfully inquire after the fulfilment of that pledge of self-devotion which Bright had given him when under the influence of a great personal calamity. He then proceeds in the remainder of the letter to discuss the vexed question of Chartism, and the attitude which the League ought to adopt towards the claim of the working men to enfranchisement. Joseph Sturge, the Birmingham Friend of anti-slavery fame, supported the League, but was trying to find common ground with the Chartists on 'organic' Reform of Parliament. His 'letter,' here referred to, was one which he had just published, erroneously charging the League with a readiness to compromise on the principles of Free Trade.

'Sturge's letter,' continued Cobden, 'is a mischief maker. Joseph has a scheme at heart for an organic [Suffrage] agitation, but he should be content to mount his hobby without running full tilt upon us. I observe that the *Nonconformist* [newspaper] is Joseph's feeler. It gives in more and more each number to the necessity of organic reform. It is a pity that paper should lose its practical character by turning aside from questions of commercial reform, which it advocates ably, to the impracticable (at present) theories of the suffrage.'

Bright in his reply to Cobden is more sympathetic with the Suffrage agitation, and we see here, in this first interchange of political correspondence, the difference on that great question which, after the Corn Laws were safely abolished, caused an important differentiation of function between the two friends. On the question whether the League should take up the Suffrage, Bright's letter runs thus:

'Much may be said on both sides. If I could believe that we shall ever obtain the *hearty* help of the masses to procure the abolition of the Bread Tax, I would gladly vote to keep on as we have hitherto moved [viz. to leave the Suffrage question alone]; I begin to doubt this somewhat, and, whilst I doubt, I do not feel much more certain that *without* their help we can ever succeed. The Suffrage question would lose us many supporters, and gain us many—but it would not lose us as many now as it would have done at an earlier point in the career of the League. I am persuaded that the conduct of Parliament on this question has made many undecided reformers more thorough-going.'

He then puts Cobden right about the *Nonconformist* newspaper. Good churchman as Cobden was, he did not know his way about Dissenting journalism and politics as thoroughly as Bright, though both perforce regarded the Nonconformist clergy and newspapers as their allies in this struggle, and the Church clergy as their foes.

'As to the *Nonconformist*, thou art mistaken in fancying J. Sturge has influenced it. J. Sturge did not subscribe to it, and I believe has had no hand in it. Miall writes his own mind I know.[1] I wrote him an article "on the Corn Law and the Poor Law," which, if he approve, he will insert next week. . . . As to my help during the winter—recent events have somewhat impaired my elasticity, and nothing but the consciousness that we are in a struggle where we must either win or be destroyed with multitudes of our fellow-men, would induce me to take any public part at present. It would be much more agreeable to spend a few months in quiet retirement.'

He chose, however, the more patriotic course. During the next few weeks he was in the thick of the autumn campaign, speaking all over the country—once at a great meeting in the Mansion House, Dublin, with the mayor in the chair. And it is written in the chronicles of the League,[2] that early in the following February he was already known as 'among the first of the leaders in the movement.'

Meanwhile he was beset by far other thoughts, which he

[1] Edward Miall (1809-81) founded the *Nonconformist* as a weekly paper in 1841. It was strongly Radical, and urged the enfranchisement of the working men. In 1842 Miall and Sturge arranged conferences at Birmingham between middle-class Radicals and the Chartist leaders, their great object being to get the middle and lower classes to combine on the Suffrage question. But this desire was not sufficiently reciprocated by the section of the Chartists led by Feargus O'Connor, and though the first conference in April, which Bright attended, was harmonious, a second conference in December failed. Gammage's *Chartism*, 198, 241-6. *Life of E. Miall*, chap. v., and *Memoirs of Joseph Sturge*, chap. xiv.

[2] *History of the League*, by Prentice, i. 307.

was able in some measure to share with his lost wife's mother.

'My dear Mother,' he wrote to Mrs. Priestman in the second week of 1842, 'my mind often wanders back to the scenes which are passed, and which the mind can only recall. I have been highly blessed; I will not complain of the present, although I am alone again. Yet, although not in a murmuring spirit, many and many a tear starts as I survey the changed circumstances.'

Two months later he writes to her again about his infant daughter:

> 'Dear Helen is very engaging. To-night, when the tea-tray came in, she drew a chair to the table, and then took my hand and pulled me towards the chair, wanting me to sit down and give her tea. We ask her what the little bird says that will sing when we go to Newcastle; she says "cuckoo," and thus the little creature grows in body and mind. So I ought to be thankful so lovely a creature is spared me.'

A few months later he wrote to his father-in-law: 'When we have the sweet and innocent company of a little child, we cannot be alone.' In the summer, when Helen goes to visit her grandparents at Newcastle, he writes to them:

> 'One Ash is quiet enough. The nursery looks as though for months or years no child's prattle had been heard in it. Not a toy is seen, no disorder is apparent; sadness only reigns. But out of doors all is glorious, and one might suppose every plant and every blade of grass doing its utmost to exalt the praises of their wondrous author:
>
> '"His praise, ye winds that from four quarters blow,
> Breathe soft or loud; and wave your tops, ye pines,
> With every plant, in sign of worship wave."'[1]

But there was another and more formidable Bright, with whom his fellow-countrymen were getting daily better acquainted; and all around him were scenes of abject misery more to be pitied, as he says in his intimate letters, than his own stricken home at One Ash. The year 1842 opened with trade half ruined. A Protectionist Duke recommended the

[1] Hymn of Adam and Eve in book v. of *Paradise Lost*.

operative classes to take an occasional pinch of curry powder in a little water to allay their inconvenient craving for food—a prescription which, though His Grace is credited with having made it in perfect good faith and charity, became an unfailing resource to League speakers so long as the controversy lasted. Statistics of the ruin and misery in the north were at this time published by the League after a careful inquiry. In Cobden's Stockport 37 spinning firms had broken since 1836, 3000 dwellings were shut up, and over 70,000 persons had received relief. Some wag wrote up 'Stockport to let.' In Manchester 116 mills were idle, 681 shops and offices untenanted, 5492 dwellings unoccupied; in one district 2000 families were without a bed; the number of criminals in prison had doubled. And so the report went on through all the great northern towns with a like tale of misery from each.

Colonel Thompson, the Peninsular veteran and author of the *Corn Law Catechism*, published in this bad January of 1842 his account of 'the siege of Bolton.'

> 'I have been at the siege of Bolton. . . . And is it not a siege? Not carried on perhaps by an enemy within gunshot, but by one working on a wider radius, and making his blockade by sea upon the means of life. . . . Anything like the squalid misery, the slow, mouldering, putrefying death by which the weak and the feeble of the working classes are perishing here, it never befell my eyes to behold,' wrote this man, who had seen Spain turned into a charnel-house. 'Did you ever set eyes on a pennyworth of mutton? Come here and you shall see how rations are served out under the Landlord's state of siege. It might bait a rat-trap. Pennyworths of mutton and halfpennyworths of bread cut off the loaf, are what the shopkeepers of Bolton deal out to the inhabitants of their Jerusalem.
>
> 'If you are curious in human misery, if you are anxious to know what a shabby tyranny can bring the rank and file to suffer, come, at your leisure, to the "leaguer" of Bolton, and see what the people of Bolton sleep upon, if they do sleep. Chopped dirt, the sweepings of a hen-house mingled with a proportion of sparrows' nests, to show that men had heard of straw, would be the best representatives of what they huddle upon in corners and call it resting. And all this because Sir Having Greedy votes in the House of Commons for closing honest trade as the means of doubling his rents.'

In these circumstances Peel summoned Parliament early in February 1842, and the principal manufacturers of all the northern shires came up in deputation from the League to demand that he should save them and their employees from ruin, by an immediate repeal of the Corn Laws. Peel had his own plans, and refused to see them. The battle had come to be one for hearth and home, even for these 'captains of industry,' any one of whom might be bankrupt before the year was out. Enraged at the Prime Minister's refusal to see them, they determined to march on the House of Commons, as if they had been so many ragged Chartists. Arm in arm they tramped down the Strand and Parliament Street, a column of five hundred well-dressed but angry citizens, each a man of note in some northern town—arousing, as they marched along, mingled feelings of awe, sympathy and merriment among the gentler cockneys, who had not yet been drawn into the full current of the League in flood. Bright was stepping along in the procession, an honoured figure among them, for he had stirred them all at a meeting at the *Crown and Anchor* the day before, rivalling the eloquence of Dan O'Connell, who had spoken after him. Arrived at Palace Yard they stood around the entrance door, scuffling with the blue-coated 'Peelers,' and shouting 'Total Repeal' and 'Cheap Food,' so that their sound was heard in the Squires' Chamber. 'It was a strange scene of excitement amongst sober-minded persons—an indication of the stronger and more dangerous excitement of the masses.' Finally they marched back up Parliament Street. Close to the entrance of Downing Street they met Sir Robert Peel driving to the House. 'He seemed to think at first that they were going to cheer him, but when he heard the angry shouts of *No Corn Law, Down with the Monopoly, Give Bread and Labour*, he leaned back in his carriage grave and pale.' Some in the procession remembered that scene with compunction in later years, when Peel lay on his deathbed, having given them all they asked, and saved them alive. But for some years to come they still thought of him as their enemy.[1]

In fact, though it was not their cue to recognise it, he was already taking the first step in the economic regeneration of England. The annual deficit in the recent Whig budgets had taught Peel that heavy duties on a thousand different articles were more ruinous to commerce and manufacture than productive to the Treasury; and he saw that the desperate expedient to which the Whigs had been driven, of increasing the

[1] *Prentice*, i. 303-11.

duties in order to make up the deficiencies of revenue, had had exactly the opposite effect. He was not the man to remain in the position in which he had described the Whig Chancellor of the Exchequer, 'seated on an empty chest by the side of bottomless deficiencies, fishing for a budget.' Peel's budget of 1842 was the beginning of the end of Protection : it introduced the income tax as a substitute for indirect taxation ; it greatly simplified the elaborate but unscientific tariff that had grown by men's negligence rather than been built up by their design ; it abolished most of the remaining export duties on manufactured goods ; it removed the weight of import duties on raw material and on manufactured articles. By these great remissions Peel lost relatively little for the Treasury, and that little he supplied by reviving the income tax in time of peace. As a consequence of this change in our fiscal system, and the simultaneous rapid increase of steam traffic, British trade—stagnant since 1815 and moribund in 1842—began to go forward on its amazing journey of Victorian prosperity. Before Peel left office in 1846, he boasted to the House of Commons that 'notwithstanding the hostile tariffs of foreign countries, the declared value of British exports has increased above ten million pounds during the period which has elapsed since the relaxation of duties on your part in 1842.' [1]

In their grasp of Free Trade principles in all matters not concerning corn, Peel, Graham, and Gladstone in his humbler sphere in the Board of Trade, were already in 1842 far in advance of their avowedly Protectionist colleagues and supporters, and of the Whig leaders also. But in the matter of corn they were fettered by their pledges, and by the country gentlemen on the benches behind them ; neither were they yet convinced in their own minds of the necessity of complete repeal. Corn still seemed to them a thing apart. Peel was still unwilling to abandon the ideal of an island that could feed itself in time of war. And he was still under the delusion that wages rose with the rise in the price of food.

And so in the great budget of 1842, though Peel took giant strides towards Free Trade in other articles, his steps towards Free Trade in corn were as delicate as those of a man feeling his way in the dark amid hidden foes. He reshuffled the sliding scale in a downward direction, but he fixed the new tariff with

[1] Exports of British produce in 1842 were £47,000,000—lower than in any of the four previous years ; in 1845 they were £60,000,000, and in 1846 they were £57,000,000. In 1912, on the same basis of calculation, they were £480,000,000.

a view to keeping the price of wheat as near to 56s. as legislation could effect. The alleged object of the tariff of 1828, now repealed, had been to keep it at 64s.

Cobden was furious. 'I ask the Right Honourable Baronet,' he cried, 'whether, while he fixes his scale of prices to secure to the Landowners 56s. per Quarter for wheat, has he any sliding scale for wages? Will he give the people a law to keep up the rate of wages?'[1] The League had set its heart on 'total and immediate' repeal of the Corn Laws, and refused to be grateful for their partial reduction, even when accompanied by the removal of heavy duties on raw material. Cobden, by a rare miscalculation, denounced the income tax as a burden on the manufacturers outweighing all the good done by other parts of the budget; though in point of fact the much abused income tax was the key that unlocked the Free Trade larder. And so, during the weeks when Peel was passing his great Free Trade measures of 1842, his effigy was being burned in the towns of North England because he still withheld corn from the people.

Bright, while he welcomed the Free Trade parts of the budget, regarded the income tax with suspicion, because its incidence favoured agriculture at the expense of manufactures; for that and other reasons he would have preferred a Property Tax as the method of levying direct taxation. He explains these views in a letter to his sister-in-law:

> 'My dear Sister Margaret,—The rest of Peel's finance proposition, as far as the reduction or change of Taxes, will be found very beneficial. . . . As to the Income Tax, my opinion is that the needful revenue would be fairly and most fairly raised if paid by property, and by individuals in proportion to their property. And at first sight an Income Tax appears very plausible—look further at it and it is seen that it cannot possibly be collected without gross wrong. . . . It is a heavy tax upon all honest men who honestly declare the amount of their income, whilst knaves can often get off by a lie or a false oath. It causes persons in sinking circumstances to pretend to an income they have not, to sustain their credit, and then to pay their Tax out of the property of their

[1] It is sometimes said that Cobden wanted low wages. The opposite is the fact. He was one of the first to popularise the idea in Parliament, and among the manufacturers, that cheap labour was less remunerative than well-paid labour. *Morley*, i. 223. The League (1838-46) always preached that Free Trade would raise wages, and that that was one of its chief recommendations.

creditors. An Income Tax takes part of income from whatever source derived, and does not take it in proportion to the amount of property. Thus £1000 income received from a Mill, as my father receives from us, is only worth say £14,000 or 14 years' purchase if the income were to be sold. But £1000 from land would sell for £30,000 or 30 years' purchase. Because in 14 or 20 years the mill would be of little value probably and Land retains its value without material change, and as population increases its value increases. One man is worth £14,000 and the other £30,000, and yet they pay the same amount of Income Tax, which is clearly unfair. A Property Tax should be an assessment upon all land and buildings, and canals and railroads, but not on property such as machinery, stock in trade, etc.

'The aristocracy have squeezed all they can out of the mass of the consumers, and now they lay their daring hands on those not wholly impoverished. Again, they exempt Farmers paying under £300 a year of rent, which is a gross piece of favouritism to their own tenants,[1] and they fix the income of farmers above £300 a year at half the rent, thus making him pay on a supposed income less than his real one is or ought to be, and saving him from any inquisition into the state of his affairs.'

Although Peel's income tax did far more good than harm, much of the criticism which Bright here makes has been endorsed by posterity, as recent legislation shows. Death duties, graduation of income tax, and differentiation between earned and unearned income, have gone some way to meet the objections that he raised. Peel, indeed, was little to blame, for he had to pilot his income tax through the landlord Parliament, and this could be done only by concessions to agriculturists at the expense of the manufacturers.

In the debates that ensued on Peel's new Corn Law, feeling in the House ran hot against Cobden, whom the country gentlemen regarded as a low-born Jack Cade, stirring up the common people to mutiny against their natural governors. The class antagonism between landlord and cotton lord came to its climax in a furious scene one night in February 1842, when Mr. Ferrand was put up after dinner by his brother squires to teach the cotton-spinners a lesson. The House was filled to overflowing, and shouted with delight, as the mill-owners

[1] Other persons paid the full income tax if they had £150 a year.

and all their doings were denounced by a vulgar and incompetent advocate. In his hatred of the new social order, Ferrand commented in the following terms on the fact that ladies had taken stalls at the recent Free Trade Bazaar :—'They have been lately exposing their wives and daughters at Manchester to the insolence of every coxcomb who chose to pay a shilling for his amusement.'

Ferrand's object was not to protect the operatives, but to ruin their employers. The solution of the social problem advocated by the high Protectionists was to close down the factories, which they regarded as a monstrous wen upon the healthy body of old England. The *Standard* newspaper wrote :—'England would be as great and prosperous as she is now, and all useful Englishmen as happy as they now are, if all the manufacturing towns and districts of the Empire were involved in one common ruin.' When Bright read this out to a great League meeting in Covent Garden Opera 'some confusion occurred from a gentleman in one of the stage boxes being mistaken for the Editor of the *Standard*.'

Another favourite quotation of Bright and other speakers on League platforms was the couplet that young Lord John Manners had produced, a Frankenstein that was to pursue its author through life :

> 'Let wealth and commerce, laws and learning die,
> But leave us still our old nobility.'

Ferrand in his speech had displayed much ignorance of factories in general and of Cobden's own business in particular, but he stumbled upon a few home truths about the truck system and the housing swindle as practised by the worst type of master. Bright, in writing to Cobden, congratulated him on having 'demolished Ferrand,' but added, 'Bolling of Bolton gives his men a key of a house when they come to work for him, and they pay rent whether they occupy or not—so the result of enquiry will not be all on one side.' It was owing to this fortunate antagonism between the country gentlemen and the manufacturers that the working people began to get their heads above water, and obtained Free Trade and Factory Acts together. The workmen themselves had then no vote, and if the wealthier classes had been united, the evils of the time would have remained unexposed and unremedied. But 'land' and 'capital' were still at daggers drawn. In Lancashire and Yorkshire one reason why the manufacturers hated the Corn Law system was that the landlords treated them socially with marked contempt, and often refused them land for their mills, houses, and cottages, even at exorbitant prices.

The men of Manchester were not slow to take up the challenge hurled at them by the country gentlemen in the House of Commons. Feeling ran so high after Ferrand's attack on the cotton-spinners, that Bright determined on the unprecedented course of calling on the merchants assembled in Manchester Exchange to turn themselves into a political meeting. He first wrote to London to ask Cobden's permission. It was a dangerous experiment, and Cobden, while giving his friend leave to make the attempt, expressed anxiety as to the result. But Bright was able to report a complete triumph :

'3 month, 1, 1842, 5 o'clock.

'The Meeting has succeeded entirely. At 1 o'clock I mounted a form in the Exchange near the door into Ducie Place, and proposed that as meetings were not permitted by the rules of that House, we should adjourn the business on to the flags in Ducie Place. I was cheered loudly—*two hisses* and *one hoot*—and the master of the room took me by the collar and pulled me down ; his red-coated *familiar* or porter was with him, but they were thrown off by my friends and threatened the police, etc. I was very cool—said I had finished—that it was not intended to hold the Meeting inside. And we immediately adjourned in great force to the flags. The whole space was crowded, and some could not get out of the Exchange by that door, the crowd was so dense. I was put into the Chair. Hy. Ashworth moved the petition. Sir T. Potter seconded it—carried unanimously. I spoke a few minutes. Ferrand was denounced as a vile blackguard, the House warned of their doings. The whole passed off with great *éclat*, and everybody seems pleased it was done. I signed the petition, and it is gone to Mark Philips [1] by this post. You must support it when presented.'

Bright's speech on the occasion described in this letter began : 'I have come here and attended 'Change for the last two years, and I have asked myself, "What kind of men are these that I see week after week on the Manchester Exchange, crawling about, grumbling at bad trade, and yet not daring to lift their hands against the cause ?"'

[1] M.P. for Manchester 1832-47.

The letter which Cobden wrote back next day, marked *Private*, is very remarkable :

'MY DEAR BRIGHT,—It is a striking illustration of the progress we have made in Lancashire to find that you were allowed to convert the Exchange market meeting into a Free Trade and anti-Tory demonstration! Go back to 1819 and imagine yourself in that position which you describe yourself to have been in on Tuesday, and, instead of there being a party of friends to have rescued you from the master, the whole of the people on 'Change would have kicked you from Ducie Place to the Police Office. If you go back only five years it was impossible to get a petition for total repeal signed in the Exchange. Verily we are not toiling in vain. Thanks for your moral courage, for which we shall often have need.

'I still think it would be a good plan for you to get a requisition signed to the Committee of the Exchange calling on them to discourage as far as possible the support of those papers whose anti-commercial and anti-manufacturing views are put forth with such offensive zeal. What fools we are of the manufacturing districts, to support such journals as the *Standard*, *Post*, etc.[1] Do you suppose that the Squires and Parsons are such blockheads as to patronise our organs ?

'I am anxious to know what course the friends of the League recommend us to take in the Country, after the decision in the House of Commons [to proceed with Peel's new Corn Law]. I am more than ever for keeping the agitation of the Corn Law apart from the Suffrage. At the same time as individually, we will go the whole hog for both.[2]

'Will you give your pen to the *Circular*[3] for the next number ? We must write up the cause now, for I fear we shall find some backwater. One of your articles should be "*Our future course.*" In which we must say that we

[1] For the *Standard's* views see p. 74 above. The *Morning Post* had written in answer to the manufacturers' demand for freedom of exchange: 'Take your manufactures away with you by all means, and exchange them anywhere you will from Tobolsk to Timbuctoo. If nothing will serve you but to eat foreign corn, away with you, you and your goods, and let us never see you more.'

[2] Cobden, however, did not individually go hard for Suffrage, either before or after 1846.

[3] The *Anti-Corn Law Circular* (later *Anti-Bread Tax Circular*), the League organ 1839-43; after 1843 it was converted into a larger paper, and called *The League*.

will not advise our friends to petition the *present* House of Commons again after this session, but that all petitions now in progress should be completed as soon as possible, and as numerously as possible, in order that we may have as strong a case against them as possible. Then you must give out that the League will throw all its energies at once into the cause, and attack the enemy by lectures and tracts, especially in the agricultural districts, and intimate that the next step must be to petition the Queen to dismiss her Ministers and dissolve Parliament. We must write with confidence and spirit now. We must be prepared for a slack shoulder from the Whig papers. The Whigs will try to snub the principle.

'By the way, [Dan] O'Connell was saying yesterday that instead of calling upon your representatives to obstruct the passing of the Corn Law Bill, the manufacturing districts ought to call for a stoppage of the supplies. This is my opinion too, and if whilst such a course was recommended the electors would unite to refuse the demand of the tax collector I should have some hopes.'

This last plan, the wildest perhaps that ever emanated from Cobden, shows the temper of that spring of 1842, when the merchant community believed that it was on the point of absolute ruin through Protection. Bright replied to his friend with another equally drastic proposal of passive resistance :

'3 month 9, 1842.

'The *Guardian* to-day says a large firm in Manchester, employing 1000 hands, closes at the end of this week. I heard also that M'Connells were about to close. Reductions in wages are the unavoidable result of this state of things. This idea has struck me, and I wish thy opinion upon it. Let a circular signed so as to give it some weight, be issued to every firm employing hands in the Cotton district, calling a special meeting at such a time and place. A deputation to be sent off to Peel to lay before him the facts, and to have authority from the meeting to declare that the property of all these parties is rapidly wasting away, that the state of Trade renders it impossible to keep up wages—that they feel themselves merely the tools in the hands of the landowners to extract the greatest possible amount of labor for the smallest possible amount of food—that this course they will no longer pursue, seeing that it will bring ruin to themselves and suffering to their workpeople, and *that unless the Govt. consent to open their trade by repealing the Corn Law they will at a given time close their works.* These views should be made public by resolutions at the meeting in order that the workpeople may see that we would keep up wages if we could. At the same time a meeting of the Yorkshire Woollen district should be held to do the same thing. This would shake Peel either from office or into a new Bill or the Total Repeal, and it would show the country to what a crisis we are arrived. But is it practicable ? To a great extent I think it is. It might be wise also for the meeting to declare that they do not wish to keep the people from their political rights [viz. the franchise], and that the Corn Law cause being most imminent must be immediately obtained.

'This, however, is matter for grave consideration. If the working people *believed* we would help them, they would now help us. There is a good article in the *Guardian* to-day, showing that the Cotton Trade pays about as much wages as all the farm laborers receive.'

Proposals to coerce the legislature by refusing taxes, or by instituting a national strike, have a strange sound in the mouths of sober men like Cobden and Bright. If Peel's budget of 1842 had not actually been doing much more for Free Trade than was yet realised, it is not improbable that resistance of some kind would soon have been resorted to by the manufacturing community. Or else, if no remedy had been applied, a great part of the people of England must, like the Irish of that day, have been compelled to seek new homes across the Atlantic, and the growth of Great Britain in wealth, population, and power must have been checked, with the most fatal results to her future position in the world.

Bright had now come round to Cobden's view on the tactical question, namely, that the League ought to leave the Suffrage question alone till the Corn Laws were settled. In a letter dated 3 Month 5, 1842, he writes to Cobden :

'We must not touch the Suffrage question. Last night I lectured to a very large meeting of working men here on "the cause of the fall of wages." I spoke 2 hours and then 1½ hours discussed with a Chartist leader the question and points raised. I am told I made many converts from their absurd views of machinery, Corn Laws, and their foolish plan of obstructing our meetings.'

Until the Free Trade budget of 1842 had been passed and had time to operate, trade continued to go from bad to worse. The summer saw the culmination of distress. 'Our mission,' wrote Bright to Mrs. Priestman in June,

> 'is to the more sensible portion of the Tory and Monopolist party, as there are evident symptoms of alarm in their camp at the continued and daily increasing distress. Government has already three towns in their keeping. At Paisley they have a Commissariat general to feed the people and persuade them to enlist, and at Stockport and Burnley an assistant poor-law commissioner to give relief from government funds.'

Two months later the misery of the working classes caused a revival of Chartism in the form of the famous 'turn-out' of August 1842. The plan was to strike, at once for higher wages and for the legal enactment of the Charter. As an effective strike the movement was absurd, for the strikers had no funds, and the employers had few orders to fulfil and little work to give. Nor was it likely that Parliament would enfranchise the working men, in order to prevent some of their number from starving themselves to death a little faster than usual. But though ridiculous as a strike, the 'turn-out' had moral dignity and effect as a national demonstration. In Lancashire at least it was unaccompanied by theft or violence, and the authorities, more liberal than those of 1819 and warned by the example of Peterloo, had the good sense to reciprocate this peaceable disposition. Carlyle, contrasting this 'Manchester Insurrection' of 1842 with the more untoward events of 1819, and that charge of the 'unspeakable County Yeomanry,' wrote:

> 'That the Manchester Insurrection stood still, on the streets, with an indisposition to fire and bloodshed, was wisdom for it even as an insurrection. And this was what these poor Manchester operatives did manage to perform. They put their huge inarticulate question, *What do you mean to do with us?* in a manner audible to every reflective soul in this kingdom; exciting deep pity in all good men, deep anxiety in all men whatever; and no conflagration or outburst of madness came to cloud that feeling anywhere, but everywhere it operates unclouded.' [1]

[1] *Past and Present*, bk. i. chap. iii.

In Rochdale, where, as elsewhere, employment had been decreasing and wages falling for years past, the 'turn-out' of August 1842 ran its course, bringing John Bright into direct and important relations with the working men of Lancashire. In a letter of August 11 he describes to Cobden the beginning of the affair in Rochdale:

'I did not suppose our prophecies were so near their fulfilment. We are in a strange state in this neighbourhood. Yesterday Oldham, Crompton and the neighbourhood were visited by the mob Government, all the mills and every description of work was stopped—all the men were turned out and, as far as could be, persuaded to join the general body. This morning about 10 o'clock, they entered Rochdale from Oldham, turning out the hands at all the mills and workshops in their progress—no opposition being made, no violence was necessary. At 11 they had passed through the town and were approaching our premises—some turned down to the Engine house and boilers and let the water out of the boilers to prevent their being started after their departure. They called to the people at work "Come out," "Come out." I was not inclined to resist, especially when the chances were all against us, and ordered the mills to be stopped. I conversed with several of them; they held a very large meeting close to the gates leading up to my house—I think 6000 or 8000 people present. They had one of our carts for a rostrum. The Chairman, I was told, was from Oldham, a good-looking and a determined-looking man about my age; the speakers were chiefly from Oldham, Shaw and Royton; the speeches were generally not violent, but resolute. They said the population were starving, wages falling and ruin before them—machinery robbed them—they would work no more until the wages of 1840 were guaranteed them with 10 hours labor per day and no more. They would be peaceable—every man would be a soldier and a policeman to keep order—they were exhorted not to taste intoxicating drinks. They had several hundreds of women with them who took up a position inside the gates on the private road up to my house. Here they sang songs, Chartist hymns I believe, but I could not tell the words as I was conversing most of the time. They moved off soon after 12 to some of the neighbouring mills. In private they told me they wished for no violence, but the time was come for a stand; they would be peaceable as long as they could, and when they could hold out no longer, they should help themselves—they would have something to eat as long as I or any one else had something.

'Now for Peel, Graham, Famine & Co., how do they feel? The villainy of the landed despots may get a shake, or it may end in deeper suffering for the unfortunate men, its victims. I know not what is in store, but the clouds are heavy just now. Will Peel dissolve the Parliament? Will the Queen's speech congratulate us on the happy effects of Peel's Corn Bill? We shall see. . . . If thou come down, don't bring Mrs. Cobden nor the young agitators.'

At a meeting of magistrates and employers, Bright tells his sister that one of those present 'was anxious some mill should start; he would engage to defend it. He seems to long to have a shot at the people; he said, "They want to obtain power and they must be put down." I rebuked him and defended the people. They ought to implore the government to repeal the Corn Law.'

Three days later he writes to Mrs. Priestman at Newcastle:

'The passive resistance revolution has commenced. We hear that in Birmingham and the neighbourhood the working people are pursuing the same course. In Yorkshire the turn-out has begun. Suffering *caused by law* has made the whole population a mass of combustible matter, and the spark now ignited may not be easily quenched. Peel almost charged the League with the insurrection, and Cobden replied that because he and the League had *foretold* it, they were charged with it! The cause was with Peel and the Aristocracy and in their Corn Laws.'

An address issued by Bright on August 17 was recognised as materially helping to bring the 'turn-out' in Lancashire to an end, without ill-feeling between masters and men, who were taught to see a common enemy in the Corn monopolists. It is an important pronouncement of Bright's political and economic views which he never altered in later life, as also of his personal relation to the working men.

'To the Working Men of Rochdale

'A deep sympathy with you in your present circumstances induces me to address you. Listen and reflect, even though you may not approve. You are suffering—you have long suffered. Your wages have for many years declined, and your position has gradually and steadily become worse. Your sufferings have naturally produced discontent, and you have turned eagerly to almost any scheme which gave hope of relief.

'Many of you know full well that neither an act of Parliament nor the act of a multitude can keep up wages. You know that trade has long been bad, and that with a bad trade wages cannot rise. If you are resolved to compel an advance of wages, you cannot compel manufacturers to give you employment. Trade must yield a profit, or it will not long be carried on.

. . . .

'Your speakers, and self-constituted leaders, urge you to give up the question of wages, and stand upon the Charter. Against obtaining the Charter the laws of nature offer no impediment, as they do against a forcible advance of wages; but to obtain the Charter now is just as impossible as to raise wages by force.

'The aristocracy are powerful and determined; and, unhappily, the middle classes are not yet intelligent enough to see the safety of extending political power to the whole people. The working classes can never gain it of themselves. Physical force you wisely repudiate. It is immoral, and you have no arms, and little organisation. Moral force can only succeed through the electors, and these are not yet convinced. The principles of the Charter will one day be established; but years may pass over, months must pass over before that day arrives. You cannot stand idle till it comes. Your only means of living are from the produce of your own labor. Unhappily, you have wives and children, and all of you have the cravings of hunger, and you must live, and, in order to live, you must work.

. . . .

'As intelligent men you know you cannot remain out; you cannot permanently raise wages by force; you cannot get the Charter now. What are you to do then? Return to your employment. It is more noble to confess your error than to persist in it, and the giving up of an error brings you nearer the truth. When you resume your labor do not give up the hope of political improvement—that would be even more to be deplored than your present movement. Cherish it still—a brighter day will come—

and you and your children will yet enjoy it. Your first step to entire freedom must be commercial freedom—freedom of industry. We must put an end to the partial famine which is destroying trade, the demand for your labor, your wages, your comforts, and your independence. The aristocracy regard the Anti-Corn Law League as their greatest enemy. That which is the greatest enemy of the remorseless aristocracy of Britain must almost of necessity be your firmest friend. Every man who tells you to support the Corn Law is your enemy—every man who hastens, by a single hour, the abolition of the Corn Law, shortens by so much the duration of your sufferings. Whilst the inhuman law exists, your wages must decline. When it is abolished, and not till then, they will rise.

'If every employer and workman in the kingdom were to swear on their bended knees that wages should not fall, they would still assuredly fall if the Corn Law continues. No power on earth can maintain your wages at their present rate, if the Corn Law be not repealed.

'To such of you who have been employed at the mills with which I am connected, I may add that as soon as you are disposed to resume your work, the doors shall be open to you. I invite you to come, and you shall be treated as, I trust, you have ever been—as I would ever wish you to treat me.—I am, with all sincerity, your friend,

'John Bright.'

Bright's prophecy that Free Trade, especially in corn, would raise wages and shorten hours was amply justified by the event. Twenty years after the Repeal of the Corn Laws he boasted to the working men of Rochdale that

'so exactly was that prophecy fulfilled, that if you will turn to the Parliamentary books, you will find that from the year 1846 to this year in which I speak, more than 400, I believe nearly 500 million pounds' worth of food, which the Corn Law was intended to prohibit, has been imported into this country and has been eaten from the tables of the English people. And, as you know, trade has so far extended within twenty years that it has surpassed beyond all calculation its extension in the previous history of England. Wages have been increased, I was going to say everywhere. I believe there is scarcely a remote agricultural parish in which wages have not been increased. But in this district, as I could show from the books of my own business, wages since that time have increased 30 to 40 per cent., although the actual production of each worker in many respects has not been increased at all, but has been diminished by the shorter hours of labor.'[1]

In the autumn and winter of 1842, Cobden and Bright toured the North of England together. 'I assure you,' Bright told his Manchester friends that Christmas,

> 'wherever we go, at every meeting that we address, for my own share I hide my diminished head. I am humiliated at the manner in which I am treated at these meetings; they look upon persons who come from the Anti-Corn Law League as the very deliverers of the commerce of their country from the shackles in which it has been so long enthralled.'

In January 1843 the two passed over the border into the native land of Adam Smith, where they found few persons in need of conversion, even among landowners. 'I believe,' Bright told the men of Manchester on his return,

> 'that the intelligence of the people in Scotland is superior to the intelligence of the people in England. I take it from these facts. Before going to the meetings, we often asked the committee or the people with whom we came in contact, "Are there any fallacies which the working people hold on this question? Have they any crotchets about machinery, or wages, or anything else?" And the universal reply was, "No; you may make a speech about what you like; they understand the question thoroughly; and it is no use confining yourself to machinery or wages, for there are few men, probably no man here, who would be taken in by such raw jests as those." . . . I told them that they were the people who should have repeal of the Union; for that, if they were separate from England, they might have a government wholly popular and intelligent, to a degree which I believe does not exist in any other country on the face of the earth. However, I

[1] *Robertson*, 111-12. In 1844 Bright paid 16s. a week to the men whom he employed (see p. 156 below, note), so in 1866 he must have been paying about 22s. Of course the real gain was that the purchasing power of wages had increased.

believe they will be disposed to press us on, and make us become more and more intelligent; and we may receive benefit from our contact with them, even though, for some ages to come, our connexion with them may be productive of evil to themselves.'

As Bright's life became more and more nomadic, his brothers Thomas and Jacob gradually took over the active management of the business, in which their father was now too old to share. Their sister Priscilla kept house for John at One Ash, and took care of the motherless Helen. About this time Bright wrote to her, 'My dearest Priscilla,—Thou art loading me with obligations daily, and I feel it very much and very often. Be assured thou hast given me only occasion for gratitude continually since thou became my companion at One Ash.' [1]

On November 19, 1842, Priscilla Bright writes to Margaret Priestman:

'... I am expecting dear John this evening—he went from Coventry to Liverpool. He had declined the latter, but some parties wrote and said if he did not go his absence would be attributed to a fear of meeting the Liverpool people, against a part of whom he had been justly, but I am not prepared to say how far politically [*sic*] severe in his short speech at a recent A. C. L. meeting in Manchester. I give him a little advice now and then upon his want of mildness, it requires no small degree of tact to win people over to opinions contrary to their own. John in his zeal sometimes forgets this, but he is very good and kind in receiving advice even from very humble individuals.'

In the following letter, of February 1843, Priscilla describes one of the series of great meetings with which the League hanselled the new Free Trade Hall, Manchester, erected in St. Peter's Fields, on the site of the 'Peterloo' massacre—a monument of fast changing times. [2]

'... On entering the room we were really awestruck

[1] To the envelope containing this letter there still adheres one of those Anti-Corn Law emblems' which the Leaguers used to stick on to the outside of their letters to advertise the cause. In this case it is a blue circular stamp with a little child praying, and the motto 'Give us this day our daily bread.'

[2] The first Free Trade Hall, a temporary wooden pavilion erected by 100 men in 11 days on the same site as the later Halls, was opened in January 1840. The 'new' Hall, opened in February 1843, was of brick, 135 feet by 105, and 27 high, with galleries: it would hold seven or eight thousand. The present stone building was erected in 1856.

with its immensity, or rather with the immense mass of human beings crowded there—all wearing but one expression of countenance—the determination to break down oppression and raise up Justice in its stead—but I need not endeavour to explain to thee the feeling which pervaded every breast there—thou hast been at one or two of the League Meetings and hast felt the Spirit which animates them. Imagine if thou canst that spirit heightened in proportion to the importance of the occasion. One gentleman told my brothers (unconscious who they were) that he left directly Mr. Bright finished speaking, certain that if he had staid a month he should have heard nothing to equal him, and more than one lady spoke similarly of him. A lady who sat next who proved to be Mrs. —— asked if we had ever heard him. She said his speech at the weekly meeting was perfectly electrical and that a lady of her acquaintance said she should never attend another meeting if he were announced as one of the speakers, as she could not bear the excitement. Mrs. —— said the chief charm of Mr. Bright was in the *simplicity* of his manner, the total absence of anything like showing off—and well might any one say so whose misfortune it has been to listen frequently to her husband. The lights going out was an interesting check to the proceedings of the evening—interesting as evincing the great coolness and good sense of the vast mass assembled together. No one manifested any particular alarm. John was wrought up by the accident and spoke in no honied strains of the evil machinations of the enemies of the cause of Corn Law Repeal. It was highly amusing to see him and George Wilson and young Rawson each holding up a farthing candle, the two former flattering and comforting the people by turns.'

When Bright wrote to Cobden about 'Peel, Graham, Famine & Co.' he scarcely did justice to the two senior partners, who were plotting against the interests of Famine at no small risk to themselves, and with scant consideration for the prejudices of 'Co.' Peel and Graham were watching, with ever increasing alarm, the incorrigible statistics of population, which would go on increasing while the wheat-growing power of the country stood still. As early as December 1842, Graham wrote to Peel:

'In truth it is a question of time. The next change in

the Corn Laws must be to an open trade; and if our population increase for two or three years at the rate of three hundred thousand per annum, you may throw open the ports and agriculture will not suffer. But the next change must be the last.'

If this letter had been published when it was written there would have been an eruption of the political Vesuvius. The Protectionist crew would have cut the throats of their officers before they had perfected their arrangements for handing over the ship to the enemy. For if it was 'a question of time,' it was not time yet by the House of Commons clock.

To men in the position in which Peel and Graham now found themselves on the Treasury Bench—beginning to think white but pledged for a while longer to talk black and act grey—it was torture to see their own incarnate conscience always agog on the benches opposite, in that precise, relentless man. Cobden began to rage like the hectic in their blood. They could have struck the man for his neat arguments—because they were coming to agree with him. This, one would suppose, is part of the psychology of Peel's outburst against Cobden in February 1843.

The immediate cause was the assassination of Peel's private secretary by a madman, who, so Peel was informed, had intended to shoot the Prime Minister himself. When, shortly afterwards, Cobden in debate said that he held Peel 'individually responsible for the present position of the country,' Peel, under the stress of strange, mixed emotions, fantastically accused Cobden of 'menacing him'—with assassination, it was implied. The Protectionist benches broke into a clamour which they hoped would be the death-knell of Cobden's character and influence. It was the kind of incident that sets half the public men of the country speaking and writing to the papers, and brings out each in the true colour of his soul. Lord John Russell spoke up for Cobden while the anger of the House was still hot against him, but the pseudo-Radical Roebuck and the inevitable Lord Brougham, while still paying lip-homage to Free Trade, seized the opportunity to deal, as they hoped, a mortal blow at the man who had replaced them in the leadership of the people, and at the organisation which bade fair to carry Free Trade out of the realm of theory into that of practice. Brougham accused the League of stirring up the people to violence and even to assassination. John Bright entered the lists against the veteran in a correspondence which was given to the world, and from which a brief extract may still be read with pleasure:

'2 month 16, 1843.

'*To Lord Brougham.*

. . . .

'I have just been reading again thy attack upon the League, and I may state freely that I think it justifies the utmost severity of language which can be used in reference to it. We have *enemies* to attack us often enough and bitterly enough, and we are not especially grateful to our professing friends, when they throw at us the slanders of the *Quarterly* and the rest of its tribe. The allusion to the late riots is a direct insinuation against the League, worthy only of its bitterest foe. It is well known that the agent of the Government did his utmost to implicate the League in those unhappy transactions, and it is as well known that he utterly and ridiculously failed. It needs no great sagacity to tell who were the real cause of those outbreaks. If the people would die *quietly*, there would be a chance of preserving the "famine law," but happily they will not; and they who maintain that accursed law, may and must take the responsibility of the dangers and evils that spring from it.

'The League was pursuing its labors—labors acknowledged by thyself to be meritorious—when thou charged them with heavy sins—may I not say atrocious crimes?—and then when they turn round and repel the charges, and say a few severe things upon thee, at least as true as what thou said of them, thou art ruffled and denouncest the pains and penalties of the House of Lords against them.'

It was said of Bright that 'if he had not been a Quaker he would have been a prize-fighter.' Be that as it may, it is a joy to see him enter the prize-ring in full Quaker costume, as he does in this letter with its 'thees' and 'thous.' Brougham was afterwards reconciled to Bright, and gave him a complete copy of his works!

On February 23 an 'extraordinary meeting' of the League was held at Manchester to send an address of confidence to Cobden, and to hurl foul scorn at those who had slandered him as an assassin. The meeting was one of the first held in the new Free Trade Hall. The chief orator was Bright; and the audience were seven to eight thousand Manchester men, whose anger and enthusiasm seemed to stiffen the muscles of their throats on this and many another night of 'tremendous cheering many times renewed.' After dealing faithfully with Brougham, he descended upon Roebuck: 'This slander was not in the House of Lords alone. There is a Brummagem Brougham in the House of Commons, who, when the whole ministerial side of the House were yelling at the man who stood there the very impersonation of justice to the people, that man stood forward and dared to throw his puny dart at Richard Cobden.' He then came on to Peel, who had originated the present campaign of slander by making it a crime in Cobden to speak of the Prime Minister as 'personally' or 'individually' 'responsible' for the state of the country.

'What shall we say,' asked Bright, 'of the leader who shrinks from the just responsibility which has been laid upon him? Did he not for ten years boast that he was building up a great party? Did he not cry "register, register, register"? And did not his followers follow out that advice? And did they not at last force themselves into the councils of the Queen? . . . I hold that his own ambition made him seek that office; he sought the power of office, the influence of office, the patronage of office, the fame of office; and if he will seek the power, and patronage, and influence, and fame of office, I, for one, will never allow him to shrink from the responsibility of office. . . . Sir Robert Peel's father was a cotton-spinner. It did not become him, therefore, to sneer at cotton factories in the manner in which he did. It became him still less to try to get rid of a powerful argument as he did. If Sir Robert Peel had been a cotton-spinner yet, if he had followed his father's trade—and I have no doubt he would have made a shrewd fellow on our exchange—if, I say, he had followed his father's trade, I have no doubt, nay, I solemnly believe, he would have been a Leaguer. Why, there can be no doubt. You have it in the *Post*, a paper of his own party; you have it in his own acknowledgments; you have it in the charges brought against him by some of the most desperate of the monopolists, that his opinions are precisely the same as the opinions of the League, but that, as Prime Minister of the landlords, his opinions were merely abstractions. If, however, he had been spinning cotton, his opinions would have been realities, and we should have had Sir Robert Peel doubtless one of the Anti-Corn Law League. When he is asked why, having those opinions, he, as head of the Government, cannot enforce them, what is his answer and the answer of his subalterns? It is, that this is not the time. I ask, when will be the time? Do you think that monopoly is about to become just, and merciful, and generous? Do you think that the Ethiopian can change his skin, and the leopard his spots? Do you think that after having gorged themselves for a few years more on the spoils of your industry, they will be more likely to surrender at discretion, and give up freely that which they now refuse to you? I tell you that it is a hypocritical pretence to say that this is not the time. It is now the time: the hour is now striking.'

In the heat of this personal controversy over Cobden there was much talk about a Government prosecution of the League champions. Bright writes to Mrs. Priestman on March 13:

'. . . as to thy fears about the Government and the League, they are not wholly groundless, I am told from other quarters—but I will try and be careful. I have no wish for martyrdom even in so good a cause. The public feeling is evidently with the League, and our cause is so obviously good that I do not think we shall be attacked by the Law. If we are, I trust you will put the best construction on our actions, and not disown me as a rebel and incendiary.'

The talk about prosecuting the League, and the fact that the talk came to nothing, were both signs of the wonder and fear which the monster now inspired. The League was a new portent in English life, introducing into politics not only new aims but new methods and a new spirit, which if successful against the old-established politicians and their methods, must needs imply a redistribution of social power. It was democracy, no longer as a vague threat for the future, but as an invading reality. In an age when political meetings were rare events, and serious politicians seldom spoke outside 'the House' except officially from the hustings—Cobden and his lieutenants addressed immense meetings night after night over a series of years. Once a month or oftener, from March 1843 until the Corn Law fell in 1846, a London opera-house was packed from floor to ceiling, from the back of the pit to the back of the stage, with an audience that was never once bored and never once lukewarm; and in the twelve weeks between December 1842 and the end of the following February, one hundred and thirty-six smaller meetings were held in London alone; in the provinces, each big city had a mass meeting nearly every month, and each market town at least once a year. In an age when political literature was limited in quantity, and perfunctory and personal in such arguments as it advanced, the League, in 1843 alone, distributed nine million carefully argued tracts, by means of a staff of eight hundred persons. In an age when finance and government were regarded as mysteries reserved for a few political families and their protégés, the League lecturers taught political economy, with its application to the year's budget, to vast audiences of merchants, clerks, and working men. All this, and much more besides in the way of monster petitions, demonstrations, industrial exhibitions, was paid for by a series of League 'funds,' rising from £5000 and £10,000 in earlier years to £50,000 in 1842-43, £100,000 in 1843-44, and £250,000 in 1845-46. The subscription lists, in which both rich and poor were equally well represented, were published at full in endless columns of the *League* newspaper—otherwise the most varied and entertaining journal devoted to one cause that has ever been written.

Two precedents had no doubt helped to suggest the idea of the League to its makers—O'Connell's Association and the Political Unions that forced through the Reform Bill of 1832. But the Political Unions had been a rough-and-ready combination, in a revolutionary crisis, to frighten the Tories into surrender; and O'Connell banded together, under the hypnotism of his personality, an oppressed race, singularly homogeneous in its social and intellectual experience. The League, on the other hand, was a means of educating the very various classes and sects of English society in town and village, up to the point of uniting them all in a common enthusiasm for a proposition in economics.[1]

In our own day we have seen several organisations somewhat similar to the League, but they have not revolutionised, though they may have developed, our methods of political warfare; upon the whole they have merely supplemented the normal activity of the two chief parties in the State. The Anti-Corn Law League, on the other hand, not only invented the modern

[1] Cavour's 'National Society,' which freed Italy, was founded in 1856 in conscious imitation of Cobden's League. Actually it was half-way in character between that and O'Connell's Association.

methods of political education, but used them to attack both the official parties, and to compel them to surrender at discretion. The Whig with his proposal for a 'fixed duty,' and the Tory with his 'sliding scale,' were both given notice to quit at the next general election, and surrendered rather than try the event against the League candidates.

If these things are considered, it is easy to understand how fools talked of prosecuting the League, and how even wise men, attached to the established parties and organs of public opinion, regarded it very much as Erasmus regarded Luther. This feeling was by no means confined to Protectionists. Macaulay had declared in favour of complete Free Trade, while his Whig colleagues were still sheltering themselves behind the 'fixed duty' compromise, but he gave offence to his Edinburgh constituents by a curt refusal to appear among them on a League platform. The *Times*, dealing out blows at Protectionist and Free Trader alike from that loftiest moral vantage-ground of one who waits for the final leap of the cat, attacked the League in March 1843, when the talk about prosecuting it was at the height, as an 'extra-constitutional association,' that 'impaired the vigour and defaced the purity of the Constitution, and destroyed or rendered useless the liberty and privileges once really and still professedly guaranteed to her subjects by the State.' The 'unconstitutional' character of the League meant that it gave a political organisation to classes that had hitherto been unheard in the national counsels. Thus it had summoned together seven hundred representatives of the Nonconformist clergy of Britain, who, narrating what each one saw in his daily ministrations, bore witness to the material conditions cutting off the mass of the population from the possibility of religious life: the *Times* had commented on this assemblage as a 'freak' and 'drollery,' no less absurd, said the great paper, than 'the British Association for the Advancement of Science,' and it proposed 'to put an extinguisher on humbugs' in both cases. With equal generosity and truth, it remarked that Lord Ducie and Mr. Cobden were decently dressed, but that none of the dissenting ministers could show a clean shirt at the Conference.[1]

In the summer of 1843 Cobden and Bright began their attack on the rural districts, and spoke face to face with the 'protected' classes. It was an easy task for them to convert the agricultural labourer. The shortest and the best speech made in the whole course of the controversy was that of a farm

[1] Leading Article, August 21, 1841

hand at one of the League meetings: 'I be protected and I be starving.'

'The Corn Law,' said Bright in a longer effort of eloquence, 'is as great a robbery of the man who follows the plough as it is of him who minds the loom, with this difference, that the man who follows the plough is, of the two, nearest the earth, and it takes less power to press him into it. . . . If there be one view of the question which stimulates me to harder work in this cause than another, it is the fearful sufferings which I know to exist amongst the rural laborers in almost every part of this kingdom. How can they be men under the circumstances in which they live? During the period of their growing up to manhood, they are employed at odd jobs about the farm or the farm-yard, for wages which are merely those of little children in Lancashire.[1] Every man who marries is considered an enemy of the parish; every child who is born into the world, instead of being a subject of rejoicing to its parents and to the community, is considered as an intruder come to compete for the little work and the small quantity of food which is left to the population. And then comes toil, year after year, long years of labor, with little remuneration; but perhaps at sixty or seventy, a gift of 20s. and a coat, or £2, from the Agricultural Society, because they have brought up a large family, and have not committed that worst of all sins, taken money from parochial rates.[2] One of their own poets has well expressed their condition:

"A blessed prospect—
To slave while there is strength—in age the workhouse
A parish shell at last, and the little bell
Toll'd hastily for a pauper's funeral."

And then a fat and sleek dean, a dignitary of the Church and a great philosopher, recommends for the consumption of the people—he did not read a paper about the supplies that were to be had in the great valley of the Mississippi—

[1] Bright Bros. at that time were paying 6s. 6d. a week to the youngest boys, and 6s. 3d. to the youngest girls whom they employed (*æt.* 13-16). Fully-grown agricultural labourers earned only 6s. or 6s. 6d. a week in many parts of England.

[2] The Leaguers used to quote the words of such a 'labourer's certificate' as the following: 'West Suffolk Agricultural Association: President, the Duke of Grafton. This is to certify that a prize of £2 was awarded to William Burch, aged eighty-two, labourer, of the Parish of Stowapland, in West Suffolk, 25th September 1840, for having brought up nine children without relief *except when flour was very dear.*' *League*, March 15, 1845.

but he said that there were swede, turnip and mangel-wurzel; and the Hereditary Earl Marshal of England, as if to out-Herod Herod himself, recommends hot water and a pinch of curry-powder. The people of England have not, even under thirty years of Corn Law influence, been sunk so low as to submit tamely to this insult and wrong. It is enough that a law should be passed to make your toil valueless, to make your skill and labor unavailing to procure for you a fair supply of the common necessaries of life—but when to this grievous iniquity they add the insult of telling you to go, like beasts that perish, to mangel-wurzel, or to something which even the beasts themselves cannot eat, then I believe the people of England will rise, and with one voice proclaim the downfall of this odious system.'

The agricultural labourer was powerless politically, and, in spite of rick-burning and poaching, was less feared than the operative of the town; but he became an important item in the League programme, as an appeal *ad misericordiam.* Week after week the *League* newspaper exposed the miseries and degradation of the average inhabitant in Dorset, Wilts, and other provinces of our rural Arcady, where, according to Protectionist speakers, all the charms of country life described by the pastoral poets were enjoyed by a stalwart peasantry—for six shillings a week! League commissioners were constantly going round the rural districts interviewing farmers, labourers, and tradesmen as to the labourers' wages, expenditure, and general habits. Pictures of the rotting hovels in which they lived were reproduced in the *League* newspaper, together with a constant flow of statistics and reports—how six shillings a week was paid in this village, seven shillings in the next, eight shillings in another; how here barley was the food of the people, and there potatoes; how fuel was usually obtained by stealth, which no one regarded as any more wrong than poaching; how the whole family income had to go in food and boots and rent, and how clothes were obtained by begging the cast-off garments of their employers and wealthier neighbours, so that 'the trade in new clothing is rapidly declining.' This exposure of the real condition of the 'happy and stalwart peasantry' was undertaken partly as an argument against the Corn Laws, and partly as a reply to Lord Ashley's attack on the treatment of the factory hands in the towns. This process of mutual exposure, vigorously conducted by the two sections of the wealthier classes, was the beginning of salvation for the oppressed millions.

Cobden and Bright were hailed as deliverers by the farm hands.

> 'We have attended meetings in those districts,' said Bright, 'and have been received with the utmost enthusiasm by these round-frocked laborers. They would have carried us from the carriage which we had travelled in, to the hustings. And if a silly squire or a foolish farmer attempted any disturbance or improper interference, these round-frocked men were all around us in an instant, ready to defend us; and I have seen them hustle many a powerful man from the field in which the meeting was being held.'

This was to be expected. But the more remarkable event was that the farmers themselves were very largely converted by the arguments of Cobden and Bright in the course of their agricultural campaign in 1843 and the two following years. From the first passing of the Waterloo Corn Law, a generation ago, the farmers had never benefited by Protection, because rents were fixed on the assumption that Protection would keep prices even higher than the point at which they were actually maintained. High prices diminished the consumption of wheat, as the people 'clemmed' or fed on turnips and potatoes; so that wheat could never be kept up at the 80s. a quarter intended by the legislators of 1815. Generally speaking, the prices of corn varied with the annual harvests of England, and the farmer's rents did not fall with prices any more than the workman's wages rose with them. The high rents were exacted as though the Corn Law were keeping up the price at 80s. A few years after the Waterloo Corn Law had begun its operation, farmers were going bankrupt 'by hundreds and thousands,' and crying out that agriculture was ruined—though every other interest had been sacrificed on its altar.

And the same things happened again under the modified Corn Laws of 1828 and 1842. Few, indeed, of the farmers were converted to Free Trade until Cobden and Bright went on their mission to the agricultural districts, but the reason why many of them were then found ready to listen, was that for thirty years the coveted fruit of Protection had been dust in their mouths. The farmer had, under the Protective system, to pay more for all he bought, whether in the way of his business or of his private expenditure, so that when Cobden made them the offer of Free Trade all round, many of them saw their salvation in that bargain. When it was no longer possible for the Protectionists to muster even a respectable minority at a farmers' meeting, when their champions no longer dared accept the challenge of Cobden and Bright to meet and argue on platforms before agricultural audiences, the landlords were left naked and no longer wholly unashamed, as the acknowledged sole beneficiaries of the Corn Laws.

The following letter of Bright's to Cobden describes the successful 'invasion' of Dorchester, the agricultural capital of the county regarded as the last lair of Protection and of landlord influence:

'5 month 15, '43.

'We have had a glorious day and such a meeting as we desired. From 2000 to 3000, the latter certainly nearest the mark, present. Murray had done his part well—good hustings on a beautiful field close to the town—a landowner, Mr. Farnall from Lyme, in the Chair. I spoke 1½ hours and Moore spoke excellently for 2 hours. A farmer named Whittle made some disturbance while I was speaking, and he was hustled out of the meeting. Then a real row commenced, and the few fools of Bankes [1] & Co. did their utmost to storm the hustings—they had but small chance. Farmers and laborers were ready to help us. The defeat of the interrupting forces was complete, and the meeting was as quiet as could be wished. Many farmers were present—many hundreds certainly—a resolution against the Corn Law was carried, only 2 men voting against it—and a petition for total and immediate repeal by a like majority. Three times three cheers were given for the deputation and the League.

'We dined at the Ordinary at Bankes' Hotel, the King's Arms, where we now are. The farmers are all very civil and friendly—this evening we have spent 3 hours with 40 of them in the room below, and the conversation has been all about the Corn Law, and I think much good has been done. The Chairman, Harry Barrard Farnall, is a landowner from Lyme, in this county—his family largely interested in land—he behaved well, and is a very intelligent and gentlemanly man. I don't think even the Tory farmers here care much for the Corn Law; except their party spirit I think they have no other motive for upholding it. . . . They say no such day has been seen at

[1] Mr. Bankes and Lord Ashley were the two Members for Dorsetshire.

Dorchester since some celebrated election many years ago.'

The League lecturers, a year or two before, had suffered outrage and insult for the Cause. But from 1843 onwards, Cobden and Bright appear to have held their meetings freely wherever they wished in agricultural England. Once, indeed, in 1843, Bright writes to his sister-in-law: 'We don't go to Bridgewater, no innkeeper daring to lend a room and the Tory Mayor refusing the Town Hall.' But this is exceptional. At Cambridge, where they go to hold a farmers' meeting in the market-place, there is no threat of violence or disturbance except from the gownsmen, 'whose *education* is exclusively under the domination of the "Church," and there we trust are learning better manners.'

Taking the country as a whole, the conversion of the farmers was mainly the work of Cobden, unequalled in political history for his power of persuasive and sympathetic argument with opponents. But his biographer has said that his alliance with Bright 'far more than doubled the power that either could have exerted without the other.' When they were together, as was usually the case, Cobden always spoke first, disarming prejudice and exposing with clear economic arguments set off in homely illustration the wrongs that farmers and labourers, or manufacturers and operatives, suffered through the working of Protection. When the audience had thus been brought round into a sympathetic state of mind, then—to use Bright's own words—'I used to get up and do a little prize-fighting.' Economic argument was not lacking in Bright's speeches, but his characteristic and vital contribution was the passion with which he reinforced reason, and the high tone of moral indignation and defiance which he infused into his listeners. And this was exactly where Cobden, the persuader, was necessarily weakest. Each supplied the defects of the other's qualities. The known friendship between them, the utter absence of rivalry and self-interest, the apostolic fervour that made these missionaries so unlike the common Whig and Tory politician, the genius and the good sense that divided them no less sharply from the Chartist orators, threw a halo round these two, and if the word in the land was 'Cobden,' the words 'Cobden and Bright' became scarcely less familiar.

No reader of Anti-Corn Law records can have failed to ask himself why William Fox was not regarded as a third with Cobden and Bright. That he very nearly was so regarded is clear, but it is equally clear that before the Corn Laws fell Bright was ahead of him in popular esteem. William Johnson Fox, originally a Unitarian minister, had become a lay politician of advanced radical views on almost all subjects, but he gained national reputation only when he spoke for the League. As an orator he was singularly like Bright in the rush of his eloquence, in his constant appeal to the moral passions of his audience, in his homely wit and his power of incisive illustration. The difference was that Fox had more power of ornate and artificial exuberance of diction, while Bright played more directly upon the simple passions. The League had the fortune to possess in its three chief speakers the three requirements of effective oratory. Cobden was argument, Bright was passion, Fox was rhetoric.

Bright's speeches on the Crimean War, the Franchise, and other questions in the 'fifties and 'sixties, if read as literature, are superior to Fox's Corn Law orations. But Bright's own Corn Law speeches do not seem to have a decided superiority over the treatment that Fox gave to the same theme. The quality of Bright's speaking, judged by high literary standards, was in the 'forties below what it subsequently became in days when he spoke seldom and prepared every speech at leisure. In the peripatetic orations delivered night after night in 1843-46, Bright had no more time than a modern election candidate to put the final touch of literary perfection on his work, though in force and volume it was unsurpassed, either by any other man or by himself in later days. And so, as we read the Corn Law speeches of Fox and of Bright, we feel unable to adjudge the palm. But the public who heard both considered Bright the greater orator, or else—it is hard to say which it was—thought him the greater man.

It would appear that though Fox spoke as much as Bright at the big meetings of the League, particularly at the Covent Garden Theatre, he was less known in the country as a whole. Bright's account of the matter, written to Fox's son in 1883, is: 'Your father was the *orator* of the League, his speeches as compositions were far better than mine—but he did not speak often.' [1] Furthermore, the sense of a superior strength and majesty in Bright was somehow conveyed to his auditors: by the sight of his glorious head poised on its massive pedestal; by the face from which listeners could never for an instant withdraw their eyes; by the beauty of his voice, which he had never need to strain; and by some emanation of personal

[1] See *Life of W. J. Fox*, by Garnett, 1910.

power which only those who have been subjected to its influence can realise, and which even they can neither describe nor define.

More than a generation after the Corn Laws had been repealed, a great Liberal meeting was advertised in Manchester with Lord Hartington in the chair, and Bright as chief speaker. Before the proceedings began, a gentleman in the audience found himself sitting behind three old working men who had walked in from a neighbouring county to hear John Bright speak once more, because they had often heard him in the Corn Law days. When they saw him come on to the platform, they all three broke down and burst into tears.

NOTE

A Typical Week's Work for the League.

[From Bright's Diary, Jan. 16-21, 1843.]

'*Monday.*—Left Edinbro' at 8. Passed the Forth; received by a crowd and music. On to Kirkcaldy, large meeting. On to Dundee, crossing the Tay—large meeting in Dundee.

Tuesday.—Posted to Perth. Town Council, etc., assembled, and short meeting with them. On to Stirling, excellent meeting, very many farmers.

Wednesday.—Posted to Glasgow. Tea-party and meeting at Young Men's Free Trade Association. Very large and excellent meeting.

Thursday.—To Edinbro', and the Colonel and I posted to Hawick, where we had a very good meeting.

Friday.—On to Carlisle (posting), and by railway to Newcastle. Excellent tea-party and meeting. Cobden joined us here from Edinbro'.

Saturday.—Rested at Summerhill to-day. My dear relatives [the Priestmans] very kind, and giving me more and more occasion to love them.'

CHAPTER V

THE BATTLE OF THE CORN LAWS—(*Continued*). II. THE OLD SPIRIT AND THE NEW IN THE SOCIETY OF FRIENDS. BRIGHT IN PARLIAMENT, 1843-45

'Rich and great people can take care of themselves; but the poor and defenceless—the men with small cottages and large families—the men who must work six days every week if they are to live in anything like comfort for a week,—these men want defenders; they want men to maintain their position in Parliament; they want men who will protest against any infringement of their rights.'—BRIGHT *at his Durham election, July* 1843.

THE time had now come when John Bright must choose whether he would enter Parliament. If he did, he must cut himself off from the conduct of the business at Rochdale and become a politician, in all probability for life. Cobden and the other chiefs of the League were urging him to come forward at the next by-election. In February 1843 it was hourly expected that a vacancy would occur either at Bolton or Sheffield, and he was pressed to stand. At that moment his brother Thomas, who alone carried on the business when he was away, was lying at death's door. Bright unfolded his perplexities to Duncan McLaren of Edinburgh, already his intimate friend and destined ere long to marry his favourite sister Priscilla. 'My brother ill—my business—my friends—and my country! What am I to decide? Cobden says I *must* go and be returned even if I stay at home half the session. The League must fight and win a battle.' A few days later (February 13), he writes to Cobden:

'I see all the necessity of our having a stirring League election to rouse up the deadness of the members, and I would make many sacrifices to bring it about—but truly I am in a dilemma from which I can see no escape. My poor brother [Thomas] is no better—I much fear he is worse, and in truth we have small hope of his recovery. My next brother Benjamin who is a partner with us is very delicate—several rheumatic fevers have left him with a heart complaint and have deprived him of energy.[1] My next brother (Jacob) is just twenty-two—only been at our business a few months—too young to manage it. The chief part of my father's property is in our mills and machinery, and the welfare of all his family depends upon their being successfully managed.

'Thou wilt understand my difficulty—as embarrassing as it was unexpected. As far as personal considerations are concerned, my staying at home will be no disappointment to me, inasmuch as only a year ago I had resolved on no account to go to Parliament, after weighing the pros and cons of that career, but as we are now placed I am conscious that I might render thee some assistance were I for a session or two in the House. I do not absolutely decide against it, even under these perplexing circumstances, altho' I confess I cannot see any clear way of following up the schemes we had laid down.'

But the seats at Bolton and Sheffield did not fall in, and before a vacancy actually occurred—at Durham in April—Thomas Bright was well again. If he had died, as he so nearly did, his brother John must needs have returned more or less completely to private life.

The conflict in Bright's mind was not merely concern for the Rochdale business; it was also a conflict between two religious ideals—on the one hand the quietist spirit of the older Friends, who sought seclusion from an evil world, and on the other the new type of Quakerism that thought it a religious duty to mix actively with the world and win it over to the principles of peace, humanity, and justice. In Britain, more perhaps than in America, the active spirit among Friends has since that time increased so much at the expense of the old, that in our day it needs imagination to realise the strong though intangible fetters that Bright had to burst when, seventy years ago, he became an agitator and proposed to become a member of Parliament. No one who belonged to that intimate and isolated Society of Friends could treat lightly the opinion of his co-religionists. Dealings with the Samaritans, except in the way of business, were little encouraged. When Bright's sister Priscilla in 1849 married Duncan McLaren, who was not a Friend, she was 'disowned' by the Society, to her own intense grief and to the bitter indignation of her brother John.

[1] He died in 1845.

There was, indeed, no such definite rule against becoming an agitator and a Member of Parliament, as there then was against marrying outside the Society. But the strict Friends and the spiritual Friends of the older generation both disapproved of John Bright's new vocation. His father, a type of the strict Friend, said to an acquaintance, 'I don't like my son pushing himself to the front like this,' but he did nothing actively to interfere. More serious because more sympathetic opposition was offered by his mother-in-law, Mrs. Priestman, a type of the spiritual Friend living under the old law. In a long correspondence she urged upon Bright the danger that the meditative life of the soul must undergo from the ceaseless intrusion of absorbing worldly cares. His reply (November 1842) to one of her letters ran as follows:

> 'I have read thy letter with much attention, and it has served to revive feelings and fears which are frequently my companions. I trust I am often deeply concerned that so much active and public occupation should not succeed in injuring better feelings and higher objects. I do not see that it is possible, nor can I discover that it would be right, for me now to withdraw from the cause in which I have so long taken so deep an interest. The work is great, and vast are the results depending upon it, and unhappily our laborers are not abundant. We have many who work harder than I do, but we have few speakers, and thus the burden is heavy upon those who are enabled to assist as public speakers. I do not, however, apprehend that this line of action is more dangerous for me than more quiet occupation in the same cause would be, and seeing that I have some power, very feeble when compared with that of some others I admit, I cannot discern that there is anything wrong in exercising it for the furtherance of a great and good object. The danger is lest this object engross all one's mind and swallow up a better object. I know that there is this danger. I hope I strive against it, and I endeavour to pray that it may not overcome me. But conscious of the increasing hazard we run owing to the long continuance of monopolies, and beholding the appalling sufferings of multitudes of my fellow-creatures, and satisfied that all benevolence and charity and the teaching of religion and of schools fall short of much of their full effect owing to the degraded and impoverished condition of the people—I should feel myself guilty, as

possessing abundance and leaving others to hunger, nakedness and immorality and deepest ignorance and crime, if I were to retire into domestic quiet and leave the struggle to be carried on entirely by others. All this is clear to me—and not less clear is the necessity of extreme care lest the one thing needful for all of us be forgotten. I trust it may not be so. I am truly grateful for thy letter and counsel. I treasure it as if it came from my own Mother, and from one dearer to me than all, for I know both would have given me counsel similar to thine.'

He countered Mrs. Priestman's affectionate warnings against his political entanglements by equally affectionate warnings against her design of leaving her family, and going at her advanced age to visit and encourage Friends in America, after the fashion of her mother and grandmother before her. Bright and his mother-in-law, as might have been foreseen, each did as they chose, and gently set aside the warnings of the other. When Bright decided to stand for Parliament he did not venture to ask for Mrs. Priestman's approval, but wrote to her: 'Don't blame me, hope for me and pray for me. The future may prove me not wholly wrong.'

And so he went forward in the new path, feeling that the Spirit of God moved him to serve tables no less than it moved the older Friends to meditation and quiet. He knew what he gained, but he knew also what he lost. As an old man he wrote the following letter to some Friends who had appointed him an Elder in the year 1875:

'The labors of my life have taken me out of the way of service for our little Church, and have, to a large extent, unfitted me for it. I feel that there is nothing above the humblest office—shall I say that of doorkeeper?—which I could properly undertake. I speak honestly, on the review of my past life and my present condition. I feel it to be absolutely impossible for me to accept the office tendered to me by the far too favorable judgment of my friends. I feel humbled by the proposition made to me, and that I am so far from the state in which it would or might seem possible for me to consider it.'

Neither in youth nor age was Bright moved to speak at the religious meetings of the Society, though he took an active part in their meetings for business. And even in the family circle, as he advanced down the vale of years, he touched on religion less often in speech or writing than he does in these earlier letters to the Priestmans. But his faith, never with him an elaborate structure of theology, did not fall away from him. Religious feeling, in its simplest form, was the very basis of his life. He was always a Friend before everything else ; and a servant of God ; a man of deep, though ever more silent devotion.

No Church or other association truly thrives unless struggles and differences are alive within it. The contest between the old and new spirit in the Society of Friends, each representing much that was good, was waged for many years in and around the Bright family. What some of the older Friends thought of John has been described in an entertaining manner by one who knew those circles well.[1]

> 'The presence of John Bright at gatherings of Friends in those days was not always a source of unmingled gratification. What had they done ? those gentle, soft-voiced people, who never imputed a motive, passed a hasty judgment, or made a rash promise, who wrapped up even their censure in elaborate sentences, who were above all things peacemakers—that from their midst should come a young man whose short words smote like sledge-hammers ; who never "believed," nor "hoped" nor "trusted," but was always quite sure that he was in the right ; who set himself in opposition to the prejudices of whole classes of English people ; who treated some leading Friends with no more reverence than he would have treated a Bishop ; and who spoke of some Quaker institutions with little more respect than of the House of Lords ! John Bright's personal appearance was conspicuous in an assembly of Friends in the North of England, where the prevailing type is tall, thin, long-faced and regular featured. The young "Tribune's" physique, his resolute carriage, the head thrown defiantly back, the sensitive mouth set as firmly as if he were facing a howling mob, or standing at the bar of a hostile court, may have resembled some of the Friends of the seventeenth century, but not those of the nineteenth. His "strength of chest and limb" suggested other leaders of men.
>
> "So sturdy Cromwell pushed broad-shouldered on,
> So burly Luther breasted Babylon."
>
> 'The *Epistle*, issued annually to members of the Society

[1] Mrs. Boyce, *Records of a Quaker Family* (The Richardsons of Cleveland).

of Friends by the Yearly Meeting, is drawn up by a Committee appointed for the purpose, and is then read over sentence by sentence to the whole assembly. The year 1843 was a time of Repeal Agitation in Ireland, of distress in England; the Chartist disturbances were then recent, and the Anti-Corn Law League was in the height of its career. One sentence in the *Yearly Meeting's Epistle* ended with the words, *We trust Friends may always be found amongst those who are quiet in the land.* John Bright sprung to his feet to express a hope that this sentence was not intended to condemn those who were striving to effect the repeal of unjust laws! The Clerk rose to call the speaker to order, but before the reproof could be uttered the young man went on, *Now the Clerk need not fear that I will introduce politics into this assembly,* and proceeded to make an effective speech, in which the word *corn* did not occur, but which was in effect a defence of the action of himself and his friends. Applause is unknown in the Yearly Meeting, but a slight tapping noise was heard as John Bright resumed his seat.'

What John Bright thought of some of the older Friends who eschewed the agitation of public causes, other than anti-slavery, can be deduced from his private correspondence of 1842-43.

'American Friends,' he writes, 'are too much like their brethren here—hold their principles so precious that they studiously try to conceal them from the public eye.'

And again:

'I intend to see Sam Gurney to tell him what is doing in the country—to see if the charity which overflows for negroes can spare a thought for Englishmen. The Friends have subscribed nothing to the Metropolitan [Anti-Corn Law] Society, although a special application has been made to them!'

In 1843 he writes to Mrs. Priestman, at a time when indignation at a Tory Bill to endow Church education had brought out into the open various Friends who had refused to agitate against the Corn Law:

'I am amused to find the fuss our Darlington friends and *relatives* are making about the Education Bill. Edward Pease, John Pease, etc., all attending a public meeting, making speeches, moving resolutions, promoting agitation, leaving their sweet retirement and the enjoyment of their *otium cum dignitate* for the tumult of political strife, and all because the Government are disposed to add another link to the fetter which has galled us. Alas! and can these men be really blind to the causes of the miseries of the people, and to the source [viz. the Corn Laws] of the physical and moral degradation which permits the heartless aristocracy of Britain to trample unpunished upon every right, human and divine? The time will come when all will have to speak. Aggression follows aggression; enthralment of the mind naturally treads upon the heels of physical prostration, and we are becoming a people powerless, spiritless, and trained to bonds and to wrong.'

The propriety of Friends taking part in politics and their right to marry non-members were not the only questions at issue within the Society. Some of the stricter rules of conduct —the Puritan inheritance of the Quakers—were being relaxed by many of the young generation. In these questions John Bright was less of a rebel than some of his brothers and sisters, particularly Jacob, who was something of an *esprit fort.* But on the whole he was in favour of the larger latitude, and stood out, here as in all things, against vain attempts to coerce.

> 'MY DEAR MOTHER,' he writes to Mrs. Priestman in October 1844, 'Jacob and Esther were at the meeting [a literary soirée in Manchester]. I did not see them after it was over till the following morning, but I believe from curiosity they stayed some time after the dancing began. They do not hold strict opinions on these matters, perhaps less so than is desirable. As they grow older they may see differently. I gave thy letter to Esther and she will see thy kind interest in her welfare. When young persons are disposed to step beyond the path prescribed, it is a difficult thing to restrain them, and not easy to tell how to interfere. If their own judgment do not suffice for a guide, I fear the counsel of others is rarely effectual.'

On another occasion, when Jacob makes up a picnic party on First day, both John and Priscilla consider the proceeding unnecessarily offensive to other Friends. But Bright was no strict Sabbatarian for the age in which he lived; in 1855 he voted for the opening of the British Museum and National Gallery on Sunday, and in after years spoke out against the complete closing of post-offices on that day. In his own home no distinction was drawn between 'Sunday books' and books that were fit to read on any day of the week.

John and Priscilla encouraged the intimacy of Helen with Cobden's little boy Richard, who already promised nobly—*si quâ fata aspera rumpas!* They were known in Free Trade circles as 'the Children of the League.' When some one, in the exclusive spirit of the older Friends, reminded the Brights that Helen and Richard would probably see less of each other when they grew up because they were of different religions, Priscilla replies:

> 'In answer to thy remark about the *impossibility* of their intimacy being maintained in after life, my opinion is that all the difficulties which appear at present will have vanished away in eighteen years' time. Friends cannot stand still in this day and the days which are approaching of general enlightenment. Christian charity is gaining ground fast; if our society will stand still, it will be lost sight of.

Priscilla and John were even outgrowing, to some degree, the objections to music that had been so carefully instilled into them. Priscilla writes from One Ash:

> '. . . The factory people all went yesterday to the Free Trade Bazaar, my brother paying for a cheap train to conduct them to Manchester. There were 700 of them, and Geo. Wilson [1] let them go in *free*. They assembled on the moor just below these gates; the women and girls went first in twos and threes, then followed a band of music, and the men and boys brought up the rear. It was really a beautiful sight. They were all so well-dressed and in such high spirits. I wished Lord Ashley and his followers could have seen them. I cannot help thinking music may be useful in bringing about a moral and intellectual regeneration of the working classes; but I did not quite like the band yesterday, it felt to me like doing a good action with a great noise.'

Strictness in dress—'the plain dress'—was still common among the older members of the Society, and in order not to offend them, John Bright wore the 'plain collar' during the first part of his public career.[2]

[1] The famous Chairman of the Council of the Anti-Corn Law League.

[2] See portrait, p. 142. After he had adopted the more ordinary coat and collar of the day, *Punch* continued to represent him in the Quaker coat he had once worn, in the broad-brimmed hat he had never worn, and also, for some unknown reason, in an eye-glass that he never wore and never would have dreamt of wearing.

Howsoever he dressed, he was a true Friend within: for to him religion was connected with freedom of growth for the individual, and with the spiritual equality of the sexes. On the subject of the clergy, he writes in his usual downright way to his sister-in-law, Margaret, who had made friends with a reverend gentleman named Browne:

> 'I hope thou wilt control thy admiration of thy friend Browne. He may be to be admired, but the system of which he is a part is the most fatal to the interests of this country and of true religion. Clergymen rarely excite my love or veneration. Their influence over the female mind of this country is destructive of truth and freedom of thought and strength of mind.'

Though widowed and stricken low, Bright was not altogether solitary of heart. His sister-in-law, Margaret Priestman, who had nursed his wife in her last illness, and his sister Priscilla, who until her marriage kept house for him at One Ash, were both very dear to him. Besides his correspondence with Mrs. Priestman, he wrote severally to Margaret and Priscilla three times a week or more when on his Corn Law tours. Both real affection and a sense of duty were required to induce a man, who in later years loved leisure sometimes almost to laziness, to keep up this double correspondence in the midst of such stress of work as fell to the lot of John Bright between 1842 and 1846. He sometimes describes to Margaret the conditions under which he is writing to her, from some hotel parlour in the south: a dozen letters on business and politics to finish for the post, an article to dash off for a newspaper,[1] his last night's speech to correct for the press, his midday or evening speech to prepare, and the journey that he must take to deliver it. Even at this period of his life, when he was speaking four or five times a week, the art in which he excelled was painfully difficult to him, in proportion to his standard of excellence. 'No faithful workman finds his task a pastime.' In the rush and hurry of the Corn Law campaign there was no time for the moody and preoccupied days that later in his life marked the gestation of his greatest orations. Yet even in 1844 Priscilla writes: 'John has been very nervous about his

[1] Bright's journalistic activities on behalf of the League were considerable. He wrote much for the *League* newspaper, and also for Miall's *Nonconformist* and many other Liberal papers. He also wrote for his little Rochdale paper *The Vicar's Lantern*, where the quarrel with the vicar over Church-rates went forward to the bitter end.

speech all day and has made me almost as bad as himself. However, he managed very well, only his remarks were some of them rather personal.'

Sometimes he wearied of the Herculean load he was carrying, sometimes he rejoiced in the sense of power well used. In July 1842 he writes to Margaret:

'We have too few workers and I am over-tasked. Going about writing, speaking, etc., with little help is very disagreeable. I long to leave this busy, turbulent scene and to join you at Tynemouth, but I see no prospect of it. Poor little Helen, I wonder if she has forgotten me?'

But in March 1843 he writes from Bristol:

'The weather is superb and is finely calculated for making *agitating* a more pleasant and healthful occupation. We have a good Anti-Corn Law feeling wheresoever we go, and the old rotten hulk of monopoly floats heavily on the waters and will before long go down.'

Whenever he came home to One Ash the presence of his little daughter did much to console him and to renew his zest for life. 'Helen is indeed a treasure,' he writes in September 1842. 'My house is changed. Each meal-time has a new charm. It seems a step up *towards* what it was ever before Helen was born.' And again—more than a year later—'Helen is a sweet darling. She learns a verse with only once or twice hearing it and repeats it with great simplicity. I cannot tell thee how I am delighted to come home and enjoy her company. Her endearing manners have more and more influence over me.'

And once in 1843 he writes to the same good friend:

'Don't give thyself trouble about me, my dear Margaret. It grieves me to hear of tears coming into thy eyes on my account. I have lost much, more than this world can ever restore, but I have much left to enjoy. To know that you care for me and think me not unworthy to have been your relative is something, and my darling Helen is something, and to be able to advance a great public good is something, and thus I think and feel that ingratitude or continued unreasonable sorrow would be wrong.'

But though he was serene, he was often very sad. A year later he writes from One Ash:

'I am alone here to-night. Darling Helen is in bed,

and it is in these quiet hours that all the past most vividly reappears and the heart fills with sympathies which may meet with no response.'

The instincts driving John Bright to serve his generation in the forefront of political life proved stronger than the opposing influence of some of his relations, and the contrary tradition prevailing among his co-religionists. The recovery of his brother Thomas from the dangerous illness from which he had suffered in February 1843, enabled John to leave the mill to his most capable management, and to fall in with the wishes of Cobden and the other Free Trade leaders, that he himself should 'have a stirring League election,' and join his friend in the House of Commons.[1] Once he had decided that such a course was right, he had no coy reluctances. His candidature for Durham was not forced upon him, but resulted from his own prompt action in going to the spot at the critical time. The appointment of the sitting member as Governor of New Zealand had come as a surprise, and the Tories hoped to get their man, Lord Dungannon, elected, before either the Whigs or the League could put up a candidate. On April 1 Bright writes to Cobden from Lancashire:

'Wilson has had letters from Durham and writes the Colonel [Thompson] to go down. Now I fear the Colonel being at Norwich will be too late, so Rawson and I have resolved to go to Durham and are now on our way, expecting to arrive at nine to-night. We will see how the wind is blowing. If it would blow the Colonel in, well and good. If it would carry me with tolerable certainty and the Colonel do not arrive, or the people prefer me to him, possibly I may stand. I can promise nothing, and can only conclude after seeing how things are there. It would be a great thing to turn out Dungannon, a Lord, in the Cathedral City.'

The next day, April 2, he was selected as candidate, and writes to his sister Priscilla in the evening: 'Thou wilt wonder to hear that I am to be put in nomination to-morrow. The Colonel has not come, and there are so many good men here, anxious and earnest and with some confidence of success that we could not run away. Forgive me if I win. For if I lose

[1] See letters, p. 100 above. John was always very grateful to his brother Thomas for enabling him to remain in public life. In his letters occur such expressions as 'Thomas is very kind and generous in his conduct to me' (1847).

thou wilt not greatly blame me perhaps.' The day after that, nomination day, he issued his address and appeared on the hustings with Lord Dungannon. His opponent had the start of a week's canvass, and the still greater advantage of the support of the Marquis of Londonderry, to whom the Durham seat was supposed to 'belong.' Bright in his address challenged this time-honoured usage of the British constitution:

> 'I need not allude to the attempt which is being made to degrade you into the convenient tool of an aristocratic family—to employ your suffrages to place a man in Parliament as a stepping-stone to the governorship of a colony, and then to hand you over, as it were by private contract, to another.'

He repeated these charges on the hustings, in Lord Dungannon's presence, and a scene took place between the two candidates, delightful to the commonalty massed below. In those days, when only a small fraction of the people were enfranchised, the hustings often afforded an opportunity for the voteless multitude, by the show of hands, to demonstrate who was the popular favourite, even though he should stand next week at the bottom of the poll. So now, the whole mass there assembled seemed to hold up its hands for Bright.[1] But at the end of the poll Lord Dungannon was in by 507 votes to 405.

The decisive character of the majority was due in part to Lord Londonderry's influence, and in part to a custom of which the beaten candidate was at the time wholly ignorant. 'The election appeared to me,' Bright afterwards declared,[2] 'to have been orderly and fair, but in this I was mistaken. There was an understanding which was not made public for a month afterwards, and then 300 men received a sovereign each for their vote. The practice was one which had existed for so many years in Durham that the electors thought that there was no harm in it,' indeed three-fifths of those who had voted in the majority took their pay. But the League was no respecter of local customs. A petition was brought, and was tried, after the practice of those days, before a committee of the House of Commons. The chairman was Lord Ashley, who hated corruption more than he loved his party. He notes in his diary of July 15:

[1] Among those who so held up their hands was a little boy sitting on his father's shoulder, afterwards well known as Dr. Spence Watson.

[2] Speech at the 'Crown and Anchor,' reported in *Times*, July 31, 1843.

'Unseated Lord Dungannon. I am resolved, whenever I have the opportunity, to run breast high against all cases of bribery. This is a perilous, a wicked system; it is corrupting our people, and spreading moral and political mischief in all directions.'[1]

The good Lord Ashley thus became instrumental in bringing into Parliament a man as zealous as himself for the welfare of the people, yet differing from him in his whole conception of society, and an opponent of those measures of factory legislation which were to Ashley what Free Trade and Franchise were to Bright. Fortunate was the election committee that could have such a chairman, and fortunate the land that could produce both Ashley and Bright, and take what was best in the advice of each.

Bright resumed the contest after the unseating of Lord Dungannon, at first with diminished enthusiasm. On the 19th of July he wrote to Mrs. Priestman from Durham:

'. . . You cannot regret more than I do that I am here again. I knew not how to escape with honor or would assuredly not have tried the Durham people again. The majority of them have no political principles and small sense of duty in this matter. I do not think we shall win, but being here we must fight it out as resolutely as we can. There are some changes in our favor.'

These changes were the longer acquaintance of the electors with Bright; the incompetence of his new opponent, Mr. Purvis; the withdrawal of Lord Londonderry into the position of neutral; and the check given to the system of bribery—counterbalanced by 'a feeling that Lord Dungannon had been hardly used,' natural to those who had taken his sovereigns. Bright in his address pointed out to the electors that whereas £1 'head money' at election time once in every four years is only five shillings a year, each of them was paying much more than that as a result of the Protectionist system which he proposed to abolish. He soon warmed to his work and took heart of grace, but not till the very last days of the fight did he expect to win. His speeches seemed to be addressed rather to the working men than to the middle class. Though he fought on the Corn Laws, he spoke less as the League candidate than as a man with a mission of his own. He announced it as the

[1] Hodder, *Life of the Seventh Earl of Shaftesbury*, 1886; vol. i. p. 495.

purpose of his life to go to the House of Commons as the champion of the working classes :

> 'I am a working man as much as you. My father was as poor as any man in this crowd. He was of your own body, entirely. He boasts not—nor do I—of birth, nor of great family distinctions. What he has made, he has made by his own industry and successful commerce. What I have comes from him, and from my own exertions. I have no interest in the extravagance of government ; I have no interest in seeking appointments under any government ; I have no interest in pandering to the views of any government ; I have nothing to gain by being the tool of any party. I come before you as the friend of my own class and order ; as one of the people ; as one who would, on all occasions, be the firm defender of your rights, and the asserter of all those privileges to which you are justly entitled. It is on these grounds that I offer myself to your notice ; it is on these grounds that I solicit your suffrages.'

The Corn Laws he put before them as a working-class question :

> 'If a man have three or four children, he has just three or four times as much interest in having the Corn Laws abolished as the man who has none. Your children will grow up to be men and women. It may be that your heads will be laid in the grave before they come to manhood or womanhood ; but they will grow up, and want employment at honest trades—want houses and furniture, food and clothing, and all the necessaries and comforts of life. They will be honest and industrious as yourselves. But the difficulties which surround you will be increased tenfold by the time they have arrived at your age. Trade will then have become still more crippled ; the supply of food still more diminished ; the taxation of the country still further increased. The great lords, and some other people, will have become still more powerful, unless the freemen and electors of Durham and of other places stand to their guns, and resolve that, whatever may come of Queen, or Lords, or Commons, or Church, or anybody—great and powerful, and noble though they be—the working classes will stand by the working classes ; and will no longer lay themselves down in the dust to be trampled

upon by the iron heel of monopoly, and have their very lives squeezed out of them by evils such as I have described.'

The result of the poll was announced on July 25—Bright 488, Purvis 410, majority 78. The following letter, written by his sister Priscilla from One Ash, tells how the news reached Bright's own people:

'Rochdale has been in such a state of excitement as I scarcely ever knew to be the case. No business has been done to-day, many have not been in bed last night. Great crowds were at the station waiting the arrival of the noon train, and when it came, not one durst put the question, though most were sanguine of success. At last someone put his head out of one of the carriages and called out "Bright," upon which the guards took off their hats, and the assembled people rent the air with applause. One man, a shoemaker of the name of Hyan, the last one would have expected taking such pains, had no sooner caught what was the majority than he set off to acquaint us. His enthusiasm *carried* him almost across the valley. My Father saw him leap the style at the bottom of the field like one enchanted or bewitched. He opened the front door calling out to us "tidings—tidings." We rushed out of the drawing-room quite terrified to hear the panting in the passage. The poor creature could only articulate "Mr. Bright—78." He was so exhausted and out of breath. Directly afterwards the omnibus man drove round quite at a gallop, and we shan't soon forget his look of astonishment and disappointment when Hyan found breath sufficient to say "You 're too late. I told the news," for he said he had come at full speed and only stopped to set down passengers at one inn.

'The work people have placed us in a somewhat trying position—they begged a holiday this afternoon, which we were all unwilling to give, for we were anxious there should be no demonstration of joy. But it was no use arguing the point with them, and they gained their wish. I hear the band—but not the bells, altho' the most enthusiastic portion of the Liberals here were so determined to ring them, provided theirs was the victory, that they made a key which would open the belfry door, provided the vicar refused them admittance; the worst of these times is the immorality which too often attends them,' adds the Quakeress, striving to mortify in herself the pride and naughtiness of heart of the victorious politician.

The capture of a Tory stronghold by the League was an event of no small importance. 'This victory could not have been attained,' so the Leaguers boasted, 'by any one even of the very *élite* of the Whig aristocracy. Lord John Russell, Lord Morpeth, Lord Howick would have failed where the Rochdale cotton-spinner has been successful.' That this was not the language of mere partisanship was shown by the altered note of the *Times*, in that epoch the most accurate of political barometers. In a leading article hostile to Bright personally, the *Times* yet acknowledged grave import in the conquest of such a seat by a man who had held up Whig and Tory alike to the scorn of the electors. Total Repeal, the great paper declared, was now only a question of time, unless it was wisely forestalled by the adoption of a moderate fixed duty in the place of the existing sliding scale. The 'moderate fixed duty,' the panacea proposed by the *Times*, the Whigs, and all lovers of half measures, was rejected not only by the League but by the Protectionists, who saw that in time of great scarcity a fixed duty would be less defensible against popular clamour than a sliding scale, and that no corn tax, if once removed, could ever be reimposed.

This *Times* 'leader' on Bright's election, which appeared on August 1, is really no less favourable to the League than the article three months later which roused the Protectionists to fury and the Free Traders to exultation by the historic phrase, 'The League is a great fact.' The 'leader' on 'the great fact' in November, like that on Bright in August, was written in favour not of Total Repeal but of a fixed duty, and still showed more fear than love of the League, saying, for instance, 'We dislike gregarious congregations of cant and cotton men.' [1]

John Bright was now entering on a new sphere of action. Without ceasing his crusade in the country, he had also to play his part in the House of Commons, where some of the greatest demagogues have failed. Would he, like Cobbett before him,

[1] The *Times* in those days was written in what we should now call a 'bright' or 'sensational' style, resembling our own *Daily Mail* or *Observer*, rather than the solemnities of the late Victorian *Times*. This sensational style had, I believe, been introduced under the influence of Moseley and of Edward Sterling, father of Carlyle's *Sterling*, the original 'thunderer,' who retired from active work about 1840-41. Delane was the editor during Bright's great period.

prove of small account in the assemblage of the gentlemen of England? Like Cobbett, he was cut off from his fellow members by class, by education, by ideas, and by his independence of party. It is difficult for us to realise the full extent of the class demarcations that subsisted then and for long afterwards. Twenty-three years after Bright's first entry into the House of Commons, at a moment when he was the most popular statesman in the land, London Society was outraged and bewildered beyond expression because Russell was known to have invited him to dinner. And London Society was closely identified with the House of Commons. If Bright had merely excelled as a mob orator, the House would have been only too glad to set him down in the list of great outsiders who had failed to pass its test. But here came the advantage of his Quaker training, his restraint, his natural good taste that only hardened in the glowing furnace of his passion, his inevitable moral ascendancy in any company in which he was found. Never popular, and always on the defensive in the House of Commons during the twenty-five years before he was sanctified by the acceptance of office, he was from first to last respected and feared by gentlemen to whom a dissenting cotton-spinner was a strange animal, but who knew a man when they saw one, and an orator when they heard one. A fine quality of the House of Commons, which it shares with any school of English boys, is the habit of judging every one within its walls, not by extraneous repute or qualification, but by his capacity for passing certain standards of the institution of which he has become a member. What precisely those standards are, it would be impertinent for any one to attempt to define who has never been on the floor of the House; but whatever they are, Bright passed them with high honours, and he was therefore allowed to tell the landlords to their faces the worst he thought of their Corn Laws, their Game Laws, and their Church establishments, and he could even find in the House, when he could find it nowhere else in the country, a hostile but respectful and admiring audience for his views on the Crimean War.

His success in the House was not obtained by flattery or by compromise. At a League banquet held at the Crown and Anchor in honour of the Durham election on the night after he had taken his seat, he described his first impressions of the scene upon which he was entering, in language prophetic of the part he was destined to play there during the next quarter of a century. 'Going into the House last night,' he said,

'the caution lately given me by a poor but honest Scotchman struck me. He said to me, "Mr. Bright, I'll give you a piece of advice. You are going into bad company; and now that you are in, remember that you stick to what you said when you were out."'

He then continues:

> 'If one had dropped from the clouds upon the floor of the House and listened to the debate last night, I never should have dreamed that there was the least distress or discontent in the country. It was true that Lord John Russell made a very clever speech and some hard hits at the ministry. . . . Then came Lord Palmerston, and he made a very clever speech, if there was no country; it would have been very well at a debating club; it had some hard cuts at the ministry, interspersed with references to Afghanistan and the Ameers of Scinde, and everything but *the condition of England question.*'

To his sister-in-law, Margaret Priestman, he wrote on the same day (July 29): 'I took my seat last night at 4 o'clock. I was not in the least overawed at the position in which I was placed. The great ones of the earth are not very great after all. I felt as if I knew all about them, their schemes, their capacities and all. Therefore I felt greatly at ease. It was a mere party debate, clever but without honesty, and without earnestness.'

His maiden speech was delivered on August 7, in a debate on the Import Duties. Though he showed some nervousness in his manner during the delivery of the first sentences, his words were bold enough. He had not been on his legs half a minute before he told the House that 'the rich here are attended to—the poor are too frequently neglected.' After a brief but powerful attack on the Corn Laws he clinched the argument with these words:

> 'A Commission has reported that the increase of our population is every year so great as to require for its support an annual increase of food equal to the whole produce of the county of Warwick. The Government has no power to add a county of Warwick every year to the country, neither has it power to arrest the increase of population. The consequences can neither be doubtful nor distant. . . . Twenty thousand pitmen in the North have lately met to fix the lowest price for which they will work, and the highest price they will pay for their food,

This may be wrong, but it is more tolerable than that several hundred land-owners should sit here to fix the lowest price they will take for the produce of their estates. You have been sowing curses, and now you wonder that curses have grown.'

Then, turning upon Sir Robert Peel, he began to prophesy:

'I should be glad to see the right hon. baronet not the Minister of the Queen merely, but the Minister of the people also. I should rejoice to see him disconnect himself from the party whose principles he declares to be unsound. I should be glad to see him bearing in mind the source from which he has sprung, the source of his power and wealth, as it is the source of much of the power and wealth and greatness of this Empire. He may have a laudable ambition—he may seek renown, but no man can be truly great who is content to serve an oligarchy who regard no interest but their own. I live in the manufacturing districts, I am well acquainted with the wishes and feelings of the population, and I do not hesitate to say, when I view the utter disregard with which they are treated by this House, that the dangers which impend are greater than those which now surround us.'

During the first seven years of Bright's parliamentary life, the House of Commons was not sitting either in its ancient or in its present home, but was billeted in temporary quarters. The government of Peel and the battle of the Corn Laws took place neither in the chamber that we know to-day, nor in the old St. Stephen's Chapel, whither Charles I. had come seeking the five members, where Walpole and the Pitts had borne sway, whence the Reform Bill had been sent up to the Lords. The fire of October 1834 had destroyed the old House of Commons, together with many of the other buildings of Westminster Palace, and until their present home was ready for occupation in 1850 the Commons sat in the old Court of Requests, on the site of the open space where the statue of Cœur de Lion rides to-day in so unparliamentary an attitude. Meanwhile the Lords, who had formerly sat in this same Court of Requests, moved to the old Painted Chamber until their new home was ready for them in 1847.

During the autumn and winter of 1843 the wind sat in the sails of the League. Its candidates continued to carry by-elections of which the most important involved the capture of the City in October. London at first had lagged behind the provinces, but the Leaguers, to use their favourite expression, had 'invaded' the capital in 1842-43. Some hundreds of meetings had been held, including the monster demonstrations every month in Covent Garden Opera House, where John Bright and William Fox delivered *urbi et orbi* their greatest efforts of oratory, still to be read word for word in the files of the old *League* newspaper. The City magnates at length began to subscribe to the League when the £100,000 Fund was opened in the autumn. In these circumstances, the death of one of the members for London gave the Free Traders an opportunity for a display of their growing power. On October 2 Bright, from London, writes to Cobden at Manchester:

> 'It is of first necessity that thou and I should work together incessantly for the City Election. Come up to-morrow night, if possible. Tell the [Manchester] Athenæum people that the matter is the all-important one and that provincials must yield to it. Come up: *we* must do it, if it be done. And Repeal is not far off when this election is won. No one dare afterwards contest a Borough against the League. *Le jour viendra.* I have not been in bed for two nights, but am not much tired.'

After nearly a month of such personal exertions by the chiefs of the League, their candidate, Pattison, was elected for the City by 6535 against Protectionist Baring's 6334.

The position of another member for the City, Lord John Russell, still bound to his 'fixed duty' formula, was now none of the most pleasant, especially when the heads of some of the great Whig families, without waiting for his lead, declared for complete Free Trade—in December 1843 Lord Morpeth, in the following June Lord Howick. In January 1844 the Marquis of Westminster sent £500 to the League funds.

While a powerful minority of the upper and landlord class was thus coming round to Free Trade, and the farmers were weakening in their opposition, the working men were becoming more and more unanimous and enthusiastic. The bankruptcy of the extreme Chartist opposition to the League was brought home to all democratic politicians by the events of August 5, 1844, when Cobden and Bright met Feargus O'Connor and his lieutenant McGrath on a platform at Northampton, and disputed with them before an audience of 6000 persons. When Cobden made his motion, the Chartists put forward their amendment, a clumsy compromise between the Protectionists and Free Traders in their body, to the effect that the Corn Laws were bad laws, but that their repeal would be injurious, if it took place before the enfranchisement of the working class, because it would make the middle class masters of the State. As the Tories present voted with the O'Connorites, the majority against this amendment was small, but the weight of argument in the discussion had, by the admission of all present, been so entirely on the side of Cobden and Bright that O'Connor's waning influence with the working men was almost destroyed by the encounter.[1]

Nevertheless 1844 was, superficially, a year of set-back for the League. All the great currents beneath were turning to swell the tide of Free Trade, but the surface was ruffled by a contrary breeze. Yet the breeze was of happy omen, for it was the wind of prosperity. A series of good harvests in England brought wheat down in 1843-45 to an average of little more than 50 shillings a quarter; trade had recovered, partly owing to the good harvests, and partly as a result of the Free Trade measures of Peel's budget of 1842. The consequent retreat of the shadow of famine from the homes of the working men, and the release of their employers from the instant fear of bankruptcy, illustrated on behalf of the League the benefits of low corn prices and of Free Trade measures, but at the same time removed the necessity for immediate rebellion against the existing system of Corn Laws. As the state of the country improved, there was a strengthening of old party ties at the expense of the League. At several by-elections in rural districts and small country towns the Free Traders failed in 1844 to repeat the successes of the previous year. 'We are sadly bothered with these elections in places where no such thing as freedom to vote exists,' wrote Bright to his sister-in-law. 'These small constituencies [2] in no degree tell what public opinion is, and yet they must be contested and in most cases without success.' The local Whigs, so Bright wrote to Duncan McLaren, generally refused to support the League candidates, whom they regarded as interlopers, and so left the humbler voters exposed to 'the vengeance of the squires' in counties, and in small towns to the various forms of intimida-

[1] Cf. Gammage's *Chartist Movement*, 253-55, to the *League*, August 10, 1844.

[2] The elections to which this letter refers were at Christchurch, where the Protectionists won by 180 votes to 84; and at Hastings, where they won by 511 to 169.

tion and bribery to which the desperate Protectionists had now full recourse. But the wiser men of all parties knew that the proud edifice of the Corn Laws, which six years before had been declared as safe as the monarchy, was now so effectively undermined that the next stress of bad weather at harvest time would bring it crashing to the ground.

Another apparent set-back to the winning cause in 1844, besides the improvement in trade and the by-elections, was the quarrel of the League with the official Whigs, despite the recent Free Trade declarations of Morpeth and Howick. The bitterness felt by the Whigs against the League at this juncture, like the bitterness of Peel against Cobden, was in part a psychological result of their consciousness that the League had the better of the argument and would soon convince their judgment against their will. When we are on the point of changing our minds we are often most angry with the persuader. And so it was with the Whigs in 1844. But there was a special reason for their irritation in the politics of Edinburgh, where Duncan McLaren, urged on by Bright, had attacked the sitting Whig Members, Craig and Macaulay, and threatened to run a League candidate. Macaulay incensed the Leaguers because, while declaring himself a Free Trader, he urged the League to join hands with the Whigs on the fixed duty compromise, which he himself regarded, not as the best, but as the best that would be practicable for years to come. In public letters written in his forcible, stabbing style, driven home with illustration and antithesis, he pointed to the recent by-elections as proof that Free Trade could only come step by step, and by the union of all Liberals to effect the gradual process. His letters, though friendly in tone, were most damaging, because they made a good case for believing that the League was not really as strong as its adherents supposed. McLaren, therefore, began to attack him in his Edinburgh constituency.

On April 25 Bright writes to McLaren :

> 'My dear Friend,—I rejoice at the result of your meeting—such a decisive demonstration cannot fail to have a powerful influence on the opinions and policy of the Whig party. They are an infatuated and imbecile party, and are every day working their own destruction. After all I have no expectation that Macaulay will resign —you may as well be prepared with a Candidate in case he should try the trick of resigning and stand again to prove his hold on your Electoral Body.'

And in July he writes again:

> 'Doubtless the Whigs hate us—nobody denies it—and yet what can be done that is not done? Most of their hatred is laid to the charge of the Leaguers of Edinbro' because they bothered Craig and Macaulay, and yet I can see no wrong you did to goad on the shufflers. Macaulay came into the House the night of the Corn Law debate and laid down on a bench up in the gallery not far from the entrance into the Library and slept or appeared to sleep there I believe for hours—the front Whig bench was wholly unoccupied during the whole night, and the whole question was treated by the Whigs and by Macaulay among the rest with the utmost contempt—and doubtless his vote was only secured by your compulsion. With the feeling now existing between the Whigs and us, no strong opposition in Parliament can be made.'

During this period of marking time, Cobden bethought him of another plan. Unless a fresh famine intervened, the Corn Laws were now reprieved till the next General Election. The efforts of the Leaguers were concentrated on preparation, in the Registration Courts and elsewhere, for that decisive event. Their candidates would certainly carry the large towns, but the great majority of the Members of Parliament were returned by counties and small towns, more or less under landlord influence. If by the Reform Act of 1832 the seats had been distributed according to population, or if the whole middle class had been enfranchised, the Corn Laws would not have stood a chance—still less if any considerable section of the working class had been given votes. But, as it was, the electoral dice were heavily loaded on the side of the monopolists. To redress the balance before the General Election, Cobden passed round word that good Free Traders were to qualify as county voters by purchasing freehold property worth 40 shillings a year. Fifty or sixty pounds could make a man a county voter. In this way they would more than outnumber the faggot votes created by the landlords, who were in the habit of 'making brothers, sons, nephews, uncles of their tenant farmers, all qualify for the same holding, and swear, if need be, that they were partners in the farm, though they were no more partners than you are.' [1]

[1] *Morley*, i. 304. The Reform Act of 1832 gave the county franchise to tenants at will, occupying at a yearly value of fifty pounds, as well as to the old 'forty-shilling freeholder.'

The idea was taken up with enthusiasm in 1844-45, and Bright, as his correspondence shows, was engaged day and night in pushing forward the 'registration' movement, as it was called, in every part of the country; in Yorkshire, Lancashire, and Cheshire alone 5000 names were by this means added to the electoral lists. This sudden increase of League votes made the Whig and Tory members less willing to face the next election with the Corn Laws still unrepealed, and no doubt in this way had a share in the final conversion of Parliament. At Christmas 1844, Bright writes to his sister-in-law Margaret: 'The registration movement is creating a great sensation, and in truth I regard it as the *ulterior measure* of our contest. We shall make short work of some of the monopolist county seats at another election.'

And on New Year's Day 1845, he adds: 'In vote-making we are doing great execution. It is now the towns against the squires, and the towns will win.'

CHAPTER VI

THE BATTLE OF THE CORN LAWS. III. THE END, 1845-46

'Peel stood up on the famous floor,
Ruled the people and fed the poor.'
BOWEN, *Harrow Song.*

IN the year 1845 Bright became the national leader of an attack on the Game Laws and the system of game-preserving. He took up the question on his own initiative, but was warmly supported by the Leaguers, who saw in it the means of further detaching the farmers from their landlords, and of adding fuel to the wrath of the whole nation against the now isolated class who withheld corn from the people.

Few, though all-powerful, were the friends of game-preserving in those days. The wealthy merchants were seldom then admitted to the joys of country-house battues, and could therefore still read with pleasure attacks on the Game Laws in the *League* and other newspapers, and could still regard the slaughter of birds with a mixture of envy, contempt, and humanitarian disapproval.[1] The squires in reality were most of them true sportsmen, who still pursued their game behind dogs from hedge to hedge and did not, in those days, leave all the real work to the beaters. They returned the scorn of the middle class on this subject with well-worn tales in the Pickwick vein about the 'snob' or city sportsman and his misadventures in the turnips or by the covert side.

But though supported by the town middle class and their press, the movement at the head of which Bright put himself was a rebellion of tenant farmers, driven by their wrongs, for the first and last time in history, to come out into the open against the squires. In the closing years of the Protectionist

[1] For instance, the death of 2517 pheasants in five days at a certain noble seat is described in the *Bury Post* (Nov. 1845) as 'wholesale slaughter.' No provincial newspaper of to-day would be so squeamish. See also *Punch's* cartoon of Prince Albert's sport, 1845, vol. viii. pp. 58-59.

régime the farmers were on bad terms with their landlords ; high rents robbed them of every advantage of protection, while they were left open to all its disadvantages. Farmers were continually being sold up, and their murmuring, though it could not be loud, was deep. One of the causes of their distress and of their alienation from the landlords lay in the wholesale destruction of their crops and pasture by pheasants and partridges, and still more by hares and rabbits. Though the French Revolution is said to have been caused in part by game preservation, game did far less damage in France in the eighteenth century than in England in the nineteenth. Some landlords gave reductions of twenty per cent. in their rents on this account,[1] but though the conduct of these men may have been fair to their farmers, it was scarcely fair to the community to destroy so much of the corn grown in the island while putting a check on foreign importation. Bright calculated that during the scarcity of 1838-42, game devoured 'as large a quantity of the produce of the soil of England as the whole amount that we imported from abroad.'

But the preserving landlords who made deductions from rent were the exception. The tenant was usually the sufferer. And it was noticeable that the farmers, the most influential section of those who tilled the soil, the cream of the 'protected' classes, found no champion in Parliament for their grievances about game, until the Free Trade cotton-spinner came into the House of Commons.

> 'The preservation of game,' Bright wrote, 'involves a list of evils to the farmer of which the loss of money is probably not the greatest. It destroys his self-respect and the independence of his character. He takes a farm and contracts to pay a rent ; he stocks it with cattle and sheep ; he ploughs and sows and reaps—his landlord also stocks the same farm with hares and rabbits and pheasants, and enjoys his battue, or sends to market the game which his tenant's produce has fed. The tenant has his servants, to superintend or conduct the operations on his farm, and to feed and protect his cattle and his flocks—the landlord has his keepers to secure his game, and these keepers are a spy upon the tenant himself, and traverse his field by day or night, as though superior to his servants and himself. In all this there is a fruitful source of depredation

[1] Mr. Pusey, M.P., allowed a rebate of £916 for damage done by game on 389 acres in the summer of 1844.

to the farmer. Men of capital and independent feeling will shun an occupation which involves so much humiliation.'

Another aspect of the Game Laws, besides the wrong done to farmers and the further reduction of the artificially limited food supply of the nation, was the demoralising character of the poaching war that raged in every county and in half the parishes of England. To poach was no doubt wrong; but to fill a thickly populated modern country with game running wild among a starving people, and to enact and enforce the harshest laws against any one who touched a head of it, was to incite to civil tumult, to make any lad of spirit think game-killing a virtue—and often indeed gamekeeper-killing less wicked than other murder. To benefit a sport enjoyed by 40,000 persons at the outside, about 5000 persons a year were fined, imprisoned or transported. The moral aspect of the game war, the bloodshed and the hanging, the fighting, the imprisonments and the breaking up of families by transportation, deeply outraged Bright's Quaker instincts.

In the winter of 1844-45 he set himself to collect evidence, and in a few months thoroughly mastered the details of agriculture in connection with the ravages of game. The landlords never caught him tripping, and were unable to laugh at him as a 'snob' out larking in the country. He was accepted in many districts as the farmer's friend. A gentleman in close touch with the rural life of Wiltshire wrote to him: 'Your name is a household word with the farmers in this district. They literally swear by you.' For several weeks, he tells us, he received and answered from thirty to sixty letters a day on the subject of the Game Laws. He interviewed countless farmers, poulterers, and other individuals of more dubious occupation: he writes to his sister-in-law that he has an appointment with 'the greatest poacher in England.' He had experiments scientifically conducted, which satisfied him that 'four and a half rabbits consume as much food as a sheep.' At length, primed with written and verbal testimony of the losses of hundreds of pounds by individual farmers, of the throwing up of farms and the bankruptcy of tenants owing to the depredations of game—armed, too, with the statistics of poaching affrays, trials and sentences—he moved in the House of Commons, on February 27, 1845, for a Select Committee to inquire into the operation of the Game Laws.

It was an arduous ordeal for so young a Member, however

self-confident and however well prepared. Both sides of the House were packed with row above row of gentlemen who only knew what was agreeable in the English game system, but knew that to perfection; their dearest recollections of boyhood were jolly days, in well-known coverts, alone or with the old keeper; as the cotton-spinner talked, there rose before each man's eyes some vision of joys deep in woodland, to many of them the best moments of life. John Bright, foreseeing the situation, wisely determined on a change in his usual method. He knew that if he used the strain of high denunciation that served him so well against the Corn Laws, he might have an orator's triumph, but he could not persuade those serried ranks, and if they could not be in part persuaded nothing on this question could be done. He did not denounce them, but appealed to their generosity and common sense. He read out facts, statistics, and stories—damning and irrefutable. In place of a peroration, he pointed out quietly before he sat down that he had brought his case before the House 'without using a single word or a single expression of harshness towards any human being.' For once he had out-Cobdened Cobden.

He had his reward. Though he had spoken through the dinner-hour, when the House was usually most empty, not half a dozen members left the crowded benches during his two hours' speech. Graham, for the Government, thanked him for his 'tone and temper,' said he had 'done justice to the gentlemen of England,' admitted that he had made out a strong case, and granted him his Select Committee. The Speaker complimented him in private.

> 'Bright,' said Cobden, 'did his work admirably, and won golden opinions from all men. His speech took the squires quite aback. It has put Bright in a right position, shown that he has power, and it will draw the sympathy of the farmers to the League. The latter conviction seemed to weigh heavily on the spirits of the squires.' [1]

The *Times* supported him, with reservation. The following extract from its 'leader' is interesting, both as an example of the boyish style of the 'thunderer' in that period when its power was at the zenith, and as a proof of the position that Bright already had acquired among his countrymen as early as February 1845:

> 'The country gentleman puts on scarlet, Mr. Bright

[1] *Morley*, i. 316.

> drab of the soberest brown. The former brings out his full-mouthed pack, the latter his not less noisy league. The one then hunts down a fox, the latter a landowner or monopolist. The sportsman bags pheasants and hares, the Quaker bishops and lords. The former rejoices to be in at the death of a fox and carries off the brush to adorn his hall; it is the acme of Mr. Bright's anticipation to witness the death-blow of a favoured class. His trenchant blade is ever at hand to lop off the whole amount of its protection, and the achievement, measured by percentages and puffed up into enormous sum totals, will, doubtless, some day hang over his mantelpiece to stimulate the hereditary prowess of future generations of Brights.'

The Select Committee of the House, thus obtained, brought to light the facts of the case as Bright had stated them. His labours on the Committee were a severe addition to his League work during the spring and summer. In March he spoke at St. Albans at 'a public dinner of 150 farmers to present a piece of plate to a farmer of the neighbourhood who had exposed his landlord's game system and been turned from his farm in consequence.' He exhorted the farmers to stand by each other, and no longer tamely to submit to anything which their landlords chose to do. At this time he saw signs of a spirit of resistance growing among the farmers, but six years later (1851) he confessed in the House of Commons that he had been forced to relinquish the agitation of the Game Laws, 'not having received that aid from the farmers which their private representations had induced me to expect.'

But his efforts had not been in vain, though no effectual legislative remedy was applied for many years to come. As a part of the Anti-Corn Law agitation, his attack had an important success. And there can be little doubt that his wide exposure of these scandals was one cause of a gradual improvement in Game Law administration and justice. Sentences on poachers began less often to bear the imprint of class vengeance. And consideration for the economic interest of the farmers became more common among their landlords. But it was not until Bright was seventy years old that Harcourt's Ground Game Act gave to the tenant certain rights of killing the hares and rabbits that preyed upon his crops. To what extent abuses of game preservation have survived the great Tribune who attacked them more than two generations ago, it boots not here to inquire.

The prospects of the Leaguers in the year 1845, prior to the unexpected events of the autumn which solved all their difficulties, were from the first better than in the previous year. It is true that the man of genius who took command of the sinking ship of Protection when the men of talent were leaving it, has told us that 'low prices, abundant harvests, and a thriving commerce had rendered appeals, varied even by the persuasive ingenuity of Mr. Cobden, a wearisome iteration.'[1] But if the iteration was wearisome—and the ever-increasing number and enthusiasm of the League meetings did not show weariness—it was wearisome to a nation already persuaded. The 'thriving commerce' was the result in part of 'abundant harvests' and in part of the great steps towards Free Trade already taken by Peel in everything except corn. The manufacturers rejoiced in the revival of trade, which at once saved their fortunes and illustrated their theories, while they had reason to hope that the first recurrence of bad times would lead at once to the triumph of their cause. On New Year's Day of 1845 Bright wrote to his sister-in-law: 'Trade continues good, and throughout the cotton district there is a manifest improvement in the condition and temper of all classes. We may hope to make this perpetual.'

'The Manchester confederates,' wrote Disraeli in a sentence that has been more often quoted than questioned, 'seemed to be least in favour with Parliament and country on the very eve of their triumph.' But if their favour with the country had grown less, it was strange that, while the last part of the hundred thousand pounds fund was being successfully collected, another quarter of a million was at Cobden's bidding, invested by Free Traders in the purchase of forty-shilling freeholds in Lancashire, Yorkshire, and Cheshire alone, besides great sums in the country at large. Meanwhile the Free Trade Bazaar in London astonished that simple era with its magnificence and variety, and paved the way for the great Exhibition of 1851. The League meetings and orations were one long crescendo. Only at the by-elections was the effect of good times so far felt that the upper tithe of the population that then had votes was less willing, in 1845, to break away from old personal and party ties and support League candidates than they had been in 1843 when faced with absolute ruin. It was generally understood that the country was converted, and it was whispered

[1] Disraeli, *Life of Lord George Bentinck*, 1852, p. 9. This wonderful 'biography' is in a class by itself with Carlyle's *Sterling*, for the biographer supplies nine-tenths of the interest.

that the official Opposition and the leading Ministers were converted too. If Cobden had any less hold on the country than before, it was because Peel was now regarded as to some degree the champion of Free Trade in his stead.[1]

Indeed, what 'the country' thinks is usually a matter of conjecture, especially when the franchise is narrow. But it can be confidently asserted that the other part of Disraeli's statement, namely, that the Leaguers on the eve of their triumph were less than formerly 'in favour with Parliament,' overlooks the facts of the case. Formerly, in 1842 and 1843, insulting demonstrations against Cobden had been rapturously applauded from both sides of the House. Such scenes were no longer possible in 1844 or 1845. And in 1845 the Leaguers in the House were more influential and popular, both with Whigs and with Ministers, than in 1844. Their quarrel with Peel and their quarrel with the Whigs had been healed by time and by a common antagonism. A secret sympathy now linked Cobden and Bright with Peel and with the front Opposition bench, while the Protectionist country gentlemen, having at length found a voice in Disraeli's revengeful wit, sat no longer in dumb mutiny behind a Minister who had long lost their hearts, and could not for much longer count upon their votes.

In 1844 Bright had been stirring up McLaren against the Whigs and Macaulay, but in the spring of 1845 he writes to him in very different terms:

> 'The cause in which we are laboring makes sensible and sure progress. The agitation has been transferred to the floor of Parliament, and has there been maintained almost incessantly since the beginning of the session. In debate we have had more than ordinary advantage over our opponents, and the Free Traders—Villiers, Cobden, Gibson, and thy correspondent—have formed if not a numerous yet a somewhat valiant party in a good cause. Lord Howick, too, has come fairly out on the principle, and Lord John Russell has made large advances towards

[1] *Punch* thus stated the situation in April 1845:

'BIGAMY

'A man, named Peel, was yesterday brought before the magistrate, Mr. Bull, at this office, charged with having intermarried with a female named Free Trade, his former wife Agriculture being still alive. Their Graces the Dukes of Buckingham and Richmond, and a gentleman, named Ferrand, proved the fact of the former marriage. A Mr. Cobden deposed that Peel had within the last two years contracted matrimony with Free Trade, a young lady to whom he was himself engaged. He complained bitterly of Peel as having stolen his sweetheart.'

us. He is now for the extinction of Protection, and pleads only for its gradual abolition, and he makes even this reservation very faintly; we learn from private sources that he is fully resolved now on the principle and only speaks "moderately" on account of his position and former statements. Thou wilt be glad also to hear that Macaulay has given up fixed duties and has expressed himself greatly dissatisfied with Lord John's slow progress from wrong to right. We have some hopes that he will give us one of his brilliant orations when Villiers brings on his motion.'

Peel, too, was coming round, like a great ship veering with the tide. In March 1845, as he sat listening to Cobden's argument against the Corn Law, he crumpled up the notes he was making for his reply. '*You* must answer this,' he said to Sidney Herbert, 'for *I* cannot.' Disraeli may have been too bitter, but he was not far wide of the mark when he said that Peel's Government, as representing the Corn Law party, was 'an organised hypocrisy.' His saying that Protection was in the same danger as 'Protestantism in 1828,' was appreciated by a generation that remembered how Peel and Wellington had carried Catholic Emancipation after opposing it for years with all their political energy.

The Budget of 1845 took Free Trade forward another immense step in articles other than corn. It was received by the Leaguers in a more friendly spirit than the Budget of 1842, for they now knew that Peel was their ally. 'The financial scheme of the Government,' wrote Bright to his sister-in-law on February 17, 'is well thought of generally—except that the squires are sulking about it. The debate to-night is on the Income Tax—shall it be continued or not? Of course Peel will succeed in carrying his measures,' and Bright for one is not going to stand in their way. It seemed that Peel, who now had the confidence of the country and the Court as well as of the House of Commons, would remain in office until he had gradually abolished the last vestiges of the Protective system. Disraeli supposed that he meant to abolish the Corn Laws in a few years' time, after another General Election in which the League would not be against him.[1] But the normal development of politics was hastened by a catastrophe of nature.

In the course of the debate on June 10, 1845, Mark Philips, senior Member for Manchester, said: 'Within a short period the

[1] Disraeli, *Bentinck*, pp. 21-22.

result of the harvest will be known, and will probably agitate the manufactures and commerce of the country to such an extent that these laws will be at once swept away.' No one took notice of the prophecy, for in June no general alarm was felt for the prospects of the ripening harvest. On August 7 Parliament was prorogued, to meet again more than five months later in a memorable hour.

A fortnight after the prorogation of Parliament Bright wrote to his sister-in-law from Rochdale:

> 'The weather is really most disastrous. It has rained almost incessantly since I left Newcastle. I felt rather sad too on leaving you. I seemed as if I had been hardly civil with any one I had come in contact with. Hard work, knocking about from pillar to post, the result of the Sunderland election and the baseness of some of the Electors [1] and some cold into the bargain upset my equanimity rather.'

He little guessed what the rain, which had begun by giving him a cold at the Sunderland by-election, would end by doing for him and for England. If he had known, he might have asked his old enemy the vicar of Rochdale to pray for its continuance. For the next month it rained, and the corn was in the ear. Day by day the farmers went out to watch the ruin of their standing crops. The rain was not the cause of the potato disease that halved the population of Ireland; the potato disease had set in earlier for mysterious reasons unconnected with the autumn weather. But the rain took away all possibility that the four million Irish and two million English who normally subsisted on potatoes could be fed next year on British corn.

Meanwhile Bright was attempting to enjoy a well-earned holiday in Scotland with two of his sisters. He records at least one fine day, but, for the most part, 'rain' and 'Scotch mist' enwrapped the scenes of old romance and crime, which were duly sought out by the brother and sisters, admirably familiar as they were with the history of Sir Walter's land. At length, having wandered as far north as Inverness, Bright found there awaiting him a letter from his friend, which read like a death-warrant to the League. Cobden announced that

[1] The local Whigs had refused to support Col. Thompson, the Leaguer, who had therefore been defeated by Hudson, the 'railway King,' by 627 to 497. At the hustings ten thousand non-voters had held up their hands for Thompson and scarcely any for his rival.

he had determined at once to retire from public life, and to devote himself to his long-neglected business as the only means of saving himself and his family from ruin.

The letter which Bright wrote back is well known to the world in Lord Morley's *Life of Cobden*. But it has equally a place in the *Life of Bright*, and those who have read it once will not be sorry to read it again:

'INVERNESS, *Sept.* 20, 1845.

'MY DEAR COBDEN,—I received your[1] letter of the 15th yesterday evening on my arrival here. Its contents have made me more sad than I can express. It seems as if this untoward event contained within it an affliction personal for myself, great public loss, a heavy blow to one for whom I feel a sincere friendship, and not a little of danger to the great cause in which we have been fellow laborers.

'I would return home without a day's delay if I had a valid excuse for my sisters who are here with me. We have now been out nearly three weeks, and may possibly be as much longer before we reach home; our plan being pretty well chalked out beforehand, I don't see how I can greatly change it without giving a sufficient reason. But it does not appear needful that you should take any hasty step in the matter. Too much is at stake both for you and for the public to make any sudden decision advisable. I may therefore be home in time for us to have some conversation before anything comes before the public. Nothing of it shall pass my lips and I would urge nothing to be done till the latest moment, in the hope that some way of escape may yet be found. I am of opinion that your retirement would be tantamount to a dissolution of the League—its main-spring would be gone. I can in no degree take your place. As a second I can fight, but there are incapacities about me of which I am fully conscious, which prevent my being more than a second in such a work as we have labored in. Don't think I wish to add to your trouble by writing thus; but I am most anxious that some delay should take place, and therefore I urge that which I fully believe, that the League's existence depends mostly upon you, and that if the shock cannot be avoided, it should be given only after the weightiest con-

[1] It is just at this date that Bright drops the Quaker dating and language from his correspondence, except in the case of letters to Friends.

sideration, and in such a way as to produce the least evil.

'Be assured that in all this disappointment you have my heartfelt sympathy. We have worked long and hard and cordially together, and I can say most truly that the more I know of you the more have I had reason to admire and esteem you, and now when a heavy cloud seems upon us, I would not wholly give up the hope that we may yet labor in the good cause until all is gained for which we have striven. You speak of the attempts which have been made to raise the passion which led to the death of Abel, and to weaken us by destroying the confidence which was needful to our successful co-operations. If such attempts have been made they have wholly failed. To help on the cause I am sure each of us would in any way have led or followed; we held our natural and just position and hence our success. For myself I know nothing that at this moment would rejoice me more, except the absence of these difficulties, than that my retirement from the field could in any way maintain you in the front rank. The victory is now in reality gained, and our object will before very long be accomplished, but it is often as difficult to secure a victory as to gain it, and the sagacity of leaders cannot be dispensed with while anything remains to be done.

'Be assured I shall think of little else but this distressing turn of affairs till I meet you; and whilst I am sorry that such should be the position of things, I cannot but applaud the determination you show to look them full in the face and to grapple with the difficulties whilst they are yet surmountable.

'I have written this letter under feelings to which I have not been able to give expression, but you will believe that I am with much sympathy and esteem,—Your sincere friend, JOHN BRIGHT.'

'A day or two later,' Cobden's biographer tells us, 'Mr. Bright changed his plans and hastened southwards. Helpful projects revolved in his mind, as he watched the post-boys before him pressing on through the steaming rain. When he reached Manchester, he and one or two friends procured the sum of money which sufficed to tide over the emergency. For the moment Cobden was free to return to the cause which was on the eve of victory.'

There was no autumn session in 1845, but events greater than parliamentary occurred in the last three months of the year. On October 13, Peel and Graham spontaneously wrote to each other private letters that crossed in the post, suggesting that the reports of the Irish potato blight would necessitate the 'removal of impediments to import' of food, and confessing a doubt whether corn duties, once remitted, could ever be reimposed.[1] The impossibility, in face of the League, of reimposing the corn duties if once they were removed as a temporary measure of famine relief, was not unpleasing to Peel and Graham so far as their own opinions were concerned, but to the majority of their supporters and colleagues it appeared as an insuperable objection to any remission of the corn duties, whatever the need of the moment might be.

On the 26th of October, Bright wrote to his sister-in-law:

> 'The Corn Laws are on their last legs, if legs they have remaining. The deficient harvest and the failure in the potato crop seem likely to do our work very shortly as far as the change in the law goes. It is expected the ports will be opened by an Order in Council, and if they are we shall make it difficult to close them again. On every hand there is an expectation that we shall have repeal next session. Our fear is of a partial measure, a fixed duty or a lower scale; but I have some faith that Peel will do the thing completely when he next touches it.'

Then followed the 'three Cabinet Councils in a week' (October 31 - November 6), at which Peel's proposals to tamper with the Corn Laws, though not yet amounting to total repeal, were rejected by all his Cabinet except Lord Aberdeen, Graham, and Sidney Herbert.[2] The rulers of the Empire, unable to agree as to how the crisis should be met, separated *re infectâ*, and went gloomily back, the Protectionists to the foxes and pheasants, and Peel and Graham to the reports from Ireland. It was generally known that they had met, but it was not known whether or on what points they had failed to agree.

But the public, meanwhile, had made up its own mind on the question: since, owing to the potato blight, there would be famine in Ireland next year, and since, owing to the same cause and to the bad wheat harvest, England herself would feel the

[1] Parker, *Life of Graham*, ii. 23.

[2] Gladstone, who would have made a fourth, had recently resigned on a point of scruple connected with Maynooth.

pinch of hunger, it was clear that the long-anticipated hour had struck, and that the Corn Laws must be abolished. While the ineffectual Cabinets were sitting in Downing Street, the League was sharpening an agitation to cut the knot of the statesmen's tangle. The spirit of 1832 was again abroad in the land. From the end of October until Christmas Cobden and Bright were traversing every corner of England, daily addressing crowded meetings of the middle and working classes, united in an invincible determination that, after three years of comparative well-being, they would not permit themselves again to be starved when there was corn to be had in the world's garners. Thus was Peel supplied with an argument that in due course turned the Free Trade minority in his Cabinet into a majority—the irrefutable argument that no Ministry could face the League in the present temper of the country.

On November 29 Bright writes to his sister-in-law from the heart of the great campaign :

> 'On 2nd day last, I was at Sheffield. Cobden and I went from Manchester by the direct railway, which is now opened except 3 miles of tunnel. When we reached its mouth we landed and walked 4 miles over a wild and bleak moor, the road being almost a sheet of ice and covered for most of the way with snow. We walked in less time than the coach took to make the journey. On the other side of the hill we entered the train for Sheffield. We had a good meeting in Sheffield ; next morning went to Leeds. The Leeds meeting was a capital one, and Lord Morpeth's letter joining the League a cheerful "fact." On 5th day, we were at Wakefield and had a good meeting, and last night at Bradford where we had the greatest *cram* I think I ever saw. On 6th day morning, before leaving Wakefield, I called on W. Leatham at the bank. He is not fully converted, but he said his mother had been, by reading my speech or speeches, but I think chiefly that spoken at the late great meeting in Manchester. I sent her a copy of the League with a report of it. She had given her son £5 to send to the League, so I thought I ought to walk up and thank her, which I did. I took dinner with them, that is with Margaret Leatham and her daughter.'

That is, I think, the first mention in Bright's letters of Elizabeth Leatham, whom he afterwards married.

He continues :

'Lord John Russell's letter is of immense importance to us, and our prospects are every day improving. The whole Whig press and the *Times* also are fairly with us, and with their writing and our speeches we shall run the monster down. On 2nd day we go to Gloster, 4th day to Stroud, 5th day to Bath, 6th day to Bristol, on the 8th of the month to Nottingham, 9th to Derby, 11th Stockport. Everywhere our meetings are greater than ever, and all the working classes are fairly uniting with us.'

The famous Edinburgh letter of Lord John Russell (November 28), to which Bright here refers, was the finest piece of statesmanship to be accredited to its author, between his part in the great Reform Bill and his management of the Italian question in 1859-60. Hitherto Lord John had been noted for the inglorious 'moderation' of his views on the Corn Law question, and his 'small fixed duty' had seemed like a small fixed idea in his brain. Now, with one stroke of the pen at Edinburgh, he brought down in ruin the already tottering fabric of monopoly. Disraeli, that impartial artist in strokes of policy, could not forbear to cheer the blow :

'It is in the season of perplexity, of hesitation, of timidity, of doubt,' so he wrote seven years after these events, 'that leading minds advance to decide and to direct. Now was the moment to strike. And without consulting his party, which for the first time he really led, and with no false delicacy for a Conservative Cabinet in convulsions, Lord John Russell expressed his opinions on public affairs in that celebrated Edinburgh epistle, which was addressed to his constituents, the citizens of London.'

In this letter Lord John made no pretence that he had not changed his mind. 'It is no longer worth while,' he wrote, 'to contend for a fixed duty.' The whole of the Whig forces swung round into line behind him. All that weight of Whig party loyalty and timidity which had hitherto retarded the cause of Free Trade in Parliament and at by-elections, now pressed down the scales on the side of Total Repeal. On this occasion Lord John had done well not to consult his colleagues, for several of them, notably Lord Palmerston, were Protectionists, and only accepted the *fait accompli* of the party mandate.

'Mr. Bright happened to be on the platform at a railway

station in Yorkshire, as Lord John Russell passed through on his way from the North to Osborne. He stepped into the carriage for a few moments. "Your letter," said Mr. Bright, "has now made the total and immediate Repeal of the Corn Law inevitable; nothing can save it."'[1]

After the official pronouncement of the Whig leader, the question between the two front benches was not whether the Corn Laws should be repealed, but who should repeal them. The League, as Cobden said, alone stood erect amid the ruins of the factions. But which of the factions was to be made the instrument of its will? On the one hand, the Whigs could best afford to neglect the Protectionist elements in their own ranks; but, on the other hand, the Tories were in office, and in a majority in the House of Commons, and nothing short of the requirements of a Tory minister would suffice to soften the hearts of the Lords, who would never pass a Repeal Bill sent them by the Whigs. It was already apparent that the Protectionists would die game. Rage at their betrayal by Peel, fomented by all Disraeli's art and power, was turning high dukes into orators of the Protection Society, and authorities of the turf into political chiefs. The Duke of Richmond and Lord George Bentinck, with a subtler spirit to prompt them, were prepared to lead those who preferred to break up their party rather than to acquiesce in a tame surrender.

In the last days of November Peel's Cabinet began another series of meetings. In view of Lord John's letter and the rising agitation in the country, the majority of the Cabinet no longer contended for the Corn Laws, and even Wellington was prepared to support Peel's Free Trade measures, much as he disliked them. 'Rotten potatoes have done it all,' he was heard to say; 'they put Peel in his d——d fright.' The question now was whether the Ministers should go forward to effect the abolition themselves,[2] or whether they should resign on account of their differences and leave the task to the Whigs.

On the morning of December 4, the world read in the *Times*' leading article that the Cabinet had decided to call Parliament together in January to repeal the Corn Laws. 'An

[1] *Morley*, i. 339. The *Life of Cobden* had the advantage of 'helpful corrections and suggestions' from Bright as it was passing through press, so it may be assumed that statements of fact concerning himself have the imprint of his authority.

[2] At this stage, before his resignation, Peel proposed that abolition should be gradual, spread over eight or ten years. See Morley, *Gladstone*, i. 286.

announcement,' said the *Times*, 'of such immeasurable importance, and to the larger part of the community so unspeakably gratifying, almost precludes the possibility of comment.' That morning Bright was with Cobden at Stroud, where the night before they had, as he writes to his sister-in-law, addressed 'a glorious meeting, all Stroud with us, both members for the Boro' present. Our cause is marching on with daily increasing force, and everything betokens an early termination of our labors. I hope Newcastle will do something with other towns in the general rising now taking place.' Then, after reading the London papers, he reopens the letter to add a postscript:

'The *Times* says the Corn Law is to be repealed the first week in the New Year. I believe this is quite true. Glorious news for us and for the world! I am almost ill with reading the announcement.'

But the news was not true. On the very day when Stroud and all England were ringing with the tidings, Peel found the opposition in his Cabinet unexpectedly harden on the part of the Duke of Buccleuch and Lord Stanley. Knowing that they represented a large section of his party outside the Cabinet, he next day secretly informed the Queen that he could no longer serve her 'in a public station.' The *Times* continued to stand by its original story, and the world to believe it for days together, while in fact the Ministers were busy resigning.[1]

Before long the secret was out. Lord John Russell was called upon to form the great Ministry that should repeal the Corn Laws. If he and his party had risen to the height of the occasion, they would stand to-day on the pedestal of fame that Peel now occupies—with this advantage that they need not, like him, have broken up their party in order to save England. Yet, when the case is fully understood, it is easy to see why Lord John shrank from the task. To overcome the resistance that the House of Lords was prepared to offer to a Repeal Bill sent up to them by the Whigs, he would have had to lead another such popular uprising as that of 1832. The Court, though it favoured Free Trade, favoured it as a Conservative measure recommended by Peel, and would have had the gravest dislike

[1] Parker, *Peel*, ii. 238-39. Delane got the information, on which he based the *Times* article of December 4, not from a lady, as tells the legend enshrined in *Diana of the Crossways*, but from Lord Aberdeen, a Free Trade member of the Cabinet. See *Greville*, December 5-9, 1845. No doubt Delane to some extent misunderstood what Aberdeen really said. But it must also be remembered that a change for the worse took place in the unity of the Cabinet on December 4 itself (see Peel's letter to the Queen of that date), a change not expected by Peel, therefore presumably not expected by Aberdeen at the time when he spoke to Delane.

to assist in coercion of the Peers. Yet Peel would not promise to induce the Peers to yield to Russell without coercion. As Minister, he could, with Wellington's help, persuade them to accept the Bill from a Tory Cabinet. But the Whigs, if they took office, would have to beat down the resistance of the Upper House by democratic force, which they themselves disliked, and which the Crown disliked still more. The Liberal party of 1868, led by the Gladstone of that era, might have welcomed such an opportunity for a fighting alliance with the people. But the Whig party of 1845, led by Russell and Palmerston, had no such ambition. And the Whig Peers were even less willing than Russell and Palmerston to enter into such a conflict with their own order. The Whig Peers, who after all would have to bear the brunt of the conflict in the upper chamber, urged Russell not to accept office. They were, indeed, overruled in the first instance by the other party chiefs in the conclave held at Russell's house on December 18. But their reluctance had taken the heart out of the proceedings, and Lord John set about forming a Ministry only because he had as yet no honourable excuse for declining the task.

Howick, who had just become by inheritance Earl Grey, was a real Free Trader and a real Liberal, far in advance of the rest of his party both as to foreign and domestic affairs. He advised Russell to put Cobden into the Cabinet, and so gain for the new Ministry the full strength of the League. Such a proposal was high treason to the Whig conception of politics. Lord John was not able to offer the Cabinet-maker any higher position than that of vice-president of the Board of Trade, which was politely declined.

The actual excuse upon which Lord John seized, in order to lay down his task of forming a Ministry, was Grey's refusal to serve if Palmerston returned to the Foreign Office. In that position Lord Palmerston, as events had proved before and were to prove again, not only gave constant trouble to the Cabinet which he declined to consult on matters of high policy, but gravely endangered the prospects of peace. Grey, like Cobden and Bright, considered that peace was all-important and that Palmerston was its worst enemy. Grey's objection to Palmerston as Foreign Minister was one which a biographer of Bright can well understand. Neither had Grey any reason to suppose, when he declined to take office, that his own absence would prevent the formation of a Cabinet. Lord John proceeded as if Grey's refusal were a mere incident, and only after some hours did he perceive in it ground for abandoning a task which he had all along been anxious to avoid. The Whig failure to take office was due, not, as is sometimes thought, to mean personal jealousies among the leaders, but to a general unwillingness to give battle to the Peers in the name of democracy. It was not the mistaken acts of this man or that—of Russell, Grey, or Palmerston—but the character and opinions of the party as a whole that led to the great refusal.[1]

And so in Disraeli's words, Lord John 'handed back with courtesy the poisoned chalice to Sir Robert.'

Meanwhile, monotonous as the war-drum, incessant as the boom of waters along the shore, the voice of the League filled the land; it had become one with the voice of all men crying 'bread.' On December 19, the day when Grey refused to serve, while the statesmen were coming and going with anxious faces in Russell's Library, a meeting such as London had never before seen was held in Covent Garden Opera House, and was addressed by Villiers, Cobden, Bright, and Fox.

> 'Notwithstanding,' said Bright, 'the hope that my friend [Cobden], who has just addressed you, has expressed, that it may not become a war of classes, I am not sure that it has not already become such, and I doubt whether it can have any other character. I believe this to be a movement of the commercial and industrial classes against the Lords and great proprietors of the soil. . . .
>
> 'This contest has now been waged for seven years; it was a serious one when it began, but it is a far more serious one now. Since the time when we first came to London to ask the attention of Parliament to the question of the Corn Law, two millions of human beings have been added to the population of the United Kingdom. The table is here as before; the food is spread in about the same quantity as before; but two millions of fresh guests have arrived, and that circumstance makes the question a serious one, both for the Government and for us. These two millions are so many arguments for the Anti-Corn Law League—so many emphatic condemnations of the policy of this iniquitous law. I see them now in my mind's eye ranged before me, old men and young children, all looking to the Government for bread; some endeavouring

[1] The two most important authorities on these transactions are the *Greville Memoirs* and the article in the first number of the *English Historical Review* (Jan. 1889), *Notes on the Greville Memoirs*, by one who got his information from Grey himself.

to resist the stroke of famine, clamorous and turbulent, but still arguing with us; some dying mute and uncomplaining. Multitudes have died of hunger in the United Kingdom since we first asked the Government to repeal the Corn Law, and although the great and powerful may not regard those who suffer mutely and die in silence, yet the recording angel will note down their patient endurance and the heavy guilt of those by whom they have been sacrificed. . . .

'We have had landlord rule longer, far longer than the life of the oldest man in this vast assembly, and I would ask you to look at the results of that rule. The landowners have had unlimited sway in Parliament and in the provinces. Abroad the history of our country is the history of war and rapine: at home, of debt, taxes, and rapine too. In all the great contests in which we have been engaged we have found that this ruling class have taken all the honours, while the people have taken all the scars. No sooner was the country freed from the horrible contest which was so long carried on with the Powers of Europe, than this law, by their partial legislation, was enacted—far more hostile to British interests than any combination of foreign powers has ever proved. We find them legislating corruptly: they pray daily that in their legislation they may discard all private ends and partial affections, and after prayers they sit down to make a law for the purpose of extorting from all the consumers of food a higher price than it is worth, that the extra price may find its way into the pockets of the proprietors of land, these proprietors being the very men by whom this infamous law is sustained. . . .

'Two centuries ago the people of this country were engaged in a fearful conflict with the Crown. A despotic and treacherous monarch assumed to himself the right to levy taxes without the consent of Parliament and the people. That assumption was resisted. This fair island became a battlefield, the kingdom was convulsed, and an ancient throne overturned. And if our forefathers, two hundred years ago, resisted that attempt—if they refused to be the bondmen of a king—shall we be the born thralls of an aristocracy like ours? Shall we, who struck the lion down—shall we pay the wolf homage? Or shall we not, by a manly and united expression of public opinion, at once, and for ever, put an end to this giant wrong?'

Two days before Christmas a great meeting was held in the Town Hall, Manchester, to inaugurate the famous 'quarter of a million pounds fund' to deal the death-blow to Monopoly. 'For an hour and a half cards were placed in the Chairman's hands, nearly as fast as he could read them, from individuals subscribing their thousands, their seven, five, four, three, two, and one hundreds, and smaller amounts.' 'Our subscription meeting is just over,' wrote Bright to his sister-in-law that evening,

> 'and we have a list of more than £60,000 given in. The meeting was the most extraordinary probably ever held in the kingdom. It lasted from 11 to 3 o'clock, on the market day. Exchange and dinner-hour alike disregarded —crowded and earnest to a degree heretofore unequalled. So in this district we are doing our duty ; 25 names or firms have given £1000 each.'

One of these was John Bright & Brothers, Rochdale, to whom a thousand pounds still represented a considerable sacrifice. For several years to come it was a question whether Bright could afford to live up in London engaged in political work.

Throughout the first half of the year 1846 the proceedings at Westminster, though apparently free discussions, were in fact overshadowed by the thought of this 'quarter of a million pound fund,' subscribed with amazing rapidity, lodged in the hands of the ablest agitators ever bred in England, and to be used for a cause now as dear to the people as life itself.

At Christmas Peel resumed office to abolish the Corn Laws. When he returned to Downing Street in noticeably high spirits, he did not foresee that he was about to break his party to pieces. It was generally expected that his new lease of power would run for another period of years, and it was with this pleasant expectation that so many Protectionist Peers pledged themselves to let the Corn Bill pass. The strength of Disraeli's party of revenge was not yet realised. All the Cabinet, with the exception of Stanley, resumed office on the basis of Total Repeal. It seemed as if the party had rallied round its chief. Gladstone, a notorious Free Trader, served in the reconstructed Cabinet with the Dukes of Wellington and Buccleuch, who helped to pass a measure in the necessity for which they did not even now believe. 'I am quite of your opinion on the subject,' said the victor of Waterloo to another Protectionist

Peer; 'it is a d——d mess, but I must look to the peace of the country and the Queen.' So he continued to sit on the Government bench, with his hat drawn over his face, apparently indifferent to all the attacks made on the Government, never saying a word in answer.[1] His attitude sufficed to secure the passage of the Corn Bill through the Lords.

Peel, too, was thinking of 'the peace of the country and the Queen,' not with more public spirit and loyalty than the Duke —for that would have been impossible—but with more intelligence and foresight.

So long as British history is read, men will dispute whether Peel did right to abolish the Corn Laws which he had so often pledged himself to maintain, and in which the majority of his followers still believed. He did not foresee that Repeal would lead to the disruption of the party, and it is probable that but for Disraeli it would not have done so, for lack of leaders of sufficient ability among the Protectionists. But that is not a complete defence of his conduct; for if he forgot Disraeli, he made a cardinal error.

His real defence is this: that the abolition of the Corn Laws mattered more to Britain, even if viewed from a Conservative standpoint, than the continued cohesion of a party which was in fact divided on the first question of the day. The schism in the Tory camp may have enabled their rivals to govern England for a few more years out of the next twenty than they would otherwise have done, but the difference between the Palmerston Whigs and the Tories was mainly one of name. On the other hand, the repeal of the Corn Law prevented the working classes from becoming revolutionaries and the middle classes from remaining radical. Peel realised that it was a case of the Houses of Parliament against the country, and that the Members of Parliament must waive their opinions in order to prevent a collision. His own opinions, indeed, were no longer those of Parliament, but those of the country. Apart, however, from the rights and wrongs of Free Trade, he saw that further resistance on the part of Parliament would be dangerous to the State. 'There is no institution of this country,' Bright had said in 1843, 'the Monarchy, the Aristocracy, the Church, or any other, whose fate, if attached to the Corn Laws, cannot be predicted.' During the session of 1846 Peel met Bright in the lobby and said to him: 'I had no conception of the intense feeling of hatred with which the Corn Law was regarded.' But he had found out in time. He had thereupon given the Whigs the

[1] Malmesbury, *Memoirs of an ex-Minister*, February 19, 1846.

opportunity of forming a Repeal government, and they had declined the task. After that, if he did not himself repeal the Corn Law, it would remain on the Statute Book, with economic and social consequences for which he was not prepared to be responsible. 'Peel can think and talk of nothing but famine,' wrote the Protectionist Earl of Malmesbury with a touch of contempt; but after all famine in both islands, foreseen, and deliberately increased by law, would have effects on the relation of governors and governed, of which a Conservative Prime Minister might pardonably 'think and talk' even to the exclusion of party interests as viewed by Taper and Tadpole.

Peel had realised that under the existing franchise the House of Commons did not represent the lower classes at all, or the middle classes more than a little. When the French constitutional monarchy fell in 1848, his comment was: 'This comes of trying to govern the country through a narrow representation in Parliament, without regarding the wishes of those outside. It is what this party behind me wanted to do in the matter of the Corn Laws, and I would not do it.' It is certainly strange that a man who lived to see so clearly that even the 'Reformed Parliament' did not represent the people enough to have ultimate authority on a great question, should himself have ever resisted the mild measure of 1832. But that is the tragedy of Peel's life: he was brought up a Tory when he was by nature a Liberal-Conservative. 'I could perhaps have parried even your power,' he wrote to Cobden, 'and carried on the Government in one sense for three or four years longer, if I could have consented to halloo on a majority in both houses to defend the Corn Law of 1842 *in all its integrity*.'[1] If he had taken that course his memory might have been held dearer by party politicians, but our island would have known no charm to ward off the continental convulsions of 1848; for that year would have found our middle and working classes united in a fierce hatred of the two Houses of Parliament.[2]

Late in January 1846 began the strangest session ever held at Westminster in modern times. The bulk of those sitting on

[1] *Morley*, i. 400, 407.

[2] These chapters on the Corn Laws were written precisely as they now stand, before the publication of vol. ii. of the *Life of Disraeli*, where the case against Peel has been so well stated by Mr. Monypenny, whose untimely death we all deplore. If many of us take a more favourable view of Peel's conduct than that taken by Mr. Monypenny, it is because we set a higher value on the economic benefits to England of complete Free Trade in corn, and because we are convinced that the Corn Laws would not have been repealed against the will of the two Houses of Parliament, except by a *tour de force* which the Whigs

the Government side of the House formed the opposition and the only opposition. The majority that kept the Tory Ministers in power was composed of the Whigs, the Leaguers, and that section of the Conservatives now first known as 'Peelites.' The moment the Corn Bill should become law, the Whigs would attempt to turn Peel out and take his place; till then they would act as his 'guard,' lest he should fall prematurely and bequeath to them the settlement of this troublesome affair.

The Leaguers in the House took little part in the debates. They had already converted Peel and all the members whom their arguments could affect; and Cobden was ill, worn out by his long exertions. During this last great session he and Bright held a watching brief for the country. But the pressure of the League was never for a moment relaxed. Outside raged the storm, while Cobden and Bright sat within like mysterious powers controlling the elements, who might, if not propitiated, let the hurricane into the House. The great object of members on both sides recently converted to Repeal was that the League should be induced to abolish itself, for then only could the old game of Whig and Tory politics be resumed in peace by the gentlemen of England. Cerberus must be given his loaf as the price of his disappearance from the scene.

Owing to the advent of Disraeli as a parliamentary power of the first class, the session did not prove as easy for the Ministry as they had hoped. 'Most of Peel's colleagues,' wrote the shrewd old Scotch Whig, Lord Campbell,

> 'would have seen him at the Devil rather than support free trade in corn as they did, had they not expected that thereby they secured to themselves their continuance in office. His and their speculations were plausible enough, and had Lord George Bentinck and Benjamin Disraeli not been members of the House of Commons, my notion is that their speculations would have turned out to be well founded. These two men, and these two alone, carried on the war *usque ad internecionem*. Their great object was (in which they fully succeeded) to make Peel personally odious to the Tory Party, to provoke him to retaliate

were unable to perform for want of influence with the Lords; and that therefore if Peel had not done it, the two Houses would soon have come into more or less violent collision with the unrepresented majority of the nation. Peel in his franker moments said this himself. At other times he made the conventional boast of statesmen that he had not yielded to agitation, but in fact his merit was that he did so yield in good time. Mr. Monypenny very rightly insists that the Irish situation was not the main or obliging factor in Peel's decision permanently to repeal the Corn Laws.

upon them, and to render a reconciliation with him utterly impossible. It is owing to them that Peel eulogised Richard Cobden, whom he had once charged with a premeditated purpose of assassination. The treat was to listen to the invectives of Benjamin Disraeli against Peel. So great was the *prestige* attached to Peel's name, that he would have continued Minister had his conduct not been thus assailed in a manner tending to make him appear odious and ridiculous.'

'Disraeli,' wrote Greville, 'hacked and mangled Peel with the most unsparing severity and positively tortured his victim. It was a miserable and degrading spectacle. The whole mass of the Protectionists cheered him with vociferous delight, making the roof ring again; and when Peel spoke they screamed and hooted at him in the most brutal manner. . . . Such treatment in a House of Commons where for years he had been an object of deference and respect nearly overcame him. The Speaker thought he would have been obliged to sit down, and expected him to burst into tears. They hunt him like a fox.'

In exact proportion to the detestation in which he was now held by the enjoyers of rent, grew the love and honour with which his wounded name was now spoken by all those classes who worked for their bread. He was never so popular in the country as during the weeks when he was hooted in the House of Commons. The session was not a month old before the Leaguers and Radicals regarded him with an affection which they had never before bestowed on any Whig or Tory Minister. On February 16, as Bright tells his sister Priscilla:

'Peel delivered the best speech I ever heard in Parliament. It was truly a magnificent speech, sustained throughout, thoroughly with us, and offering even to pass the immediate,[1] if the House are willing. Villiers, Gibson, and myself cheered continually, and I never listened to any human being speaking in public with so much delight.'

Next evening Bright was moved to join in the debates, in order that he might vindicate Peel. On these nights of con-

[1] Viz. the 'immediate repeal.' The actual measure proposed and passed, though accepted by the League as near enough to the 'total and immediate,' was not either the one or the other. A low sliding scale was to operate, of which the rates were to fall annually until the consummation was reached in February 1849; but even after that date a registration duty of 1s. a quarter was to be retained. In 1869 that too was taken off.

fusion and rage when every one wanted to explain his own position or to vituperate his own leaders, 'twenty men rise at once like a covey of partridges,' as Bright wrote to his sister; nevertheless he caught the Speaker's eye. Peel was visibly moved during his delivery of the following passage:

> 'You say the right hon. baronet is a traitor. It would ill become me to attempt his defence after the speech which he delivered last night—a speech, I will venture to say, more powerful and more to be admired than any speech which has been delivered within the memory of any man in this House. I watched the right hon. baronet as he went home last night, and for the first time I envied him his feelings. That speech was circulated by scores of thousands throughout the kingdom and throughout the world; and wherever a man is to be found who loves justice, and wherever there is a labourer whom you have trampled under foot, that speech will bring joy to the heart of the one, and hope to the breast of the other. You chose the right hon. baronet—why? Because he was the ablest man of your party. You always said so, and you will not deny it now. Why was he the ablest? Because he had great experience, profound attainments, and an honest regard for the good of the country. You placed him in office. When a man is in office he is not the same man as when in opposition. The present generation, or posterity, does not deal as mildly with men in government as with those in opposition. There are such things as the responsibilities of office. Look at the population of Lancashire and Yorkshire, and there is not a man among you who would have the valour to take office and raise the standard of Protection, and cry, "Down with the Anti-Corn Law League, and Protection for ever!" There is not a man in your ranks who would dare to sit on that bench as the Prime Minister of England pledged to maintain the existing law. The right hon. baronet took the only, the truest course—he resigned. He told you by that act: "I will no longer do your work. I will not defend your cause. The experience I have had since I came into office renders it impossible for me at once to maintain office and the Corn Laws." The right hon. baronet resigned—he was then no longer your Minister. He came back to office as the Minister of his Sovereign and of the people.'

The devotion to Peel of genuine Liberals and Free Traders was the stronger because they knew that half the Whigs would gladly betray them if they dared. As the session wore on and Disraeli's rally of Protectionist Tories took unexpected proportions, a plot was formed by a section of the Whigs headed by Palmerston to coalesce with the Protectionists, throw out Peel, and take office on the basis of the former Whig policy of 'a small fixed duty' on corn. In the opinion of those who knew the Whig coteries from inside, this plot might have succeeded, had not the party been previously committed to Free Trade by Russell's Edinburgh letter, and had not the writer of that letter been staunch to his new faith. Lord John caused a meeting of Whig Peers to be summoned at Lansdowne House on May 23 and crushed the mutiny.

When it became known that the Peers at Lansdowne House had decided to vote for Peel's Corn Bill, the Protectionists could no longer hope for success. But they could still look for revenge. The Whigs would vote against Peel the moment the Corn Bill was safely through the Lords. The story of the plot that overthrew him has been told by its principal author. 'How was Sir Robert Peel to be turned out?' wrote Disraeli in his *Life of Bentinck*:

> 'Here was a question which might well occupy the musing hours of a Whitsun recess. . . . In this state of affairs it was submitted to the consideration of Lord George Bentinck, that there appeared only one course to be taken. . . . The Government had announced their intention of moving the second reading of the Irish Coercion Bill. If this second reading were opposed both by Lord John Russell and Lord George Bentinck, the defeat of the administration seemed more than probable.'

The fact that Protectionists and Whigs had supported the Coercion Bill on its first reading did not prevent them from combining to oppose it on the second, in what the Duke called 'a blackguard combination.' The Leaguers, Radicals, and Irish who had been conscientiously opposing the Bill all through, unavoidably found themselves in the same lobby with men who in fact approved of coercion, but whose one desire was to turn out Peel. As Cobden and Bright were in the habit of voting on the merits of each question at issue, they were obliged in this division to swell the majority that hurled their favourite Minister from power.

So on the famous night of June 25, 1846, the bill repealing

the Corn Law passed the Lords, and Peel's Coercion Bill was defeated in the Commons.

It is a remarkable fact that both Cobden and Wellington privately wrote to Peel urging him to dissolve and try in the issue of a General Election the weight of his name and popularity against Whigs and Protectionists alike. He replied that if the Corn Bill had been thrown out he would have ventured on that course, but that as the Corn Bill was safe, he would not be justified in creating a further political convulsion on a personal issue. Bright did not participate with Cobden in giving this advice to Peel.

On June 29 Peel delivered his farewell speech, the last which he ever made as Minister. It contained two famous passages, which gave great offence to the Whig and Tory statesmen, and even to such staunch Free Traders as the Queen and Mr. Gladstone, but gave the most heartfelt delight to the mass of Peel's countrymen both then and in years to come. 'The name,' he said, 'which ought to be and will be associated with the success of these measures is the name of Richard Cobden. Without scruple, sir, I attribute the success of these measures to him.' And for himself Peel asked a kind of immortality which Prime Ministers had formerly neither desired nor deserved: 'I shall leave a name,' he said, 'execrated by every monopolist who maintains Protection for his own individual benefit; but it may be that I shall leave a name sometimes remembered with expressions of good-will in the abodes of those whose lot is to labour, and to earn their daily bread by the sweat of their brows, when they shall recruit their exhausted strength with abundant and untaxed food, the sweeter because no longer leavened with a sense of injustice.'

So ended the agitation which forms the first great episode in the career of John Bright. At a meeting of the Council of the League, held in Manchester Town Hall on July 2, 1846, Cobden moved and Bright seconded the motion 'that an Act of Parliament having been passed providing for the abolition of the Corn Laws in February 1849, it is deemed expedient to suspend the active operation of the Anti-Corn Law League.' One passage is specially noteworthy in Bright's speech on this occasion of leave-taking:

> 'We have taught the people of this country the value of a great principle. They have learned that there is nothing that can be held out to the intelligent people of

this kingdom so calculated to stimulate them to action, and to great and persevering action, as a great and sacred principle like that which the League has espoused. They have learned that there is in public opinion a power much greater than that residing in any particular form of government; that although you have in this kingdom a system of government which is called "popular" and "representative"—a system which is somewhat clumsily contrived, and which works with many jars and joltings—that still, under the impulse of a great principle, with great labour and with great sacrifices, all those obstacles are overcome, so that out of a machine especially contrived for the contrary, justice and freedom are at length achieved for the nation; and the people have learned something beyond this—that is, that the way to freedom is henceforward not through violence and bloodshed.'

This peaceful revolution at the expense of the landlord power in the State had social and political consequences which will appear in subsequent chapters of Bright's life. Here it is enough to note its main economic results.

In the first place, the Corn Laws were the keystone of the whole Protective system. When they were gone, there was no one to fight for the Navigation Laws, the protection of West Indian sugar, and the remaining duties on raw material and manufactures, in the way that the landlords had fought for their rents. The budgets of Peel's successors, of the Whigs and of Gladstone, which completed the Free Trade system in the course of the next fifteen years, met with no serious opposition in principle.

In the second place, Free Trade in corn at once increased the supply of food, and prevented veritable famine. In 1845 less than five million hundredweights of wheat and wheat meal had been imported; in 1847 nearly eighteen millions came in, besides the fifteen million hundredweights of maize intended to meet the requirements of the Irish famine. In this way alone was there some mitigation of the effects of two successive years of bad wheat harvest and potato blight in 1845-46, which would otherwise have caused famine in England in 1846-47. In the six years following Repeal, a larger quantity of grain was imported than had entered the country during the thirty-one years from Waterloo to the Repeal. Throughout the 'fifties and 'sixties prices in general were rising owing to gold discoveries, the Crimean War, and other causes, and the price of wheat would have risen enormously in England with the increase of population and with the purchasing power of the working class but for the free importation from abroad. While, therefore, Free Trade prevented the price of wheat from rising, and indeed caused it to fall a little, it enormously increased the consumption of wheat. 'Clemming' and living on potatoes and turnips ceased to be the rule for whole sections of the community, and bread was far more largely consumed by all. For wages, as the Free Traders had prophesied, rose fast, because trade expanded. The immense importation of food and raw material from abroad, due to Peel's budgets and the further Free Trade measures of his successors, enabled us to export our manufactured goods in return. In 1842 the exports of British produce had been worth only £47,000,000; in 1876 they were worth £200,000,000. In the same year Bright reminded his friends, the working men of Rochdale, that while their wages had increased immensely owing to the demand for labour under Free Trade, as he had told their starving fathers would certainly be the case, the consumption of foreign wheat per head of the population had increased from 42 to 197 lbs., and that there had been a similar increase in the consumption of other imported foods. 'Last year,' he said, 'there came to the ports of this country for the consumption of the people of the United Kingdom 118,000,000 hundredweights of articles of food, which were mainly prohibited under the law as it existed up to 1846.'[1]

Up to that date (1876) there was steady increase in British agricultural prosperity. For a whole generation every Protectionist prophecy of injury to agriculture proved false. 'Thirty-one years of Protection (1815-46) had added rather less than £9,000,000 to the annual value of agricultural land in Great Britain. Thirty-one years of Free Trade (1847-77), added £12,000,000 to it.'[2] Then came a change. In the late 'seventies further increases in the wheat-producing acreage of the world, further facilities of transport, flooded Britain with still greater quantities of foreign and colonial corn. The price went down yet further, to the great benefit of the community in general, but with the effect of throwing much British wheat land out of cultivation. The average price of wheat per quarter for the year 1836 to 1846 had been 57 shillings; the average price for the year 1886 to 1896 was 29 shillings, in spite

[1] Rochdale Working Men's Club, January 2, 1877. *Addresses*, p. 321. Well worth reading.

[2] Walpole, *History of England*, end of chap. xix.

of the fact that the population had doubled and that far more wheat was consumed than under the Protectionist régime.

That a part of the land should thus fall out of cultivation was an evil. But it was a worse evil that it should be cultivated under the conditions of starvation tempered by rick-burning, which was the lot of the agricultural labourer in the days of Protection; it was a worse evil that Britain's trade and industry should be strangled by taxes on food and raw material, that she should be prevented in the race of modern nations from developing in riches and power and in the well-being of her labourers in town and country. The policy adopted after Waterloo, believed in by Mr. Ferrand and Lord George Bentinck, was to insist that these islands should grow their own corn. This meant that a strict limit should be set to the increase of the town population; that the people must either emigrate or remain on the fields to starve there under their landlords. If that policy had not been reversed, Britain's wealth would not have been unlocked, she would long ago have been outstripped in power by larger countries, and her millions would have remained sunk in the degraded and miserable condition, the sight of which first aroused John Bright to become their champion.

CHAPTER VII

FACTORY ACTS. IRELAND. INDIA. SECOND MARRIAGE; PRIVATE LIFE AND CONVERSATION

'We are true ancients; we stand on the shoulders of our forefathers, and can see further.'—BRIGHT *on the Papal Aggression Bill*, 1851.

THE battle of the Corn Laws had coincided in time with one of the most critical stages in the long struggle for Government regulation of factories; and the final triumph of the League was followed in 1847 by a measure which many of the Leaguers greatly disliked, the legal limitation of factory work to ten hours per day. To attempt to explain away the fact that Bright opposed Factory legislation for adults would be as idle as to deny that these laws have since proved, in long experience, to be an essential part of our national welfare. But the reasons why he opposed them have so often been misrepresented that it is due to his memory to recall what he said and did not say on the subject.

Before coming of age he had, in his youthful eagerness, initiated a petition, at his own expense, in favour of a ten hours day for adults.[1] But by the time when he entered Parliament his views had much altered. He still admitted the justice and necessity of laws to protect children, whom he regarded as unable to fend for themselves against unkind parents or employers. Any statement that Bright ever opposed laws to protect children is untrue.

He further admitted that adults were often overworked in factories—though less often in factories than in fields and other workshops—and that many masters were to blame. But he objected to the proposed method of reform through legislative restriction of hours, which he thought an improper interference of the State between the contracting parties. He looked instead for an improvement of hours and conditions by agree-

[1] *Hansard*, 3rd series, vol. 89, pp. 1133, 1147 (February 10, 1847).

nent between the employers on one side and adults of both exes on the other.[1] No doubt he exaggerated the common ense and benevolence of masters and the bargaining power of he employee at that period of industrial history, and no doubt ie overlooked the readiness of men, and still more of women, o work voluntarily for a length of hours injurious to their own iealth. But when he said that if any one required protection y the State it was labourers in agriculture and men and women n ill-organised trades even more than factory hands, he was ight—although that argument did not prove that the Factory Acts were wrong.

His efforts were not directed to prolonging the hours of abour, which ought not, he said, to be longer than ten. 'I am quite certain,' he told the House of Commons, 'that the man who works ten hours a day is much more likely to be educated han the one who works twelve. I do not differ upon this oint. But I differ on the point whether a reduction of time ought to be carried out by the Legislature, or by a regulation etween the masters and the operatives themselves.'[2]

The occasion when he crossed swords with Lord Ashley on the floor of the House arose out of Ashley's speech in March 1844, in favour of limiting the hours of labour for women and young persons' (*aet.* 13-18) to ten hours per day. Both ides agreed that the legal limitation of hours for these classes would involve a practical limitation of the work of the whole actory to a similar time. The battle of the men was, well and wisely, being fought 'behind the women's petticoats.' Ashley in his speech exposed the evils of the factory life of North England in a tone which contrasted favourably with he venom of Mr. Ferrand the year before. But though he poke within compass he aroused Bright's wrath, and it is not iard to see why. Bright was justly convinced that, bad as he conditions of life were in the cotton factories, they were far worse in other industries, and worst of all perhaps in agriculture, whence Lord Ashley drew his income. Yet no one ever pro- osed to limit the hours of agricultural labour. He thought it unjust that a man representing Dorsetshire said nothing about he abject condition of the labourer there at six shillings to eight shillings a week, while he raised a hue and cry against

[1] *Hansard*, 3rd series, vols. 73, 89, for the speeches of 1844, 1847. See also is reply to Fielden's *Curse of the Factory System*, 1836, epitomised in Barnett Smith's *Life of Bright*, pp. 20-23. I have studied the original MS. kindly ent me by Mr. Joseph Green. It stands half-way between his views of 1832 and his views of 1844.

[2] *Ibid.*, vol. 86, p. 1059, and vol. 89, p. 1096.

masters who, like Bright himself, paid sixteen shillings to their men. And at the same time Ashley was still refusing to better the condition of Lancashire and Dorsetshire alike, by repealing the Corn Law.[1]

In all this Bright was so far right that the reason for beginning State interference with the hours of adults in the case of the factories, instead of in the case of sweated industries or agriculture, was not that conditions in the factories were worse, or even that they were as bad, but that they could be more easily regulated. Ashley himself had to some extent admitted this at the beginning of his speech in the words: 'We are called upon to give relief, not because it [the factory system] is the worst system, but because it is oppressive and yet capable of alleviation.' But few Ten Hours advocates were so far impartial as to admit even that.

Bright's speech was a defence of the factory system as he knew it, out of the reports of H.M. Inspectors, and from the wages books of his own and other firms. His argument that the cotton operatives were less badly off than other classes of working men in the country was, in all likelihood, sound. But it was not decisive on the merits of the Bill. On the principle of State regulation of hours, Bright said singularly little. His speech was nothing more than an essay on conditions of life in cotton factories.[2]

As he spoke the fire kindled. 'The noble Lord and hon.

[1] Some twelve months later Lord Ashley was converted to Repeal.

[2] In this speech (March 15, 1844) he said, with regard to his own firm:

'We employ 518 persons, and their ages and amount of wages are as follows:

		Males.	s.	d.
Age 13 to 16.	69 employed.	Average weekly earnings .	6	6
„ 17 to 21.	69 „	„ „ „ .	8	10
„ 21 and upwards.	131 „	„ „ „ .	16	0
		Females.	s.	d.
„ 13 to 16.	84 employed.	Average weekly earnings .	6	3
„ 17 to 21.	106 „	„ „ „ .	8	3
„ 21 and upwards.	59 „	„ „ „ .	11	11

After the Repeal of the Corn Laws the wages paid by Bright Bros. rose 40 per cent. in twenty years.

In another speech on the Factory question, he told the House that his family kept a children's school, reading-room, news-room, and school for adults for the benefit of their workpeople.

In January 1867, in reply to Mr. Garth's libels against John Bright (see chap xvii. below), the workpeople of Bright Bros. held a meeting in the Public Hall Rochdale, and presented an address to him, containing these words: 'Your conduct as our employers has been such as to meet with our entire approval You have always endeavoured to improve our moral, social, and intellectual well-being.'

gentlemen opposite,' he said, 'when they view from their distant eminence the state of the manufacturing districts, look through the right end of the telescope; what they see is thus brought near to them and is greatly magnified. But when they are asked to look at the rural districts, they reverse the telescope and then everything is thrown to the greatest possible distance, and is diminished as much as possible.' Fortunately for England, the right end of the telescope was held to her eye turn and turn about by both parties, in the one case by the manufacturers against the landlords, in the other by the landlords against the manufacturers. And the world's woe was at length made clear with scientific precision.

Bright's speech ended in a 'scene' with Ashley. He complained that Ashley had employed, to blacken the cause of the manufacturers, a miscreant of the name of Dodd, who had first allowed himself to be advertised by the Ten Hours party as 'The Factory Cripple,' a victim of that vile system; and had subsequently turned against Ashley and had accused his patron of not paying him what was due for his services. Ashley was hurt and appealed to the House, being apparently under the impression that the charges made against him by Dodd were being repeated by Bright. Bright explained that 'the noble Lord is entirely mistaken if he supposes that I judge his character by the character of the men in whom I tell him to put no trust.' Ashley accepted the explanation and the incident ended. According to Ashley's biographer, Bright had behaved badly and been rebuked; but Bright wrote to McLaren: 'I had a row on Friday night with Lord Ashley. I got the better of him by universal admission of the House.' The incident, in fact, reflected discredit on neither party.

Ashley's Ten Hours proposal (1844) was defeated after a close and exciting parliamentary struggle, which left the advocates of the change confident of victory in the near future. On this question parties had been entirely re-grouped. The fact that a man was Whig or Tory, Protectionist or Free Trader, was no guide as to his views on the Factory question. In the north the Ten Hours movement was led by Oastler and Sadler, Tory democrats; by Fielden, a manufacturer and a Radical; and by the Chartist and Socialist leaders. In the House, Ashley and Fielden were supported by Ferrand, the Protectionist; by O'Connell and Macaulay, Free Traders; and by Russell and Palmerston, coming round to Free Trade. Meanwhile Peel's Government in 1844, while opposing ten hours, passed a compromise Bill restricting work in factories to twelve hours. But the Ten Hours advocates returned to the charge in 1846, when Macaulay made his great speech in their favour; and they finally triumphed in the new Whig and Free Trade Parliament of 1847. By that time the backbone had gone out of the resistance; the Ten Hours Bill passed by 78 votes and became law. In 1850 Ashley's amending Act put an end to attempts to evade the Act of 1847 and made the Ten Hours Day absolute.

In 1847 Bright spoke in opposition to the successful Bill. Although, as in 1844, he devoted most of his speech to a defence of existing conditions in factories, on this second occasion he attempted an argument against the principles of the measure. But his views did not show the clearness and consistency which they always had in questions where his whole heart and mind were enlisted. He first said that he was 'not defending the principle that these persons should work twelve hours a day,' and then warned the House that if the hours were reduced from twelve to ten, wages would inevitably fall.[1] But in fact, as the Ten Hours advocates had prophesied, wages did not fall, though Bright always believed that they would have fallen if the Corn Laws had not been repealed prior to the passage of the Ten Hours Bill. Be that as it may, a very rapid rise in wages from 1850 onwards made smooth any difficulties that might have resulted from the application of the Act.

The half-dozen speeches made by Bright in the House of Commons in 1844-47 and 1850 were almost the only part that he took in the struggle. It was not thus that he treated questions where his moral and intellectual passions were fairly roused. He did not give to opposing the Factory Acts a quarter of the time and energy which he spent during the same years in attacking the Game Laws, a fiftieth part of what he afterwards devoted to winning the Franchise for the working men, or a hundredth part of what he had already spent in pulling down the Corn Monopoly. Resistance to the Factory Acts was not the kind of agitation to which a man swayed by high moral impulses is likely to sacrifice his health and leisure. But it is only fair to remember on behalf of the manufacturers that they did submit to State regulation of their business and did receive Government inspectors under their roofs before other classes of the community had been required to submit to a like inquisition. It is fortunate that the early inspectors were men of so much tact and courage, as they appear to have been. The visits of the State official soon ceased to be an object

[1] *Hansard*, 3rd series, vol. 89, pp. 1140-44.

of dread with any good master. Indeed, the conduct of the inspectors under the Act of 1833 had no doubt weakened beforehand the resistance to the later Factory legislation of 1844-50. How the inspectors would have fared if they had been sent to pry into conditions of employment in field and barn is open to conjecture. The patience of landlords and farmers was not put to that test.[1]

Another work on which John Bright was busily engaged, both before and after the repeal of the Corn Laws, was that of calling attention to the real state of the unknown island sixty miles west of Holyhead. Bright was one of the earliest and truest English friends of the native Irish, both in his attack on the Protestant ascendancy, and in his defence of the tenants against the landlord caste at a time when there was scarcely any other Englishman to defend them. His activities, long apparently so barren, sowed the seed of a better opinion in England, and bore fruit in the Irish Church and Land legislation of 1868-81, where, as in so many other matters, Gladstone carried out in the green tree what Bright had preached in the dry. The original cause that drew his attention to the miseries of Ireland—a study always uncongenial to prosperous Englishmen—was the fact that Irish misery and degradation had invaded his native district. Ever since he could remember, the edge of the black tide of Cromwell's curse had been flowing and festering under his own eyes at Rochdale and Manchester. 'Many of the evils,' he told the House of Commons, 'which in times past have been attributed to the extension of manufactures in Lancashire have arisen from the enormous immigration of a suffering and pauperised people driven for sustenance from their own country.' And when once he had, for this reason, begun the study of English dealings with Ireland, he found in it the supreme example of havoc wrought by the unchecked will of the two evil spirits he most hated—feudalism and race ascendancy.

While the Corn Law struggle was still proceeding, Bright showed that he understood the real nature of Irish discontent better than any man in the House except Disraeli, who also pointed to the evils of 'an absentee aristocracy and an alien Church.' In his election at Durham in 1843, Bright denounced the Protestant Established Church in Ireland and the tyranny

[1] On the Factory Laws, besides *Hansard* see Hutchins and Harrison, *History of Factory Legislation*, 1911; Kydd, *History of the Factory Movement*, 1857; and Hodder, *Life of Shaftesbury*.

of the evicting landlords. Though he never favoured repeal of the Union, he deeply sympathised with O'Connell, whom Peel's Government sent to trial before twelve Protestant jurors and four Protestant judges. In his private letters he wrote of the Irish Liberator as 'the man who has the affections of six millions of his countrymen and whose struggles have ever been for freedom.' Here Bright differed from Cobden, who distrusted and disliked O'Connell, in spite of the Irishman's generous advocacy of the Free Trade cause.

Bright's first important utterance on Irish Church and Land problems was made on the occasion of the Maynooth debate. In April 1845 Peel introduced his famous measure for increasing from £9000 to £26,000 a year the Government grant to Maynooth College, where the Irish priests were educated. The proposal aroused a storm of Protestant bigotry in England and Scotland, so offensive to men of sense and good-will that justice has never since been done to the very solid objections taken to the endowment of Maynooth by some who were the opposite of bigots. No doubt, as Peel and Macaulay both argued, if it was right to grant the £9000 it would be churlish to grudge £26,000 to improve the 'miserable Dotheboys Hall' which the Roman Catholics had in exchange for the seminaries taken from them at the Reformation. And Peel's endowment of Maynooth perhaps did more good than harm in Ireland as a symbol of the break-up of the tradition of Protestant ascendancy. But if John Bright and the English dissenters had not opposed this grant, it is more than probable that the British Government would have chosen the further endowment of the priesthood as the line of least resistance for pacifying Ireland, instead of taking up the real redress of grievances through Land Acts and the abolition of the Protestant Church Establishment. If 'concurrent endowment' had not been resisted *ab initio* by the dissenters, the State might gradually have been led to support a number of Churches on both sides of St. George's Channel. Indeed, Lord John Russell had already in 1843 suggested that an equalisation of religions in Ireland should be achieved not by disestablishing the Anglican Church, but by establishing the Roman at its side. Bright was determined to prevent Liberalism from going off on this false trail.

In opposing the Maynooth grant on these grounds, Bright demanded radical concessions to Irish Catholics and peasants at the expense of the Irish State Church and landlords. Peel's attempt to silence the priests by stuffing their mouths with English gold seemed to him a step away from real reform.

The danger that England, grown ashamed of governing Ireland by the sword, would proceed to govern her through the priests, was certainly no idle fear. It is a method that has since been very largely adopted, and it would have been adopted still more largely but for the resistance of such as Bright, who pointed not to the priest but to the peasant as needing relief.

John Bright began his Maynooth speech (April 16, 1845) by regretting that he would have to go into the lobby with the Protestant bigots. His reasons for opposing the grant to Maynooth were very different from theirs.

> 'Does Irish discontent,' he asked, 'arise because the priests of Maynooth are now insufficiently clad or fed? I have always thought that it arose because one-third of the people were paupers. I can easily see how, by the granting of this sum, you might hear far less in future times of the sufferings and wrongs of the people of Ireland than you have heard heretofore. For you find that one large means of influence possessed by those who have agitated for the redress of Irish wrongs is the support which the Irish Catholic clergy have given to the various associations for carrying on political agitation. And the object of this Bill is to tame down these agitators—it is a sop given to the priests. It is *hush-money*, given that they may not proclaim to the whole country, to Europe and to the world, the sufferings of the population to whom they administer the rites and the consolations of religion.'

It was not, he continued, by endowing Romanism but by disendowing Anglicanism that religious equality should be granted in Ireland.

> 'I take it that the Protestant Church of Ireland is at the root of the evils of that country. The Irish Catholics would thank us infinitely more if we were to wipe away that foul blot than they would even if Parliament were to establish the Roman Catholic Church alongside of it. They have had everything Protestant—a Protestant clique which has been dominant in the country; a Protestant Viceroy to distribute places and emoluments amongst that Protestant clique; Protestant judges who have polluted the seats of justice; Protestant magistrates before whom the Catholic peasant cannot hope for justice; they have not only Protestant but exterminating landlords, and more than that a Protestant soldiery, who at

the beck and command of a Protestant priest, have butchered and killed a Catholic peasant even in the presence of his widowed mother. The consequence of all this is the extreme discontent of the Irish people. And because this House is not prepared yet to take those measures which would be really doing justice to Ireland, your object is to take away the sympathy of the Catholic priests from the people. The object is to make the priests in Ireland as tame as those in Suffolk and Dorsetshire. The object is that when the horizon is brightened every night by incendiary fires, no priest of the paid establishment shall ever tell of the wrongs of the people among whom he is living. . . . Ireland is suffering, not from the want of another Church, but because she has already one Church too many.'

Peel's Maynooth Bill was carried by a majority of 147. There was much cross voting in all parts of the House, and for the first and last time in their lives, Cobden and Bright went into different lobbies on a big question of public policy.[1]

Then came the famine.

In 1847-48, during the worst of the famine horrors, and the futile rebellion of Smith O'Brien, Bright continued to plead the cause of Ireland in the House of Commons with arguments now familiar, then rare in the extreme.

'If Ireland has been rightly governed, if it has been wise and just to maintain the Protestant Church established there, you ought, in order to carry out your system, to establish Prelacy in Scotland and Catholicism in England; though if you were to attempt to do either the one or the other it would not be a sham but a real insurrection you would provoke.

'Driven forth by poverty, Irishmen emigrate in great numbers, and in whatever quarter of the world an Irishman sets his foot, there stands a bitter, an implacable enemy of England. That is one of the results of the widespread disaffection that exists in Ireland. There are hundreds of thousands—I suppose there are millions—of the population of the United States of America who are Irish by birth, or by immediate descent; and be it remembered, Irishmen settled in the United States have a large influence in public affairs. They sometimes sway

[1] The only other division in which they ever voted against each other was a question of expenditure at South Kensington. *Morley*, i. 327, note.

the election of members of the Legislature, and may even affect the election of the President of the Republic. There may come a time when questions of a critical nature will be agitated between the Governments of Great Britain and the United States; and it is certain that at such a time the Irish in that country will throw their whole weight into the scale against this country, and against peace with this country. These are points which it is necessary to consider, and which arise out of the lamentable condition in which Ireland is placed.

'Hon. gentlemen turn with triumph'—it was the year 1848—'to neighbouring countries, and speak in glowing terms of our glorious constitution. It is true that abroad thrones and dynasties have been overturned, whilst in England peace has reigned undisturbed. But take all the lives that have been lost in the last twelve months in Europe amidst the convulsions that have occurred, take all the cessation of trade, the destruction of industry, all the crushing of hopes and hearts, and they will not compare for an instant with the agonies which have been endured by the population of Ireland under your glorious constitution.

'We must retrace our steps—we must shun the blunders, and, I would even say, the crimes of our past legislation. We must *free the land*; and then we shall discover, and not till then, that industry hopeful and remunerated, industry free and inviolate, is the only sure foundation on which can be reared the enduring edifice of union and peace.'

When Bright that day said that they must 'free the land,' he had not yet discovered what freedom of the land in Ireland should mean. He still based much of his hopes on the Encumbered Estates Bill, shortly to become law, which did little good to Ireland. The object of this measure was to enable landlords of 'encumbered estates' to sell their land to wealthier men who would, it was expected, put capital into the land and enable the peasantry to thrive once more. Bright, like the Ministers who passed the Act, was arguing too much from his English experience. In England, then as now, the system of entail and mortgage ties up land in the hands of impoverished landlords with deleterious effects on agriculture. But in Ireland under the Encumbered Estates Act, the penniless landlords sold out indeed, but only to a new race of English exploiters and moneyed men, who looked for an eight per cent. return on their investment and raised the rents and evicted even more callously, it is said, than those whom they had bought out. It was, too often, only a change of King Log for King Stork.

In the autumn of 1849 Bright visited Ireland himself, accompanied by one of the Commissioners of the Board of Works. It was then that he realised the truth, that the first step to any 'freedom of the land' was to give the tenant security of tenure and compensation for improvements. His letters from Ireland to Cobden, whom he now enlisted as his ally in the new movement, date the small beginning of great things.

> 'The Encumbered Estates Commission will be at work in October,' he writes on September 17, 1849. 'This is something. That, however, which is most universally demanded is *security of improvements on the land*. There is a perpetual war between landlord and tenant, and to raise the rent or let to a new tenant at an increased rent when improvements are made, seems to be the almost invariable rule.[1] . . . There is a great field for usefulness in these Irish questions—the whole population are with us on the Franchise and the Tenant question, and, except the Orangemen, on the Church too. I think I shall get all the Northern tenantry to support the "Tenant Security Bill," for even *they* have no *legal* security, and now when land has been so shaken in Ireland and prices are low, their "tenant right" [Ulster custom] is of small value compared to what it was in past years.'

A week later he writes to Cobden again:

> 'Why cannot the Irish get and save money in Ireland? And why must they cross the Atlantic before they can get hold of a piece of land? Our "territorial" system is one which works a wide and silent cruelty, beggaring, demoralising and destroying multitudes of our people. I should like to join a League sworn or pledged to its entire overthrow. There are facts enough afloat that would suffice to make a revolution in opinion with regard to it, and it follows logically on the Free Trade movement.'

[1] Many an Irish tenant might have given the answer of the old Highland crofter to the Commissioners:
'Did you put up the house?' 'Ou, ay! I put up the hoose.'
'Did you put up the walls?' 'Ou, ay! I put up the wa's.'
'Didn't the landlord put up anything?' 'Ou, ay! he put up the rent.'

This new policy was taking shape in his mind under stress of deep emotions, aroused by the spectacle of that ruined country a year after the worst stages of the famine. He writes to his wife :[1]

> 'We see sad scenes by the wayside, small and wretched hovels in quarries and nooks of the roads in which some wretched family finds shelter. The children leave an impression of misery on the mind which can never be effaced. Houses unroofed and lands waste and depopulated, are the memorials of the frightful calamities through which the country has passed. The proprietors are nearly all bankrupt, great numbers of the farmers are gone away, thousands of the peasantry are in the workhouses or in their graves. I believe we can form no fair idea of what has passed in these districts within the last four years, and I see no great prospect of a solid improvement. Here we have in perfection the fruits of aristocratic and territorial usurpation and privileges.'

At Skibbereen,

> 'behind the workhouse is a small piece of land fenced off from a field, not more than a quarter of an acre ; in trenches in this space are buried 600 victims of famine and fever and cholera, buried in the rags they died in, *uncoffined and unknown*. The green corn now waves over them. It is a melancholy spot. We saw a girl trying to sell a basket of turf in the market place. It weighed 62 lbs. She had carried it on her back 8½ miles. It had been cut and dried previously. She asked 1½d. for it !'
> Even in Skibbereen the survivors 'wished to make a *demonstration* of their opinion of my efforts on behalf of Ireland.' 'Everywhere there is a feeling that Parliament is ignorant of the real grievances ; everywhere I found myself the object of more than common attention, for my speeches on Irish affairs had been read by everybody, and were generally highly approved, and no civilities were thought too much to offer me, by priest or people.'

On his return to England, the Irish inhabitants of Manchester presented him with an address in the Town Hall. He at once began to draw up a Tenants' Rights Bill, and put himself in the forefront of the movement. Unfortunately neither Whigs nor Tories would listen, and for twenty years the Encumbered

[1] For his second marriage (1847) see pp. 171-72 below.

Estates Act alone held the field, unaided or unredeemed by legislation to protect the tenant, until the era of Gladstone and the Liberal party. The reason why John Bright's appeal on behalf of the tenants was so long unheeded by the Government was quite clear to him, and he stated it in the House of Commons with his habitual frankness: 'The question,' he said in a Tenants' Right debate in February 1852, 'the question is—Can the cats wisely and judiciously legislate for the mice?'

> 'The real difficulties,' he had said in 1848, 'which beset this question do not arise from anything in Ireland, so much as from the constitution of the Government. This House and the other House of Parliament are almost exclusively aristocratic in their character. The administration is therefore necessarily the same, and on the Treasury benches aristocracy reigns supreme. No fewer than seven members of the Cabinet are members of the House of Lords; and every other member of it is either a Lord by title, or on the very threshold of the peerage by birth or marriage. I am not blaming them for this; it may even be that from neither House of Parliament can fourteen better men be chosen to take their places. But I maintain that in the present position of Ireland, and looking at human nature as it is, it is not possible that fourteen gentlemen, circumstanced as they are, can meet round the Council table, and with unbiased minds fairly discuss the question of Ireland, as it now presents itself to the House, the country, and the world.'

Such were the Whig Cabinets from which Bright tried in vain for twenty years to extract Reforms in Great Britain and Ireland. The nearest approach to attention that he ever obtained from the official Whigs for the tenants' grievances, was an interview with Lord John Russell in June 1850, noted in his journal:

> 'Conversation with Lord J. Russell on Irish Tenant question. Lord John admitted the extreme hazard of leaving the question unsettled. He said the south of Ireland might be kept quiet, they would succumb as they had always done, but the people in the north were a more sturdy race, and, if they united with the south, then the question would assume another shape that would be difficult to meet. He was evidently anxious on the question, but, not understanding it, he seems hardly to

know how to deal with it. I mentioned my having drawn a short Bill and wishing to show it to him, and he expressed a desire to see it.'

But though Russell was always ready to listen to Bright in private on the question of any Liberal Reform, he would do nothing, and the other Whigs would not even listen. Palmerston, to the end of his life, thought he had settled the question by saying, 'tenant right is landlords' wrong.'

In January 1851 Bright writes to Cobden:

> 'You see the murders in the north of Ireland. By and by it will be worth while trying my Bill or some other Bill to settle the relations of landlord and tenant. But police and troops to the disturbed districts are the old remedy, and nothing new or sensible must be tried yet.'

About the same time he wrote to Villiers:

> 'Ireland has had no rulers who ruled *for* Ireland. They have been, almost without exception, the agents of the territorial rulers of the United Kingdom, and their mission to Dublin has been fulfilled when they have maintained the tinsel dignity of the Irish Court, and prevented the factions of Ireland from devouring each other.'

In the autumn of 1852 he again visited Ireland. He writes thence to Cobden, on October 15:

> 'We must bear in mind that all we hear from Ireland—that is, all we are told of the doings and sayings of these extreme men, is told us by their armed enemies. The Irish papers are not read in England, and the *Times* is no fair exponent of the views or conduct of the Catholic party in Ireland. I find the Irish as individuals, or collected as a meeting, just about as reasonable as the English, and as willing to accept what is just in settlement of their claims.'

Meanwhile John Bright was perpetually urging the case for Irish Disestablishment, with a sympathy for the Irish point of view then extremely rare and utterly wanting to many brilliant men who accused him of British Philistinism and want of imagination.

> 'I wish,' he said in 1851, 'that honourable gentlemen could for a moment imagine themselves Irish Catholics, with this Protestant Church and this Protestant State

ruling them as the Irish Catholics have been ruled, and you will at once see that the system we have adopted would have been enough to make Catholicism not only a faith but a patriotism ; and that every Irishman who abandoned Catholicism and became a Protestant, abandoned not only his Church, but committed himself to a party who were the greatest enemies to the peace and tranquillity of his country.'

In October 1852, in a public letter to Dr. Gray, Editor of the *Freeman's Journal*, he propounded his scheme of Irish Disestablishment and Disendowment. The letter begins by repudiating Lord John Russell's former proposals for concurrent endowment, and establishment of a Catholic alongside of a Protestant Church. 'Happily for sound principles in civil government, and happily for religion itself, all parties are not agreed to do this, but are rather agreed that it shall not be done.' Bright's own proposals, however, included a gift of £1,000,000 to the Roman Catholic Church out of the sequestrated property of the disendowed Anglican Church, and proportionate sums to the other religious bodies of Ireland. The Maynooth and all other resumable or yearly grants from Government were then to be stopped. He defends this proposed arrangement in the following words :

'Now, there is not a man in the United Kingdom more averse to religious endowments by the State than I am. I object to the compulsory levying of a tax from any man to teach any religion, and still more to teach a religion in which he does not believe ; and I am of opinion that, to take a Church into the pay of the State, and to place it under the control of the State, is to deaden and corrupt the Church, and to enlist its influence on the side of all that is evil in the civil government. But in the plan now suggested the Irish sects or Churches would be left entirely free, as is the Free Church in Scotland, or the Wesleyan Methodist Church in England. The grants once made, each Church would possess absolutely its own funds, just as much as if they were the accumulations of the voluntary contributions and liberality of past generations of its members, and thus would be avoided the damage to religion and to civil government which is inseparable from what is called the union of Church and State.'

After these distributions for religious purposes 'the remaining five or seven millions, as the case may be, might, and in my opinion ought, to be reserved for purposes strictly Irish, and directed to the educational and moral improvement of the people, without respect to class or creed.'

Bright may be regarded as the father of Irish Church Disestablishment. But the scheme actually passed by Gladstone and Bright in 1869 was more generous to the disendowed Anglican Church, and it made no gifts to any other religious body.

It must be remembered that in the period following the death of O'Connell in 1847, the Irish members, mostly calling themselves 'Liberals' of a sort, were with few exceptions worthless as champions of their oppressed country. Some of them understood her case very little, and others who had placed themselves at the head of a Tenants' Rights agitation, sold the cause by corrupt bargains in the Whips' office. Hence the special value of John Bright's advocacy. He did much to initiate the Irish and British democracies into the novel belief that they had common interests and common enemies.

Bright's attention had been first turned to Ireland by the Irish problem in Lancashire; it was first turned to India by the question of the Lancashire cotton supply. He had formed for himself the opinion that the absolute dependence of our cotton industry on the supply of raw material from the Southern States of the American Union would some day prove a grave danger, the more so because the slavery question in America must ere long come to a crisis. Foreseeing in a general way the cotton famine of 1861-63 and its causes, Bright began as early as May 1847 to agitate for measures to increase the growth of cotton in India. He was on the whole supported by Lancashire opinion, but neither unanimously nor eagerly, so that the Whig Government and the East India Company found excuse to refuse, in 1850, to send a Commission to India to inquire into the matter on the spot. Peel, a fortnight before his death, told Bright that he agreed with him and had spoken privately to some members of the Government in favour of the inquiry, but in vain.

Bright had, however, obtained, in 1848, a Select Committee of the House to sift the matter so far as it was possible to examine it in England. He was Chairman, and his studies in that capacity laid the foundation of his lifelong interest in India and criticism of the Indian Government. The Report which he drew up for the Committee laid stress on the absence of railways, the badness of roads, and the system of raising revenue. All this was stated from the point of view of cotton-growing. But other aspects of our Indian affairs had already presented themselves to his mind as a result of these inquiries.

In 1853 the Whig Government passed a measure for the better government of India, which had the one supreme merit of establishing the competitive system for entrance to the Civil Service. Bright, while approving of that change, attacked the rest of the Bill on account of its inadequacy as a measure of Reform. His two chief complaints were that it retained the cumbrous system of dual government by the Court of Directors and the Board of Control, and that it made no proposal to associate the natives of India more closely with our rule out there. 'I object to the Bill,' he said, 'because it maintains a double government.'[1] He thus described one of the two bodies controlling India:

> 'There are in fact bankers and brewers, and men of all sorts in the City of London, who find it their interest to get into the Court of Directors—no matter by what channel—because it adds to the business of their bank, or whatever else may be the undertaking in which they are engaged, but who have no special qualification for the government of India.'

As to our rule beyond the ocean, he said:

> 'I am very anxious to see a very much wider employment of the most intelligent and able men amongst the native population. . . . The right hon. member for Edinburgh [Macaulay], in proposing the Indian Bill of 1833, dwelt on one of its clauses, which provided that neither colour, nor caste, nor religion, nor place of birth should be a bar to the employment of persons by the Government; whereas, as a matter of fact, from that time to this, no person in India has been so employed, who might not have been equally employed before that clause was enacted.'

One of the most acute and brilliant of parliamentary reporters[2] declared that:

[1] After the Indian Mutiny had darkly underlined his criticism of the old system, Bright said (June 1858): 'I believe everything the East India Company has said of the Board of Control—to its discredit; and I believe everything the Board of Control has said to the discredit of the East India Company.'

[2] Edward Whitty, of the *Leader*, in his anonymous *History of the Session, 1852-53*; Chapman, 1854, p. 189. For Bright's later utterances on India, see pp. 265-67 below, chap. xii.

'The India debate of June [1853] will be remembered for two of the greatest speeches delivered of late years in the House of Commons—Mr. Bright's and Mr. Disraeli's. Mr. Bright is the most English-looking man I ever saw, and Mr. Disraeli the least English-looking man I ever saw, and the characters correspond to the looks. Mr. Bright and Mr. Disraeli went into the same lobby on India, because the one looked at India like an honest Englishman, anxious that England should do her duty there; and the other like an intelligent foreign gentleman, learned in the Asian mystery, fully cognisant of British peculiarities in India, and sympathising more with the 150,000,000 of Hindoos than with the 650 members of the House of Commons who do not like trouble. After Mr. Gladstone, Mr. Bright and Mr. Disraeli are now the two greatest personages with the two greatest futures of any men of their time.'

Bright himself was not aware that any great future awaited him. Again and again between the repeal of the Corn Laws and the outbreak of the Crimean War, his intimate letters contain expressions of a desire to leave public life. He was held to his post rather by a sense of duty than by any conscious delight in his triumphs as an orator, though, like many great artists, he may have enjoyed unconsciously the pleasures of achievement. Even to a man as strong and self-sufficient as John Bright, it can never be a pleasant life to be the Ishmael of his profession. Any man—and fortunately there are always some such men in every House of Commons—who has for grave public reasons condemned himself to be a critic, and a lonely critic, of whatever Government is in power, must at moments feel fatigue and desire to be gone from an arena where the prizes are for others, whosesoever the victory. To Bright the Treasury Bench was not a goal but a target.

Until, after 1853, a marked turn for the better occurred in the fortunes of Bright Bros.,[1] his straitened circumstances afforded another argument for a return to private life. 'I must do my Parliamentary work cheaper or go out of Parliament,' he writes in 1850.

On June 10, 1847, after remaining a widower for six years, John Bright married Margaret Elizabeth Leatham. She was

[1] His brother Thomas was an exceedingly able business man. About 1848-49 the Bright Bros. added carpet-printing to their cotton-spinning business.

the daughter of William Leatham, a Friend and a banker of Wakefield. Although two of her brothers were politicians and afterwards Liberal Members of Parliament, she herself knew little or nothing of politics before her marriage. After it, she took a constant and sympathetic interest in her husband's work. She had inherited from her father a considerable portion, and this, at a time when the Rochdale business was a very lean affair, was a valuable help to her husband, who could hardly without it have been able to remain in Parliament with an increasing family. Their children, seven in number, closely occupied Mrs. Bright, and drew her husband's thoughts and affections with ever fresh bonds to One Ash. As the family grew, Bright reluctantly decided that he could not afford a house in town as well as one in Rochdale, and after 1853 his wife and children remained at home during the session. This separation was a trial to his wife—and indeed to both of them; but she recognised the necessity and bore it uncomplainingly, though she often lamented the fact. Thenceforth, in session time, Bright lived the life of a bachelor in lodgings, and was a constant denizen of the Reform Club. He went down to Rochdale for the week-end whenever it was possible; and he wrote his wife a long letter every day of his life that he was absent from her, until her death in 1878.

In these circumstances his desire to go down to One Ash to his wife and children was very great, and it is touchingly shown in his letters and journals. 'Our little children,' he writes in 1853, 'are well, and I am so happy with them that my political threatens to be lost in my domestic life, at which dear Elizabeth seems disposed to rejoice.' 'I don't like being away from thee,' he writes to his wife; 'in truth, the more we are together in our comfortable home, the less we are disposed to separate, I think. But we must take care and not become too selfish.'

During the years while sons and daughters were growing up around him, he lost many that were dear to him of his own generation. Before the end of 1853 he had lost his brothers Benjamin and Gratton, and his sisters Sophia and Esther, both of whom died shortly after they were married. And in 1851 his father died. Thus, before the Crimean War broke out, his private life had received an entirely new orientation.

In 1848 his sister Priscilla married his friend, Duncan McLaren. As McLaren was not a Friend, the Society, according to its ancient rule, cast her out. Her brother records this event, which for himself and his sister was bitter and even tragic, in the following words in his diary of April 5, 1849:

> 'To-day my dear sister Priscilla was disowned on the ground of her marriage contrary to the rules or practices of the Society. I protested against this course as unjust to her and injurious to the Society. But our Monthly Meeting seems to be unable to perceive any distinction in cases; flagrant immorality and the marriage of a member with a religious person not a member are visited with the same condemnation. The Society may well not extend. It is withering to almost nothing. Its glorious principles are made unsightly to the world. Its aspect is made repulsive. It keeps out multitudes by the imposition of tests and observances which can never be of real importance, and it excludes many from its fold who have done no moral wrong, and whose assumed error may have been highest virtue.
>
> 'The glory cannot but depart from a body which weighs principles and forms in the same balance. It does not, indeed, observe "days and months, and times and years," but it has elevated "peculiarities" into points of Christian observance, and has done that which is, to some extent, the making broad their philacteries. Can the Society reform itself, or will it slowly sink?'

The Society did in time 'reform itself' in the way Bright wished. When more liberal principles had triumphed, Mrs. McLaren, in her old age, was reinstated in the Society of Friends. John Bright's friendship with his sister continued to be most affectionate and intimate, and their correspondence long and continuous, until death divided them. Her husband, Duncan McLaren, was, next to Cobden, the man whom Bright most often consulted on political questions.

John Bright's home life at One Ash continued to be of the happiest and simplest. There was no aping the wealthier classes, even when in later years he became well off, thanks to his brother Thomas's talents for conducting the business. There was no following the fashions, but adherence rather to the old Quaker standards. Bright, when at One Ash, spent some of his time in the small library, but he usually sat in the dining-room, the pleasantest room in the house; as it was the centre of the family circle, he liked it best. On a tour abroad, he writes that he is 'abstaining from buying things, as our house is full of things.'

Many people would have thought it bare. The only expensive furniture in One Ash were the heavy carved book-cases containing twelve hundred well-bound volumes—the present with which his Anti-Corn Law admirers had rewarded him for giving up five years of his life to their cause. Careful in expenditure on his own home, to others his purse was ever open. Indeed, he allowed himself to be preyed upon by beggars to a fault. Proper remonstrances from his sons in later years were generally disregarded: 'do as I tell thee; give him the money.'

The life and conversation of which he was the centre at home or in the larger world was always simple in greatness, and truth was its keynote. He eschewed the small conventional falsehoods of which the rest of us are often guilty. He never strove to seem more friendly or more clever or better informed than he really was. If he did not know something, he would ask, without an attempt to hide his ignorance. If he did not like his interlocutor, the fact was usually apparent. To his daughter Helen, when she was a girl of thirteen, he writes bidding her 'not to write ironically, but always simply and what is literally true.' That was his own rule. The interest of his conversation, apart from the terse vigour of his language, his humour, and his good stories, arose from the fact that he never said more and seldom said less than the whole of what he thought about any subject or any person. He did not spare his own friends or party when he disagreed with them: it was about John Stuart Mill and his theoretic objections to the Ballot that he uttered a truth of wide application: 'The worst of great thinkers is they so often think wrong.'

Though in public his speech was singularly free from the accent of his native county—more so than Gladstone's—he was a great teller of Lancashire dialect stories, and of old political and coaching traditions of the days of his boyhood and youth. The Oxford philosopher, T. H. Green, one of Bright's most ardent admirers while to admire him was still 'bad form' at the university, gives this account of his conversation in 1864:

> 'I can best describe him as a great "brick." He is simple as a boy, full of fun, with a very pleasant flow of conversation and lots of good stories. He does not seem to mind what he says to anybody, but though he is sufficiently brusque, his good humour saves him from ever seeming rude.'

In Caroline Fox's *Journals* we find much the same account of his talk:

> 1861, May. 'The Brights are staying here. J. B. is great fun, always ready for a chat and a fulmination, and filling up the intervals of business with *Paradise Regained*. One likes to have his opinion on men and things, as it is strong, clear and honest, however one-sided.'

And again:

> 1868, Oct. 14. 'His conversation is so varied, he is so simple and unreserved in telling one all manner of things one wishes to hear about, and then there is such downright manliness in the whole nature of the man, which is refreshing in this rather feeble age. He had nothing for the public, though they wanted to present an address, but would talk and read poetry till ten o'clock to us.'

His conversation was not without its surprises, though they were always characteristic. When Sir Henry Hawkins was made a judge, he met Bright at dinner, and told him of his promotion, expecting to be congratulated. John Bright put his hand on his shoulder and said in a voice of deep emotion, 'Be merciful, Hawkins, be merciful.'

CHAPTER VIII

THE 'MANCHESTER SCHOOL' AND FRANCHISE REFORM. THE WHIG GOVERNMENT, 1846-52

'Colonial policy explained by Lord John Russell in a long speech; very important. Colonies at the Cape and in Australia to have legislative chambers and to have a liberal self-government. Great agreement in the House on the subject. Marvellous absence of prejudice when the objects are ten thousand miles away. Should like to move that the Bill be extended to Great Britain and Ireland.'—BRIGHT'S *Journal*, February 7, 1850.

ONE evening in the winter of 1888, during the long illness that ended in his death, John Bright recounted to those at his bedside an incident which had remained in his mind near forty years. He said that one day Thackeray met him and took off his hat with an uncommon flourish. 'Well, what 's the matter?' said Bright. 'I always feel inclined to take off my hat to you and Cobden,' replied Thackeray. 'You know just what you want and ask for it, and will doubtless get it, but so few of these fellows know what they do want.'

There was, however, one matter of supreme importance in which Bright knew what he wanted better than Cobden, and that was the extension of the Franchise to the working men. 'Why, Cobden, you haven't got faith in the working people,' he said to his friend one day. After Cobden's death there were two stories which Bright used to tell to a young Liberal Member of whom he was fond; the first was how, when his first wife died, Cobden came to him, and how they agreed to work together till the Corn Laws were repealed; and the other was how after the Corn Laws were repealed he wished to make a similar compact about the Franchise, and how Cobden refused. The difference cast no shadow on their friendship, and in no degree weakened their alliance in other causes. But it gave John Bright a function of his own in British politics. He was no longer merely the second of two.

Cobden was not indeed opposed to a further extension of

the Franchise, but he cared little about it. His plan was to work for the Reforms he advocated, especially for land reform and for retrenchment based on a pacific foreign policy, by educating the middle class up to his views, and by inducing them to continue to purchase forty-shilling freeholds in the county constituencies.[1] Bright pointed out the inadequacy of the latter method as a means of permanently controlling Parliament, and urged that a Liberal policy in home or foreign affairs was impossible until the working class was enfranchised.

On this point of political dynamics Bright was more far-seeing than his friend. If Cobden had the finer intellect, Bright had the shrewder instinct. The middle class, or rather the enfranchised part of it, having won Free Trade from the aristocracy, was preparing to amalgamate socially and politically with its late foes. Until the unenfranchised classes were admitted to full citizenship, no further serious attack was made on Church or Land monopolies in Great Britain and Ireland, or on the aristocratic control of place and power. The members of the upper middle class were undergoing a slow but enduring change in their outlook on life, that altogether unfitted them for further efforts in Radicalism. Their Nonconformist Liberalism, the cause and symbol of their rebellion against the landlord caste that had once starved and insulted them, was now, in the more prosperous times of Free Trade, gradually giving way to Churchmanship in religion and Conservatism in politics; while in social life the old simple manners yielded to an imitation of the fashionable world which Bright called by its name—'snobbery.' The nationalist passions of this middle class were easily stirred up, as the Crimean War showed, and those passions made it the tool of the aristocracy. Peace between the fashionable and the manufacturing potentates was secure so long as the Corn Laws were not revived, and the Whigs now fully realised that in defending the *fait accompli* of Free Trade they would have the advantage over that section of the aristocracy that still sighed for Protection.

For these fundamental reasons, Cobden's hopes of obtaining peace, retrenchment, and reform through the middle class were vain. Bright, who wanted to overthrow the aristocratic régime in Church and State, in Great Britain and Ireland, was prepared to take the necessary first step, namely, to enfranchise the nation as a whole. He believed in the working men, much as Cobden believed in the middle class. And he considered

[1] See pp. 122-23 above.

full citizenship as a right which ought to be denied to no man not specially disqualified.

In other matters Cobden and Bright strove not only in the same direction, but towards the same end, though Cobden showed most eagerness in preaching national economy, and Bright in attacking Church privilege. Some of the questions on which they worked together between 1846 and 1854 were resistance to military expenditure and to Palmerston's interference in European affairs which caused it; the completion of Free Trade, and the abolition of 'taxes on knowledge'; opposition to a renewal of the Corn Laws or the grant of 'compensation' to landlords and farmers; abolition of entail and of feudal restrictions on the break-up of landed estates; the defence of Roman Catholics against the 'Papal Aggression' Bill; the admission of Jews to Parliament and of dissenters to the universities. On all these and on other questions Cobden, Bright, and a handful of members who usually voted with them, operated on the flank of both parties, greatly to the scandal of the Whig Whips and the cronies of Brooks's and the Reform Club, who considered that they had a claim on all Liberal votes 'to keep in the Whigs.' But the 'Manchester School' claimed and exercised a right not only to speak but to vote on the merits of every question as it came up.

There were other groups whose political allegiance was equally uncertain, whose support might be at any moment acquired or lost by the Ministry of the day—notably the Irish Members and the 'Peelites,' the latter including Peel, Graham, Gladstone, and Sidney Herbert in the Commons and Aberdeen in the Lords. Hence the period after the abolition of the Corn Laws is one of parliamentary confusion, of weak Governments, of rapid combinations and dissolutions of political partnership. But it is not a period of important legislative Reform, because the existing electorate made no such demand.[1] Between the fall of Peel and the death of Palmerston, the prevailing character of each successive Cabinet—Whig, Whig-Peelite, and occasional Tory—was that of a liberal-minded aristocracy acting on behalf of a middle class, content to garner the fruits of recent Reforms, and to 'let sleeping dogs lie.' In short, the statesmen of this period resemble Sir Robert Walpole, though not in his corrupt methods nor unfortunately in his love of peace.

[1] The greatest Reforms of this period—the Reform of the University of Oxford and the introduction of competition for admission to the Civil Service—were not the result of popular agitation in the constituencies, but of the Liberal tendency of some of the statesmen, particularly Gladstone.

The appeal to nationalist and warlike passions was made, indeed, neither by the Peelites nor by the Protectionists, but by Palmerston and his Whig followers. This fact, together with Russell's inability to redeem his personal promise of Franchise Reform, prevented the effective alliance of John Bright with the Whig party. The author of our greatest political novel has described the effect on the Whigs of the 'Corn Law Repeal, the Manchester flood.' Before Repeal, he says: 'Whigs were, but ever since then they have walked like spectral antediluvians, or floated as dead canine bodies that are sucked away on the ebb of tides and flung back on the flow, ignorant whether they be progressive or retrograde.' [1]

If these general conditions be borne in mind, it will be easy to understand the political history of the period as reflected in Bright's letters and journals.

On July 29, 1846, a month after the abolition of the Corn Laws and the fall of Sir Robert Peel, while the Whigs were settling into the seat of Government abandoned to them through the divisions of their enemies, Bright wrote to Cobden:

> 'I had some talk with Sir R. Peel, in the division lobby. He said he had no conception of the intense feeling of hatred with which the Corn Law had been regarded, especially in Scotland. I thanked him for myself and for our friends, for his services. He said he had great satisfaction in the public approval which had been manifested of his conduct, and thought our condition now with the old Corn Law would be bad, as the potato blight was again rapidly extending.
>
> 'I confess that I am seeking the good opinion of a lady for whom I have long felt a high regard, and have some hope of being successful. This need not be published to the world, but I have been too long intimate with you not to avow it. And I know you will think I act wisely if the choice be a wise one. It is pleasant after the seven years' war of the League to look to domestic peace.'

While Bright was courting and marrying Miss Leatham, Cobden went abroad for a year to recruit his health after the 'seven years' war.' While he was away the General Election of 1847 took place. The ex-chiefs of the League were rewarded by easy returns for those great popular constituencies in the north which they had aroused to a new sense of political

[1] *Beauchamp's Career*, chap. xiv.

responsibility and power. Cobden, in his absence, was returned for the West Riding; Villiers, by the strenuous efforts of Bright,[1] was elected for South Lancashire, but was unable to sit for it as his old constituents at Wolverhampton refused to give him up. Manchester chose for its two members John Bright and Milner Gibson. They were returned unopposed on July 29, 1847.

Although no candidate was put up against Bright, the old-fashioned Whigs were very sore at the election of such a Jack Cade, and nursed the hope of revenge that was satisfied after ten years. They would have preferred to be represented by the son of a Peer, but this made Bright all the more anxious to have the seat.

> 'You are right,' he wrote to Villiers, 'in saying that the son or relation of a Peer may be as good as another man, but still I think it a great fault in our constituencies to choose such because of their rank, and to exhibit so little respect for their own class. I am sure that Manchester, other things being equal, will do more for the popular cause by not choosing a Lord than by choosing one, and considering how much political influence is vested in certain families, I think we may do better in general than, having of necessity the father in one House, to put the son into the other. And perhaps it is sometimes almost needful to fight one prejudice with another. If they run me down for want of "social position" it is a great temptation to us to try to rouse a middle-class spirit against my aristocratic opponent.'

But when nomination day came round, there was no opponent—aristocratic or other. Bright told the electors: 'My sympathies are naturally with the class with which I am connected, and I would infinitely prefer to raise the class of which I am one, than by any means whatever to creep above it or out of it.'

Bright, however, was far from discouraging all Liberal

[1] There is a long correspondence between Bright and Villiers on this subject. Villiers' election for South Lancashire was Bright's doing. If Villiers had been a mean man, he might have been jealous of Bright as one who had entered into his Anti-Corn Law labours late in the day and reaped where he had sown; but in fact a clear and intimate friendship always existed between them. In December 1852, when the Peelites were preferred to Villiers as members of the new Cabinet, Bright wrote to Lord John Russell: 'The man whom Sir R. Peel followed is somewhat better, I think, than a man who merely followed Sir R. Peel.'

members of the aristocracy from taking part in politics. In his journal of July 4, 1853, he notes :

> 'To Reform Club. Conversation with Hon. George Fitzwilliam about speaking in the House. I wondered such as he did not work and take a position in the House. Referred him to Duke of Newcastle, Sidney Herbert, Lord Stanley, as industrious and useful members of the aristocracy. Why not he? Told him if I were Lord Fitzwilliam's son, I would soon be Prime Minister and would give something of mine to the policy of the country. He said he could not speak.'

A similar exhortation in another quarter was more to the purpose. The late Duke of Devonshire, the 'Lord Hartington' of our political history, wrote, ten years after Bright's death :

> 'I remember meeting him at an inn at Lancaster, when I did not know him personally, and his asking me why I did not take any part in politics, or in the debates in the House of Commons. I told him that I could not speak. He said, "Oh, that does not matter. Lord Althorp spoke quite as badly as you, and yet he had great influence in the House of Commons." I don't know whether this had any effect in making me pay more attention to politics, but I have always remembered it.'

The future showed the comparison with Althorp to be an exceedingly apt prophecy.[1]

At the beginning of 1848 Cobden was back from his foreign tour, on which he had been enthusiastically received by the Continental Liberals on the eve of their great uprising, so different in character and result from that which their guest had brought to a triumphant issue over here. At the end of January 1848 Cobden and Bright addressed the first of many meetings in Manchester on the subject of national retrenchment.

'Cobden was rather strong,' Bright writes to Villiers. 'People rejoice that *Richard is himself again*. It was a

[1] In later life Bright used to repeat a conversation he had once had with Lord Hartington, as follows :

Bright : 'You should be careful to keep your voice *up* at the end of your sentences ; sometimes one cannot hear what you say.'

Hartington : 'It 's all very well, but it 's sometimes precious hard to know how to end a sentence.'

splendid meeting. . . . I told Cobden he had cut his cable and was afloat again. He said: "I suppose you mean that now I have put myself in the position you have been in all along?" I said: "Yes, there is a *deep gulf fixed* between you and many who have heaped adulation upon you, as deep almost as that which separated Dives from Lazarus." And I believe in my conscience that to interfere with and to control or reduce military expenditure is a more deadly sin than to insist on a free import of corn. For the land still remains to the landlord; but to Colonels and Captains there remains nothing, if regiments are disbanded and ships laid up in harbor.'

A few months later he writes to Mrs. Priestman that the new agitation for retrenchment 'will bring down on us, and especially on Cobden, all the wrath of the journals that write rather for the tax-eating than the tax-paying class.' The phrase implies a distinction between the middle and lower classes who paid taxes and the fashionable classes who received them in the form of salaries for civil and military posts under Government. In our day we can see that the effect of enfranchising the working class has not been, as Bright expected, to cut down the taxes, or the number of civil and military office-holders, but it has enabled the working class to do a little 'tax-eating' on its own behalf, through State-provided education, old age pensions, and other schemes. Owing to the extension of the Franchise advocated by Bright the balance has been redressed, not, indeed, as he expected, by emptying one scale, but by loading the other.

In his journal of this period he notes the following dinner conversation:

'Dr. —— thinks heavy taxes a blessing to a country. I asked him if he thought *foot-pads* stimulated industry as he said taxes did. He said: "No, they were irregular. The steady pressure of taxes was the best!" His wife more sensible and an amiable good person I should think.'

The years 1846-48 were years of trade depression, due to the bad harvest followed by the revolutionary wars on the Continent. 'People seem to think utter ruin would have come, but for the repeal of the Corn Law,' Bright wrote to Villiers. Owing to repeal, nothing more revolutionary occurred in England in 1848 than the flash in the pan of revived Chartist agitation. Bright was not immediately concerned in the movement, which still rejected help from the middle class. But the following letters show where his sympathies lay ; the events of the year in England and on the Continent hardened his resolution that henceforward he himself would agitate the Franchise question with no less zeal but more wisdom than the now extinguished Chartists.

(To Jonathan Priestman, 3rd month, 26, 1848.)

'Liberty is on the march, and this year promises to be a great year in European history. Our Government is blind enough, and the Parliamentary majorities are more regarded than opinion out of doors. We must have another League of some kind, and our aristocracy must be made to submit again.'

(To Mrs. Priestman, 4th month, 23, 1848.)

'In this country political agitation is not likely to be soon lulled. We shall have no violence, I think, except in Ireland, and even there I hope appearances are rather less threatening than were supposed a short time ago. But we shall have, and ought to have, a powerful agitation in favour of a real Parliamentary Reform, and to gain this would be worth some time longer of commercial depression. We have deluded ourselves with the notion that we are a free people, and have a good government and a representative system, whilst in fact our representative system is for the most part a sham, and the forms of representation are used to consolidate the supremacy of the titled and proprietary class. All this will break down by and by. From all parts of the country we hear of preliminary meetings and new organisations, Associations and Leagues, etc. The middle and working classes are beginning to see that united they may win all they require ; divided they are a prey to their insatiable enemies.

As to the renewed Chartist agitation he writes to his wife :

(6 month, 10, 1848.) 'It is all well enough for rich and comfortably off people to complain that their quiet is disturbed by the growling of millions whom they tax to an enormous amount and yet shut out from all share in the power by which taxes are imposed. Things cannot go on as they now are. And who is to change them ? Will William Henry [1] change them, or will those he associates

[1] His brother-in-law, W. H. Leatham, sometime Whig and Liberal M.P. for Wakefield and South-West Riding of Yorkshire.

with politically? Would they have passed the Reform Bill or repealed the Corn Law without the pressure of that opinion which is now considered dangerous because it demands further concessions?'

(8 month, 20, 1848.) 'The Government seem to make a great uproar about the Chartists. They have spies among those wretched fools, to stimulate them to conspiracy and to outrage, and then getting a lot of them together they pounce upon them, and imprison or transport them. This is a repetition of the old tricks of Government practised with great temporary effect in 1817 to 1820. The aristocracy want to frighten the middle classes from the pursuit of Reform, and to do this they and their emissaries stimulate a portion of the least wise of the people to menace and violence, to damage the cause of Reform, and for a time they succeed.'

(To Villiers, December 21, 1848.)

'Why not make one of the new popular party which must come out of present perplexities? We can have a party out of doors more formidable than we had in the League, and can *work the Constitution so as to reform it through itself.*'

In January 1849 a meeting was held at Manchester to inaugurate this new party or association, which Bright wished to call the 'Commons' League.' In a letter to Cobden about the arrangements for the meeting he writes: [1]

'Now with regard to the meeting in January, my notion is that the object should be general, and yet specific. General so far as the questions of Financial and Parliamentary Reform go; specific as to the measures to be taken to form and strengthen the party.'

The 'specific measures' were the further purchase of forty-shilling freehold qualifications and 'purging the register by a systematic attention to lists of voters.' Bright, while urging these 'specific measures,' regarded them as merely the means towards the enfranchisement of the remainder of the middle class and of the working men. This is what he meant when he spoke of 'working the constitution so as to reform it through itself.'

The meeting took place. Cobden, as previously agreed,

[1] December 21, 1848. For Cobden's reply see *Morley*, ii. 38-40.

spoke on Financial Reform, and John Bright on the extension of the Franchise, to an enthusiastic audience. But the new 'League' did not prosper like the old: partly because there was not yet such a popular demand for Reform as there had been for Free Trade; partly because two distinct objects were set forward—Financial and Franchise Reform; partly because the two chiefs were not in harmony as to the relative importance of these two objects.

On September 17, 1849, Bright wrote to Cobden discussing their differences:

> 'I agree with you about the forty-shilling votes, but I cannot see how the scheme is to be worked, unless there be a definite and understood object. Now you object to Parliamentary Reform as the thing to be worked for, and I am fully persuaded that there is no other object that can be started that will induce any number of *now un-enfranchised* persons to take the trouble to qualify themselves. . . . The case for Parliamentary Reform is more glaring and undeniable if possible than our Free Trade cause was.'

On December 7 he writes in a similar strain, combating Cobden's view that an extension of the system of purchasing forty-shilling freeholds was a sufficient Franchise Reform in itself. The arguments that Bright here uses are enough by themselves to prove his friend wrong, but he might have added that the class whom he and Cobden were stirring up to purchase forty-shilling freehold qualifications was destined ere long to become the backbone of the Conservative party:

> 'The forty-shilling scheme *alone* will not do the work, and *alone* it will not work extensively—there are very many districts where it will be found impracticable from the condition and value of property, or the circumstances of the people. I think you have been wrong, as I have often told you. It would have been more above board and I think more effectual to have started for Parliamentary Reform, and *for this*, to have set in motion the forty-shilling freeholds. This plan would enable us to win some counties, and to drive the factious to a capitulation, but it will not in my view ever enfranchise so many *permanently* as to make any real change in the representation. These forty-shilling properties are not held by parties who can keep them with much certainty or hand them down to a son

who may succeed on the register, but by men who have a desperate struggle to get them, a constant struggle to keep them, and whose necessities will force a sale of them far more frequently than is the case with all other kinds of property. Their small properties will be sold and gathered in one property with an unavoidable certainty and rapidity. And I think you exaggerate the extent to which people will adopt the system, especially as no definite object or battle is before them.

'I said at Oldham last night what I have said before and since the League was dissolved, that no object is worth a real and great effort short of a thorough reform in Parliament, and our object ought to be to discover the best way to that object.'

In all things else Cobden and Bright were the political twin brethren. In the daily work of the House they were a party by themselves, sometimes followed by a small fluctuating group of Radicals, but always exerting an influence out of proportion to the number of members who voted with them in a division. Intellect, character, and clear purpose such as theirs could not fail to operate on a loose crowd of office-seekers and opportunists, Whigs at a loss for a programme, and Peelites graduating in Liberalism; it was felt, even by those who liked them least, that the chiefs of the late Anti-Corn Law League represented the unenfranchised millions and the spirit of the coming age.

The complete success and popularity of Free Trade in practice added to their prestige. They had always said that wages would not fall, but rise as a consequence of Free Trade in corn, and when their prophecy proved true, the working men became so hostile to the ghost of Protection that a revival of the Corn Laws would have provoked a rebellion. Bright assisted the Whig Government in the capture of the outlying forts of Protection, that followed the fall of its corn-citadel. He assisted in the abolition of the Navigation Laws and of the protection of West Indian sugar, and in the further reduction of the timber duties.

Early in 1850 Bright writes to Cobden:

'The Protection cry seems wholly to have subsided. Every man of any mark or influence is now on the other tack: it is now to be "energy, skill, capital," etc., on which the farmers are to thrive. Disraeli appears to have gone entirely out, and the whole country is so revelling in plenty of bread—in short its mouth is "crammed full" so that it cannot speak on any subject.'

Disraeli, who had no intention of remaining 'entirely out,' was already trimming his sails to the new wind. On January 4, 1850, Bright notes in his journal:

> 'Dined at Bellamy's with Disraeli, strange fellow! Admits Protection gone. Did all he could to prevent squires and farmers making fools of themselves in the recess. When they came to *do* something on the opening of Parliament they were forced to take his proposition as an amendment, asserting only agricultural distress, and asking for relief for local burdens.'

This 'dinner at Bellamy's' is the first of many references in Bright's journal to an intimacy—it could never be called friendship, though it amounted on both sides to friendliness—between the two men in the House of Commons who were most unlike each other. Disraeli, as will appear in these pages, again and again sought Bright's company, reposed in him unasked many of his strange confidences, and made still stranger propositions of alliance. Bright so far returned the compliment as to record these evenings at greater length than any others in his journal, always with exclamations of fascinated wonder and amusement. His nature was so far from Disraeli's that he felt no need to take refuge in the peculiar abhorrence of him which Gladstone felt even at this early date. John Bright could safely listen to the siren without stopping his ears or binding himself to the mast.

On May 30, 1850, Bright notes: 'Met in the new House for first time. Impression unfavorable as to size and arrangements of the House.' It is to be presumed that Bright thought the new chamber too small, as indeed it was judged by the standard of accommodating an assembly of six hundred members. But the great tribune perhaps overlooked the importance of preserving the intimate and businesslike character of the debates, which might well have been changed into a more formal type of public oratory if the chamber had been as large as he appears to have wished.

The first great passage of arms that took place in the new lists was Lord Palmerston against all comers in the famous 'Don Pacifico' debate. On the return of the Whigs to power in July 1846, Palmerston had again become the Foreign Minister before the footlights, detested by our own and other

Courts, feared by his colleagues, but loved by the hearty, pugnacious, despot-hating Englishmen of that era. Again he had set about lecturing and interfering everywhere in Europe—Spain, Portugal, Denmark, Switzerland, Hungary, Italy—usually, though not always, on the right side, but usually, so at least his critics declared, without effect and with much danger to our own peace and prestige. That he spoke out for liberty in the evil days after 1848 was remembered to his country's credit by the oppressed peoples, but he never effected any such great thing for liberty as did Russell during his fortunate tenure of the Foreign Office in the next great crisis of Italian affairs in 1859-60. Palmerston did some good in Switzerland, but he let slip perhaps the best opportunity of this kind that he had, in failing to protest against the Russian invasion of Hungary in 1849, and even in condoning Russia's action, greatly to the indignation of Cobden and Bright. But when Austria's rebel subjects in Hungary had been suppressed by the Russian arms, Palmerston supported Turkey in her righteous refusal to surrender some Hungarian refugees to Austria and Russia. So the British fleet went to the Dardanelles ; it has often gone there on a worse errand. This incident, which aroused great enthusiasm in England, prepared the minds of many English Liberals who knew nothing about the Turkish Empire, to welcome the Crimean War five years later as a war for freedom.

Palmerston's next use of the British fleet was more questionable. He employed it to collect at Athens the dubious debts of a Portuguese Jew called Don Pacifico, who chanced to live in Gibraltar, and therefore to be a British subject. 'Civis Romanus' Palmerston called him, and sent a thrill through the hearts of our grandfathers. On his behalf Greek vessels were seized and the mediation of France was refused ; the French ambassador consequently left London. The art of the Foreign Office should be to reduce mountains to molehills, but Palmerston had turned a dirty and insignificant molehill into a volcano charged with England's thunders. He might easily have collected all the man's just debts without such vast enginery. This was the subject of the famous 'Don Pacifico' debate.

The British Conservatives of that day, Protectionist and Peelite alike, favoured a quiet Foreign Policy. The party that inherited and boasted of the peace of Waterloo adhered to the principle of the Holy Alliance—'Peace and Order,' in a form watered down to suit the British constitution. Wellington, after his crowning victory, had advised disarmament in order to reduce taxation. And still, after a generation had passed away, the Conservatives of every section—Peel, Graham and Aberdeen, Disraeli and Stanley—were all opposed to extravagant armaments and to provocative Foreign Policy, as also to the nobler element of love of liberty which Palmerston had inherited from Canning. Gladstone, who had not yet gone on his Neapolitan journey, shared these views both as to peace and 'order.'

Cobden and Bright, though they took a leading part in the magnificent reception of Kossuth in England, and openly expressed their sympathy with the Continental Liberals in their struggles against despotism, did not think that it was our business to fight for them, and in any case failed to perceive the connection of Don Pacifico's financial claims with the cause of European freedom. They found themselves, therefore, on the same side as the Conservatives in this matter, and voted accordingly. Bright specially detested Palmerston, because in home politics he was a Conservative sitting on the Liberal side of the House, and until his influence was removed from the Whig counsels, there would never be an effective Reform Bill. The 'Don Pacifico' debate was the beginning of a long battle between the Manchester School and Palmerston, which only ended in 1865 with the deaths of Palmerston and Cobden. After that, Bright, with the help of Gladstone, carried out the programme that had perforce been in abeyance while Palmerston was the presiding genius of the Whigs.

On June 21, 1850, a few days before the 'Don Pacifico' debate, Bright notes in his journal:

> 'Conversation with Disraeli. He is annoyed at this crisis; wished the *Industrial* question to be settled finally before anything of this kind had come up. Believes all his men will come up to the vote [against Palmerston], and is certain that Peel and his party will oppose the Government.
>
> 'June 22. Met Cobden and Molesworth; discussed state of affairs, and decided that we should vote against the Government on the Foreign Policy debate, to come on on Monday next. We all felt we should degrade ourselves by supporting what we wholly disapproved of, and that the question was too grave to allow of our being neutral. The result may be of great importance, but we are not responsible for these difficulties: to vote with the Government would be inconsistent with our past opinions

and policy and would destroy our self-respect and our influence for any good for the future. There is great commotion among the Whigs, and our friends of the Radical ranks at first looked at the dirty work they are to do with wry faces, but are gradually coming round to a stout defence of what they know is wrong but have not the courage to resist.

'June 25. The event of the night was Lord Palmerston's speech. He rose at a quarter to 10 and closed at 25 minutes past 2, speaking four hours and forty minutes. It was a remarkable speech, most able, saying everything that can be said for his policy, but proving conclusively how dangerous that policy is—meddling everywhere, advising, controlling, encouraging, menacing, as he pleases, in every country not of first-class power in Europe. This speech and the debate in general only make it more imperative that this mischievous system should be checked.

'June 28. Cobden spoke well and judiciously. I could not get in without putting him out, so did not speak at all. Peel made a most useful and excellent speech; no party feeling in it, and no wish to inflict damage on the Government, but an honest and simple avowal of his real opinions on the question before us. Division at four in the morning, 310 to 264, majority 46 for the Government.'

Palmerston had triumphed over Peelites, Protectionists, and 'Manchester' combined, by his graphic appeal to the nationalist passions of Englishmen, and to the generous hatred of Continental tyrannies which in that era was still associated with British Jingoism. Bright continues:

'June 29. In the evening dined with Mr. Willcox, M.P., in Dorset Square. Mr. Cockburn, M.P., there, and somewhat insolent to Cobden, telling him he was no reformer, and that he ought to be turned out of the Reform Club, because he would not vote to keep in a Liberal Government! What a strange notion of the duty of a member of Parliament these place-holders and place-seekers have! This Mr. Cockburn having been in a fright all the week for fear if the Government went out he should miss his appointment as Solicitor-General which he is expecting on the first vacancy. This evening Sir Robert Peel was thrown from his horse on Constitution Hill. The accident it is feared will prove serious.

'July 3. Startled this morning by hearing that Sir R. Peel had died last night at 10 minutes past 11. This event has shocked me very much. On reading the particulars in the *Daily News*, I could not refrain from tears; it felt as if I had lost a dear friend, so great has been my admiration for the recent career of this great statesman. . . .[1]

'This week has been remarkable for the loss sustained by the death of Sir Robert Peel, and probably on no former occasion has there been expressed so universal a sorrow on the death of any public man. Every family seems to feel the sorrow as its own. The last ten years of his life have certainly been devoted to the true interests of his country, and with extraordinary results. His labors and sacrifices on the Corn Law question have endeared him to the nation. I heard his last speech [against Palmerston's foreign policy] on the day before the fatal accident occurred: it was a great speech, in its principles, in its temper and moderation, in its tone altogether. Had he known what the morrow would bring forth, he would not have needed to omit or to add a word. Would that his dying words might sink into the hearts of statesmen and people.'

But that was not to be. Peel's death removed the only 'statesman' who combined weight and wisdom enough to have saved the country from the Crimean War.

'July 5. My recent vote against the foreign policy of the Government has been much condemned in Manchester by men who ought to know better. They seem to wear their principles but loosely and expect me to do the same. They are deluded by the notion that Palmerston is Liberal at home and abroad, and by fears that *Protection* can be restored: the first is untrue, or at least is wholly unproven, and the latter is simply childish. I cannot and will not be in Parliament a mere joint of a Whig tail.'

[1] Shortly afterwards, in a letter to Villiers, Bright writes: 'A real statesman, seeing a great emergency, and a great work for somebody to do, would not hesitate to step out, and if need be to make sacrifice of himself rather than be a party to the wretched and apparently interminable system of hushing up all disagreeable questions. Take the case of Peel. Had he fallen from his horse with the Corn Law unrepealed, or repealed in spite of him, where would have been his reputation? He lost his majority in Parliament, but he gained a tenfold majority in the country, and the act which destroyed him as a Minister built up his name for ever as a statesman.'

In a public letter to his constituents defending his action, Bright wrote :

> 'The question at issue in the late debate was mainly this : Shall the Foreign Minister of this country be permitted to interfere in the affairs of other countries in cases where the direct interests of this country do not require it ? Shall he advise, and warn, and meddle in matters which concern only the domestic and internal affairs of other countries ? I say that such a policy necessarily leads to irritation, and to quarrels with other nations, and may lead even to war ; and that it involves the necessity of maintaining greater armaments, and a heavier expenditure and taxation than would otherwise be required. It is a policy, therefore, which I cannot support under any pretence whatever. It is contrary to all I have ever declared in the Free Trade Hall, and in the many speeches in which I have touched upon this subject ; and it is contrary to the principles on which I was elected.
>
> '. . . I would not, for a moment, sit in Parliament for Manchester, or for any other constituency, if it was to be understood that I am to forget my own character and long-held principles, and what I believe to be the true interests of the country, to abandon all these, and vote as the necessities of *party* may require, at the crack of the Treasury whip.'

It was not long before the Peelites and the 'Manchester school' were again forced to oppose the Whig Government in the interests of common sense and public tranquillity. This time Lord John Russell was the sinner. The Pope had appointed some bishops to British territorial sees, and this perfectly innocent act had been announced to the world in the pretentious and provocative language usually employed by the Vatican. A Protestant hubbub at once arose, directed in part against the Pope, and in part against the Puseyite clergy in the Anglican Church. It would soon have died away like other such outbursts had not Lord John Russell taken up the cry. He wrote a letter to the Bishop of Durham, denouncing the new Papal pretensions and the 'unworthy sons of the Church of England herself.' He then proceeded to legislate against the former. This 'Durham Letter' of November 1850 was as disastrous as his 'Edinburgh Letter' of five years before had been successful. After a brief, uproarious popularity, its author found that he had thrown away his personal prestige and the votes of the Irish members. The Whig Ministry was soon staggering to its fall. The 'Ecclesiastical Titles Bill,' though passed into law by large majorities, insulted the Roman Catholics without protecting the Protestants, for if the Pope chose to make bishops no law could prevent him. *Punch*, after leading the hue and cry against the Pope and the Puseyites for a few months, at the high price of losing Dicky Doyle's services on the paper, at length summed up the situation in the famous cartoon, representing Lord John as the boy who chalked up 'No Popery' and then ran away.

Bright had not waited till the Ecclesiastical Titles Bill became unpopular before he denounced it. Indeed before the Bill had been brought in he had, in a speech to his constituents, ridiculed the then formidable agitation as resulting from the fears of 'old women of both sexes.' When Lord John introduced the Bill in February 1851, Bright characterised his speech as 'very good if delivered some 300 years ago.' It was an easy task to expose the futility and unwisdom of the Bill. 'It is a common saying,' he told the House, 'and it is an accurate saying that truth is indestructible. But let the House remember that there is another thing which is indestructible, and that is a persecuted error.' He went on thence to a general attack on Church establishments and on all State interference with religious affairs. The cry for this foolish No Popery legislation had been raised, he declared, not by the dissenters, who had, in the North of England, 'unanimously held aloof from the roar,' [1] but by the Churchmen, jealous of the rival paraphernalia of Rome, and ever prompt to invoke the aid of the secular arm, in the matter of Church-rates or otherwise.

> 'The measure,' he said, 'is nothing better than a sham. I believe the only effect of it can be an attempt to bolster up the ascendency so long maintained by the Church Establishment, an establishment, the noble Lord says, the most tolerant on earth. . . . I could show how a gentleman in a parish of this city enters, not bodily but by proxy, a meeting-house of the Society to which I belong, and annually strips it of its furniture—some forty chairs with tables, which year after year are removed to pay the minister of the most tolerant Church on earth.[2]

[1] *Greville* says, 'The dissenters have, I think, generally kept aloof.' November 21, 1850.

[2] For Church-rates.

'England shows symptoms of returning to Rome. But where are these symptoms? In the people or the clergy? Why the noble Lord's letter [the Durham Letter] tells us where it is. The noble Lord has discovered that that great institution, which was supposed to be the bulwark of Protestantism, turns out to be a huge manufactory of a national or home-made Popery.

'Not only here, but wherever they travel, these [Anglican] bishops and archbishops are surrounded with pomp and power. A bishop was sent lately to Jerusalem; and he did not travel like an ordinary man; he had a steam-frigate to himself called *The Devastation*. And when he arrived within a stone's throw, no doubt, of the house where an apostle lived, in the house of Simon the tanner, he landed under a salute of twenty-one guns.'

On May 12 Bright returned to the attack of the unfortunate Ecclesiastical Titles Bill and rent the imposture to rags.

'The Queen has not the power of making Roman Catholic bishops, and therefore the making of them by the only Power on earth that has authority to make them, is no invasion of the prerogative of the Crown.' 'I am not so presumptuous as to say to another Church that bishops are not necessary for that Church; and if bishops are necessary for the Anglican Church, who can say they are not necessary for the Church of Rome?' 'The whole matter is one of idea, of sentiment, of such fine material that it is impossible for an Act of Parliament to grapple with the case before us. I admit the insult and offensiveness of the language [of the Papal Bull]; it is repulsive to our feelings that such language should be employed. But, admitting all that, I am at a loss to discover how legislation can affect the question beneficially at all.

'The course in which the noble Lord has been so recklessly dragging us is fruitful in discord, hatred, religious animosities—it has separated Ireland from this country, has withdrawn her national sympathies from us, and has done an amount of mischief which the legislation of the next ten years cannot entirely, if at all, abate. The noble Lord has drawn up an indictment against eight millions of his countrymen; he has increased the power of the Pope over the Roman Catholics, for he has drawn closer the bonds between them and their Church and the head of their Church. The noble Lord has quoted

Queen Elizabeth and the great men of the Commonwealth, as though it were necessary now to adopt the principles which prevailed almost universally two hundred years ago. Does the noble Lord forget that we are the true ancients, that we stand on the shoulders of our forefathers and can see further ?'

In the autumn of 1851 Kossuth, the Hungarian patriot and exile, visited England, and while savagely attacked by the *Times*, received a great popular ovation which Palmerston, though Foreign Minister, endeavoured to patronise, and in which Cobden and Bright took leading parts. The following letter of Bright to Cobden (November 4, 1851) foreshadows the subsequent division of Radical feeling about the Crimean War:

'I am expected to be at the meeting in the Free Trade Hall and to speak. I am in a desperate puzzle what to do, but certainly if I speak, I shall go against any notion of *fighting* for Hungary or any other country.

'We had warm discussions last evening at the League rooms on these points—Robinson and others in favor of having a "tussle" with Russia *some time*, to put an end to Cossack domination, etc. I am very apprehensive that this Hungarian sympathy will breed a spirit which we have hoped was subsiding, and will tend to fill the people's heart with pride and self-conceit, and with a notion that it is our mission to become knights-errant in the cause of freedom to other nations, whilst we are forgetting how much we have to do at home. Besides, our friends seem to forget that until we have a revolution at home, our only instruments for regenerating other nations are a Cabinet purely aristocratic, and whose real love of liberty has never yet been proved. . . . I shall take another line at all hazards, and shall endeavor to show that by perfecting our own institutions, by promoting the intelligence, morality and health of our own country, and by treating all other nations in a just and generous and courteous manner, we shall do more for humanity than by commissioning Palmerston to regenerate Hungary by fleets in the Black Sea and the Baltic.'

After the passage of the Bill against 'Papal aggression,' and the consequent loss of the Irish vote, the days of the Whig

Government were numbered. For another year it stumbled through one crisis after another, to the inevitable catastrophe. In their weakness the Ministers tried to make terms with Bright and the Radicals by appointing a Cabinet Committee to draw up a new Reform Bill. It was Lord John Russell's doing, but Lord Palmerston, the real believer in the 'finality' of the Reform Act of 1832, grew so mutinous that the Government lost in unity as much as it gained in popularity by the new move. Bright himself gave Lord John every assistance. Throughout 1851 he was active in the House and country, organising petitions by members and constituents, and visiting the chief cities of Scotland and North England to stir up the 'leading citizens' to demand the ballot and the widest franchise that the Government could be encouraged to give. Everywhere it is his declared object to get the 'middle and working class to unite.' Cobden sat at home, a sceptical spectator of his friend's energy, patient of much exhortation and affectionate reproof.

(Bright to Cobden. Sept. 26, 1851.)

'Did you read Palmerston's speech at Tiverton? Could anything be more meagre? He studiously avoided touching upon the future, and gave no hope of anything but that the Whigs intended still to be our rulers. We must stir them up, if anything is to be done; and I confess I feel that some responsibility rests upon you and me in this matter. The time seems to me very important, and many great questions wait the solution of that which we are now approaching. Tell me what you think of all this, and *try to shake off your unbelief in political progress.* With you I shall work with hope, indeed with a certain faith; without you, I should have no spirit in any political action.'

(Oct. 24, 1851.) 'I agree with a good deal you say on the present condition of politics in this country, but by no means in your notion that we should do nothing till a popular cry forces us. In your speech after Lord John's promise of a measure of reform, you said most truly that reform was now become *the* "practical question." I think so too, and I am quite sure that, for the moment, we ought to devote ourselves entirely to this question, so far as opportunity will allow us. John Bull may be vain and stupid as he is, but we must remember that, in these exhibitions wherein he thus exhibits himself, the working classes are generally excluded, and the middle classes are only represented by the most snobbish among them.

'You write about the Land question, but what path is so easy to its solution as the procuring a Parliament which shall be really responsible to somebody, and not given up solely to the service of the private interests of a class? Did every M.P. represent a real and a free constituency, could we not discuss the Land question with a thousand times more effect in and out of the House?

'I am, therefore, satisfied that we are taking a right course. McLaren thought so distinctly. Our old friends will go with us—not every one—not the men who joined us when the [Corn Law] battle was won (though indeed the Whigs are well disposed, seeing their Chief has given the signal), but all those on whom we relied. You are living in Sussex—you see few people there—if there be a "ripple" you don't perceive it unless it is discernible in the *Times*, which is studiously keeping aloof from the question. I am mixing daily with the men whose services have been great in other times, and I see none of those reasons for melancholy which are set forth in your letter.'

The last days of the Whig Government were enlivened by open warfare between its two chiefs. The natural rivalry between Palmerston and Lord John, accentuated by the difference of opinion about Parliamentary Reform, came to a head at the close of the year. Palmerston as Foreign Secretary regarded himself as a power independent of the Cabinet, not bound to consult his colleagues before he acted, provided he could, after the event, justify himself before the House of Commons. In December 1851, misjudging for once popular opinion at home, and for once supporting a brutal act of despotic violence abroad, he hastened to express approval of Napoleon III.'s *coup d'état* without waiting for the leave of Queen or Cabinet. Lord John, strongly supported by the Queen, instantly dismissed him. This blow re-established the rule that the Foreign Minister must consult the Cabinet on important affairs. But it had not disposed of Palmerston, as Bright was sanguine enough to hope.

(To his sister, Mrs. McLaren. 12th month, 28, 1851.)

'Palmerston is at length got rid of. Cobden and I have found him out years ago, but many simpletons have fancied him a great friend of freedom abroad, though he never did anything for it at home; and that all his bustling diplomacy was a proof of England's influence on the Continent. Lord John has at last been obliged to eject him, as he should have done long since. His newspapers make a great noise, but I suspect he is finished now as an official, unless he joins Disraeli.

'Speaking of Disraeli hast thou read his character of Peel, in the *Times* of yesterday? I think it a very fair and a masterly picture of a remarkable man. Disraeli never denies any merit his opponents may possess; speaking of [W. J.] Fox to me one evening, he said: "We must go in to hear Fox; I have a great regard for Fox; Fox is a man of genius."'

(To Cobden. Jan. 3, 1852.)

'Your views of the Palmerston affair agree precisely with mine. The imposture was sure to explode, but we hardly expected Lord John to be the instrument to destroy it. The silly people who abused us so much in June 1850 [" Don Pacifico " debates] are desperately puzzled. When it was the "Whig Government" *versus* the "Manchester Party" we were a faction, etc., etc. Now it is Lord Palmerston *versus* Lord John, and the little man will beat the practised juggler in carrying with him the Whig opinion in the country; and now many persons who were almost savage against us conclude that the ex-Minister was a dangerous felon.

'I doubt if Lord John will meet Parliament, as he is— he must make a show of getting more power somewhere, and there seems only *Graham* and *you* for it; and I think more than one Cabinet will break down before Manchester is consulted. The *Times* speaks respectfully of us to-day in an article very damaging to the Government. I think they see that the concern must be changed and patched or rebuilt, and they are making ready for whatever may turn up. It is quite true that the "Woburn Bench"[1] in the House offers very little material for the salvation of a country, and Young Campbell is the only "promising young man" of that party. I feel a strong interest in what is going on, and *going to be*, for it seems to me that some of our predictions are approaching their fulfilment. The Whig section of the aristocracy does not produce men

[1] Woburn was the seat of the Duke of Bedford, head of the Russell family.

able to sustain a Cabinet as in past times; and *we* have succeeded in creating something like a party in the House and the country. . . . In former times Lord John might have patched up the concern by taking in Macaulay or Chas. Wood—but now, *with his present policy*, no man of any mark would join him from the more Liberal section of the House. I see no way to an effective Government but in a great change in the representation, and a far more Liberal policy; we may be a good way from this, but till it comes, we shall have Governments unable and unwilling to do anything real.'

Fourteen weary years were to pass before Bright saw his hopes of 'great change' fulfilled. The era of the Crimean War and of Palmerston *redivivus* was yet to intervene. On February 20, 1852, eight weeks after his dismissal from office, Palmerston showed that he was not dead by defeating Lord John on a Militia Bill, and so giving the death-blow to the Whig Government of which he had recently been a member. 'Now,' he said, 'I have had my tit for tat with John Russell.'

CHAPTER IX

THE DISRAELI INTERLUDE AND THE OBSEQUIES OF PROTECTION. THE WHIG-PEELITE COALITION AND THE 'MANCHESTER SCHOOL,' 1852-54

'The attitude of his mind was that of a solitary; reverential towards God (a very untheological deity), but by no means so towards any of God's creatures. He was very critical, and indisposed, easily, at all events, to recognise established reputations. Mobs of all sorts he hated as only a Radical can, but his particular detestation was a well-dressed mob.'—Mr. BIRRELL *at the John Bright Centenary.*

It was clear that the Whigs of the new generation were not strong enough in parliamentary talent or in popularity with the electors any longer to carry on the Government by themselves alone. But it was not so clear what party or union of parties could take their place. On the fall of Lord John Russell's Government, politicians were busy discussing every possible combination—Whig and Peelite ; Whig and Radical ; Whig, Peelite, and Radical ; Peelite and Tory ; while, as we shall presently see, Disraeli's oriental imagination conjured up a vision of the anti-Peelite Tories and the Manchester men sitting round a Cabinet table under his own suave management. For the present the anti-Peelite Tories, led by Lord Derby (late Stanley) in the Lords, and by Disraeli in the Commons, assumed office in March 1852, as caretakers till some stable combination emerged out of the political chaos.

The new Ministers postponed the General Election for as many months as they could, occupying the Treasury Bench under heavy pounding from John Bright, whose speeches when the Tories were in power were the delight of all sections of Whigs and Liberals. Again and again the challenge was issued—Is the new Government Protectionist or not? But the new Government had no intention of answering the question until a General Election had shown where the land lay. At length, in midsummer 1852, the appeal to the country was made, and resulted in a return of the same equally balanced parties and groups as in the former Parliament. To find any party strong enough to carry on the Government was as difficult as before. But at least Protection had been put out of its pain. It had once more been condemned even by the limited electorate of that period, and every one knew that the unenfranchised masses hated the memory of it more intensely every year, as Free Trade brought a fuller tide of prosperity to all.

Bright and Gibson were returned by substantial majorities for Manchester. Towards the close of the elections Bright wrote to Villiers (July 15, 1852):

> 'With the exception of Liverpool, the great constituencies are against the Derby gang, and Liverpool is a place corrupted by the old *protections*, infested with Orangeism, and afflicted with a large number of old freemen upon its register. Liverpool is too monstrous a thing to affect public opinion except adversely to its own course.
>
> '"After Lord Derby, the deluge," says Lord Maidstone, and so think many of the timid of the aristocratic and very rich classes. The "deluge" means *Manchester*, it is said—a sort of political waterspout which is to sweep away all that Peer and Parson hold dear. I don't think the time is come yet for great changes, and I hope all our changes may be gradual and so made as to bring little ill, and to carry opinion thoroughly with them. But no Government can live unless it is placed more in harmony with public opinion. Derby cannot live—Russell could not live. The County representation must be made more popular, and the people let in to share it, and the Borough representation must be given to the population. Then, and not till then, we may see an administration able and willing to make many reforms.
>
> 'At present no Government dare say a word to the Church—that overgrown and monstrous abuse assumes airs as if it were not an abuse. It is a *wen* upon the head and pretends to be the *head*, and no administration is strong enough to say a word against it. With 14,000 Dissenting Chapels in England and Wales, with two-thirds of Scotland in dissenting ranks, with five-sixths of Ireland hostile to the Church, how comes it that this scandalous abuse puts on the character of a national and useful institution? Simply because it has the Crown and the Peers on its side by tradition and the constitution,

and has gained great power in the Commons thro' our defective representation. Let the representation be amended, and then the Church will be more humble, and will submit, of necessity, to be overhauled as one of the departments of the State.'

John Bright's language against the 'political' Church is strong, but his forecast was fulfilled. Until the working men were enfranchised, the Churchmen clung to the three unjust privileges of which chiefly he complained—the Irish Church establishment, Church-rates, and the exclusion of dissenters from their share in the Universities. Within a few years of the enfranchisement of the working men (1867), the clergy were compelled to surrender every one of these monopolies, and thenceforth Bright's language about them became more moderate. But so long as the aristocratic régime lasted, whether Whigs or Tories were in office, dissenters were called on, as Bright said, 'to hope all things, to believe all things, and to endure all things.' The particular outrage that stirred him to make this famous quotation was that in 1854 Gladstone introduced a Bill to 'reform' Oxford without proposing to admit any except Churchmen to share the studies of the place.

'You do not exclude us,' said Bright, 'when you send your tax-gatherers round, or when you ask for the performance of the duties of citizenship; you do not exclude us from the statistical tables of your population, of your industry, of your wealth, or of your renown. You take all your population in and say: "This is a great and united people which are called the British people"; and you declare in your speeches and perorations that you are proud to rule over such a nation. But when you come to the question of education in the institution which you call National Universities, then you insult one-half of the population of the Country.'

Owing to Bright's protests, dissenters were graciously permitted to matriculate at Oxford (1854), but not till 1871 were they admitted to Fellowships or teaching posts. At Cambridge they had long before been allowed to matriculate, but could not take Fellowships until 1871. The Church-rate war still continued in many parishes; Lord John Russell, in a high Tory speech, refused in 1854 to abolish Church-rates, which lasted till 1868.

In these circumstances the signs and symbols of Churchmanship always reminded John Bright of the wrongs that his co-religionists were daily undergoing, and he was not to be disarmed by the smooth words and courteous manners of the denizens of Barchester, so long as in practice they refused him religious equality: 'I was at the Free Library opening last Thursday,' he writes to Cobden in 1852. 'The speeches were good, less snobbing than I looked for. I was introduced to the "Right Reverend Prelate." I can't see the use or the beauty of the apron he wears. But you will think I am prejudiced, which is probably true.' And it was a lifelong puzzle to him how 'people who can tell us so much about the next world should know so little about the present.'

The same year he writes: 'Puseyism cannot be killed off. It is too natural to man, and above all to man as priest.' He thought that quarrels between Evangelical and Puseyite ought to lead, not to 'Protestant' legislation, but to the disestablishment of 'the old political machine which has made a pretence of being a Christian Church.'

After the General Election of 1852, Bright took his holiday amid the Highland scenery that he loved. On August 26 he writes to Cobden:

> 'I met Lord John Russell at Callander. Passing the lodge at the entrance to his house, I left my card and went on to Loch Katrine, and coming back towards Callander and changing horses to go up to Loch Earnhead, we met the little man jogging along on his pony, and looking as well satisfied with himself as when he is insulting the Catholics in the House of Commons. We had some chat for ten minutes; he said he had a letter from Parker, who calculated a majority of 18 or 20 against the [Derby] Government. Lord John thought they could not go on, and I asked him if he did not think Lord Derby's successor would be in just the same predicament, and everybody else till we had a better representation? He said, "Yes, I recollect what you said about that some time ago." I told him I thought the atmosphere of the North was doing him good, and "I hoped it would brace up his politics as well as his health." He had called at the Hotel to ask us to go and dine with him, but we were on our way, and therefore could not accept the invitation.'

Bright was on more friendly terms with Lord John than

with the other Whig leaders. Palmerston could not even be civil to him. But Lord John was always ready to listen to him in private, or to correspond to any extent. Bright was at this time engaged in trying to convert him to the principle of the ballot in a series of argued letters, but in vain. Speaking in the House one day he advised Lord John to be bolder, and to lay hold of questions 'with a larger grasp.'

> 'In the cloak-room or cloisters,' he writes, 'I met Lord John on leaving the House. He said to me: "Mr. Bright, when you get a man with the grasp you speak of, the whole thing will go to pieces.' I told him we were always very civil off the stage, but in the House I thought he picked more quarrels with me than with anybody else, to which he replied laughing, "I think it is so, yes, I think it is so."'

When the Derby-Disraeli Government met the House in the autumn after the General Election of 1852, they had fully determined that they must abandon Protection. But they were naturally unwilling to go through a public eating of the leek. However, the Manchester School decided to bring up a strongly worded Free Trade Resolution; the Government must either accept it or go out. On September 7, 1852, Bright writes to Cobden:

> 'It seems to me that the best mode will be, to move the insertion of a paragraph in the address, stating the admirable success of the Free Trade policy as commenced in 1842, and affirming the propriety of maintaining it unimpaired. This will bring the Government to a point—there will be no escape, and if there be any fiery zealots of the old faith in the new Parliament we shall see how the impostors now in office can manage with them. After all, I don't feel disposed to aid in keeping Derby in, for the sake of keeping Russell out.'

This course was adopted, and Villiers, strongly backed by Cobden and Bright, moved that Corn Law Repeal had been a 'just, wise and beneficial' measure. These 'three odious epithets,' as Disraeli called them, the Ministers had not the will to accept nor the votes to reject. They must have fallen then and there had not Palmerston come to their rescue. He moved an amendment approving of Free Trade in terms to which the ex-Protectionists could agree without dishonouring their own past. They were saved for yet a few weeks.

Their fall came in December over Disraeli's Budget, when Gladstone's magnificent assault upon it first gave evidence that he was to be the greatest financier of the age, and Disraeli's historic rival. The defeat of the Budget was expected by the Chancellor of the Exchequer for at least twenty-four hours before it occurred, and on the eve of the fatal division he sent for Bright and held with him a strange colloquy. Bright, before he went to bed, wrote down what he remembered of the interview at greater length than his record of any other event in the forty years during which he kept a journal. But the interest that he felt was in Disraeli's personality, and did not arise from any serious thoughts of accepting the proffered welcome into the bosom of the Conservative party.[1]

Journal. 'Dec. 15, 1852. The debate on Mr. Disraeli's Budget is now exciting great attention. . . . He proposes to take off half the Malt Tax; this is the chief proposition of his Budget and that on which his fate will turn. This evening about nine o'clock I received a note whilst at the Reform Club from the Chancellor of the Exchequer [Disraeli] asking me to call at Grosvenor Gate to see him; this was rather in consequence of a conversation I had with him yesterday in the lobby of the House. I waited upon him soon after 10 o'clock, found him near the top of the house, in his morning gown, surrounded by books, pictures, mirrors, etc. I told him I felt in a difficult situation, seeing how entirely opposed we had been in political life. He said he would speak without reserve, as he thought that, however opposed, there had been a good deal of free conversation and he thought even some sympathy between us. He then entered on the desperate condition of their affairs, and the almost certainty of their defeat on the following night, spoke of that *infernal question,* the question of Protection; said his difficulty had been his and their promises to the country party and farmers, local burdens and now Malt Tax. He said he only touched Malt Tax because could not touch Tea duties as proposed without touching malt—was forced to try something for the farmers and to venture on malt; he had not supposed

[1] In Lord Morley's *Cobden* (end of chapter iv. of vol. ii.) the story of this interview is hinted at, no doubt from oral information received from Bright. More than a year before this interview Bright had noted: 'Amusing conversation with Disraeli in the dining-room. He spoke of the "duty of destroying the red-tapists," and urged that if the Whigs went out we should prevent their "leading the Opposition," which was our only chance of doing away their sham party.'

the opposition would be so great. If he could get a vote, a majority of *one* only, his honor would be saved and he would give up House Tax and Malt, and remodel his scheme.'

He then proceeded to lay before the Liberal economist the attractive prospect of Tory 'retrenchment.'

'He spoke of what he was proposing to do in reforming departments, of Lord Chandos's business talents in reforming Irish offices and saving money at the Horse Guards, that he intended a thorough examination by a Commission into management of dockyards, etc., and would save a very large sum. Speaking of expenditure he mentioned those *damned defences*,[1] and said he had cut and slashed them to bring the estimates for them to a more moderate sum. He entered into an examination of all our taxes and stated his views with regard to future changes and remissions.

'He spoke of his party, how well they had followed him, how faithfully they were prepared to support him. There was no jealousy—Cabinet friendly and disposed to act liberally—and he thought his party "having stood so much already" would stand a good deal more if necessary. He then adverted to his wish to get rid of the old stagers and old "red tapists" and said he could not see why we, that is Cobden, myself and Gibson—our section—should not some day be with him in a cabinet; not within 24 hours, but before long: it was quite possible and not difficult.

'I laughed at this as impossible and partly at the serious face he maintained as he explained his views. I objected that, putting aside the immorality of such changes, the constituencies would not permit it. "Oh," he said, "a man of genius and power may do anything with a large constituency; I think I could represent Manchester, and be a very popular member." I assured him he was greatly mistaken in supposing the Manchester people would be trifled with, and I asked, "How is it possible for you and us to work together?" He said we much mistook them. I said they must change their name and repudiate all their antecedents before we could ever act with them. He said there was scarcely one member of their Cabinet who would

[1] This expression, coming from Disraeli's mouth, tickled Bright so much that we find him using it, in inverted commas, in his subsequent correspondence with Cobden on questions of national economy.

not at once retire to make room for any gentlemen who would be likely to give them strength.

'He spoke of the new Administration, admitting that his defeat was certain, asked if I thought Cobden and myself were included in it, and said: "If you are included in it, or are likely to be, if you see your own game in what is going to be done, then may God help you forward, my dear Bright, and no man will be more delighted than I shall be to witness your success." He said no man knew what he had struggled against and overcome; he had been a Minister and was now about to be beaten. He had always felt the insecurity of their position, and had not removed to Downing Street on that account. He would not keep office or try to cling to it if they could not have *power*, and it was clear they had not the numbers with them to enable them to go on, and it was doubtful if they could live till Easter if they now escaped.

'I was with him from 10 to half-past 11 o'clock, and the above is a sketch of the conversation that took place. This remarkable man is ambitious, most able, and without prejudices. He conceives it right to strive for a great career with such principles as are in vogue in his age and country—says the politics and principles to suit England must be of the "English type," but having obtained power, would use it to found a great reputation on great services rendered to the country. He seems unable to comprehend the morality of our political course, and on this ground probably was induced to seek the interview with me.[1]

'Dec. 16. The debate closed this evening. Disraeli rose at 10 and spoke till near 1 o'clock—he fought for his life, and never man fought more desperately or with more skill and power. This speech was his greatest speech; he was in earnest; argument, satire, sarcasm, invective, all were abundant and of the first class. His peroration was short, to the point, and forcible; but the "numbers," as he said to me yesterday, were against him. Gladstone made a great speech in reply, only part of which I heard. The division gave 305 to 286. Government beaten and House adjourned to Monday.

'Dec. 17. Lord Derby gone to Osborne to resign.'

If Peel's spirit, like Cæsar's, was 'ranging for revenge,' it might

[1] It was probably in this interview that Disraeli said to Bright, 'We come here for Fame.' See p. 371 below. In 1854 Disraeli again suggested that Bright should become a Tory cabinet minister, see p. 242 below.

have been satisfied with this Philippi. The party that had begun its separate existence, 'signed in his spoil, and crimsoned in his lethe,' had fallen low enough. Solely because they would not accept Free Trade at Peel's hands with a good grace, the Conservatives had remained out of office for six years. And now that they themselves had perforce accepted Free Trade, they were hurled from power again for another indefinite period, because Peel's friends, the able men in whom the old party had been so rich, refused to be reconciled with the man who had made a trade of mangling their beloved chief. The enduring resentment of Peel's friends against Disraeli, that proved so important an element in the evolution of our political parties, was largely due to a belief, right or wrong, expressed by Sir James Graham to Bright more than ten years after the repeal of the Corn Laws, that 'Peel was unfortunately too sensitive, and Disraeli found this out and attacked him accordingly, without hating Peel, but as a way to his own elevation.' [Bright's journal, Jan. 15, 1857.]

It was to the Whigs that the Peelites in 1852 transferred the favour of their alliance, and the coalition Government was formed under Aberdeen. The day after Derby's resignation Bright met one of the Peelite leaders.

> 'Dec. 18. This morning I walked through the park to the club; met Sir James Graham, passing through St. James' Palace. I told him he knew our course—a good Government, acting honestly and doing well, would have our support; we should not depart from our independent line of action. He said: "I don't approve of that. I think your position in the House and the country, your popularity, the large party you influence, and your great public services, which I would be the first to recognise, all entitle you to a share in the Government, and I shall think no Government properly constituted in which you have not a part. I think it a most unsound principle that men who so greatly influence opinion should not bear a portion of the responsibilities of the executive Government; now that is my opinion." '

It was an opinion that Bright did not share. He believed that his part of honest critic was of more value to the nation than his services as a Minister could be. Till the yet distant time came round when a Government could be formed to carry Radical measures, he had no intention of accepting office even if it were offered. 'Lord Aberdeen,' he wrote to his wife on the day Lord Derby resigned, 'is to form the new Government with Peelites and Whigs. Cobden would not accept any office on any conditions, and I am still less likely than he is to be asked, or to accept if I was asked.'

> *Journal.* 'Dec. 22, 1852. Hayter came to me with message from Lord John Russell to Cobden and me, apologising in some sort for our being left out. If offered anything it should be in the Cabinet, but the difficulties insuperable now; high opinion of me—honest, consistent, etc., and hoped we should comprehend the difficulties without supposing him unmindful of our claims, all which, of course, I fully understand. I told him what we want is not office for ourselves but for men and principles such as we value, that our future course would be like our past, clear and resolute, not factious, but pursuing our own objects, etc. Saw Villiers, evidently surprised and not well pleased with things rumored. I advised him to leave the Whigs and go with us; we were the party and had the policy and principles and our time would come.

Villiers, however, contrary to Bright's advice, deigned to accept an office outside the Cabinet. Their fellow-radical Molesworth was admitted into the Cabinet itself, where in his isolation he soon took on the colour of his surroundings, and became ere long a warm supporter of the Crimean War. For the rest, Aberdeen's coalition Ministry consisted of all the most famous Peelites and Whigs sitting together under the mild Premier of whom it was not easy to be jealous. Gladstone was at the Exchequer, the place that he had won from Disraeli at the sword's point, and Gladstone's finance was destined to be the one great thing accomplished for the country by this unfortunate Ministry of All the Talents.

The new Cabinet was scarcely a week old before Bright began to press it to produce its Reform Bill; and again the unwilling Cobden was summoned to this fray.

(To Cobden, January 3, 1853.)

> 'I think I told you that I had written to Lord John Russell and that I had referred to the Reform question, urging that the more real and substantial the measure now to be carried the more conservative it would be found to have been twenty years hence. I now send you Lord John's reply, from which I gather that there is a party in the Government that will not move on unless some

pressure is applied, and that Lord John wishes the pressure not to be withheld.'

(January 5.) 'There will be a great attempt on the part of moderate Tories and Whigs, and timid men who call themselves neither Tories nor Whigs, and of the Press, to put down any independent action on the part of the Radicals. We shall be advised to trust everything to men of "long tried Statesmanship," to "a combination of talent," to a "strong Government," etc. And if we do trust everything to them, we shall be sold as usual. Our only chance of being of service is to pursue our old course—teach the people what is right, ask for what is right—and we shall move towards it, slowly it may be, but not less certainly than heretofore. Lancashire and West Riding, with all our backwardness and snobbery have done something, and may do more, and on you and me depends to a large extent what course a large party in these districts shall take.'

Cobden was willing indeed to agitate against the anti-French cry which endangered the peace of the country in 1853; he fought it manfully and not unsuccessfully, until the mysterious wisdom of our Foreign Office suddenly discovered that the 'balance of power' required us to bestir ourselves—no longer, as had hitherto been preached, against France—but as the ally of France against Russia. Cobden led the 'Peace' agitation, in opposition first to the French, and then to the Russian panic; but he would not give Bright the active help that the Franchise question demanded. He began by refusing to come to Manchester to a meeting of representative men to discuss Reform. Bright writes in reply (January 14, 1853):

'With regard to the meeting, I think you have rarely been more clearly in the wrong. . . . Indeed I think your own arguments overthrow you. The want of self-respect so often manifested by the middle classes and the retrograde nature of the composition of the new Government seem to me most cogent reasons why the meeting should be held. If the middle classes are in any degree improving, and if any considerable portion of them have *any* self-respect, it is much owing to the Free Trade discussion of the last twelve years; and what can tend so much to increase it as the teaching of men who *have* a self-respect, and who wish to inculcate the same feeling upon others? And surely if the new Government is not such as we like, unless we intend to lay down our arms, we are especially bound to show that we are alive and that we intend still to maintain our principles and our independent position in and out of Parliament. The Government are vaguely for Reform, the question is when? and how much? They are not for the Ballot, and Lord John and Graham argue against it as men do who are driven to their wits' end for something like an argument.

'The Government Press write as if *we* were "snuffed out," because Molesworth and Villiers are in the Government and we are omitted. I don't advise abdication on our part; we have worked too hard, and are too much in earnest to be justified in giving up precisely when we seem most to be wanted. Depend upon it, our Parliamentary influence is not all gained in Parliament, nor is our influence in the country all gained in the country; the one acts upon the other. The session and the recess are alike made fruitful in influence and in power to advance our views. I believe nothing would please our opponents more than we should make no sign, and seem to expire from want of earnestness to defend our principles and position.

'You are writing for Peace and are doing well, but the cause of progress generally is not less hopeful than that of peace. Our meeting would show us armed at all points, it would bind our friends together, and excite a greater vigilance on the part of the public as to the events of the coming session.

'*Personally* I would wish to have no meeting; but *personally* I would not be in public life. I would rather see more after my own interests and the interests of my children. But we are on the rails and must move on. We have work and must do it.'

Cobden, however, still refused to come to the meeting, and Bright noted in his journal:

'I think him entirely wrong and acting as if he were disposed to "abdicate" as a political leader. I am greatly annoyed at this difficulty, for it tends to show that Cobden is rather shrinking from maintaining the fight in which he has been so long engaged.'

Bright perforce held the meeting without his friend, and 'spoke on the Ballot, exhibiting the mode of voting in

Massachusetts, U.S.; the explanation produced a good effect.' Again the northern Liberals were set to work petitioning the Government for Reform.

Under pressure from Bright's agitation, the Cabinet permitted Lord John, after many delays, to produce his Reform Bill in February 1854. The Bill, though far short of the Household Suffrage carried in 1867, would have enfranchised some more of the middle classes and a section at least of the working men. Bright thought the scheme of redistribution of seats bad, but regarded the Franchise proposals as a useful half-way measure. They were, however, only too extensive, in the eyes of Lord Palmerston and others on the Government side. After being postponed again and again, the Reform project was finally dropped when the war with Russia proved a theme more attractive to so-called Liberals. 'The Glasgow war party are barely civil to us peace men,' Bright wrote to Cobden as early as November 1853; 'what a brainless lot they are, to run after everything but their own direct interests. Mrs. Jellyby in *Bleak House* is their great original, putting everything right at "Borrioboola Gha," and neglecting everything at home.' So the cause of Reform slept again for another period of years.

Bright attributed both the loss of the Reform Bill and the approaching war with Russia to the presence of the anti-Liberal Lord Palmerston in a Cabinet supposed to represent the Liberal interest.

(Jan. 12, 1854. To Villiers.)

> 'What a miserable policy it is to keep Palmerston on our side of the House. In his own place, on the other side, he would be no more capable of harm than any other clever fellow having a bad case and a party not supported by public opinion. Sitting with you [Villiers was on the Treasury Bench] he uses both sides for his purposes; it would be cheap to break up our Government to be fairly rid of him.'

One advantage was snatched for the public by Cobden and Bright, in spite of the oncoming flood of war and reaction. There was no cause that the two had more at heart than the removal of what were called the 'taxes on knowledge.' These were the taxes that made newspapers dear. They consisted of an excise duty on paper; a tax of one shilling and sixpence on every advertisement however short; and a newspaper stamp of a penny on each sheet. The combined effect of these three taxes was that the daily paper remained a luxury placed by law beyond the means of the working man and the clerk. There was no penny press, no daily provincial paper, and no daily organ of democracy such as Cobden and Bright longed to see started. The immense political influence of their enemy the *Times* was largely due to the want of competition resulting from these taxes.[1] Not only the *Times*, but the *Daily News* and *Morning Post* cost fivepence a copy. Though Bright's influence was at work in more than one provincial weekly, he had as yet no London organ and no daily paper.

Gladstone's Budgets under the Aberdeen Ministry swept away more and more of the crumbling relics of Protection, but the aristocratic Cabinet which he served, though strong for Free Trade, had no great wish to see a democratic press. The 'taxes on knowledge' would not, therefore, have been removed but for the wearisome iteration and finally the positive rebellion of Cobden and Bright. The critical stage in the affair is succinctly told in Bright's journal for 1853 :

> 'April 14. "Taxes on knowledge" discussed. Majority against the Government ; resolution to repeal advertisement duty carried. Our men frightened when they heard Disraeli was going to vote with us ! Afraid to carry their object, fearing to hurt a Government which refuses them this trifle !
>
> 'April 15. Had some talk with Sir Charles Wood [Cabinet Minister] on the vote of the preceding night, and the position of the Government and our section. I told him plainly that a large party could not be kept together without some respect being shown to every influential section of it. We wished the press to be free from taxes and no consideration of convenience to a Government would prevent our insisting upon it.
>
> 'July 14. Nothing settled yet about the advertisement duty. I have given some members of the Government to understand that we shall consider their refusal of our wishes as a proof of their desire to repudiate us, and as a declaration of war. And so it will be, and so we shall treat it.
>
> 'July 20. Mr. Gladstone announced his intention entirely

[1] 'In the early 'fifties the *Times* had an average circulation of about 60,000, nearly thrice as much as that of the *Morning Advertiser*, the *Daily News*, the *Morning Herald*, the *Morning Post*, the *Morning Chronicle*, and the *Public Ledger* all massed together.'—*English Newspapers*, H. R. Fox Bourne, vol. ii. p. 224.

to repeal the advertisement duty. So our labor has not been in vain. This is an important step towards a free press.'

Thus the advertisement duty disappeared in 1853, and two years later the newspaper stamp was abolished. From that era dates the beginning of the daily provincial press and of newspapers for the common people. In 1856 a penny journal, the *Morning Star*, came out under the editorship of Samuel Lucas, who was brother-in-law to Bright, and consulted him as to the policy of the paper on big questions. The work of freeing the press was completed in 1860-61, when the excise duty on paper was repealed, after a famous battle with the Lords.

CHAPTER X

THE CRIMEAN WAR

'Alliances are dangerous things. It is an alliance with Turkey that has drawn us into this war. I would not advise alliances with any nation, but I would cultivate friendship with all nations.'

'If this phrase of the "balance of power," the meaning of which nobody can exactly make out, is to be brought in on every occasion to stimulate this country to war, there is an end to all hope of permanent peace.'—Bright *in the House of Commons*, March 31, 1854.

It is an old, wise saying that a man's real character can be judged by his conduct when in love. But perhaps the character of a public man can best be judged when he is opposed to some violent and almost universal passion of his fellow-countrymen. Then will be seen the stuff of which he is made. He may stifle his conscience and take the popular side; or he may retire for awhile from public life; or he may find courage to face the mob by lashing himself into a frenzy of impotent rage, saying everything that will sting, and scorning to say anything that might persuade. But if he aspires to preserve his dignity, both to himself and to the world, if he hopes to emerge when the times change with reputation and influence increased, if at the height of his unpopularity he would fain say words that shall impinge even on the heated brains of the angry multitude, and leave there an impress that shall be permanent when passion has cooled, then he should take for his example the conduct and speeches of John Bright during the Crimean War.

The friendship of Cobden and Bright dated from their share in a vast popularity ending in a world-famous triumph. It was now tested and ennobled by the ordeal of a popular hatred proportioned to their former eminence. Because their two names had become a national synonym for the blessing of plentiful bread, they were now once more joined for the nation's curse that is the lot of the peace-lover in time of war. They were the 'traitors,' they were the 'Russians'; Bright was burnt in effigy; he and his friend were caricatured and vilified in the newspapers that had so often praised them; they were abused in the halls of meeting that had resounded with the thunder of their League. The Tory papers joined in the hue and cry, and their old enemies rejoiced to witness the humiliation of the calico-printer and the cotton-spinner who had dictated terms to the gentlemen of England. When the Conservative is unpopular, he can retire to the clubs and drawing-rooms of the powerful society to which he belongs, and speak there in scorn of the vagaries of the mob, whom in theory he always despises, however much in practice he may play the wooer. But when the Radical is unpopular he is naked to the blast. He may have domestic, but he has no social support or consolation; and he well knows that he is torn by his own hounds, turned out of his own temple.

After another generation of men had passed away, on the occasion of Bright's death, Mr. Gladstone delivered his eulogy in the House of Commons, and chose out for special praise his action during the Crimean War. Cobden and Bright, he said,

> 'had lived upon the confidence, the approval, the applause of the people, and the work of their lives had been to propel the life of public sentiment. Suddenly they came upon a great occasion on which they differed from the majority of their countrymen. At that time it was that, although we had known much of Mr. Bright, we learned something more. We had known his great mental gifts and powers. We had known his courage and consistency. We had known his splendid eloquence, which then was and afterwards came to be acknowledged as the loftiest which had sounded within these walls for generations. But we had not till then known how high the moral tone of these popular leaders had been elevated, and we had not known of the splendid examples they could set to the whole of their contemporaries, and to coming generations, of a readiness to part with all the sympathies and with all the support they had held so dear for the sake of right and conscientious conviction.'

Never were two men less egoistic in receipt of praise or blame. In Bright's private letters during the Crimean War, even in those to his wife and sister, and in his journal where he wrote his inmost thoughts, there is to be found no complaint, scarcely indeed a mention, of the bitter things daily said and written against him. In what he writes at this period there is always sorrow, and sometimes gloom, but it is grave regret at the public delusion and the ministerial crime; he does not seem to feel the injuries that concern himself. For these Bright had the thickest of skins. He was a prize-fighter who could 'take punishment' as well as give it. 'The goad of personal pain' never pricked him to an outcry, still less to a faltering or a desperate step. But in his letters and in his journal he constantly records his gratitude to old friends and old enemies, who came to him, like Nicodemus by night, to tell him they agreed with him against the world;[1] and he is always touched by the tolerance of the House of Commons that crowded in to hear with rapt attention his dirges over the peace they had broken, and his philippics against their idols on the Treasury Bench. Thus under a terrible strain he kept his mind healthy and his temper clear; indeed, it was on this painful question of the Crimea that his oratory reached its highest dignity and perfection. But though he showed complete self-mastery, he suffered so much from the spectacle of his country's self-inflicted woes, that just before the return of peace his health suddenly and totally gave way.

To attack the justice and wisdom of a popular war while it is still in progress requires more courage than any other act in a political society that has outgrown the assassin's dagger and the executioner's block. And it requires not only most courage but most power and skill. To perform it well is not only the rarest but one of the most valuable of public services, because to arraign an unjust and unwise war is the only way to prevent another. Bright and Cobden, by speaking out so that they were heard against the Crimean War, while it was yet in progress, were believed when it was over. In this way they did much to prevent England from taking part in the wars of the next twenty years, in every one of which she had as much concern as in the Eastern question of 1854. Had it not been for the lesson which Bright now began to teach in circumstances so unpleasant to himself, it is not improbable that we should have fought for Austria against France in 1859, or for the slave-owners against the North in 1861, or for Denmark against Germany in 1864, or again for Turkey against Russia in 1878. And if we had entered into any one of these wars, or into the

[1] *E.g.* to his sister Mrs. McLaren, 11th Month, 14, 1854:

'I daresay thou hast seen my letter on the war [to Absalom Watkin]. It has made a wonderful row among the newspapers, and with the gossips in Manchester. But it is true and unanswerable. I have had perhaps fifty letters during the week past, approving of it, six at least from clergymen of the Church of England, all of whom were strangers to me!'

Franco-German War of 1870, very little more would have been heard of the famous 'Victorian prosperity.'

The service that can be rendered by a politician of genius who, eschewing more popular and lucrative functions, will set himself to create opinion in favour of peace, cannot well be overestimated, for every country is in the hands of statesmen and journalists in whom the old leaven of Palmerston and his like is all too slowly dying, while the penalties for actual war are increasing at the accelerated pace of all modern evolution. Such a service was rendered by John Bright. He showed the world how a war can be patriotically denounced, with permanent effects upon opinion in favour of keeping peace. It is indeed no easy art. If he had taken high 'Quaker' ground, condemning all war, he would have accomplished little. But he never denied the abstract right to take up arms on good occasion, and shortly afterwards proved his good faith by supporting the suppression of the Indian Mutiny and of the slave-owners' secession in America. On the Crimean question he met the wise men of the Foreign Office and of the Treasury Bench on their own ground, and routed them on their own dispatches as reported in their own Blue Books. He showed them, in the mysteries of which they claimed to be high priests, to be the muddlers that such lofty claimants often are. He exposed the wordy superstitions of the Foreign Office for which England gave 30,000 gallant lives of her own, and sacrificed half a million lives of men of other nations, and brought misery and starvation once more to the doors of our people at home. Only the union of a clear understanding of the facts and issues with an oratory as dignified as it was telling in its emotional effects, could have driven home that most needful lesson to the rulers and people of Britain, for a while.[1]

In the early months of 1853 Prince Menschikoff, on special mission to Constantinople, raised the question of the status of the Greek Church in Turkey. Lord Stratford de Redcliffe, the British Minister to the Porte, acting without express authority

[1] During the Indian Mutiny, September 1857, Bright wrote to Joseph Sturge: 'Does our friend Southall think our Government should rest quiet, and allow every Englishman in India to be murdered. I don't think so. They must act on their principles, seeing that they admit no others. I have never advocated the extreme non-resistance principle in public or in private. I don't know whether I would logically maintain it. I opposed the Crimean War as contrary to the national interests and the principles professed and avowed by the nation, and on no other ground. It was because my arguments could not be met that I was charged with being for "peace at any price," and by this our opposition to the war was much damaged.'

from home, induced the Sultan to reject the Russian proposals. Britain thereby became a principal to this remote quarrel and took the Turkish Empire under her shield. France, the rival of Russia for the Protectorate of Christians in Turkey, made common cause with England. In July a proposed settlement of the points in dispute between Russia and Turkey, called 'the Vienna note,' was presented to the two parties concerned by England, France, Austria, and Prussia. Russia at once accepted these terms, but Turkey refused them. Her refusal of the settlement proposed to her by Great Britain was secretly prompted by the British Ambassador, Lord Stratford de Redcliffe, more warlike than the Cabinet he pretended to serve. Even his apologist, Kinglake, admits that he could not 'hide his real thoughts' about the Vienna note 'from the Turkish ministers.'

Now that Russia had accepted and Turkey refused the British terms, it was our plain duty either to compel Turkey to come into line or else to leave her to face the consequences alone. But 'alliances' do not permit either justice or expediency to stand in the way of support to the 'ally.' Our first step should have been the withdrawal of Lord Stratford; and if Lord Aberdeen had been master in the Cabinet that bears his name, this would have been done. But the withdrawal of Stratford would have led to the resignation of Palmerston and Russell, and broken up the Government. The Sultan, justly confident that whatever he did France and England would support him in the end, rejected their advice and defied Russia. The Russians had already occupied the Danubian 'Principalities,' Moldavia and Wallachia, which enjoyed an independent status, under Russian protection, beneath the suzerainty of the Porte. Turkey declared war. But serious operations did not commence, and efforts to restore peace were continued by the Powers until, on November 30, 1853, the Russian fleet in the Black Sea destroyed a Turkish squadron in the harbour of Sinope. It was an operation similar to the equally one-sided battle of Navarino a generation before, and if France and England had not on this later occasion espoused the Moslem cause, the battle of Sinope would, like the battle of Navarino, have speedily led to the liberation of large Christian populations from the Turkish yoke.[1] But on this second and less

[1] The proposals of the Czar Nicholas to England in the first weeks of 1853, had been that the 'sick man's' property should be divided up; that England might if she wished take Egypt, and that Servia, Bulgaria, and the other provinces of European Turkey should be erected into independent principalities. The proposals sound like a prophecy after the event! Yet we fought

happy occasion, the British public chose to call the affair 'the massacre of Sinope,' and denounced the Russians as savages for doing, after war had been proclaimed, what we had done at Copenhagen in time of peace—destroying a fleet at anchor under the guns of a fortress. The news of the 'massacre of Sinope' had the same effect in England as the news of the explosion of the Maine had in America many years later. War fever seized the nation. The press, hitherto by no means unanimous for war, raised a fierce outcry against Aberdeen for trying any longer to preserve peace. The divided Cabinet could scarcely have held out against the storm, even if its strongest members had been the peace advocates. In March 1854 England and France were formally at war with Russia.

The negotiations which had led to this catastrophe were analysed by John Bright in his famous 'letter to Mr. Absalom Watkin,' who had defended the war by an appeal to the law of nations as expounded by *Vattel*. Bright's letter was published in the *Times* on November 3, 1854.

> 'The question of this present war is in two parts—first, was it necessary for us to interfere by arms in a dispute between the Russians and the Turks? and secondly, having determined to interfere, under certain circumstances, why was not the whole question terminated when Russia accepted the Vienna note? The seat of war is 3000 miles away from us. We had not been attacked—not even insulted in any way. Two independent Governments had a dispute, and we thrust ourselves into the quarrel. That there was some ground for the dispute is admitted by the four Powers in the proposition of the Vienna note. But for the English Minister at Constantinople and the Cabinet at home, the dispute would have settled itself, and the last note of Prince Menschikoff would have been accepted, and no human being can point out any material difference between that note and the Vienna note, afterwards agreed upon and recommended by the Governments of England, France, Austria, and Prussia. But our Government would not allow the dispute to be settled. Lord Stratford de Redcliffe held private interviews with the Sultan—did

one war, and nearly fought another, to prevent any such settlement. For the secret agreement of 1844 between Russia and Great Britain, to act together with regard to the future of Turkey, see the *Russian Review*, July and November 1912. The policy which the Russian Government thought to be implicit in this agreement was not repudiated by our Ministers until 1853.

his utmost to alarm him—insisted on his rejection of all terms of accommodation with Russia, and promised him the armed assistance of England if war should arise.

'The Turks rejected the Russian note, and the Russians crossed the Pruth, occupying the Principalities as a "material guarantee." I do not defend this act of Russia: it has always appeared to me impolitic and immoral; but I think it likely it could be well defended out of *Vattel*, and it is at least as justifiable as the conduct of Lord John Russell and Lord Palmerston in 1850, when they sent ten or twelve ships of war to the Piræus, menacing the town with a bombardment if the dishonest pecuniary claim made by Don Pacifico were not at once satisfied.

'But the passage of the Pruth was declared by England and France and Turkey not to be a *casus belli*. Negotiations were commenced at Vienna, and the celebrated Vienna note was drawn up. This note had its origin in Paris, was agreed to by the Conference at Vienna, ratified and approved by the Cabinets of Paris and London, and pronounced by all these authorities to be such as would satisfy the honor of Russia and at the same time be compatible with the "independence and integrity" of Turkey and the honor of the Sultan. Russia accepted this note at once—accepted it, I believe, by telegraph, even before the precise words of it had been received in St. Petersburg. Everybody thought the question now settled; a Cabinet Minister assured me we should never hear another word about it; "the whole thing is at an end," he said, and so it appeared for a moment. But the Turk refused the note which had been drawn up by his own arbitrators, and which Russia had accepted. And what did the Ministers say then, and what did their organ, the *Times*, say? They said it was merely a difference about words; it was a pity the Turk made any difficulty, but it would soon be settled. But it was not settled, and why not? It is said that the Russian Government put an improper construction on the Vienna note. But it is unfortunate for those who say this, that the Turk placed precisely the same construction upon it; and further it is upon record that the French Government advised the Russian Government to accept it, on the ground that "its general sense differed in nothing from the sense of the proposition of Prince Menschikoff."[1] It is, however, easy to see why the Russian Government should, when the Turks refused the award of their own arbitrators, re-state its original claim, that it might not be damaged by whatever concession it had made in accepting the award; and this is evidently the explanation of the document issued by Count Nesselrode, about which so much has been said. But, after this, the Emperor of Russia spoke to Lord Westmoreland on the subject at Olmutz, and expressed his readiness to accept the Vienna note, with any clause which the Conference might add to it, explaining and restricting its meaning; and he urged that this should be done at once, as he was anxious that his troops should re-cross the Pruth before winter. It was in this very week that the Turks summoned a grand council, and, contrary to the advice of England and France, determined on a declaration of war.

'Now, observe the course taken by our Government. They agreed to the Vienna note; not fewer than five members of this Cabinet have filled the office of Foreign Secretary, and therefore may be supposed capable of comprehending its meaning: it was a note drawn up by the friends of Turkey, and by arbitrators self-constituted on behalf of Turkey; they urged its acceptance on the Russian Government, and the Russian Government accepted it; there was then a dispute about its precise meaning, and Russia agreed, and even proposed that the arbitrators at Vienna should amend it, by explaining it, and limiting its meaning, so that no question of its intention should henceforth exist. But, the Turks having rejected it, our Government turned round, and declared the Vienna note, their own note, entirely inadmissible, and defended the conduct of the Turks in having rejected it. The Turks declared war, against the advice of the English and French Governments—so, at least, it appears from the Blue Books; but the moment war was declared by Turkey, our Government openly applauded it. England, then, was committed to the war. She had promised armed assistance to Turkey—a country without government,

[1] Sir Spencer Walpole in his *History of England*, chap. xxiv., says: 'A microscopic examination can hardly detect any essential difference between the terms which were demanded by Menschikoff and those which were embodied in the Vienna note.' The essential parts of these two sets of proposals are there quoted textually and their purport is analysed by Sir Spencer Walpole.

and whose administration was at the mercy of contending factions; and incapable of fixing a policy for herself, she allowed herself to be dragged on by the current of events at Constantinople. She "drifted," as Lord Clarendon said, exactly describing his own position, into the war, apparently without rudder and without compass. . . .

'. . . At this moment *England is engaged in a murderous warfare with Russia, although the Russian Government accepted her own terms of peace,* and has been willing to accept them in the sense of England's own interpretation of them ever since they were offered; and at the same time England *is allied with Turkey, whose Government rejected the award of England, and who entered into the war in opposition to the advice of England.* Surely, when the Vienna note was accepted by Russia, the Turks should have been prevented from going to war, or should have been allowed to go to war at their own risk.'

This letter has yet to be answered. There were few even then who seriously attempted to defend the whole course of our negotiations. But the public was persuaded to overlook details and to take a 'broader view.' A war with Russia was said to be necessary in order to preserve 'the integrity of the Ottoman Empire,' and 'the balance of power in Europe.'

There is no party or section that is not now ashamed of our defence of that chamber of horrors euphemistically termed 'integrity of the Ottoman Empire.' It was indeed the 'wrong horse,' as one of its latest defenders at length most honourably confessed. But in 1854 Cobden and Bright were the only men of mark who had looked behind the curtain at Turkish misrule; Cobden as a young man had travelled observantly in Turkey, and prior to the Corn Law campaign had published a pamphlet telling the truth about its internal condition. But Palmerston still spoke of 'the progressively liberal system of Turkey.' 'It is startling,' Lord Morley writes, 'to look back upon the bullying contempt which the man who was blind permitted himself to show to the man who could see.' Bright and Cobden considered that the war had been undertaken not merely unnecessarily but on the wrong side, because our troops were being used to keep the Christian populations subject to the Turk. While we were addressing our ultimatum to Russia in February 1854, Bright met Lord Shaftesbury and told the great evangelist 'that we had restored the Pope to his throne and now we were going to fight for Mahomet.' And in his public letter to Absalom Watkin, quoted above, he continues:

> '... we are not only at war with Russia, but with all the Christian population of the Turkish Empire, and we are building up our Eastern Policy on a false foundation—namely, on the perpetual maintenance of the most immoral and filthy of all despotisms over one of the fairest portions of the earth which it has desolated, and over a population it has degraded but has not been able to destroy.'

Cobden and Bright were the first to bring forward this aspect of the Balkan question, which Gladstone long afterwards made the predominant aspect in the mind of the country.

But the Crimean War still finds defenders, no longer on the ground that it protected the Turk, but because it restored 'the balance of power,' or in Lord John Russell's antique phrase, preserved 'the liberties of Europe.' Whether or not John Bright went too far in saying that the 'balance of power' and the 'liberties of Europe' are in all cases a rhapsody of words used to delude the people into a warlike policy, at least it is difficult to see in the Czar Nicholas a Louis XIV. or Napoleon I. overshadowing the Western world. Immediately before and immediately after the Crimean War it was Napoleon III. who seemed to us to be the danger to this delicate 'balance of power'; yet we chose him as an ally in this conflict undertaken to adjust the balance. And even during the brief period of the Russian panic, the ministers, journals, and public who cried for war to restrain the danger of Muscovite predominance showed that they did not really believe in such danger, for they treated Russia as a second-class power, grossly underestimated her ability to defend even her own territory, sent in the first instance a wholly inadequate force to the Crimea, and confidently expected as a preliminary to further operations the immediate fall of the great fortress that in fact required for its reduction the efforts of the whole war. The truth was, as Bright saw and said from the first, that the Russian power of offence against civilised Europe was very small, but her power of dull resistance to invasion was as great as it had always been in the days of Charles XII. or Napoleon. To make war on her was wrong because she was not dangerous to Western Europe, and unwise because she could not herself be subdued.

A third argument for the war, besides the 'integrity of the

Ottoman Empire' and the 'balance of power,' was the argument that we may call the 'Liberal' argument. The war feeling in England was created by the Whig leaders, especially by Palmerston, and by the *Daily News* and the Radical press, followed by the Tories who hated the peace-loving Aberdeen as the representative of Peel.[1] The feeling against Russia drew its origin from a healthy dislike of despotism, prevalent among the English middle class during the Victorian era. The congenital lunatic in Tennyson's 'Maud,' who represents the spirit of the Crimean War party in all its aspects, loves war for its own sake and rebukes the 'love of peace that was full of wrongs and shames,' and expects to cure our social evils by a regimen of war fever and war taxation; he is deeply shocked by the moral turpitude of the peace party led by John Bright,

> 'This broad-brimm'd hawker of holy things,
> Whose ear is cramm'd with his cotton, and rings
> Even in dreams to the chink of his pence';

but he also hates the Czar for more sensible reasons, disliking that

> 'An infant civilisation be ruled with rod or with knout,'

and he is determined to wage war in order

> 'That an iron tyranny now should bend or cease.'

The feeling against despotism was directed against Russia rather than against Turkey, because Russia had helped Austria to suppress the Hungarians in 1849, and Turkey had sheltered Kossuth and the Hungarian refugees.[2] This seemed, though it was not, a good reason for Liberals to fight for the Turk.

It is indeed true that an unexpected by-result of the Crimean War helped the cause of liberty. Austria, by remaining neutral, incurred the resentment of Russia on the one side and of England and France on the other; she was therefore left

[1] *Greville Memoirs*, September 26, 1853. 'Day after day the Radical and Tory papers, animated by very different sentiments and motives, pour forth the most virulent abuse of the Emperor of Russia, of Austria, and of this Government, especially of Aberdeen.'

'October 4, 1853. Palmerston is lauded to the skies by all the Radicals who are admirers of Kossuth and Mazzini, who want to renew the scenes and attempts of 1848, and who fancy that if Palmerston were at the head of the Government he would play into their hands.'

'July 9, 1854. The Tories, agreeing in nothing else, concur with the Radicals in hating Aberdeen because he represents the Peel party, and is Minister as the successor of Sir Robert Peel, for whose memory their hatred is as intense as it was for his person when he was alive.'

[2] See p. 188 above.

friendless when the Italian question came up again in 1859-60. And Cavour's astute alliance of Piedmont with France and England, half-way through the Crimean War, prepared the way for the liberation of Italy. But although the Crimean War by chance helped Italy to obtain freedom, it was not because our statesmen had succeeded in their policy, but because they had failed. For they tried hard to obtain as their ally in the Crimea, not Piedmont, but Austria, the tyrant of Italy and of Hungary. If France and England had succeeded in their prolonged efforts to induce Austria to join in the attack on Russia, no more sympathy with Italy and Hungary would have been permitted in Downing Street or Paris for the next generation. By the greatest good fortune Austria remained neutral, so that in the end the Crimean War was by chance of some use to somebody—namely, to Cavour. It is an ill wind that blows no one any good. But it was not for the freedom of Italians or Magyars, but for the enslavement of Greeks and Bulgarians, that our troops were sent to fight.

'Our countrymen,' Bright wrote to a public meeting in April 1854,

> 'our countrymen fancy they are fighting for freedom because the Russian Government is a despotism: they forget that the object of their solicitude is no less a despot: that their chief ally [Napoleon III.] but the other day overthrew a republic, and imprisoned or expatriated the members of a freely-elected Parliament; that they are alternately coaxing and bullying Austria, whose regard for freedom and justice Hungary and Italy can attest, to join them in this holy war, and that the chief result of their success, if success be possible, will be to perpetuate the domination of a handful of the followers of Mahomet over many millions of Christians throughout the provinces of European Turkey. . . . The people, or a portion of them, are drunk with a confused notion of fighting with Russia; they confound the blowing up of ships and the slaughter of thousands with the cause of freedom, as if there were any connection in matters wholly apart.'

The infamous treatment of Poland was quoted by the war party to excite hatred against the Czar. But when in 1855 Napoleon III. vaguely proposed to extend the operations of war to Poland, our Government shrank back with not unnatural alarm from so vast an undertaking. Indeed, Lord Palmerston characterised the idea of helping Poland as 'positive madness.' Both he and Russell, to the disgust of their Radical supporters, denied that the war was to benefit either the Poles or the Hungarians. The other country besides Turkey for whom the Ministers declared that we were fighting was—not Italy, still less England—but 'Germany,' who herself refused to enter into the quarrel. 'Be it remembered,' said Lord John, 'that we are seeking no object of our own. The cause is one, in the first place, of the independence of Turkey. . . . It is to maintain the independence not only of Turkey, but of Germany and of all European nations.'

John Bright (June 1855) seized hold of this extraordinary utterance :

> 'To me,' he said, 'it was really frightful to hear the noble Lord tell the House that we are not fighting for ourselves, but for Germany. . . . What a notion a man must have of the duties of the twenty-seven millions of people living in these islands, if he thinks they ought to come forward as the defenders of the sixty millions of people in Germany, that the blood of England is not the property of the people of England, and that the sacred treasure of the bravery, resolution, and unfaltering courage of the people of England is to be squandered in a contest in which the noble Lord says we have no interest, for the preservation of the independence of Germany, and of the integrity, civilisation, and something else of all Europe.'

His final summary of the whole issue, at the end of his 'letter to Mr. Absalom Watkin'[1] (November 1854), is a fine example of rhetoric as the handmaid of argument.

> 'My doctrine would have been non-intervention in this case. The danger of the Russian power was a phantom ; the necessity of permanently upholding the Mahometan rule in Europe is an absurdity. Our love for civilisation, when we subject the Greeks and Christians to the Turks, is a sham ; and our sacrifices for freedom, when working out the behests of the Emperor of the French and coaxing Austria to help us, is a pitiful imposture. The evils of non-intervention were remote and vague, and could neither be weighed nor described in any accurate terms. The good we can judge something of already, by estimating the cost of a contrary policy. And what is that cost ? War in the north [Baltic] and south of Europe, threatening

[1] See p. 220 above.

to involve every country of Europe. Many, perhaps fifty millions sterling, in the course of expenditure by this country alone, to be raised from the taxes of a people whose extrication from ignorance and poverty can only be hoped for from the continuance of peace.[1] The disturbance of trade throughout the world, the derangement of monetary affairs, and difficulties and ruin to thousands of families. Another year of high prices of food, notwithstanding a full harvest in England, chiefly because war interferes with imports, and we have declared our principal foreign food-growers to be our enemies.[2] The loss of human life to an enormous extent. Many thousands of our own countrymen have already perished of pestilence and in the field; and hundreds, perhaps thousands, of English families will be plunged into sorrow, as a part of the penalty to be paid for the folly of the nation and its rulers.

'When the time comes for the "inquisition for blood," who shall answer for these things? You have read the tidings from the Crimea; you have, perhaps, shuddered at the slaughter; you remember the terrific picture—I speak not of the battle, and the charge, and the tumultuous excitement of the conflict, but of the field after the battle—Russians in their frenzy or their terror shooting Englishmen who would have offered them water to quench their agony of thirst; Englishmen, in crowds, rifling the pockets of the men they had slain or wounded, taking their few shillings or roubles, and discovering among the plunder of the stiffening corpses images of the "Virgin and the Child." You have read this, and your imagination has followed the fearful details. This is war—every crime which human nature can commit or imagine, every horror it can perpetrate or suffer; and this it is which our Christian Government recklessly plunges into, and which so many of our countrymen at this moment think it patriotic to applaud! You must excuse me if I cannot go with you. I will have no part in this terrible crime. My hands shall be unstained with the blood which is being shed. The necessity of maintaining themselves in office may influence an administration; delusions may

[1] Speaking of the war taxation, he said in the House: 'Gentlemen, I congratulate you, that every man of you has a Turk upon his shoulders.'

[2] More corn then came from Russia than from America. The war sent up the price of wheat to 72s. in 1854, and 74s. in 1855 (average).

mislead a people; *Vattel* may afford you a law and a defence; but no respect for men who form a Government, no regard I have for "going with the stream," and no fear of being deemed wanting in patriotism, shall influence me in favor of a policy which, in my conscience, I believe to be as criminal before God as it is destructive to the true interest of my country.'

So ended the famous letter that appeared in the *Times* on the day before the battle of Inkerman was fought in the fogs at dawn. Our statesmen and our generals had failed us, but the race was not dwindling down that could find in her hour of need one man to write such a letter against the errors of a whole nation, and a few thousand men to fight such a battle against the attack of a whole army.

Such were the general aspects of the case against the Crimean War as John Bright saw it, and as many more see it to-day. It remains to trace the chronological sequence of events, as they appear in his letters, journals, and speeches, from the first foreshadowing of war at Christmas 1853 onwards.

(Dec. 24, 1853. To Cobden.)

'All that is passing around us only shows how fearfully unsound our people are on war and intervention, and how necessary it is to teach them by a free press,[1] and other means. The London papers, *Daily News* and *Herald*, are now running at Prince Albert because he wants peace. How odd if you and I should have to defend the policy of Aberdeen and the Court in the coming session.'

(Dec. 27.) 'As for you and me—we are in a minority apparently and the session looks unpleasant enough as it approaches. We shall almost be hooted down in the House, I expect, for the Tories are for war, partly because the Government has been supposed to be for peace. And if war begins, then nine-tenths of the men on our side will back the Government and shout even more vociferously than the Tories. Losing a Reform Bill and gaining a war. I don't see how we could be worse placed. Though the *end* may show that we are now right, yet the *end* is not yet, and in the meantime we shall have much to suffer and much to despond about. How men can prefer the certain

[1] See p. 213 above.

and enormous evils of a war, to the dim and vague prospect of remote injury from Russian aggrandisement, is beyond my understanding. The nation seems little wiser than in 1793 and we may soon be as unpopular as Fox was, and yet be as much right as he was. I feel rather sick of public life, and indeed of the follies of my country.'

(Dec. 30.) 'This old aristocracy and Church-ridden, and tradition-ridden country will never grow wiser. Whilst we are fighting for supremacy in Europe the [United] States are *working*, and not fighting for it, but winning it all over the world.'

His journals at the time of the outbreak of the war show that in private conversation many public men of all parties confessed to him that they shared his views, but they did not feel impelled, as he did, to proclaim them in public.

Journal. 'Feb. 8, 1854. Conversation with Lords Aberdeen and Granville[1] on Eastern Question; both as strong for peace as I am, but thinking the country violent for war. I blamed the Government for having committed themselves to intervention and for not having extricated themselves when the Turk began the war against their advice; both evidently felt that an error had been committed. Aberdeen said "the independence and integrity of Turkey" was a phrase which had no meaning, it could not be; peace might have been made half a dozen times over if Turk more reasonable and not under the influence of fanatical party acting in the belief that, having England and France to back them, it was a grand opportunity for them to fight Russia. Aberdeen thought Russia did not want more territory, but sought *influence*, and was really for peace if escape could be made for her. He told the Queen that loyalty was found with the Radicals at Manchester, alluding to my speech at the recent meeting there, rather than with the Tories and the Tory press! I asked if we could learn anything further very soon.

[1] Lord Granville, then a member of Lord Aberdeen's Cabinet, was in later years the Foreign Minister after Bright's own heart, and his personal friend. In 1889, after Bright's death, he said in the House of Lords: 'I have known Mr. Bright between forty and fifty years. That acquaintance, with other circumstances, prevented my ever feeling that prejudice which there is no doubt at one time was felt against Mr. Bright. I always felt for him a great esteem and regard, and I might mention that even as far back as 1853 I asked Lord Aberdeen why he did not invite Mr. Bright at that time to join the Government.'

He said, "No—not for some time," and then, turning to Lord Granville, he said, "You know how I should bet upon it," to which Granville replied, "Yes, and Palmerston thinks still we shall have peace." I told them men in high office did wrong in letting the public go wrong without fully explaining a question and putting them right, and advocated the freedom of the press from penny stamp as a means of liberating the press from Pall Mall cliques. . . . This is written immediately on my return to my lodgings.'

'March 16. Reform Club, reading over debates on Russian and Turkish question in 1791; Fox and Burke and Whitbread strong against England supporting Turks against Russia. Yesterday had a talk with Disraeli in the Library; he insists that war is the result of the Coalition; any Government with a united policy under one head would have preserved the peace.[1] We spoke of his shilling edition of his novels; he said he had sold more than 300,000 copies in less than a year, that 400,000 copies would give him a profit equal to his salary as Chancellor of the Exchequer!

'Up till half-past three, writing a long letter to Lord Aberdeen on behalf of peace, urging the acceptance of new propositions said to have been offered through Prussia on behalf of Russia, reminding him of his heavy responsibility, and pointing out that it would be more glorious to fall in the endeavor to preserve peace than to reign through the calamities of war. I have written this letter under a pressure of anxiety I could not withstand; it may do no good, but the smallest effort though unsuccessful should not be neglected.'

This letter referred to a hope held out by the newspapers that was in fact imaginary. No 'new propositions' had been made. But the personal phrases of the letter and its most kind reception by the Premier are not without interest.

'My Lord,' Bright began,—'In addressing you I am taking a liberty which possibly you may condemn, and which many people, were they aware of it, would certainly condemn. Nevertheless as I believe you are a Minister, honest and moral in your conduct of public affairs, and as I write in the interests of humanity and peace, I feel as if I cannot refrain from this intrusion on you.'

[1] Six months later he notes: 'Met with Disraeli in St. James's Street. His view of the war unfavorable and particularly of the Crimean expedition.'

Towards the close of the letter he says:

'I need not tell you that *you* have more interest in preserving peace, in one sense, than any other man in this kingdom. Your administration will not be known in our annals as the *Russell* or the *Palmerston*, but as the *Aberdeen* administration, and, as Prime Minister, on you will mainly rest the blame or the praise which this generation and which posterity and impartial history will award to the policy which is now to be pursued. . . . I venture thus freely to address you, believing that my motives will not be misunderstood. My writing is unknown to any one but myself, and I know too well the unusual nature of the step I am taking to expect any reply.'

Journal. 'March 21, 1854. Among my letters, one from Lord Aberdeen, very friendly and expressing the "deep impression" my letter had made on his mind, inviting me to call upon him. There is much frankness and simplicity in the language and correspondence of the Prime Minister.

'March 22. To Argyll House to see Lord Aberdeen—expressed his fear that hostilities with Russia were now unavoidable; his great sorrow at this result; when offered the premiership was sensible of his deficiencies and unfitness for the position; accepted it reluctantly as it was wholly unexpected by him; consoled himself with thought that at least he could preserve peace, and yet, step by step we had approached the verge of war; *his grief was such that at times he felt as if every drop of blood that would be shed would rest upon his head.* Spoke of the Newspaper Press; I pointed out how much it is in the hands of individuals and cliques, referred to the *Morning Post*, Palmerston's paper, and its abuse of Lord Aberdeen, and urged that the repeal of the Stamp was the only mode of improving the character of the English Press. . . . He did not wish English troops to come into contact with Greek insurgents; admitted that the consular statements as to internal condition of Turkey were much worse even than appeared in blue books, as the worst parts were necessarily omitted to avoid damaging the case of the Turks.

'I left Lord Aberdeen with the belief that he is sincerely anxious to avert the horrible calamity impending over Europe, but I suspect he is not sufficiently master of his own Cabinet, and has been dragged by his colleagues into a course which is entirely opposed to his own convictions.[1]

'March 24. Conversation with Mr. Walter of the *Times* on the war—urged him to seize any chance of preserving or making peace—remarked upon the *Times* being browbeaten into a support of the war. He said when the country would go for war, it was not worth while to oppose it, hurting themselves and doing no good.'

A month later Bright records in his journal a conversation with Delane, the editor of the *Times*, 'on the war. His opinion as to its non-necessity agrees precisely with my own.'

Three weeks before war was declared, a banquet was given at the Reform Club by the Liberal party to Sir Charles Napier, chosen for the command of our fleet in the Baltic. Lord Palmerston took the chair; and two other Cabinet Ministers (Bright's old friend Molesworth and Sir James Graham, both of whom might have known better) took part in the hilarious and undignified proceedings. Graham had the ill taste in his after-dinner speech to announce that 'My gallant friend (Sir Charles Napier) says when he goes to the Baltic he will declare war; I as First Lord of the Admiralty give him free consent to do so.' There was much premature boasting of the kind which our countrymen are supposed to make it a point of honour to avoid. Everybody, with the important exception of Sir Charles Napier himself, seems to have made as certain of taking Cronstadt and Sweaborg as ever the French made certain of reaching Berlin. All this was very little to Bright's taste. He notes in his journal:

'March 9. Slept little last night, thinking of the recent dinner to Sir C. Napier at the Reform Club and the discreditable speeches made at it. Excited and not well.'

'March 13. House at four o'clock—spoke in condemnation of the dinner to Sir Charles Napier at the Reform Club, blamed Palmerston, Graham and Molesworth for attending it, and denounced the reckless levity manifested on the subject of war by the Ministers of a civilised and Christian nation. Palmerston, very insolent in his reply, called me the honourable and "reverend" member;

[1] More than a year later (April 27, 1855), Bright notes in his journal: 'Called on Lord Aberdeen. He evidently much conscious of the misfortune of the war; "he was the greatest culprit" among those to be blamed; he knew people were not to be forgiven "on the ground of good intentions"; "many reasons why he had not resigned": the Queen thought "he might preserve peace," or failing that "might soonest restore peace."'

he was called to order by Cobden, and made a most lame and ineffective speech as was admitted by all his friends in the House. Molesworth very angry and very bitter—"owed no allegiance to me," admitted that I was "an able man," but "full of illiberal and narrow-minded prejudices." The three Ministers evidently in a desperate mess and made worse by their wretched attempts to get out of it.'

Macaulay, who had no reason to like Bright, who chose Palmerston as his favourite among surviving statesmen, and who supported the war, none the less wrote of the incident:

'I heard Bright say everything that I thought, and I heard Palmerston and Graham expose themselves lamentably. Palmerston's want of temper, judgment, and good-breeding was almost incredible. I came home quite dispirited.'

On March 29 war was declared, and two days later came the first of Bright's great Crimean speeches. In this he attacked the principle of waging war for 'the balance of power' and the system of European alliances which gave away our freedom of action and involved us in war whenever it suited the book of our 'ally,' in this case of the Turk. 'I spoke,' he notes,

'more than an hour and a half; well listened to and with effect on many members, judging from their warm congratulations when I sat down. From this and other evidence I am satisfied there are many calm thinking men in the House who condemn the war but feel it difficult to oppose it. Palmerston spoke later in the evening, flippant and superficial as usual in his attack on me. Time will show who is right in this war policy. Rothschild speaking to Gibson to-night said a country with £800,000,000 of debt should have considered much and seriously before it involved itself in another war.'

'April 26. Day of Humiliation and Prayer on account of war with Russia. It is wonderful what an amount of hypocrisy or of ignorance there is in this proceeding. The Government secures the co-operation of the State Church and thus attempts to obtain the concurrence and sympathy of the "religious public" to their wicked policy. Humiliation is indeed admirably suited to the occasion, for what feeling is more appropriate when we engage in the slaughter of our fellow men—for no definite object, for no object in which we have any real interest, from whom we have received no injury, nor indeed so much as an insult. Prayer for success seems much like a gang of burglars seeking the Divine blessing upon their guilty enterprises. The public sentiment is demoralised and Christianity is impeded and its character tarnished by impieties of this kind.'

On August 9, 1854, he notes in his journal the close of a

'miserable session; much labor and no result; politics gloomy; Europe overrun by war or despotism and England no wiser than in the last generation. I have withstood the war clamor and am in a small minority apparently, but hope sometimes for better times; my position in the House not worse but better, notwithstanding my opposition to policy of Government and House. Have met with many marks of respect and good feeling from men of all parties in the House, and have much reason to be content with what has taken place there so far as I am personally concerned.'

Thus it was in the House. But in the press and in the country Bright was assailed with floods of abuse which he took as indifferently as the air he breathed, seldom mentioning it in his letters or journal. When on September 18 a meeting was held at Manchester to condemn his conduct, he marched in by the public entrance, shouldered his way to the platform, and faced his accusers. No one on either side could get a hearing, and when the Mayor tried to take the sense of the meeting he could only declare the parties equally balanced. Bright says that his friends were 'greatly pleased with the result'; it is doubtful whether he could have divided the vote in a public meeting outside his own constituency.

During the spring and summer of 1854 warlike operations had been confined to the great things that Sir Charles Napier did not attempt to do in the Baltic, to the chagrin of his sanguine friends of the Reform Club. On the shores of the Black Sea, Russia, to avoid complications with Austria, had withdrawn from the Danubian Principalities. It was only in the autumn of 1854 that the war began in earnest, with the landing of the French and English armies in the Crimea, the battle of the Alma, the investment of Sebastopol from the south, the approach of vast armies from the interior of Russia, and the heroic defence of our weakened lines at Balaclava and Inkerman. Then followed the horrors of the Crimean winter. But before the catastrophe of a new Walcheren could be consummated, the *Times* correspondent, Dr. Russell, boldly supported by his paper, had exposed to the indignant public at home the fact that their army was being destroyed by aristocratic and official ineptitude. The exposure was in more ways than one a step towards democracy; and the class that had hitherto exercised the right to throw away British armies without being called to account, considered Dr. Russell's letters as an impertinent intrusion on the decencies of public life. Cobden and Bright had expected that the democratic movement in England would be put back, perhaps for a generation, by war fever and the admiration of the upper class, which is a common symptom of that disease. And if the Crimean War had been as well conducted by Ministers and generals as it was well fought by the private soldiers, the political history of England might for some considerable period have taken a more aristocratic turn. The actual revival of democracy under Bright's leadership from 1858 onwards, culminating in the triumphant winning of the Franchise in 1867, was in no small measure due to the proved incompetence of the aristocrats, even at their own trade of war. 'Reform' seemed indeed necessary for a system of Government which could not, until it had been hauled over the coals by the *Times*, supply adequate food and shelter to an army of 25,000 men eight miles from a harbour where our fleet lay.

Bright left to others, of whom there were plenty, the task of exposing the 'incompetency, lethargy, aristocratic hauteur, official indifference, favour, routine, perverseness, and stupidity which revel and riot in the camp before Sebastopol.' [1] He took upon himself the task which no one else could adequately fulfil of impressing on the conscience of the nation that its miseries and losses were the result of the criminal act of plunging into an unnecessary war. In that mournful Christmas session he wreaked the vengeance of Peace on the Ministers who had violated her with such merry hearts. It was on December 22, 1854, at the close of a debate on a measure for the Enlistment of Foreigners, that John Bright rose and addressed to a silent and crowded house, and to the Treasury Bench packed with the famous men against whom his indictment was laid, an oration which held that hostile audience spellbound. No

[1] *Times*, leading article, December 23, 1854.

difference in mere opinion could dispel the charm, when purest passion spoke through the forms of perfect art.

He began by reviewing again in detail the negotiations that had led to all these woes, ending with the incontrovertible conclusion: 'You are making war against the Government which accepted your own terms of peace.' Then he turned upon the Treasury Bench:

> 'When I look at gentlemen on that Bench, and consider all their policy has brought about within the last twelve months, I scarcely dare trust myself to speak of them, either in or out of their presence. We all know what we have lost in this House. Here, sitting near me, very often sat the member for Frome [Colonel Boyle]. I met him, a short time before he went out, at Mr. Westerton's, the bookseller, near Hyde Park Corner. I asked him whether he was going out. He answered he was afraid he was; not afraid in the sense of personal fear—he knew not that; but he said, with a look and a tone I shall never forget, "It is no light matter for a man who has a wife and five little children." The stormy Euxine is his grave; his wife is a widow, his children fatherless. On the other side of the House sat a member, with whom I was not acquainted, who has lost his life, and another of whom I knew something [Colonel Blair]. Who is there that does not recollect his frank, amiable, and manly countenance? I doubt whether there were any men on either side of the House who were more capable of fixing the good-will and affection of those with whom they were associated. Well, but the place that knew them shall know them no more for ever.
>
> . . . . . .
>
> 'I was in the House of Lords when the vote of thanks was moved. In the gallery were many ladies, three-fourths of whom were dressed in the deepest mourning. Is this nothing? And in every village, cottages are to be found into which sorrow has entered, and, as I believe, through the policy of the Ministry, which might have been avoided. No one supposes that the Government wished to spread the pall of sorrow over the land; but this we had a right to expect, that they would at least show becoming gravity in discussing a subject, the appalling consequences of which may come home to individuals and to the nation. I recollect when Sir Robert Peel addressed the House on a dispute

which threatened hostilities with the United States—I recollect the gravity of his countenance, the solemnity of his tone, his whole demeanour showing that he felt in his soul the responsibility that rested on him. I have seen this, and I have seen the present Ministry. There was the buffoonery at the Reform Club. Was that becoming a matter of this grave nature ? Has there been a solemnity of manner in the speeches heard in connection with this war, and have Ministers shown themselves statesmen and Christian men when speaking on a subject of this nature ?

'It is very easy for the noble Lord, the member for Tiverton [Palmerston], to rise and say that I am against war under all circumstances ; and that if an enemy were to land on our shores, I should make a calculation as to whether it would be cheaper to take him in or keep him out, and that my opinion on this question is not to be considered either by Parliament or the country. I am not afraid of discussing the war with the noble Lord on his own principles. I understand the Blue Books as well as he ; and, leaving out all fantastic and visionary notions about what will become of us if something is not done to destroy or to cripple Russia, I say—and I say it with as much confidence as I ever said anything in my life—that the war cannot be justified out of these documents ; and that impartial history will teach this to posterity if we do not comprehend it now.

'I am not, nor did I ever pretend to be, a statesman ; and that character is so tainted and so equivocal in our day that I am not sure that a pure and honourable ambition would aspire to it. I have not enjoyed for thirty years, like these noble Lords, the honours and emoluments of office. I have not set my sails to every passing breeze. I am a plain and simple citizen, sent here by one of the foremost constituencies of the Empire, representing feebly, perhaps, but honestly, I dare aver, the opinions of very many, and the true interests of all those who have sent me here. Let it not be said that I am alone in my condemnation of this war, and of this incapable and guilty Administration. And even if I were alone, if mine were a solitary voice, raised amid the din of arms and the clamours of a venal press, I should have the consolation I have to-night—and which I trust will be mine to the last moment of my existence—the priceless consolation that no word of mine has tended to promote the squandering of my country's treasure or the spilling of one single drop of my country's blood.'

The House, we are told by one who saw it all, gave their antagonist 'the most deferential attention, deepening every instant, until it reached a climax probably unparalleled in the recollection of any individual present.' Before he had gone half-way through his speech, while he was still talking of the Vienna note and the occupation of the Principalities, half the Ministers had turned round in their seats, to gaze in motionless fascination at their terrible assailant. Lord John sat with his face in his hands, giving an occasional nervous laugh, not of merriment, until the words on Colonel Boyle and the 'stormy Euxine' hushed every lighter sound. Mr. Gladstone was in deep and apparent distress. What, if anything, Lord Palmerston felt was concealed as usual beneath his tilted hat. When John Bright sat down there was some 'loud cheering' on the Opposition side of the House. Then followed silence, broken by cries for 'Gladstone' to answer him. Never was there a speech that more called for reply. But no Minister rose, and the House trooped out to a division.

CHAPTER XI

THE CRIMEAN WAR—(*Concluded*), 1855

'At length, after infinite effort, the two parties come into actual juxtaposition; and Thirty stands fronting Thirty, each with a gun in his hand. Straightway the word "Fire!" is given: and they blow the souls out of one another; and in place of sixty brisk, useful craftsmen, the world has sixty dead carcases, which it must bury and anew shed tears for. Had these men any quarrel? Busy as the Devil is, not the smallest! They lived far enough apart; were the entirest strangers; nay, in so wide a Universe, there was even, unconsciously, by Commerce some mutual helpfulness between them. How then? Simpleton! their Governors had fallen out; and, instead of shooting one another, had the cunning to make these poor blockheads shoot.'—CARLYLE, *Sartor Resartus*, bk. ii. chap. viii.

HITHERTO John Bright had been engaged solely in denouncing the war. From the beginning of 1855 he turned all his energy to forwarding the return of peace. For this purpose, when occasion required, he changed the note of his oratory from denunciation to conciliatory appeal even in addressing Palmerston; he let no feeling of self-righteousness prevent him from working with any of those who had made or had supported the war—Russell, Disraeli, or Gladstone—as soon as they were ready to speak out for peace.

In the last days of January 1855 Aberdeen's Ministry of All the Talents fell, on account of their mismanagement of the invasion of the Crimea. Roebuck's motion for a committee of inquiry was carried against them by 157 votes, and they resigned. Bright wrote to his sister Priscilla:

> 'Our *Statesmen* have brought the country to humiliation not equalled since the American War; and surely things would not have been worse, or so bad, had *Manchester men*, who are not *statesmen*, had the guidance of public affairs. . . . An invasion of Russia by this country is an act of madness, and there is no honor or success possible in such an undertaking.'

It is remarkable that although the combined Whig and Peelite Cabinet had been ruined by that most unpopular of all Ministerial failures, misconduct of a war, the credit of the Anti-Peelite Tories was so low that Derby and Disraeli could not even at this juncture undertake to form a Government. After some weeks of confused palavering it emerged that the public looked to Palmerston as the only man who could pull the cart out of the Balaclava mud, in spite of the fact that he had been a leading member of the fallen Ministry. It would appear from the following passage in Bright's journal that he did not share the public enthusiasm for the new Premier:

> 'Feb. 14. Palmerston Prime Minister! What a hoax! The aged charlatan has at length attained the great object of his long and unscrupulous ambition. He is believed in by a shallow portion of the public, and he has had the advantage of a "cry" from a portion of the Press, but it passes my comprehension how the country is to be saved from its disasters and disgrace by a man who is over seventy years of age, who has never been known to do anything on which a solid reputation could be built, and whose colleagues are, with one exception, the very men under whose Government every thing has been mismanaged.'
>
> 'Feb. 16. Palmerston's first night a failure. His speech not well received, and his promises with regard to army reforms not clear and satisfactory. The House bewildered and disorganised.'

The Palmerston Ministry was compelled against its will, by the House and country in revolt, to permit Roebuck's Committee to hold its inquest. As the year 1855 went on, great improvements were made in the condition of our troops in the Crimea. How much if at all this beneficent change was due to the substitution of Palmerston for Aberdeen as Prime Minister, it is difficult to say. It was chiefly due to the *Times*, the public, and the House of Commons. The revelations of Roebuck's Committee put the people of England quite out of love with the class by which they were then governed.

> 'I read through the report of the Sebastopol Committee,' Bright writes to his wife; 'it is a melancholy narrative, and should condemn every member of the Government of Lord Aberdeen to perpetual exclusion from office. There is one fact stated, that in the month of November (1854) in the hospital at Scutari, there were

2000 patients, suffering from wounds and disease, and that in *that whole month only six shirts were washed!* Can any one conceive the horrors which are included in this fearful statement? . . . There seems to me a shocking indifference in the public mind as to the loss of life, even of their own countrymen in the Crimea; in the Clubs and at the House men talk of such an one as being "hit" or "knocked over," just as if they were discussing a question of sporting at the expense of some dumb animals.

'This morning I have been reading the book of Ruth and some of the book of Samuel. What a charm there is in these narratives! Nothing can surpass it. Old Eli heard unmoved of the death of his two sons, but "when he heard that the Ark of God was taken" he fell backwards.'[1]

Journal. 'Feb. 20. Talk with Disraeli. He thought one or two speeches weekly like the one I made before Christmas would break up the Government in a month. I said I wanted *peace*, not to break up Government, but if they would not make peace, then I would make war upon them. He returned to an old topic, on my saying I thought they (Derby party) would come in soon; he could not see why I should not join Lord Derby's Cabinet! I smiled, and said I could never lift up my head after such an act; it would destroy me. He thought Palmerston done; "you may see the breed, but the action and power are gone." Cobden showed me a note written by Mr. Delane of the *Times* to Mr. Caird, in which he said: "Cobden and Bright would be our Ministers now, but for their principle of peace at all price, against which I have done all I can to warn them."'

Two days later he writes to his wife:

'I suspect the country will be tired of our "Statesmen" by and by, if things are not brought into order. They tell us we should have been Ministers if we had not opposed the "policy of the country"—as if office could compensate a man for the guilt of a participation in this war!'

In February 1855 occurred the first diplomatic opportunity

[1] Readers well enough acquainted with the traditions of London Society fifty years ago to have heard of the 'tall man,' Jacob Omnium, will be amused by the following passage in this letter: 'I walked up into Piccadilly with "Jacob Omnium," the *great* man thou saw get out of the train at Bletchley. I fancy he has been a good deal in tropical climates, which perhaps may account for the luxuriance of his growth!'

of treating with Russia, and for the next twelve months the question of prolonging or terminating the war divided the statesmen and parties who had begun it. What Bright called in the House of Commons "the unspeakable madness of invading Russia" was now apparent. The hopes of dismembering Russia, or of taking away from her the Crimea, had vanished. No country engaged in the war now expected any great gain, but the difficulty of making peace lay in saving the face of all parties. Unfortunately the obvious way to save the face of England and France was to continue the war until Sebastopol fell—and then hand it back to Russia. To make peace on terms, however good, before the fall of Sebastopol would look like military failure. Such was the instinctive feeling of the war party in England during the spring and summer of 1855, and this sentiment, it cannot be doubted, was shared by the new Premier.

The first abortive stage in the negotiations was Lord John Russell's mission to Vienna. In February 1855 Palmerston sent Lord John as the British representative to the Peace Conference held at the Austrian capital. Peace and war hung in the balance, and Bright entertained hopes that Palmerston would consent to end the waste of blood and treasure.

Bright was now a suppliant for peace, and the conciliatory tone of his speech on February 23, even when he turned to address Palmerston himself, was in contrast to the philippic at Christmas. Both orations were perfect of their kind. But the dove is better liked than the eagle, and the speech in February was, of course, the more popular of the two. It did not accomplish its purpose, because Palmerston had not taken office to make peace without Sebastopol; but it gave Bright an immense personal success in striking contrast to the shattered laurels fallen from the brows of so many senators that year. The speech made and still keeps its reputation mainly by a single sentence. One of the half-dozen most famous phrases that ever passed the lips of an English orator, it owes nothing to political aptitude of the moment, but everything to intrinsic beauty and eternal truth.

> 'I cannot but notice,' he said, 'in speaking to gentlemen who sit on either side of this House, or in speaking to any one I meet between this House and any of those localities we frequent when this House is up—I cannot, I say, but notice that an uneasy feeling exists as to the news which may arrive by the very next mail from the East. I do

not suppose that your troops are to be beaten in actual conflict with the foe, or that they will be driven into the sea; but I am certain that many homes in England in which there now exists a fond hope that the distant one may return—many such homes may be rendered desolate when the next mail shall arrive. *The Angel of Death has been abroad throughout the land; you may almost hear the beating of his wings.* There is no one, as when the first-born were slain of old, to sprinkle with blood the lintel and the two sideposts of our doors, that he may spare and pass on; he takes his victims from the castle of the noble, the mansion of the wealthy, and the cottage of the poor and the lowly, and it is on behalf of all these classes that I make this solemn appeal.

'I tell the noble Lord [Palmerston] that if he be ready honestly and frankly to endeavour, by the negotiations about to be opened at Vienna to put an end to this war, no word of mine, no vote of mine, will be given to shake his power for one single moment, or to change his position in this House. I am sure that the noble Lord is not inaccessible to appeals made to him from honest motives and with no unfriendly feeling. The noble Lord has been for more than forty years a member of this House. Before I was born, he sat upon the Treasury Bench, and he has spent his life in the service of his country. He is no longer young, and his life has extended almost to the term allotted to man. I would ask, I would entreat the noble Lord to take a course which, when he looks back upon his whole political career—whatever he may therein find to be pleased with, whatever to regret—cannot but be a source of gratification to him. By adopting that course he would have the satisfaction of reflecting that, having obtained the object of his laudable ambition—having become the foremost subject of the Crown, the director of, it may be, the destinies of his country, and the presiding genius in her councils, he had achieved a still higher and nobler ambition, that he had returned the sword to the scabbard—that at his word torrents of blood had ceased to flow, that he had restored tranquillity to Europe, and saved this country from the indescribable calamities of war.'

Although he had complained to his wife that his brother Members talked of their friends being 'knocked over' in the war, most of them, we may be sure, had the old English trick of gruff, shamefaced compassion. They were all, as he said, waiting for the Eastern mails; and when he spoke that next sentence, it seemed that the House was hushed to listen for the beating of the wings. He afterwards said to his sister, Mrs. McLaren, that the figure of the Angel of Death 'came to me very simply and naturally. I was lying awake in bed in the morning, thinking of my speech and of all the calamities which the war had brought about, when suddenly the idea, without being sought for by me, flashed upon my mind. I did not think anything more about it except that it was true, and I was surprised at the effect which it produced on the House of Commons.'[1] After the speech—so Bright told Spence Watson—'I went into Bellamy's to have a chop, and Dizzy came and sat down beside me, and he said, "Bright, I would give all that I ever had to have made that speech you made just now." And I just said to him, "Well, you might have made it if you had been honest."'

When he reached home that night, he made the following entry in his journal:

> 'The House very full, and every gallery and place full. I spoke for about half an hour for peace, arguing that Palmerston and Lord John Russell were mostly responsible for the war, and could most easily extricate us from it, that while negotiations were going on and peace possible, I would not oppose Palmerston, and appealed to him to crown his long life by aiding the restoration of peace. I was overloaded with compliments. Sir Charles Wood said to me, "Portions of your speech were more eloquent than anything I ever heard before in my life." And other expressions of admiration and approval from great numbers. I have thought about this very much: how much there is of food for vanity and self-love, and how a foolish pride may be created and fostered by it. I have felt its influence, for it is something rare that one from so humble a beginning, born and reared in an almost singular retirement, of a sect by many ridiculed and despised, without real trained education, and without wealth, and without political influence of any kind, should be permitted with any effect and with any acceptance to speak to an assembly so critical, often so hostile to my views, and so powerful in everything affecting the interests not of England only, but of the world. I would wish to avoid vanity, and to be

[1] Barry O'Brien's *Bright*, p. 250.

rather grateful that I am permitted and enabled to speak in such an assembly on behalf of peace, and of political morality, and to feel how solemn is the responsibility of such a position.

'25th. Danby Seymour and Sir Erskine Perry called—long conversation with them—Perry compliments me; says everybody expects me to be in the (not this) Cabinet; great changes coming; Whig party worn out; no office, even highest, to which I may not aspire, etc.

'I spoke of my sect and principles as great obstacles to any official career, which he and Seymour would not admit. I suspect they know little of the influence of the oligarchy which has ruled this country since 1688. My taking a Cabinet office would be deemed little less than a revolution, if I maintained any decent consistency; besides is it not as useful to teach the truth to the people from an independent and unofficial position? Time will show.'

Palmerston may have been flattered or grimly amused, but he was certainly not persuaded by Bright's appeals to his better self, and he took care that the Vienna conferences should break down. Russia had indeed consented to three out of the four points demanded by the allies;[1] and she was ready to treat on the basis of the fourth point—the termination of Russian naval predominance in the Black Sea—but a dispute arose as to the means of effecting it. Lord John Russell thought that the Austrian proposal for a compromise on the point ought to be accepted, but Palmerston insisted on its rejection. At the same time he would have nothing to say to Napoleon III.'s schemes for helping Poland. Our Ministers talked glibly of the war continuing for another five years, in order to get a paper promise from Russia that she would not float warships in the Black Sea.

So on June 7 John Bright made another onslaught, this time with much sympathy and even support in many quarters of the House. The Peelites, especially Gladstone, might now almost be reckoned as his allies, working to put an end to the war they had helped to begin. 'If I spoke only for the sake of vanity and love of applause,' he wrote to his wife, 'I ought to be content with the reception the House gave me. Thou wilt see I did not forget the Ministers.' Indeed, he had not for-

[1] Viz. (1) Substitution of a European for a Russian guarantee of the autonomy of the Danubian Principalities. (2) Free Navigation of the Danube. (3) Abandonment by Russia of all claim to protect Christian subjects of Turkey.

gotten them: this was the occasion on which he called Palmerston 'a man who has experience, but who with experience has not gained wisdom, a man who has age, but who, with age, has not the gravity of age.'

This speech on June 7 exposed with just foresight the folly of fighting year after year to obtain that agreement about the ships in the Black Sea, which, though won after the fall of Sebastopol, was torn up by Russia in 1870 as so much waste paper.

> 'Some honourable gentlemen talk as if Russia were a Power which you could take to Bow Street, and bind over before some stipendiary magistrate to keep the peace for six months. Russia is a great Power, as England is, and in treating with her you must consider that the Russian Government has to consult its own dignity, its own interests, and public opinion, just as much at least as the Government of this country. . . . To ask from an independent Power that it should limit its force is to assail its rights of sovereignty on its own territory. If any diplomatist from this country, under the same circumstances as Russia was placed in, had consented to terms such as the noble Lord had endeavoured to force upon Russia—I say, that if he entered the door of this House, he would be met by one universal shout of execration, and, as a public man, would be ruined for ever.'

It was for this object that Ministers declared themselves ready to continue the war for five more years, which would involve the expenditure of another four hundred millions of pounds:

> 'We have had,' said Bright, 'for twelve years past a gradual reduction of taxation, and there has been an immense improvement in the physical, intellectual, and moral condition of the people of this country; while for the last two years we have commenced a career of reimposing taxes, have had to apply for a loan, and if this war goes on extensive loans are still in prospect. Honourable members may think this is nothing. They say it is a "low" view of the case. But these things are the foundations of your national greatness, and of your national duration.
>
> 'I recollect reading in the *Life of Necker* that an aristocratic lady came to him when he was Finance Minister of

Louis XVI., and asked him to give her a thousand crowns from the public treasury, not an unusual demand in those days. Necker refused to give the money. The lady started with astonishment—she had an eye to the vast funds of the State—and she asked, "What can a thousand crowns be to the King?" Necker's answer was "Madam! A thousand crowns are the taxes of a whole village." I ask honourable gentlemen what are the taxes of a whole village and what they mean? They mean bareness of furniture, of clothing, and of the table in many a cottage in Lancashire, in Suffolk and in Dorsetshire. They mean an absence of medical attendance for a sick wife, an absence of the school pence of three or four little children—hopeless toil to the father of a family, penury through his life, a cheerless age and at last

"The little bell
Toll'd hastily for a pauper's funeral."

'That is what taxes mean.

'Is war the only thing a nation enters upon in which the cost is never to be reckoned? Is it nothing that in twelve months you have sacrificed 20,000 or 30,000 men, who a year ago were your own fellow-citizens, living in your midst, and interested, as you are, in all the social and political occurrences of the day. . . . The four nations engaged in this war have already lost so many men, that if you were to go from Chelsea to Blackwall, and from Highgate to Norwood, and take every man of a fighting age and put him to death—if you did this you would not sacrifice a larger number of lives than have already been sacrificed in these twelve months of war.'

It was at this date, perhaps, that the foundations were laid for the alliance with Gladstone, the great fact of Bright's later life.[1] On August 3 he notes in his journal: 'Gladstone made a speech of the highest class, proving his superiority over all other men in the House. His case against the Government for going on with the war irresistible, and felt to be so.' A week later he writes to Villiers: 'I find in Manchester that the men deeply committed to the war are desperate with Gladstone and Lord John Russell, seeing that they shrink from the ruinous policy which so many have been bent upon pursuing.'

[1] Gladstone was no longer in the Government. He had resigned for reasons referred to in the Note at the end of this chapter.

On August 9 he notes :

'By train to Manchester and home. What a relief to be free of this lamentable session! *War is the grave of all good*, whether in administration or legislation, and it throws power into the hands of the most worthless of the class of statesmen. Hence a session with no result and a Palmerston in the place of Prime Minister.'

Right or wrong, Palmerston was taking the popular course in prolonging the war until after the fall of Sebastopol, which fortunately took place that autumn. On September 21 Bright writes to Cobden :

'In the train last evening from Wigan was a young man going to Leeds. We talked on the war. He argued that the people were not likely to be in the wrong when so moved, instancing the Corn Law agitation. He admitted they were wrong on the Papal aggression however, but he said, "Did we not throw up our caps for Cobden and John Bright, and should we not go with them now, if we thought they were right?" I told him they did not trust men of their own order, but preferred Palmerston and Russell, and I thought there was too much of the flunkey in them ever to go right when men of that class had an interest in leading them wrong. He did not know me, or appear to suspect me, though he knew I was getting out at Rochdale, so it was amusing enough.

'. . . I am in danger of becoming not so much *hopeless* as *indifferent*, from the folly of our countrymen. Honest public life seems to yield little to the country or to those who pursue it. Why then not abandon public life, unless with consciences more pliant, we can work for its honors and emoluments like other men, without reference to strict principle, or to the public interests? The *Times* says that men cannot aspire to share Government without regarding popularity, which is true ; but putting Government apart, can men be very useful without popularity, and is popularity compatible with doing right?

'Our good friend Whitehead of Rawtenstall says, "If we keep right, things will come right"; so let us hope it may be so.'

(Oct. 8. To Cobden.)

'The *Times* is more than usually savage and insulting with me. I should like to go over the *Times* of 1853, and to extract passages against the Turk, against the war, in favor of Russia, etc., and then to read them out, and to state boldly that they were written by the very same hands that have written their recent articles in favor of the war. I dare say no good comes of this; or of any attack against the Press, and we only make enemies by it. But yet there is a pleasure in exposing the treachery of these guides of the people.[1]

'The *Press* [a Disraeli paper] is writing for peace. I wish it represented the large party who sit opposite to us in the House, or the Tory party in the constituencies.

'I would act on that question with any set of men that would try to put an end to the war, and I am sure Gladstone would do the same.'

The fall of Sebastopol opened the way to negotiations at the new year that led to peace before the spring of 1856. When these negotiations began Bright wrote a private letter to Sir George Grey, the man he most trusted in the Cabinet, though they were not on terms of personal intimacy:

'Private.

'Jany. 2nd, 1856.

'My dear Sir,—Will you permit me to write to you somewhat of that which has been pressing upon me for many weeks past?

'. . . I assume that there are men in the Cabinet willing to offer and accept moderate terms. The question is, will these men stand firm, or will they yield on this momentous point? If Lord Aberdeen and Mr. Gladstone had acted up to their convictions in 1853, there would have been no war, or they would not have been responsible for it. If Lord J. Russell had acted on his convictions after his return from Vienna, he would not have placed himself in a position where his best friends have found it impossible to defend him. If the moderate men in the Cabinet now dare to act up to their convictions, we shall probably have peace—if not, then recklessness may carry the day, and the end none of us can foresee, and few dare even to speculate upon. . . . It is not a question of a

[1] Bright once said in a speech: 'The *Times* says I repeat myself; the *Times* says I am guilty of what it calls tautology; the *Times* says I am always saying the same thing. What I complain of in the *Times* is that it *never* says the same thing.'

£5 or a £7 suffrage, but a question of the destruction of human life—of the sacrifice, it may be, of hundreds of thousands of lives. Who shall answer for these things? To save a Government—to obey the howlings of the newspapers—to shun a transient unpopularity—are poor excuses for the crime and agonies of "one more campaign."

'By insisting on making peace on moderate and reasonable terms, you would either force your Cabinet to that course, or break it up. If the latter result followed, I think a new Government would come in more free from Guildhall dinner speeches, and more able to discuss and arrange terms of peace.

'Depend upon it, if you think peace might now be made, and you yield to the obstinacy of others who do not wish for peace, you will bring yourselves into the position of Lord Aberdeen, and Mr. Gladstone, and Lord John Russell, and you will have no excuse. To involve a country in debt and peril, and to bring about or permit multitudes of men to be slaughtered, and whole regions to be desolated, for the sake of acting harmoniously with colleagues in a Government, is not a weakness only—it is a crime for which our language has no name.'

On January 28, while peace and war still hung in the balance, John Bright addressed a crowded meeting of his constituents in the Corn Exchange, Manchester, with vigour and success, but 'at the close of the meeting it was remarked that he was flushed in the face and suffering from the excitement of the effort.' For more than two years to come he was *hors de combat* as a politician, and during the early months of his illness it was doubtful whether he would ever regain the use of his working faculties. When, therefore, peace was signed in March 1856 he was a stricken man.

The evils of a war do not end with the conclusion of peace. As late as November 1857 Bright wrote to Villiers: 'The Russian War spent about 500 millions of the floating capital of Europe. I should not mourn much if the innocent did not suffer with the guilty. Lancashire is getting rapidly to three days per week of working and wages and *food*, and the winter promises to be dark in more senses than one. I suppose the Parliamentary Jester [1] will still jest, and the representatives of the people will still laugh.' And again he writes to the same correspondent: 'I suspect the hundred millions sterling we

[1] Palmerston.

squandered in the Russian War would be welcome now. But it can no more be recovered than the souls of the 50,000 Englishmen who died to make Palmerston Prime Minister.'

Twenty years later Bright was passing through London with Philip, his youngest boy. They drove by the Guards' Monument in Pall Mall, one of the few public memorials in London that show any appositeness of feeling for the men or events commemorated: three bearded privates in their bear-skins and greatcoats stand with heads bowed, in sorrow for their comrades fallen at Inkerman, while a Victory in mourning crowns them from above. No general or statesman is honoured in the word CRIMEA at the base. As father and son drove by that day, the Rochdale lad, looking out eagerly at the great city, asked the meaning of that word. Bright was silent for a moment, and then said 'A CRIME.' He offered no further explanation, and the boy, a little frightened by something in his father's voice, asked no more, but always remembered what he did not then understand.

NOTE

Bright's Usual Seat in the House of Commons

The present chamber was first occupied in May 1850 (see pp. 118, 187 above), and Bright first sat on the Treasury Bench in 1869. His 'great period' as a House of Commons speaker lies mostly between those two dates. When the Whigs or Liberals were in office, as they usually were during that period, he sat 'on the second bench below the gangway, Ministerial side, nearest to the Ministerial benches,' in the place now (1912) occupied by the leader of the Labour party.

The following letter of Mr. Gladstone's is not without 'House of Commons' interest. It is dated 'Downing Street, Feb. 22, 1855, midnight,' and was written by Gladstone when he and the other Peelites resigned from Palmerston's Ministry, owing to the submission of the new Premier to Roebuck's Crimean Committee of Inquiry which he and the Peelites had resisted when recently in office under Aberdeen:

> 'My dear Sir,' writes Gladstone to Bright, 'it has been, I believe, the understood usage of the House of Commons, though it was departed from in the case of Lord John Russell, that ex-Ministers, quitting the Government for some special cause, should make their explanations from the upper end of the second Bench (on the Ministerial side) below the gangway: and there is much convenience in a fixed position, as it cuts off at least one source of gratuitous and idle speculation.
>
> 'I hope you will not think I am taking too great a liberty if at the request of Sir J. Graham and Mr. Herbert I make the request of you and your friends, Mr. Cobden and Mr. Gibson, that we may be allowed without any discourtesy towards you to occupy that spot at least for to-morrow evening? I address myself to you as (I think) the most constant attendant of the House, in the hope that you will kindly make our apologies to them.
>
> 'I remain, my dear Sir,
> 'Faithfully yours,
> 'W. E. Gladstone.'

On the 23rd, Graham, rising from Bright's usual place, explained the cause of his own and his friends' resignations; then Bright rose from further down the same bench and made his 'Angel of Death' speech.

CHAPTER XII

FIRST ILLNESS, 1856-58. DEFEAT AT MANCHESTER AND ELECTION FOR BIRMINGHAM. INDIA. THE BIRMINGHAM SPEECHES AND REOPENING OF THE FRANCHISE AGITATION

'For thou hast been
As one, in suffering all, that suffers nothing,
A man that fortune's buffets and rewards
Hast ta'en with equal thanks: and blest are those
Whose blood and judgement are so well commingled
That they are not a pipe for fortune's finger
To sound what stop she please.'—*Hamlet*, III. 2.

JOHN BRIGHT's first illness, which kept him out of the public arena during the whole of the years of 1856 and 1857, marks not merely an interval, but a natural division and fresh starting-point in his life. During his absence from the House his connection with Manchester ended and his connection with Birmingham began. And when he returned to his full activities, he at once gave to the agitation for enfranchising the working man an importance in the public mind that it never before had. It was at his first Birmingham meetings, in October 1858, that he brought to close grips the tussle of the British democracy with the aristocracy in possession. In the ten years' contest that followed, the chief incident was the relation of the two parties over here to the kindred struggle then being fought out with fiercer weapons in America. John Bright won through to victory, and saw the harvesting of his life's work in the Franchise Act of 1867 and Gladstone's first Ministry of the great reforms.

Bright used to attribute his illness to the misery which he had endured during the Crimean War. And indeed no reason can be assigned for it, other than overwork and public cares. The doctors gave it no specific name, but in our day it would popularly be called a 'nervous break-down.' Great physical weakness, frequent severe headaches and inability to do mental work, were its chief symptoms, though his brain was in no sense or degree deranged.[1] During the first twelve months, hope and fear were evenly balanced with regard to his ultimate recovery.

Much of the first period of his enforced leisure he spent in the Highlands of Scotland with his daughter Helen, now a most companionable girl of fifteen. As a boy at school he had fished in the streams of the Pennine moorland, and now, after a long interval of years, he again began to practise the gentle art destined to be his chief recreation during the latter half of his life. His letters, over a long period of years, prove that he often caught a fair number of trout and of salmon. But it was not so much his own skill and success as the calm and beauty of the secret places of nature that drew him year after year to the Highland rivers. Shooting, or any pursuit of larger and more sensitive creatures, was repugnant to his feelings and even to his principles.[2]

In November 1856 the doctors ordered him off to Algiers. He did not like the place and was in low spirits there, partly because none of his family were with him, his wife being kept at home by their numerous family of small children. But at Christmas he returned to the South of France to meet Helen. 'I am glad to be again on this side of the sea,' he writes on landing at Marseilles, 'and the expectation of seeing dear Helen so soon makes my heart light, and my journeying a pleasure.' They went together to Rome, and thenceforward, whenever he could forget politics, he enjoyed life as every Englishman must do who travels in Italy with a loved companion.

In his journal he writes that on the night when he reached Rome, January 26, 1857, 'I dreamt I was at the opening of

[1] On January 17, 1859, John Bright delighted the people of Bradford by saying in his speech: 'One Scotch Lord told a great audience that I have been afflicted by a visitation of Providence and that I am suffering from disease of the brain. His friends can tell whether that is a complaint with which he is ever likely to be afflicted.'

[2] Note in John Bright's handwriting, 1881: 'Mr. Bright has always preferred Scotland to those portions of the Continent most frequented by English travellers. That the salmon river has charms for him need not be denied. It was in 1856 during his long illness that, at the urgent recommendation of the late Dr. M'Leod of Ben Rhydding, he began to cast a fly on the pools and streams of the Scottish rivers. From this exercise, from spending many hours almost daily on the river's bank, he recovered the health he had lost in the long nights in the House of Commons, and in the fierce political conflicts of the time. It was not the instinct of the sportsman, but the search for health which connected Mr. Bright with so many of the rivers of Scotland.'

the session, and heard Roebuck speak. My old labors sometimes seem to haunt me, and I am very sad at being excluded from the field where so much is to be done or attempted.' On January 28 he writes, for no eye but his own:

'It is a year to-day since my last speech in Manchester. I was ill then, and should not have undertaken the labor which the meeting in the Corn Exchange threw upon me.[1] I dare not, however, regret what was done; it was the pouring forth, if I may so speak, of what was in my heart, and of what filled my very soul at the time; and if it prove the last speech, and I am no more able to tell the truth to my countrymen from the platform, I will not regret the effort there made, terrible as is the price it has cost me. I have worked *in earnest* in the political field, and if any meaner motive has ever stimulated or guided me, if ambition, or any love of display or of popularity has at any time led me on, of which I am little conscious, I think I can honestly say that a love of what I have believed to be the truth, a strong desire for the good and true greatness of my country, and an unchangeable hostility to the selfishness and fraud which distinguish the government of the English oligarchy, have been the main-spring of my public and political conduct. I have not sought that which is to be gained by submission to the ruling parties, and I have endeavored to act uninfluenced by the clamor or the momentary and impulsive applause of the people. I look with gloomy forebodings on the consequences which may and which probably must result from the follies and the crimes into which ignorance and passion so frequently lead or impel my countrymen. I write this surrounded by the ruins of the once mistress of the world, and from her history, and indeed from all history, I learn that loud boasting, great wealth, great power, extended dominion, successive conquests, mighty fleets and armies, are not immoveable foundations of national greatness. I would rather rely on an educated and moral people, and on a system of government, free at home, and scrupulously moral and just in its dealings with every other government and people.'

He saw with keen interest the sights of Rome, ancient and modern. He witnessed the antique and modish gaieties of a

[1] See p. 251 above.

carnival. He detected and approved the mutiny smouldering in the hearts of the people against their priest rulers. He heard, with quiet distaste, 'Dr. Manning, not long ago of the English State Church,' preach Mariolatry to a fashionable English audience, and came away with the conviction that 'he was a very good speaker, if you don't listen to what he says.' He felt the melancholy of Rome and its ruins with all the depth of his nature; but he did not embrace the true antiquarian spirit, as we gather from a letter to his wife written after more than a month's residence in the world of statues and excavations:

> 'I cannot look *back* with the delight which some men seem to feel. The view is a sad and gloomy one, full of crimes and of the sufferings of humanity. Ancient Rome was great, even pre-eminent in crime. She conquered and plundered the world, and she lies now, visited with a just retribution, a ruin. And may not another space of centuries, or even a shorter period, make as complete an overthrow of the Empire of Modern Rome as the past 1500 years have worked in the aspect of the Ancient Capital of the world? And the lesson of what has befallen Rome should not be lost, tho' doubtless it will be wholly lost on our own country, for men will not look back that they may the better look forward, and they flatter themselves that tho' all before them have died, yet that immortality of power and fame and prosperity is for them! It is pleasanter for me to dwell upon the future of nations than the past, if I see an opening for what may be called the wiser life of nations. I prefer therefore to dwell on the growing greatness of the populations in America and Australia. I would rather spend three months in the United States of America than in the States of the Church.'

Yet he never went to America.

In his graver utterances during this winter, he seems to express something more like despair with regard to the future of England than at any other period of his life, before or after. The folly and waste of the Crimean War still lay heavy on his spirit, and he knew not how soon England might again break the peace of Europe; he doubted whether he would ever be well enough to take part in politics again; and the apparent failure of the cause of Franchise Reform, after so many futile endeavours to get itself under weigh, augured ill for the prospects of democracy in the Old World. It is often darkest near the dawn, and he did not foresee that a dozen years would lead the cause of Reform to victory, and that England would avoid the wars of Europe during the remainder of his long life.

But John Bright had still another depth to go down before he reached the trough and upward curve of fortune's wave. While he was wandering through the sunlit cities where patrician and plebeian, Guelf and Ghibelin had fought out their street factions long ago, he and his party were being expelled from the city whence they drew their name and mandate, and his friends were falling before Palmerston in the polling-booths of Yorkshire and Lancashire.

It is probable that every man, even the most hearty Imperialist, who to-day studies the treatment of China by Palmerston in the affair of the *Arrow*, will arrive at the conclusion that he abused the strength of Britain, and brought on a war originating from an unworthy quarrel. This view was taken not only by Cobden but by Disraeli's Conservative party, by the Peelites and by Lord John Russell. A combination of these forces passed Cobden's vote of censure on the Chinese policy of the Government by a majority of sixteen on February 26, 1857. The news rejoiced Bright at Rome, but was quickly followed by rumours of a dissolution. Palmerston determined to appeal to the Jingo passions of the electorate. He recovered his majority, and extinguished at the polls the weakest of the parties allied against him—the 'Manchester School.' Fox was unseated at Oldham, Miall at Rochdale, Cobden himself at Huddersfield. The fate of Bright and Gibson at Manchester concerns us more particularly.

Even at the date of Bright's first and unopposed election for the cotton capital ten years before, in the honeymoon of Anti-Corn Law triumph, there had been murmurings against him among the Manchester Whigs, on the ground that he was too radical and too obnoxious to the aristocracy.[1] This feeling of discontent with their Member had increased with the passing years, as Free Trade became ever more secure and the great merchants became more conservative and more closely bound by social ties to the landed magnates who had so lately been their bitterest foes. Bright's look-out ahead for the new democracy, and his endeavour to bring the working men into the political arena, were repugnant to not a few of the Manchester grandees. When he opposed the national sentiment

[1] See p. 180 above.

over the Crimean War, these malcontents saw their opportunity to get rid of him. The election of 1857 was fought in Manchester equally on a review of Bright's past conduct during the Crimea, and of his present attitude, expressed in letters from Italy, on Palmerston and the Chinese question. To secure his defeat the Tories instead of running Conservative candidates supported Sir John Potter and James Aspinall Turner, who stood as Palmerstonian Whigs. The old Liberal party of Manchester was divided against itself, and the Tory vote was bound to decide the contest.[1]

In Bright's absence, Cobden came over from his own losing battle at Huddersfield and spoke for his friend at Manchester. Never were the two more dear to each other than in this period of public and private disaster. The tragedy of Cobden's life—the death of his only son, Richard, on the threshold of a noble career—had coincided in time with John Bright's illness, and was but a year old when their common unpopularity culminated in the disasters of the 'Chinese' election.[2] Bright writes to his wife from Italy: 'Cobden's speech was only too kind and laudatory. But what he says of our political brotherhood is quite true. I only know how I have gained in political experience through our long friendship. How base the *Times* is towards Cobden. I loathe the compliments it pays me at his expense, because I know him and his worth.'

During the last days of the Manchester election Bright and his daughter travelled from Rome to Florence. Helen had for some days been ill of a fever caught in their lodgings in one of the streets off the Corso, then the visitors' quarter of Rome. Her father nursed her with a woman's tenderness, but took her off on the journey to Florence perhaps unwisely soon. During the three days' drive across the Campagna and through the Apennines, she slept long with her head upon his shoulder, and

[1] The Liberal split was illustrated by the different sides taken by the Philips brothers. Mark Philips, Member for Manchester 1832-47, a prominent Unitarian, Liberal, and champion of the League, offered in 1857 to propose Potter and Turner at the hustings. His younger brother, Robert Needham Philips, threatened in return to come over to Manchester from his own contest at Bury to propose Bright and Gibson. So the Philips brothers 'paired' and took no active part at the hustings.

[2] In November 1856 Cobden had written to a friend: 'Perhaps there never were two men who lived in such transparent intimacy of mind as Bright and myself. Next to the loss of my boy, I have had no sorrow so constant and great as from his illness. The two together make me feel quite unnerved. Bright's loss, if permanent, is a public calamity. If you could take the opinion of the whole House, he would be pronounced, by a large majority, to combine more earnestness, courage, honesty, and eloquence than any other man. But we will not speak of him as of the past. God grant that he may recover!'—*Morley*, vol. ii. chap. vii.

he gave her food with his own hand. At Siena the railway north began, and he took her straight on to comfortable quarters in Florence. There he received the news of the Manchester election.

Sir John Potter .	8368
Jas. Aspinall Turner	7854
T. Milner Gibson .	5588
John Bright . .	5458

On March 31 Bright wrote to his wife:

'Late last night I received the news of the result of the election. So thy wish is accomplished, and I am free, without having run away from my post! The news scarcely affected me in the least. I was partly prepared for it by the delay in receiving it. And the simple fact of my being out of Parliament, I need hardly tell thee, does not cost me a thought. I grieve for Gibson and Wilson and our good friends, and I am sorry for the pain it will cause to Priscilla and many of my relatives, but after all, it is but a trifle, not worth thinking about. Honest men are not in demand just now. Shams are more needed for the foolish notions that are abroad—perhaps wiser times may come.'

In April he wrote to Cobden from Venice a letter full of courage,[1] admitting 'the sudden break up of the *School* of which we have been the chief professors,' but reviewing the prospects of the future hopefully, recalling the triumphs of progress in recent years, and prophesying great improvements in the Franchise, in Church questions and in foreign policy, as soon as Palmerston should disappear—as he soon must in the order of nature or of politics. 'He will not last long as Minister or as man. I see no one ready to accept his mantle when it drops from him. Ten years hence those who live so long may see a complete change on the questions on which the public mind has been recently so active and so much mistaken.' The writer but not the reader of these words lived the ten years and saw the prophecy fulfilled.

In Cavour's Piedmont, then the only free State in Italy and the best-governed country in Europe, Bright noted with pleasure that 'people take increasing interest in elections, and appreciate more their free constitution.' He enjoyed an inter-

[1] Printed at full in *Morley*, vol. ii. chap. viii.

view with Cavour, the only 'statesman' whom he really admired between the death of Peel and the Presidency of Lincoln. He noted Cavour's 'eye expressing mildness and firmness, and a mouth very pleasing but showing strength. He has the appearance of an intelligent English gentleman farmer, rather than of a *fine* and subtle Italian.'

By midsummer John Bright was back in the Highlands of Scotland, fishing. Hope was gradually maturing into expectation that he would ere long be strong enough to resume his work in life, when an opportunity occurred for immediate re-election without any present effort on his own part. One of the two sitting Members for Birmingham had died, and the Liberals of the Midland capital decided to offer the seat to John Bright, and to pay all his election expenses. Joseph and Charles Sturge, Mr. Manton and Mr. J. S. Wright, were among the first and most generous movers of this scheme, and Mr. Thomas Lloyd carried through the negotiations as Chairman of the Election Committee. Neither John Bright nor his relations had any previous connection with Birmingham, and they had approached no one in the matter. Indeed, the offer was so unexpected that on the day when it was made Bright was lost to the world in some remote Highland glen. With the help of his brother-in-law, Duncan McLaren, he was found and informed of the offer, and brought back to McLaren's house at Edinburgh. There he received from the Chairman of the Birmingham Committee a telegram charged with obvious anxiety; it was clear that his candidature would depend on the answer he sent, for it was the first days of August 1857; the English were still on the Ridge before Delhi and the bagpipes had not yet been heard at Lucknow:

> 'Will you resist the measures considered necessary by the Military Authorities for suppressing the present revolt against the British rule in India? This revolt may have been provoked by misgovernment and ought to be followed by Reform, but how is the present Insurrection to be suppressed? Answer speedily; want for immediate use.'

Bright replied by wire:

> 'The success of the Indian revolt would lead to anarchy in India, and I conceive that it is mercy to India to suppress it. I should not resist the measures considered necessary to suppress it. I should insist on an improved Government for India for the future.'

No one doubted that this was Bright's inmost conviction, although his re-entry into political life depended on his giving an answer to this effect. It is no disparagement of our public men to say that few if any others would have escaped suspicion so completely in a case so nice. Bright, though vigilantly critical of our rule in India, throughout his life took a more active and hopeful interest in its prospects than Cobden was ever able to do.[1] Bright held that, however doubtful the wisdom or morality of our first going there, we had incurred duties to India which we were now bound to fulfil, and that we might fulfil them successfully if we could avoid the pitfalls of racial and bureaucratic arrogance. 'I accept,' he had said, 'the possession of India as a fact. There we are; we do not know how to leave it, and therefore let us see if we do not know how to govern it.'

From Edinburgh Bright went south as far as Tamworth to meet his Election Committee, but his health did not permit him to address a public meeting, or even to make entry into Birmingham. When it was known that he was standing, the Conservative candidate withdrew, and he was elected unopposed.

No public man has ever been treated better by his constituents. If the story of Burke and Bristol stands for the mixed good and evil of that married state of a great man with a great city, Bright and Birmingham stand for a perfect form of the union. He was never asked to contribute to his expenses. Here, as formerly at Durham and Manchester, he refused, and soon ceased to be asked, to subscribe to bazaars, hospitals, and churches or other local objects. He was always a 'distinguished stranger' in Birmingham. He came down once or twice a year and made his great orations in the Town Hall, a full return, so his audience thought, for all the advantages that he drew from his connection with their city. He took no part in Birmingham local politics. And so, when in later years another great man, who was anything but a 'distinguished stranger' in Birmingham, became his colleague in the representation, their several lines of action ran parallel and never clashed, though their opinions on many subjects stood far asunder.

He had indeed found, by a process of natural selection, the constituency best able to serve him as a place of arms whence

[1] In 1877 (December 4) Bright writes to Mr. Thomas Bayley Potter, M.P. for Rochdale: 'Our dear friend Cobden would never touch India in any shape, always giving as his reason that we have no business there.'

to conquer England in the coming battle for democratic Reform. Birmingham of the 'sixties was almost as well suited to lend force to the Franchise agitation, as Manchester of the 'forties had been suited to lend force to the Free Trade movement. The social and economic cause of the different political atmosphere in the two cities was analysed by Cobden in a letter commenting on Bright's first election for Birmingham:

> 'The honest and independent course taken by the people at Birmingham, their exemption from aristocratic snobbery, and their fair appreciation of a democratic son of the people, confirm me in the opinion I have always had that the social and political state of that town is far more healthy than that of Manchester; and it arises from the fact that the industry of the hardware district is carried on by small manufacturers, employing a few men and boys each, sometimes only an apprentice or two; whilst the great capitalists in Manchester form an aristocracy, individual members of which wield an influence over sometimes two thousand persons. The former state of society is more natural and healthy in a moral and political sense. There is a freer intercourse between all classes than in the Lancashire town,[1] where a great and impassable gulf separates the workman from his employer. The great capitalist class formed an excellent basis for the Anti-Corn Law movement, for they had inexhaustible purses, which they opened freely in a contest where not only their pecuniary interests but their pride as "an order" was at stake. But I very much doubt whether such a state of society is favorable to a democratic political movement, and this view I have urged upon Wilson and Bright ever since the League was, or ought to have been, abolished. If Bright should recover his health and be able to head a party for Parliamentary Reform, in my opinion Birmingham will be a better home for him than Manchester.'[2]

During the decade of slumber and growth that followed the Crimean War, the sham fights on the floor of the House of Commons were devoid of reality and of bitterness, except in recurrent episodes of the lifelong duel between Palmerston and the chiefs of the Manchester School. But even that duel was less tragic than comic, resembling the alternate rise and

[1] Viz. in Manchester. Not in the smaller Lancashire towns, where employers and workmen were nearer to each other. See pp. 16-17 above.

[2] *Morley*, vol. ii. chap. viii.

fall of Punch and the Policeman, in rapid exchange of knock-down blows, each less fatal than appears at the first moment to the applauding spectators. Hardly had the men of peace crept back at by-elections into the arena whence they had been expelled by Palmerston's 'Chinese' dissolution, than we find them again heading the alliance of his enemies, and again defeating his Government, this time fatally to its continuance. Cobden had not yet returned to the House, but Bright and Gibson, the rejected of Manchester, had secured other seats, and on February 19, 1858, Gibson moved an amendment to the second reading of Palmerston's Conspiracy to Murder Bill. The amendment was seconded in silence by Bright, still too unwell to speak, and carried by 19 votes. 'I was a teller,' he wrote to Cobden next day, 'and Gibson and I walked to the Table to read the condemnation of the hoary sinner, which was received with immense cheering by the majority.'

The combination of parties—Tories, Peelites, Russell-Whigs, and 'Manchester' schoolmen—was the same as that which had beaten Palmerston on Cobden's Chinese motion a year before, but on this occasion he could not hope to appeal from the House to the nationalist passions of the electors, because Milner Gibson's charge against him on this occasion was neglect of the honour of England. The complaint was that his Foreign Secretary had left unanswered the rather insolent dispatch of Napoleon III.'s minister, on the subject of the Orsini bomb outrage which had been plotted by refugees in England.[1] The question whether it would have been better to answer the dispatch instead of ignoring it, is a question of diplomatic method rather than of large public principle. Bright, whose opinions on the subject were never recorded at length, probably did not greatly care about the question, though he thought Palmerston had chosen the wrong course. His chief desire was not to see the dispatch answered, but to see the Premier turned out. Till he was gone, there was no place for a real Liberal party, led by men free from Palmerston's invincible repugnance to retrenchment and reform.

[1] Gibson's amendment (to Palmerston's motion for the second reading of the Conspiracy to Murder Bill) was: 'This House hears with much concern that it is alleged that recent attempts upon the life of the Emperor of the French have been devised in England, and expresses its detestation of such guilty enterprises; that this House is ready at all times to assist in remedying any defects in the Criminal Law which after due investigation are proved to exist, yet it cannot but regret that H.M. Government, previously to inviting the House to amend the law of conspiracy, has not felt it to be their duty to make some reply to the important dispatch received from the French Government dated Paris, January 20, 1858, which has been laid before Parliament.'

The immediate outcome of Palmerston's fall, in the formation of another short-lived Derby-Disraeli Cabinet, did not disturb Bright, who foresaw that the Conservatives were not strong enough to do any harm, and that they would soon be out again. His only anxiety was lest Gladstone should join this Ministry of Tory caretakers, for already he dimly discerned in Gladstone his own future ally and the leader of the Liberal party to be. 'I think,' Bright wrote to him, 'I am not mistaken in the opinion I have formed of the direction in which your views have for some years been tending. You know well enough the direction in which the opinions of the country are tending. The minority which invites you to join it, if honest, must go or wish to go in an opposite direction, and it cannot therefore govern the country. Will you unite yourself with what must be, from the beginning, an inevitable failure?' Gladstone was careful to avoid the snare, and refused Derby's invitation to take office in a Conservative Cabinet.[1]

In the summer of 1858 the Government of India was set upon a new basis. The old 'dual control' which Bright had so long attacked [2] was abolished after the experience of the Mutiny, and the powers and territories of the East India Company were vested in the Crown. In the debates on these memorable changes, Bright propounded to the House of Commons his scheme for decentralisation and admission of natives to the Council, as a first step on the path of teaching the Indians to govern themselves.

> 'I would propose that we should have Presidencies, and not an Empire. . . . I would propose to have at least five Presidencies in India, and I would have the Governments of those Presidencies perfectly equal in rank and in salary. The capitals of those Presidencies would probably be Calcutta, Madras, Bombay, Agra, and Lahore. I will take the Presidency of Madras as an illustration. . . . It has a Governor and a Council. I would give to it a Governor and a Council still, but would confine all their duties to the Presidency of Madras, and I would treat it just as if Madras was the only portion of India connected with this country. I would have its finance, its taxation, its justice,

[1] The whole letter (February 21, 1858) and Gladstone's answer will be found in Morley's *Gladstone*, bk. IV. chap. ix., and Gladstone's biographer adds, 'We may well believe that' this 'sagacious letter from Mr. Bright made its mark upon his meditations.'

[2] See chap. vii., p. 170 above.

and its police departments, as well as its public works and military department, precisely the same as if it were a State having no connection with any other part of India, and recognised only as a dependency of this country.'

He proposed that the office of Viceroy should be abolished. 'If the Governor of each Presidency,' he went on, 'were to have in his Council some of the officials of his Government, some of the non-official Europeans resident in the Presidency, and two or three at least of the intelligent natives of the Presidency in whom the people would have some confidence, you would have begun that which will be of inestimable value hereafter—you would have begun to *unite the government with the governed.*'

Bright believed that England would withdraw from India at some distant day—after 'generations,' he said. But however distant that day might be, he thought that we could not begin to prepare for it too soon, because the task of teaching India to stand alone after we were gone must needs be long and gradual. Near the end of his life, in December 1877, he repeated his views in favour of decentralisation, and connected them with the distant future in the following words:

> 'While the Government [by Presidencies] would necessarily or probably be much better, you would teach the people of these Presidencies to consider themselves, as generations passed on, as the subjects and the people of that State. And thus if the time should come—and it will come, for I agree with Lord Lawrence that no man who examines the question can doubt that some time it must come—when the power of England, from some cause or other, is withdrawn from India, then each one of these States would be able to sustain itself as a compact, as a self-governing community. You would have five or six great States there, as you have five or six great States in Europe; but that would be a thousand times better than our being withdrawn from it now when there is no coherence amongst those twenty nations, and when we should find the whole country, in all probability, lapse into chaos and anarchy, and into sanguinary and interminable warfare.'

There is little doubt that Bright was wrong when he proposed to abolish the central government of India; but in the light of subsequent experience there is equally little doubt that decentralisation was the right policy, although he proposed to carry it too far. Decentralisation and admission of natives to the Councils have in recent years been adopted, as the means of 'uniting the government with the governed,' and may be carried yet further in time to come. The words of the famous dispatch of the Government of India, published in December 1911, proclaim first the adoption and then the limitation of Bright's policy :

> 'The only possible solution of the difficulty would appear to be gradually to give the Provinces a larger measure of self-government, until at last India would consist of a number of administrations, autonomous in all provincial affairs, with the Government of India above them all, and possessing power to interfere in cases of misgovernment, but ordinarily restricting their functions to matters of Imperial concern.'

Bright was one of the first, perhaps the very first, of politicians resident in England to grasp the necessity for treating the natives of India with personal respect and sympathy. It was easy and natural for a Quaker to take a coloured man by the hand. 'I would not,' he said in 1858, 'I would not permit any man in my presence, without rebuke, to indulge in the calumnies and expressions of contempt which I have recently heard poured forth without measure upon the whole population of India.' Throughout his public life he was the personal friend of Indian politicians and reformers, who when they came to England found in him ready sympathy and sound moderating advice. Bright's attitude to India and its problems was in those days as rare as his understanding of the Irish land question. In the earlier half of his career he was a generation ahead of others in sympathetic foresight with regard both to Ireland and to India. So little is it true that he suffered, as some would have us believe, from a British Philistine's want of imagination and from a 'cotton-spinner's' provinciality of outlook. He saw what others did not see, and though there were some things to which he was blind, who knows but that some truths have escaped even the omniscient understanding of his critics ? It is possible for a pair of honest eyes to see as far from Lancashire as from London.

In the parliamentary session of 1858 Bright had been a convalescent on half work. But in the autumn and winter he took the field in earnest. His speeches at half a dozen great meetings in the country marked not only his return with undiminished powers to the forefront of the battle, but a new era in the Franchise movement. Hitherto the introduction of new Reform Bills had been a custom of the House of Commons rather than a question in the country. The official parties found it a useful stage property, but they meant nothing by it, except perhaps some very moderate change in the franchise which would not greatly alter the balance of classes. But after 1858, though this trifling by Whigs and Tories continued for a while longer in Parliament, the real movement was outside, in a serious agitation by the working classes and the unenfranchised part of the middle class to demand the vote. This movement was stirred up by Bright, the only politician of the first rank who took part in it. He connected the demand for Franchise Reform with ample denunciation of the existing aristocratic régime in political, administrative, and social life. He preached a democratic crusade against the privileged orders. He was accused of 'setting class against class.' Not otherwise would household franchise have been won.

Once more, as at the time of the Crimea, John Bright deliberately turned away from the path that would have led him speedily to a place among the Whig Cabinet Ministers. He preferred to remain in the wilderness, until he could lead the whole people into the promised land. His great reputation in the House of Commons and the golden opinions that he had won even among the 'statesmen' whom he had denounced during the Crimea, were soon discounted when it was perceived that illness had not tamed him, that he had chosen for himself the tasks of the 'demagogue' and that he was marshalling the hosts against the citadels of privilege. The toleration with which he had from time to time been regarded by the Whig and Tory press underwent a marked decline, and he became the butt of obloquy in the social world, the universities,[1] and all the quarters where the upper class and their dependents foregathered. The first blows of his new attack were delivered at Birmingham on October 27 and 29, 1858, and they resounded throughout the country with mingled scandal, clamour, and applause.

On October 27 he met his new constituents for the first time. Though he had once and again spoken for a few minutes in the House, he had made no great oration since the beginning of his illness nearly three years before. Not only in Birmingham but throughout the country there was much speculation and

[1] In 1858 the philosopher, T. H. Green, brought forward a motion eulogistic of Bright in the Oxford Union. He writes that it was 'frantically opposed, and after two days' discussion I found myself in a minority of two. I am almost ashamed to belong to a university which is in such a state of darkness.'

excitement as to what he would say. 'The *Times* reporter,' he writes to his wife, 'called this morning to ask when I thought the meeting would be over, that he might arrange for their special engine! Other men, I mean our public men, must be very little, if I am so great.' When the body of the Town Hall was emptied of chairs, 5000 of the citizens could stand shoulder to shoulder, and listen to him there.[1] This night for the first time, and on many a night to come, that great audience swayed, like a cornfield beneath the wind, under the gusts of cheering and laughter that shook them as he spoke. Although, when he began, they seemed packed as tightly as human beings can stand and breathe, yet more than once, in some storm of emotion, the front of the mass swung forward and the rear backward, leaving a broad strip of floor bare to view, like an island of sea-sand revealed for a moment when the waves are sucked down by the tide. And the magic that swayed them was not some hard appeal to the lower part of their nature, but drew its compelling virtue from the simplest invocation of moral principles, in words which survive the speaker as part of the wealth of our mother tongue. No class ever had nobler teaching than the working men of this island during the years while Bright was their champion, while he was being abused by dunces from public school and college, as a vulgar demagogue who could not scan a line of Virgil.

The opening passage of his first Birmingham speech made a profound impression on those who heard it:

> 'If I exhibit embarrassment in rising to address you, I must ask for your forbearance, for, in truth, as I cast my eyes over this great assembly, I feel myself almost bewildered and oppressed with a consciousness of my incapacity to fulfil properly the duty which devolves upon me to-night. It is now nearly three years since I was permitted, and, indeed, since I was able, to stand upon any public platform to address any public meeting of my countrymen; and during that period I have passed through a new and a great experience. From apparent health I have been brought down to a condition of weakness exceeding the weakness of a little child, in which I could neither read nor write, nor converse for more than a few

[1] Bright put it at 6000. The floor below the platform was larger than it is now; it has since been encroached upon at both ends. The audience used to be packed so tight, when Bright was advertised to speak, that it was impossible for men to get their hands up if once they had them down. The heat, for those on the floor, would have been considered unendurable in any less cause than listening to Bright.

minutes without distress and without peril; and from that condition, by degrees so fine as to be imperceptible even to myself, I have been restored to the comparative health in which you now behold me.'

Then after a pause he added:

> 'In remembrance of all this, is it wrong in me to acknowledge here, in the presence of you all, with reverent and thankful heart, the signal favour which has been extended to me by the great Supreme?'

The Rev. Robert W. Dale, the famous Congregational minister of Birmingham, who was present, has recorded that

> 'the hush which had fallen on the vast and excited assembly as soon as he began to speak deepened into awe. We had expected a fierce assault on the "obstinacy" and "iniquity" of the defenders of what the orator afterwards described as "the fabric of privilege," but the storms of political passion were for a moment stilled; we suddenly found ourselves in the presence of the Eternal, and some of us, perhaps, rebuked ourselves in the words of the patriarch, "Surely, the Lord is in this place, and I knew it not."'

But those who had come to hear the speaker denounce 'privilege' had not long to wait. He first declared himself unrepentant with regard to the Crimea. 'Now, after all is over except the tax-gatherer, and the sorrows of those who have lost their friends in the war,' he could perceive no advantage won in return for the 400,000 lives lost—of which he estimated the British portion at 40,000, as many as all 'the grown men of Birmingham from eighteen years of age to fifty!'

He then unrolled his scheme for Parliamentary Reform. 'Wherever you go in Great Britain or Ireland, five out of every six men you meet have no vote.' His remedy fell short of manhood suffrage, which he knew would frighten people too much to be practicable at present.[1] He proposed to extend the £10 household franchise from the boroughs to the counties; and to adopt in the boroughs themselves the rating franchise which had existed for parish purposes at least since the time of

[1] 'I am not working for failure, but for success, and for a real gain, and I must go the way to get it. I am sure the putting manhood suffrage in the Bill is not the way. This has been done by the Chartists, and by the Complete Suffragists, but what has become of their Bills?' [Bright to Joseph Sturge, 2 month, 25, 1858.]

Queen Elizabeth. By his scheme 'every householder, of course, because every householder is rated for the poor, shall have a vote,' whether his rates are paid personally or through the landlord. He proposed also a 'lodger' franchise in the boroughs for every one renting an apartment for £10. This scheme, first put forward by Bright in this Birmingham speech of October 1858, was embodied by him next session in a carefully drawn Bill which was much circulated and discussed. The proposals are, with very slight and quite immaterial changes, the basis of the enfranchising Act passed nine years later, under the auspices of Disraeli. Lord Cranborne was speaking by the book when he said in his wrath that, if the adoption of the principles of Mr. Bright were a triumph, then 'in the whole course of your annals the Conservative Party has won no triumph so signal as this.' That was in 1867; in 1858 Tories and Whigs were equally far from approving the 'Birmingham' Reform Bill. Yet even then Arthur Clough wrote: 'Bright's agitation will bear fruit. He is scoffed at in the metropolitan papers and at all clubs. But his hold on the country is such as no M.P. whatever, except himself, possesses.'

Next he expounded to his Birmingham audience a scheme of redistribution, which he declared to be scarcely second in importance to the broadening of the franchise. He showed that the great cities were grossly under-represented, and were outvoted by the landed interest with its hold on the country seats and corrupt boroughs. 'There are in the House of Commons at present 330 Members, more than half the House, whose whole number of constituents do not amount to more than 180,000, and there are at the same time in Parliament 24 Members whose constituents are upwards of 200,000 in number.' He called on the middle class, under-represented and largely unenfranchised, to unite with the working men to vindicate their common rights. The hour had come and the man. The era of Chartism and mutual class suspicion had passed away; far in the future lay the time when 'labour politics' would come into collision with 'middle class conservatism.' The times were ripe for a union of the Radical part of the middle class with the working men; and Bright was born and bred to preside over such a junction of forces, already incarnate in the vast Birmingham audience to which he spoke.

He proceeded to scotch the immortal fallacy that rich men are better fitted to vote than poor men.

'They say we must not on any account "Americanise"

our institutions. . . . They tell us in America numbers overwhelm property and education. Well, but numbers have not overwhelmed property and education in England, and yet look at legislation in England. Look at our wars, look at our debt, look at our taxes, look at this great fact—that every improvement of the last forty years has been an improvement which numbers, and numbers only, have wrested from the property, and what they call the education of the country. Our education is fairly represented by our Universities, but I say now, as I have said before, that if the Legislature of England, if the Parliament of England, had been guided for thirty years past according to the counsels of the representatives from the Universities, England, instead of being a country of law and of order, would have been long before this a country of anarchy and of revolution.'

Following the same train of argument, he showed the peculiar unfitness of the hereditary Peer to legislate. He drew his famous picture of the life of a Lord, showing how the subservience of all around and the luxury to which the child of fortune has been accustomed from his nursery onwards, unfits him to understand the needs of the nation. Such bold reasoning delighted the men of Birmingham, but was regarded as worse than high treason by the politicians of the day at Westminster. He did not mend matters by ending his attack on the House of Lords by reference to 'another kind of Peer, that creature of—what shall I say?—of monstrous, nay, even of adulterous birth—the spiritual Peer.'

His peroration, reminding the men of Birmingham of what their fathers had done to pass the Reform Bill of 1832, was received with ecstatic enthusiasm:

'Shall we then, I ask you, even for a moment, be hopeless of our great cause? I feel almost ashamed even to argue it to such a meeting as this. I call to mind where I am, and who are those whom I see before me. Am I not in the town of Birmingham—England's central capital; and do not these eyes look upon the sons of those who, not thirty years ago, shook the fabric of privilege to its base? Not a few of the strong men of that time are now white with age. They approach the confines of their mortal day. Its evening is cheered with the remembrance of that great contest, and they rejoice in the freedom they have won. Shall their sons be less noble than they? Shall the fire which they kindled be extinguished with you? I see your answer in every face. You are resolved that the legacy which they bequeathed to you, you will hand down in an accumulated wealth of freedom to your children. As for me, my voice is feeble. I feel now sensibly and painfully that I am not what I was. I speak with diminished fire; I act with a lessened force; but as I am, my countrymen and my constituents, I will, if you will let me, be found in your ranks in the impending struggle.'[1]

In John Bright's creed, the cause of democratic franchise was closely connected with that of economy and peace. He regarded our warlike foreign policy as the result of our aristocratic system of Government. The House of Commons was chiefly aristocratic and for the rest almost entirely plutocratic; the Foreign Office was a strict aristocratic preserve. He believed that if the influence of the working men began to be felt on foreign policy, it would make for peace, and therefore also for retrenchment. His first speech at the Birmingham Town Hall had been devoted mainly to Franchise Reform; two days later, on October 29, at a banquet in the same building, he spoke on foreign policy, connecting it closely with the Franchise agitation.

After showing that Walpole and Peel were both strong upholders of the peaceful views for holding which he was himself called 'unpatriotic,' he proceeded to arraign the theory of the 'balance of power.' We had entered into the Crimean War to 'balance' Russia, and were now bidden, on behalf of this same delicate 'balance,' to embroil ourselves with France, whom we had chosen as our ally in that so recent war. 'The balance of power,' he said, 'is like perpetual motion, or any of those impossible things which some men are always racking their brains and spending their time and money to accomplish.' War was fatal to domestic liberty and democracy, and to the well-being of the poor, as had been proved between 1793 and 1815.

[1] The phrases about his own 'diminished fire' and 'lessened force' had been thought out before he tried the great adventure of addressing this meeting, for the words had actually been written out in full as an essential part of his peroration, which he had set down word for word at the end of his notes, according to his usual custom. These expressions are therefore no evidence that he had felt conscious of lessened power while he was actually speaking. It is true that his brother-in-law, Edward Leatham, used to say he never spoke so well after his illness as he had spoken during the Crimea, but others thought Leatham wrong. He had some trouble with his voice in making his speeches of this winter, 1858-59: 'cutting with a blunt knife,' he called it.

War and great armaments gave to the upper class the monopoly of power and supplied their sons with a multitude of well-paid posts. 'This excessive love for "the balance of power" is neither more nor less than a gigantic system of out-door relief for the aristocracy of Great Britain.'

Lord John Russell had recently been addressing a meeting largely composed of working men, whom he had exhorted to feel proud of belonging to an Empire which, in Great Britain and India together, 'enjoyed a revenue of £100,000,000 a year.' 'The State indeed, of which Lord John Russell is a part,' so ran Bright's shrewd comment, 'may enjoy a revenue of £100,000,000, but I am afraid the working men can only be said to enjoy it in the sense in which men not very choice in their expressions say that for a long time they have "enjoyed very bad health."' At the time Bright made these speeches, the working men had nothing to do with the taxes except to pay their share of them. They had no votes, and consequently they got no special advantages from taxation, such as free education or old age pensions.

The train of thought and feeling which the Roman ruins had aroused in Bright the year before,[1] had been awakened in his memory by a recent newspaper attack on his doctrines, in which the editor had held up ancient Rome as the proper example for modern England.

> 'I do not think,' he told the men of Birmingham, 'that examples taken from pagan, sanguinary Rome, are proper models for the imitation of a Christian country, nor would I limit my hopes of the greatness of England even to the long duration of 800 years. But what is Rome now? The great city is dead. A poet has described her as "the lone mother of dead Empires." Her language even is dead. Her very tombs are empty; the ashes of her most illustrious citizens are dispersed—
>
> "The Scipios' tomb contains no ashes now."
>
> Yet I am asked, I, who am one of the legislators of a Christian country, to measure my policy by the policy of ancient and pagan Rome!
>
> 'I believe there is no permanent greatness to a nation except it be based upon morality. I do not care for military greatness or military renown. I care for the

[1] See his journal and letters, pp. 256-257 above. He had read *Childe Harold* aloud to his daughter while they were at Rome in 1857.

condition of the people among whom I live. There is no man in England who is less likely to speak irreverently of the Crown and Monarchy of England than I am; but crowns, coronets, mitres, military display, the pomp of war, wide colonies, and a huge Empire, are, in my view, all trifles light as air, and not worth considering, unless with them you can have a fair share of comfort, contentment, and happiness among the great body of the people. Palaces, baronial castles, great halls, stately mansions, do not make a nation. *The nation in every country dwells in the cottage*; and unless the light of your constitution can shine there, unless the beauty of your legislation and the excellence of your statesmanship are impressed there on the feelings and condition of the people, rely upon it you have yet to learn the duties of Government.

'The most ancient of profane historians has told us that the Scythians of his time were a very warlike people, and that they elevated an old cimeter upon a platform as a symbol of Mars, for to Mars alone, I believe, they built altars and offered sacrifices. To this cimeter they offered sacrifices of horses and cattle, the main wealth of the country, and more costly sacrifices than to all the rest of their gods. I often ask myself whether we are at all advanced in one respect beyond those Scythians. What are our contributions to charity, to education, to morality, to religion, to justice, and to civil government, when compared with the wealth we expend in sacrifices to the old cimeter? . . . The moral law was not written for men alone in their individual character, but it was written as well for nations, and for nations great as this of which we are citizens. If nations reject and deride that moral law, there is a penalty which will inevitably follow. It may not come at once, it may not come in our lifetime; but, rely upon it, the great Italian is not a poet only, but a prophet, when he says:

> "The sword of heaven is not in haste to smite,
> Nor yet doth linger."

We have experience, we have beacons, we have landmarks enough. We know what the past has cost us, we know how much and how far we have wandered, but we are not left without a guide. It is true we have not, as an ancient people had, Urim and Thummim—those oraculous gems on Aaron's breast—from which to take counsel, but we have the unchangeable and eternal principles of the moral law to guide us, and only so far as we walk by that guidance can we be permanently a great nation, or our people a happy people.'

These doctrines, as regards Parliamentary Reform and foreign policy, were repeated during the next two months at great meetings in Manchester, Edinburgh, Glasgow, and Bradford. The effect of this winter's campaign was immense, and aroused a degree of attention, friendly and hostile, reflected in the cartoons of *Punch*, which treated him for some months as its principal personage. He was frequently, but without the smallest reason, accused of Republicanism. Even so sensible an old gentleman as Lord Chief-Justice Campbell wrote: 'I begin to be afraid that I may live to see John Bright President of the Anglican Republic.' His speeches, reported word for word in the newspapers, and afterwards sold as pamphlets, were read by every one interested in politics.

From the day that Peel had stopped the mouth of the Anti-Corn Law League, there had been some return in politics to the quiet old fashion of former years. Political literature was no longer systematically distributed; no longer were hundreds of small, unreported meetings held in town and village, as they had been in the great days of the League, and as they now are even in normal times. In the 'fifties and 'sixties a political meeting was a noticeable event, and whenever a politician of the first rank made a long speech, he was reported and read at full, not merely in excerpts and headlines. Full reports of great speeches were eagerly awaited and read by a political nation that had very little else in the way of politics brought to its door. For the same reason parliamentary debates were better reported and more closely followed than they are in our own time, although the general level of political interest and understanding is higher to-day, if all ranks of society are taken into account.

This state of things set a premium on careful oratory that would not only move the audience but would read well in the paper next morning and in the pamphlet next month. For all these purposes Bright's art was supreme. He moved his audiences more than Gladstone, though he instructed them less; and yet his speeches formed a body of literature which spread his ideas among students of all classes. Since quality rather than quantity in speaking was then required to make an effective politician, Bright was able to indulge his natural preference for leisurely prepared speeches, which stand the tests of literature as well as those of oratory. At the same time his immunity from the cares of office, and of party leadership, gave him that leisure without which art can scarcely reach perfection, and that licence to utter the thought that was within him which gave to his words an intellectual freedom and a moral power, necessarily rare among politicians bound by the convenience of their party and the opinions of their fellow-countrymen.

One passage from the speech that he made at Glasgow in December 1858, two months after the opening of the campaign at Birmingham, represents his double message of Peace and Democracy with a singular force :

> 'Mr. Disraeli said that expenditure depended on policy, by which he meant that our public expenditure depended on our foreign policy. . . .
>
> 'But when you come to our foreign policy, you are no longer Englishmen ; you are no longer free ; you are recommended not to inquire. If you do, you are told you cannot understand it ; you are snubbed, you are hustled aside. We are told that the matter is too deep for common understandings like ours—that there is great mystery about it. We have what is called diplomacy. We have a great many lords engaged in what they call diplomacy. We have a lord in Paris, we have another in Madrid, another in Berlin, another (at least we had till very lately) in Vienna, and another lord in Constantinople ; and we have another at Washington ; in fact, almost all over the world ; particularly where the society is most pleasant and the climate most agreeable, there is almost certain to be an English nobleman to represent the English Foreign Office, but you never know what he is doing. And out of all this comes the supposed necessity for armaments twice as large as were necessary twenty-five years ago ; and yet you have no control over, and know nothing of the matter. . . .
>
> 'It is a curious thing to observe the evils which nations live under, and the submissive spirit with which they yield to them. I have often compared, in my own mind, the people of England with the people of ancient Egypt, and the Foreign Office of this country with the temples of the Egyptians. We are told by those who pass up and down the Nile that on its banks are grand temples with stately statues and massive and lofty columns, statues each one

of which would have appeared almost to have exhausted a quarry in its production. You have, further, vast chambers and gloomy passages; and some innermost recess, some holy of holies, in which, when you arrive at it, you find some loathsome reptile which a nation reverenced and revered, and bowed itself down to worship. In our Foreign Office we have no massive columns; we have no statues; but we have a mystery as profound; and in the innermost recesses of it we find some miserable intrigue, in defence of which your fleets are traversing every ocean, your armies are perishing in every clime, and the precious blood of our country's children is squandered as though it had no price. I hope that an improved representation will change all this; that the great portion of our expenditure which is incurred in carrying out the secret and irresponsible doings of our Foreign Office will be placed directly under the free control of a Parliament elected by the great body of the people of the United Kingdom.'

If we have not, since that day, been plunged into another European War for 'some miserable intrigue,' like that for which Lords Stratford de Redcliffe and Palmerston plunged us into the Crimea, it is largely due to the increased weight of the working men in our political system, and to the doctrine which Bright preached, and other statesmen have from time to time adopted, that Britain's greatest interest is Peace.

CHAPTER XIII

PALMERSTON, GLADSTONE, AND THE 'MANCHESTER SCHOOL.' THE 'INEVITABLE WAR' AVERTED. THE FRENCH TREATY AND THE PAPER DUTY, 1859-61

'I see how unlucky have been your elections. I have learned not to make myself unhappy on these matters. They are trifles, and don't much impede or hasten the world's march. At the age of fifty we discover that not much is done in a lifetime, and yet that, notwithstanding all the immeasurable ignorance and stupidity of the majority of the race, there is a gradual and sensible victory being gained over barbarism and wrong of every kind. I think we may, in some sort, console ourselves. If we can't win as fast as we wish, we know that our opponents can't in the long run win at all.'—John Bright *to his sister*, Mrs. McLaren, *on his fiftieth birthday*, Nov. 16, 1861.

The Conservative Government, having obtained power solely through the divisions of its enemies, proved unable, as Bright had foreseen, to stay long in office. In February 1859 Disraeli introduced a Franchise Bill very different from that which eight years afterwards he passed into law. The author of *Sybil* had not yet educated either himself or his party to the point of regarding the rich and the poor politically as one 'nation.' The Bill did not gives votes to the working men, and did not increase the representation of the towns. The franchise was to be extended 'laterally,' not downwards. It was proposed to increase the number of the county voters dependent on the landlords, without affording them the protection of the ballot; and to create a number of franchises—'fancy franchises' was the name which Bright fastened on the proposal—for doctors, clergy, graduates, East India Stock holders, State pensioners of £20 a year and upwards, and other nondescript superior persons.

The Whigs and Radicals forgot their grievances against each other in opposition to the Bill. Bright attacked it vigorously, and urged the claims of a real extension of the franchise to new classes. He told honourable Members that if they would now give the vote to the working man, twenty years later they would find that they had thereby secured the basis of society. 'I assure you that resistance is not always Conservative. I profess to be, in intention, as Conservative as you—I believe infinitely more so, if you look twenty or thirty years into the future. Was not Free Trade Conservative? And yet you resisted it to the last. Is not prosperity Conservative? Is not peace Conservative?' Much alarm was felt at this period about Trade Unionism, for it was an era of strikes. Bright warned his countrymen that the Trade Union movement would become revolutionary if the wage-earners were 'condemned to remain a separate and suspected order in our social system,' and that industrial war would go from bad to worse so long as 'the class receiving wages is shut out from the questions and the interests which occupy the minds and engage the energies of the employing class.' [1]

On the last day of March 1859, the 'fancy franchise' Bill was defeated by 39 votes, and a dissolution followed.

Cobden, still without a seat, was absent in America, but at Bright's instigation the electors of Rochdale restored him to Parliament without a contest. Bright himself was opposed by Thomas Dyke Acland, the younger, who stood as a Liberal-Conservative. When the Devonshire candidate first reached Birmingham, he was encouraged to believed that 'Anti-Bright is the strong feeling and they are ready to vote for a broomstick to shake him off.' Acland was undeceived at his first ward meeting, where, as he records, 'the first thing they did was to turn my chairman out of the chair and put one of their own in.' He made an able and gentlemanly fight against a not very tolerant majority, but only secured 1544 votes against Bright and Scholefield, who were elected by 4282 and 4425 respectively. In this contest a young man named Joseph Chamberlain was canvassing for Acland, in opposition to the 'Quaker's' views on foreign policy.

The General Election gave a few more seats to the Conservative Government, but not enough to maintain it in office if the various sections of Liberals were to unite. When politicians came up to London early in June, Bright was much sought after. During the continued absence of Cobden in America, Bright had a dominating influence over the Radical vote in the House, and every one told him that 'the fate of the Government was in his hands.' On June 3 he met Russell by appointment. The Whig leaders, although they could not obtain office without his support, did not propose to reward him with

[1] See his letter dated November 3, 1860.

a share in the spoil. And on his side Bright asked, not for office, but for a positive undertaking that, if Derby and Disraeli were turned out by his help, Palmerston and Russell would keep England clear of any participation in the war then raging in Italy. As Russell and Bright were talking together that morning, the French and Italians were crossing the Ticino to fight the battle of Magenta and deliver Milan from the Austrians. Russell gave Bright a solemn promise to observe English neutrality, and added with perfect truth that there was no question of England interfering on the French side; that the only fear was lest she should intervene on the Austrian side; and that this could only occur if the Derby-Disraeli Government retained power. Both Liberal and Conservative statesmen were anti-French in feeling, but in the minds of Palmerston and Russell this was counterbalanced, as regards the war now on hand, by anti-Austrian and pro-Italian sentiment not shared by the Conservatives. So Lord John could safely promise Bright that he would observe neutrality in the war; he also held out hopes, which proved vain, that there would be a good Reform Bill and that Palmerston would 'go up to the Lords.'

Three days later a party meeting was held at Willis's Rooms, at which 270 Liberal Members were present. 'Palmerston spoke, then Russell, then calls for me, and I spoke. Afterwards other Members.' The alliance was thus publicly sealed and ratified. Bright already understood that he was not to be given office, because of the scandal created by his speeches in the country during the last winter.

On June 9 young Lord Hartington moved an amendment to the Address, expressing want of confidence in the Ministry. Bright spoke in support, declaring that he distrusted the Conservatives' neutrality in the Italian War, that their Reform Bill had been a sham, and that the General Election had left them in a minority. Next evening, in a House of 643 Members voting, the Ministry was defeated by 13, and resigned the following day. When the figures of this close division, in which Bright had been the deciding factor, were read out in the House, Cavour's representative threw up his hat and cheered in the lobby. The Italian had good reason to be pleased, for the division brought Lord John Russell to the Foreign Office. During the next eighteen months Italy's freedom was at stake; and it was secured for ever, in no small degree by the benevolent neutrality of the new Government in Downing Street.

The business of Cabinet making began, and on June 15

Bright received the following letter. It was from Lord John, and was a sequel to their conversation of June 3:

'My dear Mr. Bright,—Till yesterday I could not properly communicate with you.

'Lord Palmerston having been entrusted by the Queen with the formation of a Government, it was for me to consider whether I could join it. I thought it impossible to insist on his going to the House of Lords, if he did not choose to go [to] that House.

'The only thing which remained for consideration was whether there was any office which I could take, which would be a security for my influence over a Liberal course. It struck me that if I accepted the Foreign Office, I might steer a course which should be free from personal adulation of the Emperor of the French on the one hand, and of undue favour to Austria on the other. Such a course might prevent Germany from rushing to war, and thus contribute to future peace at an early period.

'With respect to reform, I told Lord Palmerston that if the Bill of the Government when prepared should not appear to me a sound and satisfactory measure, I reserved to myself the power of resigning office before it was introduced.

'Seats in the Cabinet were to be offered to Mr. Cobden and Mr. Milner Gibson. You will not be surprised that Lord Palmerston said he regretted that the course you had taken, not with regard to the reform of the House of Commons, but with regard to other institutions, considered essential by the great majority of Englishmen, prevented his proposing to you to join his Cabinet.—I remain, Yrs. very truly, J. Russell.'

The 'institutions' which Bright had been attacking in his Birmingham speeches were, not the Crown, but the House of Lords and aristocratic influence everywhere.[1]

Bright wrote in his journal that evening: 'This is amusing, and I suppose the excuse will serve its purpose. Palmerston

[1] This is the only possible interpretation of the letter, and Bright so interpreted it, in his speech of January 18, 1865, at Birmingham. Cobden, when pressed by Palmerston to accept office himself, urged that the exclusion of Bright was unfair, because in his Birmingham speeches he had 'carefully avoided personalities.' Palmerston replied: 'It is not personalities that are complained of. A public man is right in attacking persons. But it is his attacks on *classes* that have given offence on powerful bodies, who can make their resentment felt.'

would not have raised himself in my opinion by offering me office, and I could not have accepted it or anything else at his hands.' A fortnight later Palmerston wished to offer Bright the consolation prize of a Privy Councillorship, but the Queen demurred. 'It would,' she wrote, 'be impossible to allege any service Mr. Bright has rendered, and if the honour were looked upon as a reward for his systematic attacks upon the institutions of the country, a very erroneous impression might be produced as to the feeling which the Queen or her Government entertain towards these institutions.'

Cobden, on board an Atlantic steamer, did not know that the Derby Cabinet had fallen, and that all England, impatiently awaiting his arrival, was speculating whether or not he would accept office. When he landed at Liverpool on June 29, letters from Palmerston and Russell were put into his hands. 'Recent speeches,' Russell wrote, 'have prevented the offer of a Cabinet office to Mr. Bright. This is much to be regretted; but if you accept, his accession may take place hereafter. If you refuse, I do not see the prospect of amalgamating the Liberal party during my lifetime.' But in fact it was during Palmerston's—not Russell's—lifetime that the amalgamation of the Liberal party was bound to be a hope deferred.

The great body of Cobden's admirers and friends petitioned him, both publicly and privately, to accept office. But his best friend hoped that he would refuse, though he did no more than 'place all the facts before him, leaving his own judgment to decide.' 'We now know,' writes Cobden's biographer, 'that Mr. Bright's sagacity was not at fault. If Cobden had taken office at Midsummer, he would certainly have been out by Christmas.'

The first two years of the new Whig Cabinet (June 1859-61), saw a terrible danger draw near and recede. The panic-mongers, headed by Palmerston himself, long held the country on the verge of war with France, for no reason except the utterly false belief that Napoleon intended to attack us, though in fact desire for friendship with England was the fixed point in his otherwise erratic schemes. Such a war would have made an end of 'Victorian prosperity' and of much else besides. It was averted by Gladstone, Cobden, and Bright, in the sweat and agony of a contest still to be read in the anxious and often despairing letters that passed between the three. Their struggle to avert war is largely forgotten because it was successful. But the positive prizes they secured in place of war—Cobden's Commercial Treaty and Gladstone's Budgets of 1860-61, including the repeal of the Paper Duties—are remembered as the crown of Palmerston's Premiership, though certainly not of his policy.[1]

In this domestic and foreign crisis, Gladstone on the Treasury Bench consulted and worked with Bright below the gangway. It was in the darkest months of anxiety and suspense in 1860 that their political friendship first took solid form. The alliance can be given no earlier date, for as late as June 1859, when the Cabinet was being formed, Bright had written to Horsman: 'The appointment of our eccentric friend Gladstone seems to me wholly unjustifiable, and shows a preference for opponents which supporters are not likely to admire.'[2] Six months later Bright held very different language. He notes in his journal (February 24, 1860): 'Gladstone's speech on Budget and Treaty admirable; sound and liberal and moral. How infinitely he excels the ordinary race of statesmen.'

Russell kept his promise to Bright that England should remain neutral during the Franco-Austrian war. Peace was soon restored by the Treaty of Villafranca in July 1859. That treaty, momentarily so disappointing, ultimately so useful to the Italian cause, was the signal over here for an outburst of pro-Italian feeling, no longer incompatible with the prevailing antagonism to France. France had deserted Italy, men said, and was now preparing to attack England. It was alleged that the number of Napoleon's ships was close on the number of our own, and that we had no effective army for a second line of defence. It was also said that Napoleon III. intended to use his forces to conquer this island. So far was this from the truth, that England's friendship was in fact the pivot of his foreign policy.

The anti-French panic, whipped up by Palmerston and the *Times*, and running straight for war, was countered by a quiet and characteristic move of Cobden. While the storm of panic was blowing big guns in England, he carried through at Paris

[1] In 1863 Bright saw with amusement a picture painted for the Speaker, in which 'the Cabinet was on the Treasury Bench, Palmerston speaking, Cobden and I up behind Ministers as if we were supporters, which we are not. On the Table "French Commercial Treaty" lying open as if the glory of Palmerston's Government, when Cobden and I know he did all he dared to make the Treaty miscarry.'

[2] The sharpness of this saying contrasts with Bright's letter to Gladstone in February 1858, see p. 265 above. The explanation was that Gladstone had either abstained or voted for the late Tory Government in the divisions that brought about its fall.

negotiations for a Commercial Treaty with France. The much abused Napoleon was one of the few Free Traders in his own dominions, and Cobden tried upon him with success that personal fascination that seldom failed with emperor or clown.

The Commercial Treaty belongs to the life of Cobden, but Bright's modest share in it has been told by himself in his journal of January 25, 1860:

> 'The Commercial Treaty with France signed yesterday by Cobden on behalf of this Government—a wonderful event, and may have great and blessed results. It has come about curiously. Near the end of last session, I made a speech on expenditure and taxation, and urged Free Trade with France—recommended reduction of Wine Duties, etc., as the best means of putting an end to the chances of war. When this speech reached Paris, M. Chevalier, the eminent French economist, wrote to Cobden, expressing his high approval of it, and his opinion that something might be done, wishing that Cobden and I should see M. Persigny, the French Ambassador, who would be very favorable to a better trade policy between France and England. Cobden saw him, but I did not. Mrs. Cobden and her children being in Paris, Cobden was to spend the autumn there, and, with the aid of M. Chevalier, he succeeded in inducing the Emperor to consider the question of the French Tariff, and by his judgment, patience, intelligence, and tact has brought about a treaty, invaluable, as I hope and believe, to both countries and to Europe. It is a crowning reputation for him, and will compensate for many anxieties he has suffered of late. Lords and diplomatists, spending £15,000 a year, have been in Paris for half a century past, and have done nothing: Cobden, a simple citizen, unpaid, unofficial, but earnest and disinterested, has done all. If our statesmen were such as he, what would not England become! I rejoice in his success as if some great blessing had happened to myself. Such events are compensations for the disappointments and wearisome labors of public life.'

The story of the two years' struggle that raged round the closely connected questions of peace and war, Commercial Treaty and Paper Duties, can be followed in Bright's letters to Cobden. These, we may be sure, left no *nuance* of the writer's thoughts and feelings concealed.

Oct.-Nov. 1859. 'The Reform question here is an ugly

one for our oligarchy. A war with France would, in their eyes, be a cheap price to pay for a few years' respite only from the hated Reform.' 'I presume they want a war with France, and as the former one was so successful, postponing Reform for forty years, they think the experiment worth trying again. If they do, posterity will see what we can only foretell.'

Nov. 15, 1859. 'I was in London a fortnight ago, and last Friday week I called on Sidney Herbert at the War Office about some soldiers whose discharge I was endeavoring to obtain. I found him talking in the tone of that foolish old Admiral who bores us so much in the House: "no reliance can be placed on that fellow over the water"—"he undertook four things, and he has done two of them, he has humbled Russia and Austria, and it may be England next"—"things are looking very squally," etc. This was his language.[1] I told him he was in an atmosphere of armaments and war, and that his judgment was affected by it. . . . The suspicion about the French is great and widespread—the *Times* and almost all the London papers, by lies and insinuations of every kind, do their best to increase it. Our plan [Commercial Treaty] is the only remedy that I know of, and if it be not adopted, war I think will not long be avoided. To partially break down the Custom House barriers between the two nations is the only peace security we can have, and if the French Government made a bold step in that direction now, and Gladstone made a corresponding move in the wine duties and in some minor articles, I think public opinion would change, and the dangers ahead might be averted. I suspect, however, that it is opposed to the policy of the English Oligarchy and Court to smooth the way between England and France, and that they would prefer always to have that kind of suspicion which seems to justify great armaments, great taxes, a busy Foreign Office, and the

[1] It was this year that Tennyson, in his song for the Rifle Volunteers, wrote of Napoleon III.:

> 'True that we have a faithful ally,
> But only the Devil knows what he means.'

Whatever we may think of Bright's dislike of the Volunteer movement, we must bear in mind that the movement, however desirable, originated in a complete misinterpretation of Napoleon III.'s intentions towards England. As late as August 1861, Bright writes to Cobden: 'It is considered anti-national and wanting in patriotism *to hope even* that the French do not intend war against us, and that we may never have to resist an invasion from them.'

distraction of the public mind from home affairs. Mr. Gladstone will honestly go with us, if he has the courage—for without much courage he cannot succeed.'

Feb. 5, 1860. 'All that has happened since the announcement of the [Commercial] Treaty proves how accurately I have taken the measure of the House of Commons and the ruling class here. Mr. Gladstone is as enthusiastic about it as you or I can or could be. Lord John Russell is really glad about it and speaks of it with a look of exultation rather unusual with him. There may be others in the Government who are pleased, as, of course, our friend Milner Gibson is—but I have not seen much evidence of it. Cardwell is in good spirits. Villiers, who is desperately and absurdly anti-French, and indeed almost anti-everything we wish for, talks against it, as if to make a Treaty were contrary to Free Trade. The tone in Parliament is not warm or cordial on your great work—they don't like the work itself, and they don't like the man who has done the work. I never saw anything before that so conclusively showed the bias of Parliament against a real pacification, with reduced armaments, estimates and taxes, as the feeling manifested during the last fortnight. I am quite sure that the prospect of more trade with France is unpleasant to the ruling class. . . . In Lancashire and Yorkshire, and indeed throughout the country—and in the city of London, I believe one opinion only is expressed, that of admiration at your success, and of thankfulness that there is a prospect of more peaceful times. This opinion will, I am convinced, be felt in Parliament when the Treaty and the Budget come to be discussed, and the threatened hostility of the Tories will prove too feeble to do harm. I feel daily and hourly some exultation that your labors and mine do still produce some result. . . . I think Alderman Salomons says you should be made a Baronet! What a glory! And how Aldermanic the suggestion!'

They were not yet out of the wood. The provisions of the Commercial Treaty had yet to pass the House of Commons. In so far as the new Budget was Free Trade it was acceptable to the Parliament of that date, but so far as it made for reconciliation with France it was suspect.

Feb. 8, 1860. 'The resolutions to be moved on the 16th. There is a bad spirit in the House; the devil shows himself almost more than ever; the "services" and the tax-eaters, the courtiers and the war men, are all hard hit by the Treaty and hate it even more than they dare tell. In the country there is a different feeling, but, during the delay, the *Times* does its utmost to poison the public mind. Gladstone's illness is very unfortunate—he has had a smart attack on the chest, and it may impair his power very much. I know not who can supply his place, if he fails—for the *old, old Whigs* know little of political economy and care little about taxes—except that the people should be content to pay them.

'Do what you think best. I know the Government people, or some of them, wish you to come. *I wish you were here*—but I do not like to trouble you by urging you to come.'

Cobden, however, remained at Paris, and Gladstone won his own battle. Bright writes to Cobden:

Feb. 26, 1860. 'Just what I expected has happened. The great Free Trade propositions have borne down all opposition, and in the country no meeting of any kind could be held without a direct vote of approval of Gladstone's measures taken as a whole. Town Councils, Chambers of Commerce, and public meetings have been almost unanimous, and many votes of thanks have been passed to you for your services in connection with the Treaty. I have never seen a case in which a good cause, backed by public opinion, has made a more striking change in the tone, the speeches, and the votes of the House. Gladstone seems very happy.'

Then fresh trouble arose. King Victor Emmanuel, in order to buy from France permission to annex more integral parts of Italy, ceded Savoy and Nice to Napoleon. England's sympathies were right about the Italian question, but her understanding of it left something to be desired. All the good and bad passions of our countrymen blazed up in anger as fierce and ill-informed as the anger of Garibaldi himself when he heard that the French were to have the two provinces. Again we were on the verge of war with France, this time on account of Savoy. Bright flung himself into the breach and put in a plea for the common-sense policy of minding our own business, in a speech which was loudly denounced as 'un-English.' 'Perish Savoy,' he said to the House of Commons on March 2,

'I say, perish Savoy—though Savoy, I believe, will not perish and will not suffer—rather than that we, the representatives of the people of England, should involve the Government of this country with the people and Government of France in a matter in which we have really no interest whatever.' 'Unless it can be shown that there is any direct and obvious interest which this country has in any of the foreign questions which are so constantly discussed, what an absurd spectacle do we offer to Europe with all these repeated discussions.'

This attack on the habit indulged by Palmerstonian England of perpetually lecturing and shaking the birch at Continental powers grown too big for the part of naughty boy, is the central doctrine so wittily set forth by Matthew Arnold many years later in *Friendship's Garland*. John Bright, being a dissenter, and not having been to Oxford, never got the credit for having understood the doctrines of Sweetness and Light in this matter, though in fact he was the first to preach them.

Fortunately for ourselves and for Italy, we managed to swallow our pride over the question of Nice and Savoy, and adopted Bright's 'un-English' policy.

The next event was that the Lords threw out the Repeal of the Paper Duty, thereby reclaiming control over finance. In so doing they were abetted by Palmerston himself, who thought it the ideal arrangement for the country that he should be in office, but that the Lords should reject any Liberal measure which his Government might be so ill-advised as to introduce. On May 20 Bright wrote to Cobden:

> 'You have seen Derby's threat to throw out the Paper Duties Bill in the Lords. I think the crisis one of great importance. The *Court* is not friendly to this Government, that I am sure of, it is anti-French to a strong and most dangerous degree. The "services" and the "interior" oligarchy look with alarm on Reform, and on any further approach to direct Taxation—they are determined to destroy the Government or rather Mr. Gladstone, who is just now the object of their bitterest hate. The Treaty, the Budget, the Reform Bill, are regarded with animosity, and I believe in my conscience that war with anybody, or anything, but especially with France, would be considered a blessing if it saved them from these hateful measures. . . .
>
> 'The vile agents for the furtherance of war do all they

can to create the belief that "there can be no security for peace so long as a Buonaparte is on the throne of France." It is the old story, and the holy alliance is to be brought back from its grave :—our Court and the Russian Court, and all they can influence, and a portion of our Press, the *Times* leading them. I cannot think that the Government as a Government is in this conspiracy, but there are members of it who would like to go with the Court; but it cannot depart from a policy of peace without breaking up, for there are some men in it who mean what is right.

'I had a talk with Disraeli on Thursday night; he talks rather at random often, and it is hard to say when he is in earnest. He said: "You brought in a Government to give you Reform and peace, and you will get no Reform, and within six months you will be at war: *war is inevitable.*" I blamed him for being a party to the murder of the Cheap Press, thro' this proceeding of Lord Derby. He laughed and "chaffed" about it; said he read the *Star* more than any other paper, it was the best paper published, etc.'

Bright himself could ask for nothing finer than Gladstone's wrath when he found that the Lords had rejected his Paper Duty Repeal, and that the Prime Minister and the House of Commons were minded tamely to acquiesce in this resumption of hereditary control over the people's taxes. 'I told Walpole,' writes Bright, 'that if Coke and Selden and Glanville and Pym and such men, whose names are associated with the ancient defence of the Commons, could come back now, they would spit on the Committee [of privilege]—and Gladstone said "Yes, and roll it in the mud and the House of Commons with it." '

Palmerston, with unpardonable treachery to his own Cabinet, wrote to the Queen that if the Lords threw out the Repeal of the Paper Duty 'they would perform a good public service.' And the steps which he took against them when they had performed that service, were proportionately mild.

(Bright to Cobden. July 15.)

'Gladstone has been in a painful and critical position; from day to day it has been doubtful if he could remain under a leader who has used him so treacherously. On the last night of the debate, before I spoke, Lord John beckoned me out of the House, and told me how difficult was the position, and suggested that, if I agreed with him in not wishing to brings things to a crisis, I should not say anything to render Gladstone's continuance in office less possible. I told him I should leave matters in that particular as they were, and not add intentionally to the mischief which was already extensive enough. . . . There is great dissatisfaction with Palmerston on our side of the House, and in the country; and but for Gladstone and Gibson, I think all our "below the gangway" party would overturn the Government, on the first opportunity. I have not sought to aggravate this feeling just now, for I think a change of Government would bring us into many perils. I suppose the Government will go on to next session—I hope so—that you may not be disturbed, and that the Paper Duties may be got rid of. I believe their repeal will be an immense thing to destroy the unwholesome supremacy of the wretches who direct the *Times*, and I think a change of Government might prevent it for some time to come. It will be a great aid to the popular party throughout the country.'

(Aug. 13.) 'Our friends in the Government are in a miserable position. You will have seen my speech on the privilege question on Friday night, and Palmerston's angry and insolent reply. Gladstone and Gibson sat there, in a pitiable submission to their master, condemning in their hearts everything he said, as much as I did.'

A few days later Gladstone wrote to Bright on the subject of the revived control of the Lords over finance: 'Nothing can in my eyes attenuate the magnitude of the event. Notwithstanding the Treaty, notwithstanding the progress towards freedom and peace in Italy, it has left, for us, a great black mark on the year 1860, and both the House of Commons and its members are smaller than they were.' 'The Commons,' Bright wrote to McLaren, 'are now but a *sub* to the Lords, as the Kitchen is to the Drawing-Room.' 'To-day we begin to pay Taxes at the dictation of the Lords! How are the mighty fallen!'

But the end was not yet.

In the middle of September, shortly after Garibaldi's triumphant entry into Naples, Bright writes to Cobden:

'The public eye is looking rather to Italy than to anything at home; we seem on a platform watching the progress of a singular revolution. We see Governments decayed and rotten, only needing to be touched to fall to pieces; people long subject to bad and insulting rule, manifesting a moderation and a wisdom unlooked for; and a leader, but the other day without money, or men, or power of any kind, becoming the Dictator and Arbiter of the fate of millions. The whole thing is very strange—I rejoice that so little blood is spent—but I am not without fear as to the result. Heretofore the "royalties" of Europe have not permitted changes of this kind to be perfected, and I am doubting now if they will not, at some point, unite and suppress that which must be to the majority of them a matter of dread. I think the Emperor of the French has behaved with great moderation and much wisdom since Villafranca.'

(Oct. 10.) 'I observe your remarks about the iron-cased ships. We have built sailing ships—then steamers—then gun boats—and now I suppose we are to spend some millions on ships in armour. I see no end to it. The greatest mechanical intellects of our time are absorbed in the question how to complete instruments of defence and destruction, and there seems no limit to their discoveries or projects, so long as France and England shall lead in great armaments, and in the attempt to dominate over the world. What a glorious isolation is that of the United States. Until we adopt their principle, I see no security for peace for us or for Europe—for until then, every disturbance in Europe is made the pretext for a greater expenditure here, and we are constantly in a state of preparation to plunge into the chaos of any Continental entanglement.'

In January 1861 he wrote to Mr. Gladstone:

'Some members have insisted upon it that no good will be done till some arrangement is made with France as to naval armaments. This might easily be done if the difficulty on this side the Channel were no greater than that on the other side. I am convinced that Mr. Cobden could arrange the whole matter with the Emperor in one tenth of the time he spent on the Commercial Treaty, if he knew he would be heartily and honestly supported by the English Court and Government. . . . Only this year, what has been done? The Treaty and the abolition of Passports—and Mr. Cobden now tells me he has obtained the consent of the French Post Office to an increase in the weight of letters passing through the French post, and he has written to Rowland Hill to urge him at once to have the arrangement concluded. More, much more may be done. I believe there has *never before, in any time*, been a Government in France more willing to act honorably and amicably with England, and that anything we can reasonably ask will be conceded. At least 15 millions a year might be saved to the two countries at once by such an arrangement as I speak of, besides the increasing peril of war from these frightful preparations, and this incessant military excitement.'

The suggestion for a limitation of armaments by mutual agreement was no mere Quaker fantasy. Six months after Bright had written this letter (July 26), Disraeli spoke in the House in favour of a reduction of naval expenditure by an understanding with France as to the relative size of the two navies. Disraeli said that the wish for such an understanding had been 'candidly expressed' by France. And indeed as early as January 1849 Napoleon, when President of the French Republic, had offered to make almost any reduction we might suggest in naval armaments, provided we reduced our own in somewhat the same proportion. Lord Palmerston had declined the offer.[1]

In February 1861 Lord John Russell threw over Parliamentary Reform, in spite of the hopes that he had held out to Bright in his letter of June 15, 1859.[2] Since Palmerston would not have allowed any real extension of the suffrage to the working classes, it was perhaps as well that the question should be altogether laid aside in Parliament, till Bright's agitation in the country had become irresistible, and till Gladstone stood in Palmerston's place. A bad Reform Bill might have been worse than none.

(Bright's Journal. Feb. 5, 1861.)

'Lord John Russell threw over the Reform question in a speech of offensive tone and language. I replied, and spoke on the general question. I had great difficulty in restraining my indignation at his conduct. I shall keep no terms with this Government for the future. It is base,

[1] This appears clearly in the F.O. papers, as has been pointed out to me by Rev. F. A. Simpson of Trinity College, Cambridge, author of the *Rise of Louis Napoleon*.

[2] See p. 282 above.

as was the former Government of Lord Palmerston. How long Mr. Gladstone and Mr. Gibson will go through the mire with them I know not.'

For the next four years the pleasant personal intercourse that had existed between Russell and Bright was broken off. Bright thought that Lord John had not behaved well about Reform, and avoided his company without being positively rude. There is no evidence that Lord John noticed the change.[1]

Yet even now Bright's political sagacity, which in spite of his fiery indignations was seldom at fault, prompted him not to overturn the Government unless and until it failed to settle the Paper Duty question and re-establish the Commons' control over finance. He writes to Cobden: 'I have not seen Gibson since his friend and patron threw over the Reform cause. He may expect Gladstone to repeal the Paper Duty. If he does, I can understand his sticking to the ship.'

And in fact Gladstone had bethought him of a plan. He put together all his financial proposals for the year 1861 into one Bill, which the Lords must either accept or reject as a whole. They had not claimed the right to amend money Bills, and they must now either throw out the whole Budget or accept the repeal of the Paper Duties. On April 15 Gladstone wrote to Bright a letter marked 'very private': 'It is our intention to adopt a mode of *procedure* in regard to financial matters this year, which, among other advantages, will materially tend to prevent a recurrence by the Lords to the great operation of 1860. But I most earnestly hope that nothing will be said to-day which can put upon it an invidious construction. I would indeed hope more than this; namely, that, if we do what is right and effectual, we should all through say the very least possible about it. All, however, that I venture to ask for to-day is that you will use your influence, or if need be give an example, in favour of treating this part of the subject to-day with an absolute forbearance.'

So, at Gladstone's request, the great triumph was not hailed by Bright and the Radicals with any provocative demonstra-

[1] Bright's journal, March 2, 1864: 'Received this morning invitation from Lord Russell to dinner for the 12th. Since his abandonment of the cause of Reform have not had any intercourse with him, and since his acceptance of a Peerage have not ever seen him except once or twice in the House of Lords. Another engagement for the 12th to dine with Mr. Everest will prevent my dining with him.' In 1866 Bright dined with Russell, who was bitterly attacked by London Society for receiving the demagogue at his house.

tions of joy. But they had reason for profound satisfaction. Gladstone's stroke opened out the paths to a better future. The Lords' control over finance was gone for ever, unless they should some day be mad enough to throw out the whole Budget of the year ; cheap paper was obtained, ensuring an epoch of cheap books and cheap journals ; and a 'statesman' of mature age had most miraculously blossomed out into a Radical hero —a man crafty, resolute, eloquent, capacious of mind, and prepared to devote his long experience of great affairs and his unrivalled genius to no cause save that of the people.

CHAPTER XIV

THE AMERICAN CIVIL WAR

'Whereas one Alfred Rubery was convicted on or about the twelfth day of October 1863, in the Circuit Court of the United States for the District of California, of engaging in, and giving aid and comfort to the existing rebellion against the Government of this country, and sentenced to ten years' imprisonment, and to pay a fine of ten thousand dollars;

'And whereas, the said Alfred Rubery is of the immature age of twenty years, and of highly respectable parentage;

'And whereas, the said Alfred Rubery is a subject of Great Britain, and his pardon is desired by John Bright, of England;

'Now therefore, be it known that I, Abraham Lincoln, President of the United States of America, these and divers other considerations me thereunto moving, and especially as a public mark of the esteem held by the United States of America for the high character and steady friendship of the said John Bright, do hereby grant a pardon to the said Alfred Rubery, the same to begin and take effect on the twentieth day of January 1864, on condition that he leave the country within thirty days from and after that date.'[1]

During the most fateful years of the nineteenth century, when no one knew from month to month whether England would not lend her aid to the secession of the slave-owners from President Lincoln's Government, the nicely balanced scales were turned in favour of peace, not by the action of a political party, but by the efforts of individual men—Prince Albert, the Duke of Argyll, Forster, Goldwin Smith, Mill, Cobden, and Leslie Stephen, among whom John Bright was in this struggle the first and the foremost. When the 'statesmen,' the Parliament, and the press of oligarchic England made the country appear favourable to the South, Bright and his friends roused the unenfranchised masses to proclaim their sympathy with freedom across the Atlantic, and so prevented by a hair's

[1] Rubery had been engaged in a plot to seize a vessel in San Francisco for the purpose of going out as a privateer on behalf of Jefferson Davis. The judge who tried him and the two Senators for California reported that there was great indignation at the crime, but that the people would be satisfied with the pardon 'if granted at the request of Mr. Bright, who is a true friend of their country.'

breadth a war that would have turned the world's course into a new and disastrous direction. More was at issue than the extinction of all possibility of future friendship between England and free America, though that alone would have been stake enough. More even was at issue than the good name of England, which would have perished on the day when the Union Jack was unfurled beside the flag of the slave-owners. The issue was nothing less than the world-wide revival of slavery. If the South had with British help established her independence, slavery would have grown apace not only in all the Western Hemisphere south of the Potomac, but in Africa and in every land where the low development of one race puts it at the mercy of another. If, as so nearly happened, a great American Republic had been formed by British aid, with slavery for its sole *raison d'être* as an independent State, the example would have spread like the plague in a world ever susceptible to such infection.[1] 'If we interfere,' so Bright wrote to Cobden in October 1861, 'we shall not only create the great slave nation, but be compelled to guarantee its permanence, and to accept a protectorate of slavedom, as we are now burdened with the *integrity* of Turkey.'

It is easy to see this now, and to whiten the tomb of 'Father Abraham.' But John Bright saw it then, when the wise were blind; and he made half England see.

When the fathers of the American Commonwealth made their famous Declaration that all men were created equal, the words sounded strange on the lips of slave-owners. Slavery, however, was then on the decline among the revolting colonists, and was regarded by them with disfavour. One of their grievances against George III. was that he had refused to sanction the suppression of the trans-Atlantic slave-trade. It was expected that slavery would disappear by a gradual process. The Quakers, taught by John Woolman, had set on foot a movement towards manumission, and no violent passion had been aroused on the opposite side. Slavery was then chiefly domestic, and was not the sole basis of the Southern economic system. But in the following generation a great change took place. The invention of the cotton-gin in 1793 enabled the Southern States to produce cotton for the Lancashire looms on an enormous and ever-increasing scale. By the middle of the nineteenth century 'cotton was king,' and the Southern

[1] Even as it is, we know by recent experience what the modern cosmopolitan capitalist can do in the Congo and Peru.

planters had persuaded themselves that cotton could not be grown by free labour. The modern commercial spirit of wholesale production had made alliance with slavery, giving to that 'peculiar institution' a magnitude and a potency that destroyed every other principle in the life of the South.

A recent American historian, after an impartial examination of the facts, has drawn an authoritative picture of the plantation system.[1] Being human, the Southerners were usually kind to the negroes whom they kept as inmates of their own houses. But these 'household servants were different in all respects from the field hands.' The slaves on the plantation were systematically and of set economic purpose underfed, ill-clothed, ill-housed, and overworked. In Louisiana the owners of plantations openly admitted that 'they found it the best economy to work off their stock of negroes about once in seven years and then buy an entire set of new hands.' The slaves were abandoned to the mercy of the overseers, the refuse of mankind, disliked by the very planters who were under the necessity of employing them. A vice inherent in slavery is that the slave has no motive to work except the lash. Flogging was an essential part of the system, without which it would not have been profitable; there was no other choice between flogging the negroes or making them free. Morality among the blacks was discouraged. Their women were used to breed ever more slaves; they were sold, advertised, and priced for their qualities as brood-mares. The breaking up of negro families by sale, though frowned upon by many of the best Southerners, was a common feature of the system. The slave auctions did most to create abolitionist feeling in the North, because they were more in evidence than the secret horrors of the plantations. 'The greatest orator I ever heard,' said John Randolph, 'was a woman. She was a slave. She was a mother, and her rostrum was the auction-block.'

Slavery degraded the white man, to whom it sacrificed the black. The vast majority even of the white population, significantly spoken of as 'mean whites,' had lost their hold on the best tracts of land; but so long as they could feel superior to the negro, they were content to live abject lives, beneath a small oligarchy who alone reaped the financial benefits of slave labour. Other benefits there were none. Art, literature, learning, science withered away. Crafts and

[1] Rhodes, *History of the United States*, 1850-77, vol. i. chap. iv. The statements in my text are based on that highly documented work, the recognised authority on the subject.

manufactures could not flourish down South. The Southerners were Free Traders, not because they were above Protection, but because they were below it, having no manufactures to protect.[1]

As the nineteenth century wore on, the Southern writers and politicians taught themselves to think of everything human and divine in terms of slavery. Slavery became to them what superstition is to the fanatic, an obsession extinguishing or absorbing every other thought. At length it stepped out into the open and took the offensive. It claimed to be no longer the exception but the rule; not the vanishing past but the coming future. It boasted that it would reconquer mankind, and it did for a while reconquer the American Commonwealth. In the 'fifties the political machine of United States politics was seized on by the Southern politicians, who used it to propagate their ideals in the North, to erect the slave system in the new States of the West, and to extend the area southwards by force of arms into Mexico. They established a complete system of terrorism. Down South no one could speak against slavery without being lynched, and the statute law of some States assigned the death penalty for any one circulating anti-slavery literature even among the whites.

In 1856 the character of the Southern domination of the Republic was brought home to the people of the North by a remarkable incident. Preston Brooks, a Carolinian member of the House of Representatives, strode into the United States Senate, and with a heavy weapon struck Charles Sumner from behind on the head, as he sat there at his desk. Brooks intended to kill him, and actually disabled him for several years to come. The ladies and gentlemen of the South passionately applauded the deed. Sumner shortly afterwards became Bright's friend and correspondent.

At length the slave-owners exhausted the apparently inexhaustible patience of their countrymen. The North determined not indeed to abolish slavery in the South, but to prevent its indefinite extension into the West, and to put an end to the subservience of the Republic to the slavery politicians. On this platform Abraham Lincoln was chosen at the Presidential Election of 1860. Thereupon the Southern States seceded from the Union, and proclaimed the Independence of their own

[1] The remarks in these two paragraphs are not true of the Border States, particularly not of Virginia, where the plantation system proper was not found. But they are true of the cotton-growing States that dragged Virginia into the Secession.

Confederacy under President Jefferson Davis. Whatever may have been the legal or moral rights of Secession abstractly considered under the old constitution, the cause of Secession was slavery, and slavery alone.

This state of society and politics, which was hidden from the view of the English aristocracy and Foreign Office, was familiar to John Bright, both in its broad outlines and in the progress of its daily happenings. The words that he afterwards used at the public breakfast given in England in honour of the anti-slavery advocate, Lloyd Garrison, admirably resume the situation that caused the war :

> 'Thus, in spite of all that persecutions could do, opinion grew in the North in favour of freedom ; but in the South, alas ! in favour of that most devilish delusion that slavery was a Divine institution. The moment that idea took possession of the South, war was inevitable. Neither fact nor argument, nor counsel, nor philosophy, nor religion, could by any possibility affect the discussion of the question when once the Church leaders of the South had taught their people that slavery was a Divine institution ; for then they took their stand on other and different, and what they in their blindness thought higher grounds, and they said, "Evil ! be thou my good" ; and so they exchanged light for darkness, and freedom for bondage, and good for evil, and, if you like, heaven for hell. Of course, unless there was some stupendous miracle, greater than any that is on record even in the inspired writings, it was impossible that war should not spring out of that state of things ; and the political slave-holders, that "dreadful brotherhood, in whom all turbulent passions were let loose," the moment they found that the Presidential Election of 1860 was adverse to the cause of slavery, took up arms to sustain their cherished and endangered system. Then came the outbreak which had been so often foretold, so often menaced ; and the ground reeled under the nation during four years of agony, until at last, after the smoke of the battle-field had cleared away, the horrid shape which had cast its shadow over a whole Continent had vanished, and was gone for ever.'

There is little wonder that Americans were angry when England appeared to favour such a cause as the Slave-owners' Rebellion. Charles Dickens, whose *Martin Chuzzlewit* was read everywhere both in England and the United States, and a whole host of minor English authors dealing in the detraction of things trans-Atlantic, had described the Americans in general not only as 'Yankees' with characteristic 'Yankee' faults, but also as slave-owners. That the 'Yankees' and the slave-owners were two mutually exclusive societies had not dawned upon the British intelligence prior to 1861. But when at length the 'Yankee' went to war with the slave-owner, it was the slave-owner who was pronounced the 'gentleman,' and the 'Yankee' who was voted a bully for interfering with him. But this error was, as we shall see, far from universal in England, and where it existed it was not wholly without excuse.

The people of the South had fine redeeming qualities, and at the outbreak of the war these more admirable features of Southern Society were those best known in England. The quality most easily observed and appreciated by travellers in a country is the courtesy of its inhabitants. Not only true Virginian gentlemen of the school of Washington, such as Lee and 'Stonewall' Jackson, but even the cotton planters down South, exhibited to their English guests the fine careless courtesy natural to leisured aristocrats.

Again, the Southern cavaliers and their poor white retainers were more martial by disposition and way of life than many of the clerks and farmers of the North, when first they obeyed Lincoln's call to arms. Braver men than the Southerners never marched to war. As a result of the first great battle at Bull Run (July 1861), they acquired in England a reputation for greater valour than their opponents. This first impression, only very gradually effaced by the Northern armies in years of steady heroism, created sympathy for the 'gallant little South.' Since the North was trying to conquer and hold down the South, she appeared to superficial British spectators in the unpleasing light of an aggressor who has overrated his power of attack. It was admitted that if the North chose to let the South go, the war would stop. It was therefore the North that insisted on the continuation of the war. This argument told heavily in England, where it was generally believed that the South could not be conquered, and that if conquered it could not be held down. Why therefore continue the war? Such reasoning was more than plausible, and would indeed have been conclusive, had it not been based on an underestimate of the power of the North, very natural after Bull Run. Until that initial Northern defeat, Southern sympathy had not been strong in England. But such was the impression created by the battle that, forty days after Bull Run, Bright himself wrote to Cobden: 'I think the accounts from the States indicate that the North will have to submit to some recognition of the South. The North can raise money and I do not believe the South can. Still, the disasters caused by the war, and the hopelessness of a real union after what has passed, must turn the minds of all sensible men in the North to some mode of extrication other than that of conquest.' If Bright himself could in a moment of weakness write thus,[1] it may be pardoned to the English in general if they thought that the North had undertaken a task as hopeless as that in which George III. had failed—the subjugation of a hostile and united population. What is less to be excused is that the majority of the English wealthy class rejoiced in the checkmate of the North, and openly expressed their hope that the slavers would triumph. But such were not the sentiments of the majority of English people.

Apart from the fear that the North had undertaken an impossible task, the real Southern sympathy in England, which Bright from first to last combated with all his strength, arose from three distinct sources, which we may call the Free Trade, the Liberal, and the Conservative points of view.

First and least important was the sympathy of some Free Traders with the South, because the North stood for tariffs and the South for a free exchange of its only considerable product, raw cotton. Cobden was at first slightly affected by this, and still more by the desire to see the horrors of war avoided, and to see the free North separated from the contamination of the Southern slave-owners—a wish shared by many who hated the slave system. Bright, in February 1861, writes to Cobden: 'I agree with you as to the grandeur of the free States, free from political brotherhood with the South. Still, it was a noble prospect to see a great Continent under one central Republican Government, and I cannot help hoping it may be realised.' Some time in the year 1861 Bright, in a notable conversation, won Cobden round from his misgivings, and enlisted him thenceforward as an earnest champion of the North.[2]

Bright always treated the 'Free Trade' argument for the South with the contempt it deserved. 'Your friend,' he writes to Cobden (October 3, 1861), 'is either a fool, or he takes you and me to be fools when he objects to my statement that the Southern State is intended to be built up on the perpetual enslavement of millions of men. Surely the whole question is

[1] For a letter of the same date to Sumner, see p. 311 below.

[2] *Morley*, ii. 373. *Motley's Letters*, ii. 204-5.

one of slavery: the North was divided between those who would abolish, those who would control it, and those who would tolerate it for the sake of Union. The South was and is against its abolition, and against its limitation, and prefers its perpetual existence to the Union itself. And now even the writers and speakers of the South insist upon it that all social organisation is wrong which is not based on slavery. He speaks of the *Free Traders assembled at Richmond* as if the freedom of individual industry were not the basis of all freedom.' Yet in his letters to Sumner[1] Bright took care to tell the American Government, with no less than his usual candour, that their 'foolish tariff' was in part responsible for such feeling against the North as was to be found in the English middle class.

Beside the 'Free Trade' feeling, there was a 'Liberal' feeling for the South, just as there had been a 'Liberal' feeling for the Crimean War. The democratic historian Grote had no sympathy with the North. Gladstone and his friend Acton regarded the Southern States as a nation 'rightly struggling to be free.' If the slavery question were left out of account, 'State Rights' might be argued with greater or less justice against the Unionist ideal, but to leave slavery out of account in this case was the least pardonable error of Gladstone's whole career. He went down the wrong course further than his Whig colleagues and further than the leaders of the Conservative opposition.

But although Gladstone in his 'Liberal' zeal for the South went further than Palmerston and Derby in their Conservative sympathy with the same cause, it is none the less true that Conservative and anti-democratic feeling was, in the case of normal men, a much more powerful factor than Liberal feeling in creating English sympathy with the South. The Conservative classes, Tory and Whig, were nervously aware that Bright's

[1] Bright's letters to Charles Sumner, Chairman of the Senate Committee on Foreign Relations, were read to President Lincoln and Secretary Seward. And they were sometimes read aloud in the U.S. Cabinet, in particular those on the *Trent* affair. The same is true of Cobden's letters to Sumner. Sumner says this (Pierce's *Sumner*, vol. iv.), and so does Bright in his journal, where, after Lincoln's death he notes: 'I have had no direct communication with the late President, but my letters to Mr. Charles Sumner, as well as those from Mr. Cobden, were frequently read by him, and he sent me, through Mr. Sumner, in his own handwriting, a draft resolution which he suggested as likely to be useful if adopted at public meetings held in this country in favor of the North [*see opposite*]. It referred to the question of slavery, and the impossibility of our recognising a new state based on the foundation of human bondage.' My thanks are due to Mr. Rhodes, the historian of the American Civil War, and to Mr. William C. Lane, Librarian of Harvard University, for enabling me to see copies of Bright's letters to Sumner, before they were printed in the *Massachusetts Historical Society Proceedings*, 1911-12, where they can now be found.

democratic movement was threatening their own monopoly of political power. If democracy triumphed in America, nothing could long delay its advent over here. But if democracy in America failed, the reaction would be strongly felt in Europe, and most of all in Great Britain. The American historian Motley, a favourite of London Society in spite of the land he hailed from and the opinions he professed, for once found residence in England unbearable, owing to the irrepressible rejoicing of his high-born friends over the misfortunes of his country. He traced their feeling to its source. After Bull Run he wrote: 'The real secret of the exultation which manifests itself in the *Times* and other organs over our troubles and disasters, is their hatred, not to America so much as to democracy in England.' A no less competent observer, Charles Francis Adams, the great American minister over here, who shares with Bright the chief merit in keeping the peace between the two countries, was deeply impressed by the connection between English and American politics. During the last part of the war, he used to say that if the North won John Bright would be the most powerful man in England. And the event proved Adams to be right.[1]

If all England had been hostile to the North, the most fatal results must have followed. It was, indeed, only the wealthier classes that went wrong; but at that time they nearly monopolised the press,[2] as well as the political power. Their monopoly was, however, no longer complete. The Reform Act of 1832, the victory of the Anti-Corn Law League, and Bright's more recent agitation for further Reform, had made democracy a force to be reckoned with. If England had in 1770 possessed institutions as representative as those of 1861, there would have been no American Revolution. If in 1861 she had possessed institutions as democratic as those of our own day, there would have been no *Alabama* and no effective 'Southern sympathy.'

The belief held over here that the war was not about slavery

[1] For the history of English opinion during the war see Rhodes, *History of the United States*, vol. iv. chaps. xvii., xxi.; and the excellent life of *Charles Francis Adams*, by his son of the same three names.

[2] The *Daily News* and *Spectator* did yeoman's service for the North. But the London press was predominantly Southern, and the *Times* counted in America for more than all the rest of the British press put together. Four years of leading articles sneering at every action and every motive of the Northern statesmen 'irritated Americans,' as Mr. Rhodes tells us, 'more than any speech of Palmerston, any dispatch of Earl Russell, and I think I may safely add any violation of Great Britain's neutrality. Let one imagine how different would have been the feeling between the two English-speaking nations had the ability and influence of this newspaper been on the side of the North.'

was so erroneous that few Americans thought it to be sincere. But the English who held it had more real excuse than the Northerners allowed. President Lincoln, during the first year and a half of the war, refused to proclaim the manumission of the negroes, and declared that it was for the Union and the Union alone that the North was fighting. To people who knew this fact and nothing more about the political situation in America, it was natural to mistake the issues. But when at length, in October 1862, Lincoln proclaimed the freedom of the slaves in the South, he dealt a very serious blow to sympathies with the South in England. From that time forward our Southern party, being forced against their will into the position of a pro-slavery party, declined every month in power.

The House of Commons, Whig and Tory, represented the attitude, not of England, but of Clubland. The majority of the Members were actuated by mixed feelings. Their dislike of wanton cruelty told against the slave-owners, but their no less characteristic preference for polished manners and aristocratic views of life made them dislike and distrust Lincoln, while they spoke of the Southerners as *gentlemen*, as *cavaliers*, as *men that we can make our friends*. Bright appealed from the one set of feelings to the other in his speech of June 30, 1863, successfully treading ground on which few speakers could have ventured. He reminded the House that in the Slave States of America every year there are

> 'one hundred and fifty thousand children born into the world—born with the badge and the doom of slavery—born to the liability by law, and by custom, and by the devilish cupidity of man—to the lash and to the chain and to the branding-iron, and to be taken from their families and carried they know not where.
>
> 'I want to know whether you feel as I feel upon this question. When I can get down to my home from this House, I find half a dozen little children playing upon my hearth. How many members are there who cannot say with me that the most innocent, the most pure, the most holy joy which in their past years they have felt, or in their future years they have hoped for, has arisen from contact and association with our precious children? Well, then, if that be so—if, when the hand of Death takes one of those flowers from our dwelling, our heart is overwhelmed with sorrow, and our household is covered with gloom; what would it be if our children were brought up to this

infernal system—one hundred and fifty thousand of them every year brought into the world in these Slave States, amongst these *gentlemen*, amongst this *chivalry*, amongst these *men that we can make our friends*?'

In the House of Commons Bright, by such appeals, could do no more than stem the tide. As in the Corn Law days, his more active propaganda was in the country, rousing up a public opinion which in course of time reacted on the House and on the Government.

After Lincoln had proclaimed the Southern slaves free, the Nonconformists became strong partisans of the North. Spurgeon, then at the height of his great influence, made the thousands congregated in his Tabernacle pray together: 'God bless and strengthen the North; give victory to their arms. Bondage and the lash can claim no sympathy from us.' Exeter Hall, which has 'brayed' as often on the right side as on the wrong, witnessed on behalf of the North 'a more earnest demonstration of public opinion than had been known in London since the days of the Anti-Corn Law League.' 'I know nothing in my political experience as striking,' wrote Cobden, who had seen some striking popular movements in his day. The working men throughout the country, instructed by Bright, saw in the Southern Confederacy the men who would degrade labour to a chattel of the capitalist, and in the great Northern Republic the central force of democracy whose fall would involve the baffling of their own hopes of enfranchisement. In short, the same hopes and fears with regard to the near future in England attached our wealthy class to Jefferson Davis, and our artisan class to Abraham Lincoln, while the middle class was divided.

But there was another element in the case besides political sympathy. The free States of the American Union were then what Canada is to-day, the land to which British workmen were emigrating in great numbers every year. Family ties bound many humble homes in England to the men who were fighting under Grant, and to the women who were praying for their victorious return; while on the other hand the intermarriage of our aristocracy with Americans was less common than it has since become.

The various reasons moving the different classes to take sides in this foreign controversy were summed up by John Bright in his speech to the Trade Unions of London in St. James's Hall, March 1863:

'Privilege thinks it has a great interest in this contest, and every morning, with blatant voice, it comes into your streets and curses the American Republic. Privilege has beheld an afflicting spectacle for many years past. It has beheld thirty millions of men, happy and prosperous, without emperor, without king, without the surroundings of a court, without nobles, except such as are made by eminence in intellect and virtue, without State bishops and State priests,

"Sole venders of the lore which works salvation,"

without great armies and great navies, without great debt and without great taxes. Privilege has shuddered at what might happen to old Europe if this grand experiment should succeed. But you, the workers—you, striving after a better time—you, struggling upwards towards the light, with slow and painful steps, you have no cause to look with jealousy upon a country which, amongst all the great nations of the globe, is that one where labour has met with the highest honour, and where it has reaped its greatest reward. Are you aware of the fact, that in fifteen years, which is but as yesterday when it is past, two and a half millions of your countrymen have found a home in the United States—that a population equal nearly, if not quite, to the population of this great city—itself equal to no mean kingdom—has emigrated from these shores? In the United States there has been, as you know, an open door for every man—and millions have entered into it, and have found rest.

'Now, take the two sections of the country which are engaged in this fearful struggle. In the one labour is honoured more than elsewhere in the world; there, more than in any other country, men rise to competence and independence; a career is open; the pursuit of happiness is not hopelessly thwarted by the law. In the other section of that country, labour is not only not honoured, but it is degraded. The labourer is made a chattel. He is no more his own than the horse that drags a carriage through the next street; nor is his wife, nor is his child, nor is anything that is his, his own.

'There may be men—rich men—in this city of London, who will buy in the slave-owners' loan, and who, for the chance of more gain than honest dealing will afford them, will help a conspiracy whose fundamental institution, whose corner-stone, is declared to be felony, and infamous by the statutes of their country.

'I speak not to these men—I leave them to their conscience in that hour which comes to all of us, when conscience speaks and the soul is no longer deaf to her voice. I speak rather to you, the working men of London, the representatives, as you are here to-night, of the feelings and the interests of the millions who cannot hear my voice. I wish you to be true to yourselves. Dynasties may fall, aristocracies may perish, privilege will vanish into the dim past; but you, your children, and your children's children, will remain, and from you the English people will be continued to succeeding generations.

'You wish the freedom of your country. You wish it for yourselves. You strive for it in many ways. Do not then give the hand of fellowship to the worst foes of freedom that the world has ever seen, and do not, I beseech you, bring down a curse upon your cause which no after-penitence can ever lift from it. You will not do this. I have faith in you. Impartial history will tell that, when your statesmen were hostile or coldly neutral, when many of your rich men were corrupt, when your press—which ought to have instructed and defended—was mainly written to betray, the fate of a Continent and of its vast population being in peril, you clung to freedom with an unfaltering trust that God in His infinite mercy will yet make it the heritage of all His children.'

The most touching example of this loyalty to the cause of freedom was shown by the working men and women of Lancashire. The war threw the cotton operatives out of work, yet they and their families would not ask the Government to end the war by helping the slave-owners. Owing to the Northern blockade of the Southern ports cotton could not reach England from what was then almost the sole source of supply. Yet the starving workmen of Lancashire repudiated the demand of the wealthy men of London and Liverpool that our fleet should break the blockade. The Southerners' dearest hope was that England would be starved into coming to their rescue, and they even burnt their own cotton in order to hasten the end. Yet those very Englishmen on whom the starvation fell were the most steadfast on the side of the North. One by one the Lancashire mills, including the Brights' at Rochdale, closed their doors as the supply of cotton languished and ceased.

The bulk of the population was supported on the charity of their employers and neighbours, hard hit as they were themselves. And all England came to the rescue with abundant generosity, irrespective of class or party, or of sympathy with North or South. The Earl of Derby took the lead in the relief work, as became a great Lancashire magnate. Every one behaved in a manner worthy of the citizens of a great and free nation. Through all the prolonged distress there was no rioting, because the mill hands had the wit to perceive that they were not the victims of injustice. The moral and intellectual qualities of Lancashire were displayed to the world, and had their effect on opinion in both hemispheres.

The spectacle deeply affected Americans, and did much to counteract the anger they felt with England. On December 6, 1862, Bright wrote to Sumner : ‘ Our people will be kept alive by the contributions of the country. I see that some one in the States has proposed to send something to our aid. If a few cargoes of flour could come, say 50,000 barrels, as a gift from persons in your Northern States to the Lancashire working men, it would have a prodigious effect in your favor here. Our working class is with you, and against the South, but such a token of your good will would cover with confusion all who talk against you.’ He was urgent that help should come from America, not in subscriptions to a fund over here, but in substance tangible to eye and hand and mouth.

His advice was taken. Three large ships were loaded with flour at New York, and sent over to the Mersey, whence the *Alabama* had sailed a few months before. Such was America’s reply to the work of the Liverpool shipbuilders in destroying her mercantile marine. The ‘ American flour ’ entered many Lancashire homes, a token of friendship from the North, itself stricken and impoverished by war, to those Englishmen who could not be allured by the hope of gain or terrified by the presence of famine into aiding the slave-owners’ rebellion against mankind.[1]

The changes and chances of the Four Years’ War in America, and of the answering struggle over here to preserve peace with

[1] Mr. George Ingham, for fifty or sixty years in the employment of Bright Bros., told me that a barrel from the American gift long afterwards stood in the mill at Rochdale. He said that schools for the men and sewing classes for the women unemployed during the cotton famine were organised; and what was then learnt gave many people their subsequent start in life. Referring to the cotton famine, he said to me twice ‘ It was not all evil.’

the North, the vicissitudes of despair and hope in this twofold contest for everything that John Bright valued in the life of nations, will best appear from his own letters, particularly those which he wrote to Charles Sumner for the eye of President Lincoln.

(To Sumner. Sept. 6, 1861. After the initial defeat of the North at Bull Run.)

'Public opinion here is in a languid and confused state. The upper and ruling class have some satisfaction, I suspect, in your troubles. They think two nations on your Northern Continent more easy to deal with than one, and they see without grief that democracy may get into trouble, and war, and debt and taxes, as aristocracy has done for their country.

'The middle class wish abolition to come out of your contentions, but they are irritated by your foolish Tariff, and having so lately become Free Traders themselves, of course they are great purists now, and severely condemn you. I have not, so far, seen any considerable manifestation of a disposition to urge our Government to interfere in your affairs, and yet with some doubtless there is a hope that France and England will not permit their cotton manufacture to be starved out by your contest. There is a great anxiety as to what is coming. I preach the doctrine that the success of the North is our nearest way to a remedy, but there are those who hold a contrary opinion.

'Lords Palmerston and Russell in public speak in a friendly tone, and I have been disposed to believe in the honest disposition of the latter, but I do not like the moving of troops to Canada, for it indicates some idea of trouble in the future. They may only fear it, acting on ancient tradition, and may not *intend* it. Still with our upper class hostility to your country and Government, with the wonderful folly of your Tariff telling against you here and with the damage arising from the blockade of the Southern ports, you will easily understand that the feeling here is not so thorough and cordial to you as I could wish it to be. . . . Many who cavil at you now say, "If the war were for liberating the slave, then we could see something worth fighting for, and we could sympathise with the North." I cannot urge you to this course, the remedy for slavery would be almost worse than the disease, and yet how can such a disease be got rid of without some desperate remedy ?

. . . .

'I cannot see how the South with its vast territory is to be subdued, if there be any of that unanimity among its population which is said to exist and of which there are some proofs. If it be subdued, I cannot see in the future a contented section of your great country made up of States now passing thro' the crisis of a Civil War, with every ferocious passion excited against the North—and the prospect being so dark, looking through the storm of war, I am hoping for something which will enable you to negotiate. I have no sympathy with the South; their folly seems to be extreme, and I think their leading men who have made this insurrection are traitors to human nature itself. They have sought to overthrow the most free Government and the noblest constitution the world has ever seen, and they wish to decree the perpetual bondage of many millions of human beings. Whatever of evil comes to them through the war, they will have richly deserved it. But I dread the results of the war to the North. Debt, taxes, army, and the corruption which grows inevitably in times when so much of public money is being expended, are fearful things. We have had them and have them now in this country. I hope they may never grow to such rank luxuriance in yours.

'And now, after writing all this, I leave the matter as I found it. "All that we know is, nothing can be known." I can give no advice, I can find no way of escape. The devil of slavery has been cherished and now threatens to destroy you; if he is to be driven out, as in old time, he will tear and rend you.

'Whatever is done and whatsoever comes, I need not tell you that I am for the Government which was founded by your great men of eighty years ago, and that all my sympathies and hopes are with those who are for freedom.'

(To Sumner. Nov. 20, 1861.)

'I shall be very glad to know what you think in regard to the possibility of peace on the basis of a secession. All I see and hear from you forbids me to imagine such a thing to be likely. . . . It is unfortunate that nothing is done to change the reckless tone of your *New York Herald* [towards England]. Between it and the *Times* of London there is great mischief done in both countries. . . . It has been a misfortune that so little has been said to instruct the public on the true bearings of your question, for it is incredible almost how ignorant even our middle and upper class is with regard to your position. The sympathies of the great body of the people here are, I think, quite right, although some papers supposed to be read by them are wrong. . . . There is nothing that you can do that would more restore sympathy between England and the States than the repeal of the monstrous and absurd Tariff. It gives all the speakers and writers for the South an extraordinary advantage in this country.'

Christmas 1861 was the moment of greatest danger in the relations of England and America. Two Southern Commissioners, Mason and Slidell, had been sent by Jefferson Davis to rouse England and France to war against the North. Mason, who was coming to this country to match himself against the grave astuteness of the American Minister, Charles Francis Adams, proved in the event so unfitted for his task, that Lincoln would have done well to have paid his passage. But before he reached our coasts he nearly occasioned the war that he was sent to stir up. On November 8, 1861, he and Slidell were taken off the British ship *Trent* by an over-zealous Northerner, Captain Wilkes, of the *San Jacinto*. In demanding the release of the two men, England stood up for the law of nations and for the just rights of her own flag. Fortunately Russell, not Palmerston, was Foreign Minister, and under the steadying influence of Prince Albert, who from his death-bed exerted himself in the cause of peace, Russell eventually so framed our demands as to enable the Americans without derogation to acknowledge themselves in the wrong, if they were disposed to do justice. But for weeks peace and war hung in the balance.

Early in the crisis, on December 4, 1861, John Bright spoke at Rochdale in favour of peace and arbitration on the *Trent* affair; he pleaded the case of the North against the slave-owners in a manner that did much to form a Northern party in England. The last words of this speech will be long remembered:

'Now, whether the Union will be restored or not, or the South achieve an unhonoured independence or not, I know not, and I predict not. But this I think I know—that in a few years, a very few years, the twenty millions of freemen in the North will be thirty millions, or even fifty millions—a population equal to or exceeding that of this kingdom. When that time comes, I pray that it may not be said amongst them that, in the darkest hour of their country's trials, England, the land of their fathers, looked on with icy coldness and saw unmoved the perils and calamities of their children. As for me, I have but this to say: I am but one in this audience, and but one in the citizenship of this country; but if all other tongues are silent, mine shall speak for that policy which gives hope to the bondsmen of the South, and which tends to generous thoughts, and generous words, and generous deeds, between the two great nations who speak the English language, and from their origin are alike entitled to the English name.'

It was the first, or at least the clearest note of battle for the North that had been sounded over here. The historian Motley, who had recently left England to serve his country in the United States Legation at Vienna, wrote to Bright: 'When I first read your speech at Rochdale, I wished to write and thank you for it at once. But I found myself too agitated to do so. I laid it aside for two days, and I have now just read it all through again. I should perhaps have been inclined to dwell more, in writing to you, upon the breadth and accuracy of view, the thorough grasp of the subject and the lucid flow of argument by which your speech was characterised. But the peculiar circumstances under which it was delivered make it impossible for me to express my emotions in any other way than in one honest burst of gratitude to the speaker—Thank God! our noble mother tongue is not entirely given over to revilings and denunciations of those who speak it beyond the sea. And I honour you more than I can tell, for your courage in thus standing up, in the midst of the tempest of unreasoning wrath now sweeping over England, to defend not an unpopular but apparently a hated cause.' [1]

Although he stood up for what was righteous in the American cause, John Bright told the American Government that it must not venture to put itself in the wrong. His letters to Sumner on the all-important question of the *Trent* were read aloud in

[1] In the course of this letter the historian of the Dutch Republic says: 'Imagine what may be the sensations of some of our descendants, fifty years hence, if they should learn, by some research into forgotten rubbish, that it was the current opinion of the statesmen and public writers in England in the year 1861 that negro slavery had nothing whatever to do with the American Civil War.'

Lincoln's Cabinet, in the meetings that decided the issue of peace or war with England.

(To Sumner. Dec. 5, 1861.)

'If I were Minister or President in your country, I would write the most complete answer the case is capable of, and in a friendly and courteous tone, send it to this country. I would say that if after this your view of the case is not accepted, you are ready to refer the matter to any Sovereign or two Sovereigns, or Governments of Europe, or to any other eligible tribunal, and to abide by the decision, and you will rejoice to join with the leading European Governments in amendments and modifications of international law in respect to the powers of belligerents and the rights of neutrals. . . .

'You know that I write to you with as much earnest wish for your national welfare as if I were a native and citizen of your country. I dread the consequences of war quite as much for your sakes as for our own. So great will be my horror of such a strife that I believe I shall retire from public life entirely, and no longer give myself to the vain hope of doing good among the fools and dupes and knaves with whom it is my misfortune to live, should war take place between your country and mine.

'I need not tell you, who are much better acquainted with modern history than I am, that Nations *drift* into wars, as we drifted into the late war with Russia, often thro' the want of a resolute hand at some moment early in the quarrel. So now, a courageous stroke not of arms, but of moral action, may save you and us. I suppose the act of your Captain Wilkes was not directly authorised by your Government; if so, the difficulty will be smaller. . . .

'It is common here to say that your Government cannot resist the mob violence by which it is surrounded. I do not believe this, and I know that our Government is often driven along by the force of the genteel and aristocratic mob which it mainly represents. But now in this crisis, I fervently hope that you may act firmly and courteously. Any moderate course you may take will meet with great support here, and in the English Cabinet there are, as I certainly know, some who will gladly accept any fair proposition for friendly arrangement from your side.'

(Dec. 7.)

'I have no doubt you will be able to produce strong cases from English practice in support of the present case, but I doubt if any number of these will change opinion here. It will be said, and is said already, that if we did wrong fifty years ago, it is no reason why you should do wrong now. The law is the law and it shall not be broken, and we take our law officers' law for our law. Now what is to be done? You must put the matter in such a shape as to save your honor, and to put our Government in the wrong if they refuse your proposition. . . .

'At all hazards you must not let this matter grow to a war with England, even if you are right and we are wrong. War will be fatal to your idea of restoring the Union, and we know not what may survive its evil influences. I am not now considering its effects here—they may be serious enough, but I am looking alone to your great country, the hope of freedom and humanity, and I implore you not on any feeling that nothing can be conceded, and that England is arrogant and seeking a quarrel, to play the game of every enemy of your country. Nations in great crises and difficulties have often done that which in their prosperous and powerful hour they would not have done, and they have done it without humiliation or disgrace. You may disappoint your enemies by the moderation and reasonableness of your conduct, and every honest and good man in England will applaud your wisdom. Put all the fire-eaters in the wrong, and Europe will admire the sagacity of your Government.'

(To Cobden. Dec. 9.)

'I look to a retirement from Parliament and to a time of economy and care for one's family if war actually takes place. I will not kill myself with proving it wicked as I nearly did seven years ago [Crimea]. . . . I spent a long evening with Mr. Adams. I found him quiet and serious. He believed the seizure of the Commissioners to be without authority from the Government and he thought the act unfortunate and impolitic.'

(To Sumner. Dec. 14.)

'If you are resolved to succeed against the South, *have no war with England*; make every concession that can be made; don't even hesitate to tell the world *that you will even concede what two years ago no Power would have asked of you,* rather than give another nation a pretence for assisting in the breaking up of your country. The time will probably come when you can safely disregard the menaces of the English oligarchy ; now it is your interest to baffle it, even by any concession which is not disgraceful.'

(To Sumner, Dec. 21.)

'This week the country has been shocked by the death of Prince Albert, but our war journals have not suspended their mischievous labors. There has, however, been more manifestation of opinion in favor of peace, and of moderate counsels, and of arbitration in case your Government cannot accept the opinion of our law officers on the unhappy *Trent* affair.'

(To Louis Mallet. Dec. 23.)

'The Palmerston Papers, *Times* and *Post* chiefly, are in terror lest war should not come, and I think it will not come. There is no unanimity in its favor in the country. The most influential journals in the Provinces are for arbitration and moderation, and there is nothing like the blind feeling there was for the Russian War.'

In the last week of the old year, President Lincoln's Cabinet, after long and doubtful debate, decided not even to ask for arbitration, but to give up Mason and Slidell.

(To Sumner. Jan. 11, 1862.)

'Your letter of the 23rd ult. reached me on the 7th of this month. It showed such evidences of anxiety on your part that it made me intensely anxious, and I was not prepared for the tidings of the following day, which announced the settlement of the question which was the main cause of immediate danger. I need not tell you how much I rejoice, or how much I admire the dignity and tact with which the matter has been dealt with in the dispatch of your Government so far as I have yet seen of it. The war-mongers here are baffled for the time, and I cannot but believe that a more healthy opinion is gradually extending itself on all matters connected with your great struggle.'

During the *Trent* affair Lincoln's Government had received from Cobden the same counsels of moderation as from Bright.

But Cobden went further, urging them to abandon the blockade of the Southern ports, in order to avert all pretext for interference by England and France. In this he was not supported by Bright, who writes to Sumner:

(Dec. 21, 1861.)

'Mr. Cobden writes to me again about the blockade. It would indeed be fortunate if you could permit the trade to be reopened; but I tell him I do not see how it can be done if the struggle is to be continued. Mr. Cobden too condemns the stopping of the ports by sinking ships laden with stones, as being barbarous and permanently hostile to commerce. But *war* is *barbarous*, and this is but an act of war.'

As early as 1847 Bright had prophesied that the Nemesis of slavery in America would some day cause such a convulsion as to impede our cotton supply from that quarter. He had vainly exhorted his countrymen to provide against the danger that he foresaw, by planting cotton in India while there was yet time.[1] His Manchester opponents and those who succeeded him in the representation of the city had refused to help him in this matter, and now the wheel had come full circle.

(To his wife. 7th month, 19, 1862.)

'It is a sort of retribution on these Manchester people who are now howling for cotton, that they are now represented by a man who crawled on his belly in the mud before the East India Directors, and refused out of pure flunkeyism and spite of me, to do the only thing that could have averted the terrible disaster which is overtaking the great Manchester interest. If I did not grieve for the ignorant and powerless workers, I could almost be content to see the sufferings of those who, when time permitted it, refused to help to provide for their own safety.'

Bright knew that the cotton famine would be long and severe, for he did not look forward to the early termination of the war. To Sumner he writes in October 1862:

'I begin to believe that another crop of cotton from slave labor will never again be grown on your Northern Continent. Terribly as this would make me and mine and multitudes suffer, I cannot wish it otherwise.'

[1] See p. 169 above.

Cotton was now being grown in India to meet the sudden need. To Villiers he writes:

> 'I think these extraordinary prices will bring more cotton from India, especially if none of your colleagues make fools of themselves by predicting the early termination of the war, and the willingness of the United States people to allow their country to be dismembered.'

For eighteen months the cotton famine was at its height. Then, very gradually, cotton began to come in from India and other hastily organised new sources of supply. Before the end of the war, the worst was already over in Lancashire.[1]

Bright was a man of peace. But he was not for peace at the price of slavery. If his letters in the autumn of 1861 indicated some doubt as to the possibility of subduing the South by arms after Bull Run, a very remarkable hardening in his view is to be observed in 1862, long before the tide turned in favour of the North at Gettysburg. He who had stood in the breach against the Crimean War, and against the threat of war with France, now writes to urge Lincoln's Government that the most bloody contest of modern times should not be brought to an end unless and until slavery were abolished. To use the phrase of Carlyle, Bright had 'swallowed formulas'—even those of peace. On every question he looked to the heart of the matter. Nothing, neither Free Trade nor even his own deep pity for the hundreds of thousands slain and maimed and bereaved, could make him overlook the great issue, between the abolition of slavery on the one hand, and on the other its sanctification in America, and probably therefore its gradual extension over the whole tropical world. There is a ring of Cromwell's voice in some of Bright's utterances on this war.

(To Sumner. Feb. 27, 1862.)

> 'I fear to hear of any surrender on the part of the South at present, fearing that men would be so glad to have peace that they would admit the Slave States again in their fellowship, and that twenty years hence, you might find the old disturber still present with you. When the white flag is hoisted from the South, and when you come to negotiate—then will be the time of real danger, and it

[1] The first cotton procured from India was found hard to work and was not liked. Bright used to tell a story of a Lancashire prayer meeting at which the following petition was offered up: 'O Lord, we beseech Thee send us cotton;—but O Lord, *not Shoorat*.'

may require more statesmanship to make peace, and more firmness, than it has required to carry on this gigantic war. But I will have faith. I believe a higher power than that of President and Congress watches over the interests of mankind in these great passages of the history of our race, and I will trust that in this supreme hour of your country's being, it will not fail you.'

(July 14.)

'Nothing in public affairs has ever before made me so anxious as your great conflict. I wish it to end well, but I am not anxious about its ending suddenly. For the fate of your "Black Nation" must now be decided, and I cannot think that God has permitted this fearful war to be waged without a plan for the redemption of the four millions of his creatures whose wrongs and sorrows have hitherto appealed to man in vain.'

And after the tide of war had begun to turn, he continues in the same strain:

(To Villiers. July 29, 1863.)

'I am not anxious to see the conspiracy in the States break down too rapidly. It needs as many plagues as Pharaoh suffered from, to force the corrupt portion of the Northern people to let the negro go.'

(Aug. 5.)

'I have letters from the States. The rebel forces lost 83,000 men during the first half of July, and set free even a larger number of the U.S. forces by the surrender of Vicksburg and Port Hudson. Mr. Sumner fears they are going on too fast: so do I. I want no end of the war, and no compromise, and no re-union till the negro is made free beyond all chance of failure.'

(To Sumner. Sept. 11, 1863.)

'The Union is only good and great when a Union of Freedom, and any compromise which gives up the [Emancipation] Proclamation will be the most deplorable event in history. It will be a curse on your reputation which no time can remove.'

In July 1862, by a grievous and bitterly repented error of Russell's, the *Alabama* was allowed to sail from Liverpool docks.

Once at sea, she hoisted the Southern flag and began her long and destructive warfare on the commerce of the United States. In October of that year Mr. Gladstone, then Chancellor of the Exchequer, declared at Newcastle that Jefferson Davis had made an army, was making a navy, and had 'made a nation.' Another crisis was on hand as dangerous as that of the *Trent*, with England this time as the offender. Bright was again active in preserving peace. He pointed out to the American statesmen that Russell 'had actually issued an order for the arrest of the *Alabama*, which was evaded by the vessel's being, as it were, smuggled out to sea before she was ready and before she was expected to go.'

(To Sumner. Oct. 10, 1862.)

'I write to you from a feeling of anxiety. You will see what is being said here by public men who speak on your question, and most of all, and *worst of all*, by our old acquaintance and friend Mr. Gladstone. He has made a vile speech at Newcastle full of insulting pity for the North, and of praise and support for the South. He is unstable as water in some things; he is for union and freedom in Italy, and for disunion and bondage in America. A handful of Italians in prison in Naples without formal trial shocked his soul so much that he wrote a pamphlet, and has made many speeches upon it, but he has no word of sympathy or of hope for the four millions of the bondsmen of the South! I have known for months past that he talked of an European remonstrance, or mediation, or recognition, or some mischief of that kind, but I did not expect that he would step out openly as the defender and eulogist of Jefferson Davis, and his fellow conspirators against God and man.'

The danger of war caused by the *Alabama* and by Gladstone's speech was greatly relieved by Lincoln's Proclamation (October 1862), of liberty for the slaves in the South, to date from the new year. It was welcomed by an uprising of all the better elements in English life.[1] Bright and Adams were not slow to let America hear of the change in English sentiment.

(Bright to Sumner. Dec. 6, 1862.)

'The anti-slavery sentiment here has been more called forth of late, especially since the Proclamation was issued,

[1] See p. 306 above.

and I am confident that every day the supporters of the South among us find themselves in greater difficulty, owing to the course taken by your Government in reference to the Negro question.

'Then, there is the French mediation proposition which, utterly silly as it was, might have led to great mischief if our Government had been prevailed upon to indorse it. I can assure you that the refusal of Lord Russell to unite with France in that matter has been cordially approved throughout the country, and even by those who, like Mr. Gladstone, believe your undertaking hopeless, and many of whom doubtless wish that you may ultimately fail in your efforts to restore the Union. . . . The Proclamation, like everything else you have done, has been misrepresented—but it has had a large effect here, and men are looking with great interest to the 1st January [when the slaves were to be considered free] and hoping that the President may be firm.'

(Jan. 30, 1863.)

'Our Southern Newspapers are surprised and puzzled at the expression of opinion in favor of the North. . . . I think in every town in the kingdom a public meeting would go by an overwhelming majority in favor of President Lincoln and of the North. I hope what is doing may have an effect on our Cabinet and on the Parliament.'

(To Cyrus W. Field.[1] Feb. 27, 1863.)

'Opinion here has changed greatly. In almost every town great meetings are being held to pass resolutions in favor of the North, and the advocates of the South are pretty much put down.'

It is due to our country that Americans should note, what their own historians have pointed out, that this change for the better in English opinion followed on Lincoln's Proclamation of freedom for the slave, and preceded by several months the first great successes of the Northern arms. The mass of the people were converted to the Northern cause when the North pronounced the doom of slavery. The upper classes followed, when the North had won.

In spite of this movement of opinion there was still great

[1] American advocate of friendship with England, and in particular of the Atlantic cable.

danger of a breach between England and the North. The Lairds were building 'rams' at Birkenhead to follow up the *Alabama*, and Russell had not yet evidence enough of their destination to lay hands upon them. The blockade of the Southern ports by the Northern ships was jealously watched by the British fleet, eager to find a pretext for interference in some illegal action by the Northern captains.[1] So Bright was perpetually at work keeping the peace.

(To Sumner. Ap. 24, 1863.)

> 'There seems mischief brewing between your Government and ours. You are justly irritated about the Pirate ships; and efforts are made here to create anger about the seizure of vessels from England to Matamoras. . . . Irritation is inevitable, from the legal and necessary conduct of your war-vessels, but the greatest care should be taken to use their powers, even their legal powers, with the greatest moderation. Whether a ship more or less breaks the blockade is of no real importance to you, or to us, but whether you should be interfered with in your efforts to suppress the Southern insurrection by a war with England, is of importance to you and us that words cannot describe. With the jealousy which exists here, in regard to all you do, and with the evident wish to damage you on the part of the powerful party here, I can only hope that your Government will keep strictly within known and acknowledged law and thus baffle its enemies, whether at home or abroad.'

On June 30, 1863, the pseudo-Radical Roebuck proposed in the House of Commons an alliance with the Emperor Napoleon for the purpose of interfering on behalf of the South. But the rooted English suspicion of Napoleon for once served the cause of peace. Although it was the general belief that Lee was on the point of capturing Washington and that the Northern cause was lost, the Government and the House of Commons rejected the proposal and stood firm for neutrality, while John Bright poured out on Roebuck a deluge of weighty ridicule from which he never fully recovered. 'He shook him

[1] A British naval officer who served in the Mediterranean in 1860, and in American waters during the following years, told me that the feeling for Garibaldi in 1860 was quite unanimous on board the British fleet, and that the feeling for the South two years later was equally unanimous; he said they were all agog to find occasion to interfere with the blockade, and believed that they had been sent out to begin war.

as a terrier shakes a rat,' said one who heard the debate. Next week the tide of war turned sullenly. Lee's invasion of the North was repulsed at Gettysburg, while a thousand miles away to the west Grant captured Vicksburg and restored the free use of the Mississippi to the Union Government.

(To Sumner. July 31, 1863.)

'I need not tell you with what feelings of gratification and relief I have received the news of your recent successes. The debate on the foolish Roebuck proposition took place when there was much gloom over your prospects, and the friends of Secesh here were rejoicing in the belief that your last hour had come. How soon are the clouds cleared away; and how great is now the despondency of those who have dishonored themselves by their hatred of your people and Government. The [Southern] loan is down near 20 per cent. in a little more than a week and is now, I suspect, unsaleable, and people are rubbing their eyes, and wondering where the invincible South is gone to. Our Pro-slavery newspapers are desperately puzzled and the whole mass of opinion is in confusion.'

In September Russell, under skilful and constant pressure from Adams, refused to repeat his *Alabama* mistake, and stopped the sailing of the Laird rams from Birkenhead.

(To Sumner. Sept. 11, 1863.)

'You will hear by the mail that the iron-clad steam rams are detained by the Government. . . . I suppose the changed position of your affairs has helped our Foreign Office to the decision they have come to! Lord Russell has just made a short speech at Dundee, and he has said nothing foolish, which shows that there is an opening of the eyes among our statesmen, as to the prospects of your war.'

(Feb. 18, 1864.)

'You will have noticed the tone taken by our Attorney General and Lord Palmerston a few days ago in speaking of your prize courts and your dealing with international law. Nothing could be more friendly—it was all I could wish for. But what a miserable thing to see our friendliness and our justice depending on your strength! When you seemed weak and staggering under the weight of the insurrection, the Prime Minister and his law officer continued to insult you; when you are strong and the revolt is staggering under your blows, they speak gently and pay you compliments. This statesmanship is a very low morality, and I despise it from my heart.'

The Northern sympathisers in England were not lacking in zeal or knowledge. We read in Bright's journal for March 9, 1864:

'Mrs. Adams spoke of Mr. Stanley,[1] son of Lord Stanley of Alderley, his earnestness about America and his zeal for the North; she said his talk was rapid and earnest, "would take my hair off my head," knows every minute detail of U.S. affairs, "knows more than Mr. Adams *a pile*" (*i.e.* a heap or great quantity more than Mr. Adams), of details of geography, etc. Mr. Adams wishes this Government to remain in; it is working fairly now with America.'[2]

[June 1.] 'Called at St. James's Hotel on ——, an American lady; not a very pleasant visit; boasting of her loyalty to her country, but loud in her abuse of Mr. Lincoln and all connected with his Government. I told her such language was offensive to us from an Englishman, and I did not wish to hear it from an American.'

In the year 1864 the attack was no longer made by the Southern, but everywhere by the Northern armies; yet although the war in the West prospered, Grant's frontal attacks on Lee's position before Richmond were sanguinary and apparently fruitless. In September Bright writes to Sumner:

'There is great uncertainty of opinion. It fluctuates with the varying news from week to week, and men become puzzled with the long-continued strife. For myself I am rendered unhappy very often by your disasters, and all my efforts to harden myself against the anxiety which oppresses me are unsuccessful.'

He hopes for the re-election of Lincoln as President; it will 'tell Europe that the country is to be restored and slavery is to be destroyed, and it will say the same thing to all Southern people.'

That Christmas saw the beginning of the end. Sherman

[1] Edward Lyulph Stanley, present Lord Sheffield, 1912.

[2] As early as May 1863, Bright wrote to Sumner about Russell: 'I am not sure that if we change him we shall get a better man in his place.'

with the Western army abandoned his communications and vanished for some weeks into the unknown.

(To Villiers. Dec. 27, 1864.)

> 'Sherman's march is full of interest as an exploit of war. Perhaps to-morrow, and almost certainly by the end of the week, we shall have further particulars and we may comprehend more of his plan.'

Sherman was marching to the Eastern seaboard, breaking the back of the Southern Confederacy as he went.

> 'By and by,' continues Bright to Villiers, 'I hope that the chiefs of the rebellion will have an opportunity of seeing their friends in England "face to face." Jeff. Davis and Co. under the gallery of the House would be exciting, and Mr. Gladstone and Robert Cecil [1] and the rest of their friends might shake hands with them. A pleasant sight, would it not be?'

In the spring of 1865 Grant moved forward again on Richmond, and this time Lee could offer but feeble resistance. At Appomattox Court House he surrendered, and the war was at an end.

The news of this great public salvation found Bright bowed down by many private sorrows. One of these he had related to Sumner but a week before: 'Cobden is taken from us. It seemed that half my life were buried with him in that grave.' Then came the glad tidings that he would have loved to share with his friend. In his private journal he wrote down his inmost thought:

> 'News received of the surrender of Lee and his army to General Grant. This may be taken to be the end of this great and wicked rebellion. Slavery has measured itself with freedom, and slavery has perished in the struggle. How often have I longed and prayed for this result, and how much have I suffered from anxiety whilst it has been slowly working out, I only know! This great triumph of the Republic is the event of our age. The friends of freedom everywhere should thank God and take courage—they may believe that the world is not forsaken by Him who made it and who rules it.'

A few days later came the news that Lincoln had been murdered in the hour of his own and his country's triumph.

[1] Afterwards the famous Lord Salisbury.

(Journal. April 29, 1865.)

'Whilst at Dolgelly on the 27th heard of the shocking tragedy in Washington—the murder of President Lincoln. For an hour or near it, I felt stunned and *ill*. . . . I will not write an eulogy on the character of President Lincoln —there will be many to do that now he is dead. *I have spoken of him when living*. . . . In him I have observed a singular resolution honestly to do his duty, a great courage—shewn in the fact that in his speeches and writings, no word of passion, or of panic, or of ill-will, has ever escaped him—a great gentleness of temper and nobleness of soul, proved by the absence of irritation and menace under circumstances of the most desperate provocation, and a pity and mercifulness to his enemies which seemed drawn as from the very fount of Christian charity and love. His *simplicity* for a time did much to hide his *greatness*, but all good men everywhere will mourn for him, and history will place him high among the best and noblest of men.'

On the same day he wrote to Sumner:

'For fifty years, I think, no other event has created such a sensation in this country as the great crime which has robbed you of your President. The whole people positively mourn, and it would seem as if again we were one nation with you, so universal is the grief, and the horror of the deed, of which Washington has been the scene. I have had a month of extraordinary suffering—the death of Mr. Cobden, then the death of my brother-in-law, Mr. Lucas of the *Morning Star*, then this new and inconceivable calamity. I feel as if all were unstable, and that nothing can stand.

'When I read that the President had gone to Richmond without a guard, I felt that he ran a risk to which he ought not to have subjected himself. In times of great excitement, dangerous men become more dangerous, partly vicious, and partly mad, and men of great mark become the objects of their hate and passion. The deed is done, and it is now too late to take precautions.

'It is easy to kill a President, but it is not easy to destroy a nation.'

NOTE

The Proposal that Bright should visit the United States

It is a strange fact that John Bright never crossed the Atlantic. He was neither a good sailor nor a passionate traveller, and the magnificent reception that he would have had in the United States any year after 1861 had no attraction for him. He was often told, after Lincoln's death, that he was 'the most popular man in America,' and was much pressed by newspapers and private persons to visit the States. But John Bright was a democrat who sympathised with the masses without desiring their applause. On July 31, 1863, a few days after Gettysburg, he writes to an American friend, Mr. Forbes:

> 'I fear I am getting too far on in life to cross the ocean, unless I saw some prospect of being useful, and had some duty clearly before me. It is a subject of constant regret that I have not paid a visit to the States years ago. Mr. Walker and many others alarm me by telling me I should have a reception that would astonish me. What they promise me would be a great affliction, for I am not ambitious of demonstrations on my behalf.'

In 1879 he was invited over to the White House by the President, but declined the invitation. Shortly afterwards Mr. E. J. Broadfield, on a visit to America, was told there that 'if John Bright came, we would scatter flowers before him all the way from Chicago to the sea.' As his wife had died, and his children were getting married, it was suggested that travel might give him company and distraction. But he wrote to Mr. Broadfield, in April 1880:

> 'I envy you your trip to the great Republic of the West. I wish I were some years younger; I also would trust myself to one of the great boats now crossing the Atlantic. As it is I must try to be content at home. As age comes on, the youthful longing for travel lessens and disappears, and lonely as I now am at home, I should feel much more lonely abroad.'

One of John Bright's daughters, writing of life at One Ash during the American Civil War, describes the intense feeling of his family and circle:

> 'We used to live for the transatlantic steamers that twice a week brought the anxiously expected news. America and its history, past and in the making, was the breath of our nostrils. It was a great time in Rochdale, with all its cotton workers in enforced idleness and so alive to the reason: a meeting was called in the town by a Liverpool Association of Southern sympathies, formed to promote the breaking up of the blockade. The lecturer delivered his address, and the meeting passed a Resolution censuring him for endeavouring to mislead them.'

CHAPTER XV

ENGLISH AFFAIRS CONTEMPORARY WITH THE AMERICAN WAR. THE APPROACH OF GREAT CHANGES. THE DEATH OF COBDEN

'If Bright had not kept his light burning through the thick darkness of the Palmerstonian régime, I know not whether the nation would have emerged from its political apathy during this generation. For many years he stood virtually alone:

> "Against example good,
> Against allurement, custom, and a world
> Offended, fearless of reproach and scorn."

And this is the man who, the "educated Liberals" tell us, is not a statesman. I want to know who shall have most credit for statesmanship, men who "take upon them the mystery of things, as if they were God's spies," and who yet cannot see one inch beyond their nose, men who for years past have been writing themselves down asses in prophecies which the next week's news refuted, or the man who throughout his career, whether in regard to the Crimean War, or India, or America, has showed a foresight that has been verified by events. They call him a demagogue, but whom does that name best fit? Men whose trade is to prophesy smooth things to any one who has aught to give, or one who has been a butt for more insult and contumely than any one in this generation? They say he is a revolutionist, when they themselves advocate a system which by treating five-sixths of the people as political aliens, leads, by inexorable necessity, to revolution.'—T. H. GREEN, *the Philosopher. Speech to the Oxford Reform League*, 1867.

NEW figures, bodying forth the new age, were one by one growing visible by the lights of Westminster. None of them, except Lord Hartington, came from the 'great Whig Houses' to whom the recent past had belonged. Conspicuous among the signs of the times stood the bearded Radical from Yorkshire, W. E. Forster, formerly of Bright's religion and still emphatically of his politics. Forster had come to the front in a way that does him eternal honour, in defending the cause of the American democracy against the Southern sympathisers. In the approaching crisis of English Reform he was to fight as Bright's younger comrade-in-arms; like Bright, he was a man altogether 'unfashionable' in appearance and opinions; and, like Bright, he derived his influence in the State from the enthusiasm aroused by his presence at mass meetings of workmen in the North.

A type very different from Forster, but equally characteristic of the new age, was young Mr. Goschen, famous for his volume on finance. His first appearance as a rising Liberal we find noticed in Bright's journal for February 4, 1864:

> 'Debate on Address. Mr. Goschen, M.P. for the City, seconded address, spoke well; one sentence aimed at me, and cheered by Opposition. This Oxford "young man of great promise" has, I suppose, already found out the way to please the aristocratic order. It shows a disposition which does not promise honesty or generosity in his Liberalism. The future will prove what he is.'

Then, again, there was James Stansfeld, Member for Halifax, of much the same origin and opinions as Forster and Bright, but already occupying a modest place on the Treasury Bench. Ever since 1847 he had been on intimate terms with Mazzini, who often had letters addressed to him under a pseudonym at Stansfeld's house. This fact was brought to light in March 1864, at the time when a certain Greco was being tried in France on the charge of conspiring to murder Napoleon III. A document was found in Greco's possession bearing the words, '*Mr. Flower*, 35 Thurloe Square.' *Mr. Flower* was a pseudonym of Mazzini's and the address was Stansfeld's. There was no evidence that Greco had ever written to Mazzini, there or elsewhere. Mazzini denied all knowledge of the plot against Napoleon, and Stansfeld denied all acquaintance with the conspirators or with the contents of Mazzini's letters. But Disraeli, in one of his high, artificial passions, accused him of being the medium of correspondence with the assassins of Europe; the Tories were hard on the track, and loudly gave tongue as they ran their quarry down. The House was excited and out of hand. Palmerston's Government, which stood firmly by its cadet, was on the brink of defeat and Stansfeld of political ruin, when Bright arose and in a noble speech turned the tide of debate and of feeling. His last words before he sat down had their effect: 'I am no partisan of the Government; I have never, since a short time after its formation, looked forward with dismay to its dissolution. But if I were as hungry as the hungriest person opposite to place myself on the Treasury Bench, I would be ashamed to make my way to it over the character, the reputation, the happiness, and the future of the last appointed and youngest Member of that Government.' Thanks to Bright, the Government secured a majority of ten votes. Mr. Stansfeld, though not driven out, thought it best to resign; but his honour and his career were saved, and indeed he was shortly afterwards back in office. He expressed his gratitude to Bright in the following letter of March 18:

'My dear Mr. Bright,—I must write to tell you of the deep and affectionate gratitude which I feel for the words you spoke last night. It is not because of their effect that I so write, though my belief is that in all probability they saved me from the mortification of being the cause of a serious blow and defeat of the Government. It is because of the unspeakable relief that amidst the humiliating scene, some one, thank God, should have been there with power and character and a manhood which no one else could have equalled, to chastise the cowardice and the hypocrisy of this attack. May I add that it has but intensified a feeling I have always had towards you, and never more so than when I have differed and discussed, for to differ with you and not to care about that difference is impossible to me.'

Next month was brightened by a more pleasant reminder of the Italian question, the visit of Garibaldi to England. On April 11, 1864, he entered London in such popular triumph as no English hero has enjoyed in those streets. 'The people,' wrote Bright, 'numbers without number, made a grand display. I have seen nothing equal to it before.' Two days later Bright was present at one of the strangest scenes in history, the reception, at Stafford House, of the battered old guerilla in his red shirt, by the governing families of England.

(Journal. April 13.)

'To Stafford House reception in honor of General Garibaldi. Going up stairs from the hall, met Lord Derby coming down; at the top of the staircase met Lord Russell. In the company saw nearly all the Ministers, Duke of Argyll, Lord Granville, Palmerston, Gladstone, Cardwell, Villiers and Gibson. Duke of Argyll introduced me to Garibaldi; he was walking along the balcony overlooking the hall, leaning on the arm of the Duchess of Sutherland. I shook hands with him. He said, "I am very glad to know you." I said, "We are glad to see you here, but I am afraid the kindness of your friends will be too much for you." He said, "And it is all so new to me." Soon after he left the company, as he retires early. From the balcony I saw him limping down the staircase into and across the hall, leaning on the arm of the graceful Duchess of Sutherland. Her face is intelligent and very charming; his rather weather-beaten, but indicating a most kind and generous heart. The house is very grand; hall, staircase, and reception rooms, on a magnificent scale, exceeding that of any other house I have been in in this country. The Duke and Duchess of Argyll were very civil to me;[1] she is of the good breed of the Howards, and, so far as my experience goes, they are all kind and good people. I had a long talk with Mr. Gladstone, among other topics upon Ireland and the Irish Church; he thought when the Liberal party is restored to life, that question would come up for settlement, and he should regard it as one of the great purposes of the party, although it would necessarily separate him from the University of Oxford.'

Never was prophecy more exactly fulfilled. It was not without fitness that the first outlining of the terms of political alliance between Bright and Gladstone, which shortly afterwards produced the modern Liberal party, should take place in Stafford House on the day of Garibaldi's reception. For the success of the Italian Revolution, like the victory of the North in America, helped to create over here the atmosphere in which democracy triumphed. The enthusiasm aroused by Garibaldi's visit among the millions of unenfranchised working men alarmed both Whigs and Tories. Some of the Tories muttered mild deprecation of Garibaldi, while the Whigs received him into their houses and tried to guard him from contact with the people, to whom he might act as flame to tinder. His reception even in London had been terrible. What then would happen if he went the round of Birmingham, Lancashire, and the northern manufacturing centres? Fears of this sort were added to other reasons why Palmerston's Government wished to prevent his longer stay in England, and above all, his projected tour in the provinces.[2]

[1] The Duke was strong for the North in the American quarrel.

[2] The evidence in Guerzoni's *Garibaldi* makes it certain that it was not merely anxiety for Garibaldi's health that caused the Government, through Gladstone, to induce him to abandon his northern tour.

(Journal. April 13.)

'Lord Stanley said to me a day or two ago, "I wonder if it ever occurs to the Duke of Sutherland that if Garibaldi had his way, there would be no Dukes of Sutherland." It is Garibaldi's magnanimous disinterestedness which gains him such universal sympathy, though I suspect some of his aristocratic friends here rather patronise him to keep him from alliances of a democratic character.'

A week later Cobden and Bright met Garibaldi at Mr. Seely's house in London:

(Journal. April 19.)

'Garibaldi said to us: "I am of your principles, for if I am a soldier, I am a soldier of peace." There is a singular kindness and gentleness, and dreamy enthusiasm in his face and in his eye, and a charming simplicity about him. He is going away. It is said, and doubtless truly, that the Government wants him out of the country. They fear he may excite political feeling in the provinces, or his presence here is annoying to the French or Austrians, or the Queen is irritated at the manner in which he has been received. Perhaps there is truth in each of these stories. His going thus suddenly will give great dissatisfaction to the country, and may have an effect on the Administration.'

Scarcely had Garibaldi gone back to tend his goats on Caprera, when the inhabitants of this larger island were set skipping by a speech of Mr. Gladstone. On May 11, 1864, he uttered in the House of Commons what was perhaps the most sensational in effect of all the sentences that ever fell from his lips. 'I venture to say that every man who is not presumably incapacitated by some consideration of personal unfitness or of political danger, is morally entitled to come within the pale of the constitution.' Having so said, he began after his manner to qualify and refine upon his words, but all in vain. He had pronounced in favour of enfranchising the working men. He confessed that he had 'unwarily set the Thames on fire.' London society, still in that day a well-defined and most potent circle, could talk of little else but Gladstone's dangerous lunacy. He had revived the doctrine of Tom Paine, said Disraeli—Disraeli who, three years later, presided over the passage into law of this dreaded doctrine, whether it were Tom Paine's or John Bright's. Palmerston, as Prime Minister, wrote to Gladstone to expostulate, declaring that it was 'more like the sort of speech with which Bright would have introduced the Reform Bill which he would like to propose, than the sort of speech which might have been expected from the Treasury Bench in the present state of things.' But what was the 'present state of things'? Other, perhaps, than could be seen by a veteran who had first held office among the High Tories before the Peninsular War.

On the same day Bright was writing to his wife:

> 'Gladstone made a memorable speech yesterday. It makes a new era in the Reform question, and shows what he is looking towards in the future. The *Times* is wroth with him this morning, and he will be more than ever the dread of the aristocratic mob of the West End of London. I was silent, wishing others to come in. I think the political prospect is brighter than for some time. Palmerston in truth only stops the way for a time.'

In one sphere of action, no less vital to the well-being of the people than that of the franchise itself, Palmerston, though he still reigned, had already ceased to govern. His lifelong policy of interference in the affairs of Europe was brought to a humiliating close in June 1864, when the House of Commons, in obedience to a strong expression of public opinion, refused to allow him and Russell to go to war with the German powers on behalf of Denmark. The fact that we had no army fit to put into line against the Prussian and Austrian, and the consideration that the quarrel was none of our business, and that the rights of it were by no means all on Denmark's side, would not have deterred those believers in 'the balance of power,' but for the positive refusal of their countrymen to be dragged to a ruinous conflict in obedience to some formula of the Foreign Office. The Queen's German proclivities also helped the cause of peace.

It was a great triumph for Cobden and Bright. 'It is evident,' the latter noted in his journal, 'that our years of preaching on Foreign policy and non-intervention have not been without effect.' And a few months later he said to his Birmingham constituents:

> 'The theory of the balance of power is pretty nearly dead and buried. You cannot comprehend at a thought what is meant by that balance of power. If the record

could be brought before you—but it is not possible to the eye of humanity to scan the scroll upon which are recorded the sufferings which the theory of the balance of power has entailed upon this country. It rises up before me when I think of it as a ghastly phantom which during one hundred and seventy years, whilst it has been worshipped in this country, has loaded the nation with debt and with taxes, has sacrificed the lives of hundreds of thousands of Englishmen, has desolated the homes of millions of families, and has left us, as the great result of the profligate expenditure which it has caused, a doubled peerage at one end of the social scale, and far more than a doubled pauperism at the other. I am very glad to be here to-night, amongst other things, to be able to say that we may rejoice that this foul idol—fouler than any heathen tribe ever worshipped—has at last been thrown down, and that there is one superstition less which has its hold upon the minds of English statesmen and of the English people.'

The idol, having thus fallen in 1864, remained prostrate as Dagon during the Continental wars of 1866 and 1870, enabling England to wax in prosperity and peace. Then, during the Russo-Turkish War, Disraeli set up the fetish once more, and called on England to bow down to it and worship, with the result that Macedonia was put back for a generation under the Turk. Then again, in the latter years of Gladstone and Salisbury, the balance of power was relegated to the lumber heap, or at least concealed in the attic, and Bright's doctrines prevailed in the foreign policy of Liberal and Conservative alike. Whether or not in our own day the idol has been refurbished is a point of moment to us all.

In the autumn of 1864 a heavy and unexpected blow fell upon John Bright and his wife. Their third son, Leonard, a bright, engaging little fellow of five and a half years, died at Llandudno of scarlet fever, after a few days' illness. He was a child of great promise, of a most lovable nature, given to quaint and original sayings; and his likeness to his father, both in features and expression, was sometimes almost startling. It is a curious fact that three close friends—Cobden, Milner Gibson, and Bright—each lost a young son suddenly from scarlet fever. To his elder children, away at school, all tenderly attached to their little brother, Bright wrote the following letter in the fulness of his heart:

'CHESTER, 11 mo. 11, '64.

'MY DARLING M.,—We have thought much of thee, for we know how thy loving heart must be almost broken by the sudden loss we have all sustained. . . . I must tell thee of the sad duties of yesterday. Not being able to have our precious child buried at home, we thought it best to place him in the ancient churchyard of St. Tudno's on the Orme's Head, where all of us have so often walked.[1] We were nearly an hour in our slow journey up the mountain. Thou knows the little Church stands with one side to the sea; we crossed the yard below the Church, that is, having the Church on our left hand, and at the far corner, that is, the corner furthest from Llandudno and nearest the sea, we found the little grave made. It is alongside that of a young man from Manchester who was killed in 8th month last by a fall from the rocks at the Little Orme's Head and between it and the boundary wall of the yard.

'The grave was not deep, not more than 5 ft. deep, the little coffin was let down into it and Mama and I stood by, looking down upon it, our eyes running with tears and our hearts ready to break. The day was fine—the sea perfectly calm—there were several vessels in sight, some very near; on the mountain there were sheep and we heard the bleating of one of them as tho' seeking for companionship and comfort. The wildness and desolation of the place were relieved by the calm and mildness of the day, and we thought that but for the distance from home, there could be no more desirable place for the remains of our precious child to rest in. We were a small party—very lonely—we remained but a few minutes looking down upon his last resting-place, who, not a week ago, was apparently full of life and health—and then we turned away with a wish to bow to the dispensation of God, which had taken from us the sweet and precious child we loved so tenderly. I found it impossible to stay longer in Llandudno; everything reminded me of our loss in such a way that my heart seemed ready to burst as I walked its now quiet streets, and we resolved to come away to-day. Everybody was kind to us—many had noticed our darling child—he had walked with me to the news-room or with Mama to market, and all knew our loss and were kind and sym-

[1] Till the children grew up, John Bright always had a month's yearly holiday with the whole family at Llandudno, so that its neighbourhood was full of associations to them all.

pathising as they looked upon us or spoke to us. We left Llandudno this morning. It was most lovely; the Orme's Head was decorated with a new beauty, as if in harmony with the new and solemn interest it now has in our eyes and in our thoughts. The sun lit up every point and every recess in the gray old rocks and gave a warmth and a glow such as is rarely seen upon them; and as we came on towards Conway, the delicate colors of the rock and of the sky were so intermingled that it was difficult to say where the rock ended and the sky began.

'And thus we left our darling Leonard in his loneliness and peace! But we felt that there only was the outward form in which he had lived his short and bright and happy life with us—that elsewhere was the soul, the life which fevers cannot kill, and which will live for ever in the blessed and unchanging rest and bliss to which he has been so early called. If thou could have seen him as his pure soul was passing away, it would not have seemed as it were death that had struck him, but rather that some angelic nature had beckoned him upwards—it was not gloom, or terror or suffering, or even deprivation of life—but it was the departure of all sign of fever and suffering, and the advent of a look of more than earthly purity, perfection and beauty—to me it seemed not death, but rather a transformation before our eyes and in our very presence.

'My darling M., I write out of the fulness of my heart, but I tell thee little of all I have really felt. We have had a great lesson during the past week—a lesson on the power and the goodness of God. We have not rebelled against His dispensation, we try to submit to it. Not our will, but His will be done. We feel that one of our dear children is in that haven towards which we fondly hope they may all tend, and that they and we may one time meet there. . . . I hope thou wilt be comforted, as we are comforted to some degree. We will love each other and cherish the memory of the sweet child whom God has taken to Himself.

'Send this on to the boys. Mama's dear dear love and mine always, Thy loving Father,

'JOHN BRIGHT.'

The friendship of Cobden and Bright knew no shadow from

the beginning to the end. Cobden's want of faith in the extension of the franchise had never been a cause of coldness between them, and after a period of frank expostulation on the subject by Bright,[1] both had long ago accepted a natural differentiation of their functions in life. In everything else they stood shoulder to shoulder. In December 1863, little more than a year before death parted them, Cobden, in defence of his friend, had entered on the famous public controversy with Delane of the *Times*.[2] The dispute had arisen over Bright's rural land policy, which the *Times* had incorrectly described as a violent scheme of confiscation, to divide the lands of the rich among the poor. In reality the land policy, both of Bright and of Cobden, was this: to denounce the existing unequal division of land, and the perpetual accumulation of great estates in the hands of single persons, and to point out that the English peasant, almost alone among the peasantry of the world, was a landless man. But neither Cobden nor Bright had any more drastic remedy for the disease they diagnosed than the abolition of entail and of other artificial restrictions on the break-up of estates, and the enactment of legal facilities for land transfer. Bright, indeed, was the first English politician of note to recommend tenant right and land purchase for Ireland. But he had no such definite proposals for England. He argued, however, that the extension of the franchise to the agricultural labourers would eventually lead to great improvements in their condition, and that when they had been armed with the vote, 'they would be redeemed from that poverty and serfdom which up to this time have been their lot.'[3]

When the *Times* misrepresented Bright as having proposed violent confiscation, Cobden's anger on his friend's behalf led him to attack and tear down the fictitious anonymity of Delane. Bright made fun of the great man before the audience of the Birmingham Town Hall, called him 'the Man in the Mask,' and told the following story at his expense:

> 'I recollect a description which I am sure will suit Mr. Delane admirably. It was published some time ago in the city of New York, and described a notorious politician there who, if I am not mistaken, has been at the elbow of the New York correspondent of the *Times* for the last twelve months—with what happy success to the forecast

[1] *E.g.* pp. 184-86, 196-97, 209-11 above.

[2] It has been recorded at full in chap. xvii. of the *Life of Cobden*, vol. ii.

[3] See his speech at Rochdale, November 24, 1863, and at Birmingham, January 26, 1864.

and honesty of that paper we all know. It was said of him that "he was a just man and a righteous man, and he walked uprightly *before the world*, but when he was *not* before the world his walk was *slantindicular*."'

Bright used to say that if he felt at all doubtful as to the wisdom or morality of anything he had said in a speech, he had only to wait till the next morning for the verdict of the *Times*; if it condemned him, he felt contented that he was right; if it praised him, he was uneasy. Already the abolition of the 'taxes on knowledge,' as Cobden and Bright had prophesied, had brought into the field a cheap press which had destroyed much of the former power of the Thunderer. During this controversy with Delane, Cobden declared that: 'a few years ago the *Times* possessed almost a monopoly of publicity. Four-fifths of the daily newspaper circulation issued from its press. *Now* it constitutes, probably, one-tenth of our diurnal journalism.'

This amusing controversy with the *Times*, and the victory of peace in the Danish question, were the last battles that Cobden and Bright fought together. The one, now, was taken, and the other left.

(Journal. April 1, 1865.)

'Called at Suffolk Street to enquire about my poor friend Cobden. Did not see him. Mr. Fisher told him I was in the house. He turned to Dr. Roberts and said, "Doctor, I am in your hands, and perhaps in those of death, ought I to run the risk of any excitement?" Dr. Roberts thought not, and thus I missed the chance of seeing him again when he could have known me. I was very sad.

'At 8 o'clock next morning, being Sunday, April 2nd, I heard the bell ring, and sprang up to dress, conscious of the ill-tidings that were coming. A note from young Mr. Fisher asked me to come down as my poor friend was worse and sinking. I was with him soon after 8 o'clock. There was no apparent pain, not a limb stirred; he lay breathing out his precious life, and for three and a quarter hours I watched my greatest friend of more than 20 years as his life ebbed away.

'At a quarter past 11 o'clock the breathing ceased—there was a moment of suspense—a pallor spread over the face and the manly and gentle spirit of one of the noblest of men passed away to the rewards which surely wait upon a life passed in works of good to mankind, a life of unselfish benevolence, and of unspotted honor.

'It was a scene never to be forgotten—his hands were still warm, and the warmth of life was still on his forehead after life had fled. We stood and looked, and wept with almost breaking hearts, and then came away with a burden of grief hard to bear. I pressed his hand for the last time, and kissed his forehead, and left him with a sense of the loss I have suffered.

'To Gordon St. Found McLaren and Priscilla there. We all wept as though one of the dearest of our circle had been taken.'

To his wife, who was at Rochdale, he wrote: 'Yesterday and to-day I seem to suffer as I did at Llandudno, but without thee to help me.' And to his friend, Mr. Thomasson: 'I feel now as if I had lost a brother, and as though in my political life I am now almost alone.'

(Journal.) 'April 3rd. House, great sorrow manifested on all sides. Palmerston and Disraeli spoke in fitting language of the loss the House has sustained. I wish his eulogy could have been spoken by men more in harmony with his own great and good character. I thought the House expected something from me. I was bowed down with grief—my eyes were filled with tears. I stood up trembling, and with my heart bursting and my head on fire. I pressed my forehead with my right hand to steady my brain. I said: "It may be expected that I should say something on this sad event, but I feel that I cannot speak. Every mark of sympathy shewn by the House is most grateful to my heart, but the time since I was present when the manliest and gentlest spirit which ever tenanted and animated a human form took its flight, is so short that I leave to a calmer moment what I may have to say to my countrymen on the lesson which is to be learned from the life and character of my friend. He has been my friend and as my brother for more than 20 years, and I did not know how much I loved him till I found that I had lost him." I sat down sobbing with grief, and trembling with excitement and passionate sorrow. There were many Members present whose eyes were filled with tears—such a time has probably never been known before in the House of Commons.'

'April 4th. To Suffolk St. Found the poor girls in

grief and excitement. N. almost delirious. I took her out for four hours. Walked with her in Hyde Park, then called at a shop at Piccadilly and bought her a sweet nosegay—a red rose, a white rose, and some lilies of the valley, which she longed for to place on the bosom of her father. I took her to Suffolk St., and went with her into the chamber, and saw her place it over the heart which had loved her so tenderly. At half-past six saw the sad family off for the Waterloo Station.

'April 5th. House at 11. Found a letter from Lord Kinnaird with an apology for an unkind remark he made upon me some years ago, and which has caused estrangement between us ; he wishes all to be forgotten before we meet at the funeral of my lost friend. I must write to thank him for his letter ; he is, I believe, a good man.

'April 6th. By 5.30 train to Midhurst, at Dunford about 7. Mrs. Cobden calm, and bearing up well, the children also, except N., whose sufferings have been extreme. I seemed to have more influence with her than any of her family, and I tried to soothe her.

'April 7th. This morning I spent a long time, probably near two hours, in the library, where the coffin was, with the children. J. was there with me, and said she often read the "Sermon on the Mount" to her father, "he always said it was so very beautiful."

'I saw little at the Church, for I could not look up into the faces of so many I knew. The Church is new and very nice ; everything around it seems arranged to please the eye. The landscape is very charming, and the sunshine seemed to fight against the sorrow in our hearts. There were many hundreds of persons present. I was one of the pall-bearers, Mr. Gladstone and I walking foremost, Mr. Villiers and Mr. Gibson next, and others following.

'When the coffin was being placed in the vault, I could hold out no longer, and my anguish found some vent in passionate sobs and tears. I think I am becoming weaker that I am thus affected. Generally men seem to become harder and less given to tears as they grow older. In me it is not so. It may be that this event, almost unconsciously to myself, brings me nearer to my own end, and points to the time when I must follow the path which all must tread. . . . In the evening I found N. walking alone in the field above the house. She "could just see Lavington Church" from that high ground. I took her home and tried to comfort her young but almost broken heart.'

Finally, looking back on Cobden's death, he writes in his journal:

'The friend of 25 years is gone, and I can no more ask counsel of him, or give him help. We have striven together for freedom and justice, and have done something for both that cannot be undone. Henceforth, if any henceforth is permitted to me, I must work alone, but I feel as if I could do little more, for, as I looked into that vault at Lavington, it seemed to me that half my public life was buried there. But I will thank God that I have had such a friend, and that I have been permitted to be the friend of such a man.'

CHAPTER XVI

DEATH OF PALMERSTON. THE NEW ERA. IRELAND AGAIN. GLADSTONE'S REFORM BILL DESTROYED BY THE 'CAVE OF ADULLAM.' 1865—JUNE 1866

'A political leader does well to strive to keep our democracy historic. John Bright would have been a worthy comrade of John Hampden, John Selden and John Pym. He had the very spirit of the Puritan leaders. He had their brave and honest heart, their sound and steady judgment, their manly hatred of oppression, of bad laws and bad government; and besides that, it was true of Bright as was said of John Pym that "he had the civic temper and the habit of looking for wisdom as the result of common debate." It was that which made him glory in the House of Commons. No man so profoundly honoured the great possibilities of the Mother of Parliaments.'—JOHN MORLEY *at the unveiling of Bright's Statue, Rochdale,* 1891.

FROM the grave of his friend John Bright turned to face the crisis which should decide the triumph or the failure of his life's work. He had waited long, often disappointed, seldom impatient, during twenty years, sowing seed and watching for it to grow. But in the half-dozen years now at hand, the institutions of his country were about to be remodelled almost after his own heart. The popular forces which, after the Chartist collapse, he had reawakened and trained in constitutional methods, he was now to apply as the driving force of a splendid new machine—Gladstone's parliamentary and legislative genius.

The first short step in this onward path was the General Election of July 1865. Palmerston preserved his majority over the Tories, and the Radical element in that majority gained rather than lost ground. Veteran Members from Scotland and the north came up to the new House of Commons to remind it that the under-represented industrial half of the kingdom was strong for Bright and Reform, while the electoral victories of John Stuart Mill and Tom Hughes were a further sign of the democratic advance. But the greatest rejoicing among Reformers was caused by the defeat of their own man, Gladstone, for Oxford University, and his consequent election for South Lancashire, whither, as he said, he came down 'unmuzzled.' His constituents were no longer to be the clergy.

> It is a national gain,' wrote Bright to J. E. Rogers, 'that Mr. Gladstone has left Oxford and come to South Lancashire. His connection with Oxford did something to drag the old University on, but the labor was not worth the power expended. So long as the Church is a State Church depending on the law and on the patronage of the squires, I do not see how the clergy can become anything but what they are, a force almost unanimously hostile to all Liberal advancement. I am sure that Mr. Gladstone is happier in his new position, altho' he may have felt a pang at parting with his old friends. I think we are very near a step in reform.'

And to Charles Villiers, who was in the Government, he writes on July 27 :

> 'The elections are over, and nobody has been able to discover the great Tory reaction. I am writing to various persons urging various modes of action. Some propose a strong M.P. deputation to your chief [Palmerston] on the subject of Reform, to insist on the Bill of 1860, and on its being faithfully adhered to and carried. Mr. Gladstone's election here [Lancashire] may help in the same direction. . . . The *Times* as usual, seeks to serve its patrons whom Delane meets in the dining rooms of the West End, and proposes £20 for the counties—enough perhaps to give some counties to the Whigs—but not enough to give them to the people. But the *Times* is always wrong, and events generally settle themselves in opposition to its counsel. I wish to urge you to adhere to the Bill of 1860 on the Suffrage—unless you can go to Household Suffrage. I am sure that anything less will be folly, and will probably end in the ruin of the Government.'

The Government would not have been permitted to listen to the advice of John Bright, had it not been for the death of Lord Palmerston in the following October. He died in office, and it almost seemed as if he had been born there ; for he had served the Tories during the last twenty years of their political monopoly, that ended with the First Reform Bill, and afterwards the Whigs throughout the long era of their ascendancy. A biographer of Bright must needs dwell on the case against

Palmerston—that being a Conservative in home affairs, he insisted on leading the Liberals 'from behind,' and that in foreign affairs he fostered the warlike and interfering spirit of his countrymen. But an Englishman and a lover of Italy can still be proud of the last and most grandly careless of that stalwart race of gentlemen, who first beat the man they called 'Bonaparte,' and then snapped their fingers in the face of the priests and despots who succeeded him in the lordship of Europe.

The good Lord Shaftesbury, who mourned for Palmerston as his 'dear, true, and private friend,' tells us that he had but two real enemies, Bright and Gladstone. 'Once he said to me, though he seldom dealt in predictions, "Gladstone will soon have it all his own way; and, whenever he gets my place, we shall have strange doings." He rarely spoke severely of any one. Bright and Gladstone were the only two of whom he used strong language.'

It is not, then, to Bright that we need look for an eulogy of Palmerston. He wrote to Charles Sturge:

> 'The old Minister is gone at last. I wish there were more to be said in his praise. We are breaking with the old generation and I hope we shall see new and better principles and policy in the ascendant. I think the present Cabinet with merely a new chief cannot go on doing nothing. It cannot be provided with another chief who can keep so many people quiet as Lord Palmerston was able to do.'

Lord Palmerston was succeeded as Premier by Earl Russell, and as leader of the House by Mr. Gladstone; both changes opened the path to Reform. Bright determined to forgive Russell for deserting Reform in 1861, and to hope better of him for the future. 'As to Lord Russell,' he wrote to Charles Villiers, 'I do not believe him to be a bad man; of his class I think him one of the best in intention and certainly the best on Reform. But he is often capricious and sometimes feeble. He is now in power and we must do the best we can.' In letters to Villiers, and probably also in conversation with others, he let the reconstructed Government know that his support of them would entirely depend on the line they took about Reform. 'You will have to *think yourselves awake* before February, and the dawdling system of the last five years may not keep the concern afloat for another period.' He urged the Government to bring in a good Franchise Bill, and to press it upon the unwilling Members of their party, not as involving an immediate dissolution of the Parliament so recently elected, but on the contrary, as the only alternative to a punitive dissolution, in case they rejected the Bill. The common theory that the passage of a Franchise Act must lead at once to a General Election, he showed to be a false deduction from the inapplicable precedent of 1832.

(To Villiers. Nov. 22, 1865.)

'If I were the Minister bringing in the Bill, and resolved to carry it, I would allow it to be known that if a dissolution were needful to carry it, that measure would be resorted to, but that if the Bill passed, it was not intended immediately to have a new Election. In the case of the Bill of 1832 a new Election was necessary. That Bill was a revolution—so much was swept away, and so much was new, that it would have been absurd and impossible to go on with the old Parliament, but now it is not a *revolution* that is coming, but a *progress* on the old foundation—and nobody would feel much aggrieved, I think, if the exercise of his newly acquired right to vote were postponed till some accident brought about a General Election.'

Redistribution, which Bright in his campaign of 1858 had treated as no less important than the extension of the Franchise,[1] seems at this later period to have occupied a less prominent place in his mind. At any rate he was anxious to have the Suffrage extended first, because then a more just redistribution would follow afterwards.

(To Villiers. July 27, 1865.)

'I would not touch the distribution of seats in the Bill. That question only doubles your difficulties and it can be dealt with much better in a Parliament elected on the wider suffrage.'

(To Chas. Sturge. 12 month, 21, 1865.)

'As to Reformers who object to the Suffrage till they get electoral districts, all I can say is they don't understand their business, or what is the use of a wedge in mechanics. The Suffrage is the only thing possible or probable now, and I have advised the Government for ten years past to do the Suffrage alone in their first measure. And I am prepared to defend this course before all the

[1] See p. 271 above.

radicals in England. It is the only way ever to get anything until the Revolution of violence comes, which I do not wish to see. If the Government be honest and firm they may carry a fair measure of Suffrage, but any distribution of seats might now[1] be all in favor of the counties, or if not would destroy the Government and the Bill would fail.'

'Mr. Bright,' wrote his enemy, the *Saturday Review*, in the first week of 1866, 'Mr. Bright governs although he does not reign. When at this critical time he declares his views on Reform, the Cabinet cannot avoid being to some extent guided by his views.'

During the Christmas and New Year of 1865-66, while Russell and Gladstone were preparing their Reform Bill with one eye on Bright and one on their supporters among the 'old, old Whigs,' public opinion began to be moved with regard to Jamaica and the doings of Governor Eyre. John Bright from the first was in the forefront of the battle against the Governor, who, after quelling a negro insurrection with energy and promptitude, had been guilty of cruelty and illegality in indiscriminate vengeance wrought not on the guilty alone.[2] The regiment of scientific and literary men of the first rank who were then the boast of England, enlisted with zeal on the one and the other side. Except Tyndall, the men of finest scientific mind—Darwin, Huxley, Mill, Leslie Stephen, Sir Charles Lyell—ranged themselves on the side of law and humanity, while those whose cue it sometimes was to complain of the hardness of the scientific attitude to life—Carlyle, Ruskin, Kingsley, Tennyson—showed by their own conduct how prone sentimentalists are to inconsiderate worship of brute force and the

[1] 'Now': viz. if settled by the present unreformed House.

[2] The Government Commission of Inquiry's Report (Blue Book, 1866, vol. xxx.-Evidence, vol. xxxi.) must be studied by any one venturing to form a judgment on the question. One of the Commissioners appointed by the Government was Russell Gurney, an eminent Conservative M.P. and Recorder at London. The three Commissioners unanimously reported that Eyre had, 'with skill, promptitude and vigour,' suppressed a rising that would have become very dangerous if it had spread: but 'that the continuance of martial law' was 'for a longer than the necessary period'; 'that the punishment of death [439 cases] was unnecessarily frequent; that the floggings [600 cases] were reckless, and at Bath positively barbarous; that the burning of 1000 houses was wanton and cruel.' As to the much argued case of Gordon, they wrote: 'On the assumption that, if there was in fact a wide conspiracy, Mr. G. W. Gordon must have been a party to it, the conclusion at which we have arrived in his case is decisive as to the non-existence of such a conspiracy.'

'strong man.' The excited feelings of the English artisans against Governor Eyre gave a foretaste of their temper in the coming struggle for their own rights as citizens. The Tories were fierce on the other side, and most bitter personally against Charles Buxton and John Bright, although the Tory leaders did not take up Eyre's cause with any zeal. Gladstone, in this most dangerous affair, showed equal courage and wisdom. The expediency, if not the justice of the case, was met by a compromise in accordance with the strength of the two parties. On the one hand, Governor Eyre was recalled; but on the other hand, the 'Jamaica Committee' failed in the attempt to prosecute him for murder. Bright had from the first moment urged his recall in private letters to Members of the Government; and he stood in with the attempt to prosecute him, on the ground that 'the blood of Gordon and of many less known men cries to heaven for vengeance.'

It was not only on the Reform but on the Irish question that John Bright was now beginning to dominate the heart and mind of Liberals, especially of Mr. Gladstone. In 1865, the era of Fenian outrage and conspiracy, attention was again, after a long interval, attracted to the woes of Ireland. Early in 1866 a Bill was introduced to suspend Habeas Corpus for her benefit. Bright made this the occasion, not to oppose the Bill, but to make a solemn appeal for something more than coercion, for large remedial legislation on Irish Church and land, such as he had urged for many years past. Times were beginning to change, and now there were some in the House, and some even on the Treasury Bench, who listened to him, critically indeed, but with the ever-increasing conviction that he was generally in the right. His speech on February 17, 1866, reduced many who heard him to tears, and Leslie Stephen in the gallery, though he probably remained dry-eyed, wrote of it as 'the finest speech I ever heard.' The fact that Bright had been saying these things for twenty years and that all his evil prophecies had come true, lent weight and dignity to his fresh appeal. It aroused against the speaker much indignation, but it was soon to bear fruit.

> 'An hon. Member from Ireland a few nights ago referred to the character of the Irish people. He said, and I believe it is true, that there is no Christian nation with which we are acquainted, amongst the people of which crime of the ordinary character, as we reckon it in this country, is so

rare as it is amongst his countrymen. He might have said, also, that there is no people—whatever they may be at home—more industrious than his countrymen in every other country but their own. He might have said more; that they are a people of a cheerful and joyous temperament. He might have said more than this—that they are singularly grateful for kindnesses shown to them, and that of all the people of our race they are filled with the strongest sentiment of veneration. And yet, with such materials and with such a people, after centuries of Government—after sixty-five years of Government by this House—you have them embittered against your rule, and anxious only to throw off the authority of the Crown and Queen of these realms. I believe that if the majority of the people of Ireland, counted fairly out, had their will, and if they had the power, they would unmoor the island from its fastenings in the deep, and move it at least 2000 miles to the West. . . .

'I have not risen to blame the Secretary of State or to blame his Colleagues for the act of to-day. But what I complain of is this: there is no statesmanship merely in acts of force and acts of repression. And more than that, I have not observed since I have been in Parliament anything on this Irish question that approaches to the dignity of statesmanship. There have been Acts for the suspension of the Habeas Corpus Act, like that which we are now discussing; but there has been no statesmanship. Men, the most clumsy and brutal, can do these things; but we want men of higher temper—men of higher genius—men of higher patriotism to deal with the affairs of Ireland.

'I put the question to the Chancellor of the Exchequer [Gladstone]. He is the only man of this Government whom I have heard of late years who has spoken as if he comprehended this question, and he made a speech in the last session of Parliament which was not without its influence both in England and in Ireland. I should like to ask him whether this Irish question is above the stature of himself and of his Colleagues? If it be, I ask them to come down from the high places which they occupy, and try to learn the art of legislation and Government before they practise it.

'I myself believe, if we could divest ourselves of the feelings engendered by party strife, we might come to some better result. Take the Chancellor of the Exchequer. Is there in any legislative assembly in the world a man, as the world judges, of more transcendent capacity? I will say even, is there a man with a more honest wish to do good to the country in which he occupies so conspicuous a place? Take the right hon. gentleman opposite, the leader of the Opposition [Disraeli]—is there in any legislative assembly in the world, at this moment, a man leading an Opposition of more genius for his position? Well, but these men—great men whom we on this side and you on that side, to a large extent, admire and follow—fight for office, and the result is they sit alternately, one on this side and one on that. But suppose it were possible for these men, with their intellects, with their far-reaching vision, to examine this question thoroughly; and—whether this leads to office and to the miserable notoriety that men call fame which springs from office, or not—to say for once: "If it be possible, we will act with loyalty to the Sovereign and justice to the people; and if it be possible, we will make Ireland a strength and not a weakness to the British Empire." It is from this fighting with party, and for party, and for the gains which party gives, that there is so little result from the great intellect of such men as these. Like the captive Samson of old—

> "They grind in brazen fetters, under task,
> With their Heaven-gifted strength,"

and the country and the world gain little by those faculties which God has given them for the blessing of the country and the world.'

Gladstone heard this speech, and not with the ear alone.

Next autumn (October 30, 1866) Bright spoke in Dublin, laying down the programme of England's future course of reparation.

'You will recollect,' he said, 'that when the ancient Hebrew prophet prayed in his captivity he prayed with his window opened towards Jerusalem. You know that the followers of Mahommed, when they pray, turn their faces toward Mecca. When the Irish peasant asks for food, and freedom, and blessing, his eye follows the setting sun; the aspirations of his heart reach beyond the wide Atlantic, and in spirit he grasps hands with the great Republic of the West. If this be so, I say, then, that the disease is not only serious, but it is even desperate; but desperate as it is, I believe there is a certain remedy for it, if the people and the Parliament of the United Kingdom are willing to apply it.'

The remedy he declared to be the disestablishment of the alien Church, and the buying out of the alien aristocracy. He repeated his old arguments for Irish disestablishment, and demanded a 'Parliamentary Commission empowered to buy up the large estates in Ireland belonging to the English nobility, for the purpose of selling them on easy terms to the occupiers of the farms and to the tenantry of Ireland.'

The great operations of 1866-67, which ended in household suffrage for the boroughs, commenced in March 1866 with the introduction of a much more limited measure by Mr. Gladstone. He proposed to reduce the occupation franchise from £50 to £14 in the counties, and from £10 to £7 in the boroughs. If the Conservative party, and the anti-democratic Whigs led by Robert Lowe, had accepted this compromise, they would have excluded the bulk of the working class from the franchise for another long period of years.[1] Bright was not exaggerating when he said in April 1866, 'I believe there never was a Bill submitted to this House by a Government connected with the Liberal party which it was more clearly the duty and the interest of what is called the Conservative party to support.' And it is highly probable that the Conservatives would have submitted to this Bill but for the example of resistance set them by Robert Lowe from the back benches on the Government side. As it was, the ill-calculated resistance of the Conservative party and of the Whig rump, though for a short time successful, led speedily to an uprising in the country, headed by Bright, so formidable that Disraeli himself was fain in 1867 to go much further than Gladstone in 1866, and by a

[1] Bright's calculations as to the effect of the Bill of 1866 were as follows: 'The Chancellor of the Exchequer says when this Bill is passed there will be 330,000 working men upon the register. I say there will be 179,000. Call them for easier recollection 180,000. The newly admitted by this Bill will be 116,000. What will be the gross effect? The whole number of borough electors in England and Wales, if this Bill should pass, upon the calculation of the Blue Book, will be 691,000, of whom 180,000 only, or about one-fourth will be working men, and therefore that portion of the people which forms at least three-fourths of the whole population will only have one-fourth of the electoral power in the boroughs, and no power whatever worth reckoning in the counties. There will be in England and Wales more than four million of them left out.' (H. of C., Ap. 23, 1866.)

measure of household franchise in the towns to give votes to the great body of the working men.

It was the cue of those who attacked Gladstone's Bill of 1866 to name Bright as the author of it. But he declared that there was nothing in it which he had recommended. Seeing, however, that it was the best that he could get, he called on the people to give it their full support.

> 'The Franchise Bill now before Parliament,' he wrote in a public letter of March 25, 'is a perfectly honest Bill. It will, if it becomes law, give votes extensively to the middle classes, both in counties and boroughs, and it will overthrow the principle of working class exclusion which was established by the Reform Bill of 1832. It will admit to the franchise so many of the working men in all important and populous boroughs, that they, as a class, will no longer feel themselves intentionally excluded and insulted by the law.
>
> 'I say the Bill is an honest Bill; and if it is the least the Government could offer, it may be that it is the greatest which the Government could carry through Parliament. . . . It appeals to the middle and working classes alike. It is a measure of enfranchisement to both of them, and they should heartily unite in an effort to make it a law.'

The fact that the middle class had been left only half enfranchised and very much under-represented in seats by the Act of 1832 made it easy for Gladstone and Bright to unite the middle with the working class behind the new Reform Bill. But the only real opposition to it, as Bright wrote, was directed

> 'against the admission of any portion of the working men to the suffrage. The Tory party, and those from the Liberal ranks who join it, are animated by an unchangeable hostility to any Bill which gives the franchise to the working men. They object to any transfer of power from those who now possess it, and they object to share their power with any increased number of their countrymen who form the working class. They regard the workmen here as the southern planter regards the negroes who were so lately his slaves. They can no longer be bought or sold; so far they are free men. They may work and pay taxes; but they must not vote. They must obey the laws, but must have no share in selecting the men who are to make them. The future position of the millions of working men in the

United Kingdom is now determined, if the opposition of the Tory party is to prevail—it is precisely that fixed by the southern planter for the negro. Millions of workmen will bear this in mind; they will now know the point or the gulf which separates one party from the other in the House of Commons.'

These words mark the temper which the controversy had assumed. The aristocratic champions, who might wisely have accepted Gladstone's Bill as the vaccination of the State with democracy to avert the real disease, chose to fight the enfranchisement even of a small minority of working men, as a matter of principle. In those days it was still possible for a politician to utter aloud any unfavourable views which he might hold about the working classes without committing political suicide, and Robert Lowe, never deficient in courage, expressed his views to the House as follows, on March 13:

> 'Let any gentleman consider the constituencies he has had the honour to be concerned with. If you want venality, if you want ignorance, if you want drunkenness and facility to be intimidated, or if, on the other hand, you want impulsive, unreflecting, and violent people, where do you look for them in the constituencies? Do you go to the top, or to the bottom?'

These words, widely advertised by Bright in every speech he made, printed on Reforming leaflets and hung up in the workshops, rallied the artisans to the defence of the feeble Reform Bill of 1866, when they saw the opposition to it take the form of insult to their class.[1] The demand for the Bill, the whole Bill, and a great deal more than the Bill, waxed louder and more loud as the year went on. The controversy raged on the abstract question of the fitness of the working man for the vote. Bright, Forster, and Fawcett quoted the conduct of the Lancashire operatives during the cotton famine and contrasted it in point of civic virtue and political wisdom with the desire of so many of the upper classes for war on behalf of the slave-owners.

[1] It is perfectly true, as Lowe explained, that he had not said that the working class as a whole was venal, drunken, and ignorant. But he had used the alleged venality, drunkenness, and ignorance of the poorer part of the existing electorate as an argument against a further extension of the franchise among the working class. The inference was clear, even if the use made of his words was sometimes not too scrupulous. What specially angered Bright was the 'frantic violence' with which the majority of the House of Commons had cheered these words of Lowe's. The anti-democratic case in the years 1866-67 will be found in the *Life of Viscount Sherbrooke* (Lowe), by Patchett Martin, vol. ii.

Gladstone too, though he could not use that particular argument, spoke up against calumniating 'our own flesh and blood.'

As the desire for Reform grew hotter in the country, the fear of it threw an ever colder chill over the West End and the House of Commons. The opposition to the Bill was led, if not indeed originated, by Robert Lowe, from the benches behind the Government. The white-haired scholar, a man, like Burke, with a Liberal past, and like Burke, reinspired by a burning zeal against democracy on general philosophic grounds, sounded the trumpet-call to the slumbering hosts of Conservatism. His speeches, equally sincere and ornate, contained many Latin quotations, which Bright listened to sulkily and only Gladstone could effectively cap. Such a portent on the Ministerial benches, white-shining like the day star, gave to the Conservative Opposition their chance of defeating the Government, and they decided to go in against the Bill.

Then began a battle of giants. The leading combatants never left the House, and every one knew where to look for them. Nothing but the gangway separated Bright and Lowe, the two champions who represented the forces of democracy and aristocracy, now come to grips. They sat at the contiguous ends of the two second benches above the floor, and Mill exactly behind and above Bright, in constant communication with him. On the other side of the House, at the end of the front Opposition bench below the gangway, sat Lord Robert Cecil, the soul of the resistance on the Conservative side of the House to working class enfranchisement,[1] while across the table Gladstone and Disraeli eyed each other, the greatest pair of parliamentary rivals since Fox and Pitt. If the time was great in its issues, the men who had to deal with it were themselves of no puny stature.

The ardours of that session, when something real was at stake, were new to fashionable Members accustomed to the ease and gaiety of the Palmerstonian régime. With mutiny in the ranks, Brand, the Liberal Whip, had his task cut out. Men began to dine in the House—or to eat biscuits on the benches, or sitting on the crowded steps of the gangway. And indeed the House was worth staying in for those who loved either oratory or excitement. The attack on the Bill was conducted as an attack on Bright, and the charge against Gladstone was that he had become Bright's instrument. This year and the next were the fiery ordeal through which Bright won his way

[1] The future Lord Salisbury sat in this conspicuous position next to Lord Robert Montagu, and people used to talk of 'the two Lord Roberts.'

to acceptance even by the highest in the land, and acquired that odour of sanctity in which the last twenty years of his life were spent. The ordeal, though short, was sharp. Though so near to the era of his canonisation, Bright in 1866 was more unpopular among the upper class than even he had been before. The wealthy and high-born saw their power threatened, and turned savagely on the man who had trained the mob to agitate by peaceful and effective methods. It was owing to Bright and Gladstone that they had to deal with something much more difficult to handle than Chartism. Gladstone, traitor though he was, was privileged, for he was one of themselves, and he was hedged round by the divinity of an old Minister of State. But the cotton-spinner was fair game. It was indeed not easy to be impertinent to Bright face to face, for he was the most formidable of men and gave as good as he got, whether in debate, in the lobbies, or in the Reform Club. He knew how to preserve the dignity of his unofficial and unchartered greatness. But behind his back, and in newspapers and speeches, he was denounced as if he had been the modern Catiline.

'I am the great terror of the squires,' he wrote to his wife; 'they seem to be seized with a sort of bucolic mania in dealing with me.' At a party at the Duke of Devonshire's that season, a young Liberal Member, much at home in Society, overheard a noble politician exclaim, on perceiving John Bright in the room, 'I did not think the Duke would have insulted his guests by asking that man here.' When, after many private qualms,[1] Bright made up his mind to accept an invitation to dine with Russell at Chesham Place, London society was furious with the Prime Minister for receiving the demagogue under his roof. The incident is referred to in *Ladies in Parliament*, a piece in which one of the youngest Liberals in the House drew a picture of that London season and session, when the *ancien régime* in Society and politics began to suffer change to something less easy and idle. The verses tell how

> '. . . satirists confine their art to cutting jokes on Beales,
> Or snap like angry puppies round a mightier tribune's heels:[2]

---

[1] To his wife, 2 month, 10, 1866: 'I have not decided about the Russell invitation to dinner, and wish such engagements could cease. But I cannot be, or seem to be, uncivil, and may probably accept this one. I fear I shall have to blame the Government, and though the association of dining will not cause me to swerve, still, I would rather not be found condemning strongly those with whom I am occasionally sitting at the same board.'

[2] Mr. Edmund Beales was President of the Reform League, referred to later on in these lines as 'The League.' The 'mightier tribune' and the 'block of rugged Saxon oak' both mean John Bright.

Discussing whether he can scan and understand the lines
About the wooden Horse of Troy, and when and where he dines:
Though gentlemen should blush to talk as if they cared a button
Because one night in Chesham Place he ate his slice of mutton.

'Since ever party strife began the world is still the same,
And Radicals from age to age are held the fairest game.
E'en thus the Prince of Attic drolls, who dearly loved to sup
With those who gave the fattest eels and choicest Samian cup,
Expended his immortal fun on that unhappy tanner
Who twenty centuries ago was waving Gladstone's banner:
And in the troubled days of Rome each curled and scented jackass
Who lounged along the Sacred Way heehawed at Caius Gracchus.
So now all paltry jesters run their maiden wit to flesh on
A block of rugged Saxon oak, that shews no light impression;
At which whoe'er aspires to chop had better guard his eye,
And towards the nearest cover bolt, if once the splinters fly.

'Then surely it were best to drop an over-worried bone,
And, if we 've nothing new to say, just let the League alone;
Or work another vein, and quiz those patrons of their race
Who like the honest working-man, but like him in his place;
Who, proud of rivalling the pig which started for Dundalk
Because it thought that Paddy wished towards Carlingford to walk,
In slavish contradiction all their private judgment smother,
And blindly take one course because John Bright prefers another.'

John Bright was a match for Lowe in oratory, and in that kind of chaff which goes down best with the House of Commons. His jokes were not too frequent and they invariably came off. Even the Conservative Opposition and Mr. Lowe himself were laughing aloud during his 'Cave of Adullam' speech of March 13. On that night, when he coined the happy phrase for the Liberal dissentient body, it as yet consisted only of the quarrelsome Horsman and the fiery Lowe. Bright complained that certain Members returned from Australia took 'a Botany Bay view of the great bulk of their countrymen,' and by their abuse of the working men did far more than he had ever done to 'set class against class.'

'The right hon. gentleman below me [Mr. Horsman] said a little against the Government and a little against the Bill, but had last night a field-night for an attack upon so humble an individual as myself. The right hon. gentleman is the first of the new party who has expressed his great grief, who has retired into what may be called his political *Cave of Adullam*, and he has called about him every one that was in distress, and every one that was discontented.[1] The right hon. gentleman has been anxious to form a party in this House. There is scarcely any one on this side of the House who is able to address the House with effect, or to take much part in our debates, whom he has not tried to bring over to his party or cabal; and at last the right hon. gentleman has succeeded in hooking the right hon. gentleman the member for Calne [Lowe]. I know there was an opinion expressed many years ago by a member of the Treasury Bench and of the Cabinet, that two men would make a party. When a party is formed of two men so amiable, so discreet, as the two right hon. gentlemen, we may hope to see for the first time in Parliament a party perfectly harmonious and distinguished by mutual and unbroken trust. But there is one difficulty which it is impossible to remove. This party of two reminds me of the Scotch terrier, which was so covered with hair that you could not tell which was the head and which was the tail of it.'

The House broke out into a storm of laughter at the Scotch terrier. But as the days went by, it was soon clear that Lowe's end of the terrier contained the head, and a good one too. And ere long the 'Cave of Adullam' had more than two inhabitants. Bright was soon writing in his private letters of the 'forty traitors' and the 'forty thieves.'

The 'cave' was inhabited very largely by men, like Lord Grosvenor, well known in London society, of which the House of Commons was still almost as much the heart and centre as it had been in the days of the Walpoles. It was a marked thing if a great noble did not put his son into the House, whether as Whig or Tory. The younger men on the Government side in the Parliament of 1865-68 were most of them of established social position, and generally speaking not of any very marked ability. It was only the following Parliament, the first elected after the passage of the Reform Bill, that displayed a changed social tone in the House, and introduced a whole troop of able Liberals marked out for future prominence—like Henry Campbell [Bannerman], William Harcourt, Wilfrid Lawson, A. J. Mundella, Charles Dilke, and Henry James. Though Lowe himself was no more an aristocrat than Burke, his Adullamites

[1] The French scientific historian, M. Seignobos, has thus explained to his fellow-countrymen the strange political term coined by Bright: '*Allusion à un passage de la Bible. Adullam avait voulu tuer David.*' (*Hist. Politique de l'Europe Contemporaine*, 1897, p. 60.)

were for the most part a last rally of aristocrats of the Whig decadence.

After a long losing battle, the Government was defeated on the anniversary of Waterloo, by eleven votes, in favour of an amendment that destroyed the first principle of their Reform Bill. Bright wished the Government to follow the precedent of Earl Grey in similar circumstances in 1831, and appeal to the electorate. On June 24 he wrote to Mr. Gladstone:

> 'I have thought much of our last conversation and remain confirmed in my opinion that the true policy is to have a new Parliament. Resignation I only dread, or dread chiefly, in the fear that the Tory Government if formed might conspire with the "40 thieves" to force a Reform Bill which would be worse than nothing. Mr. Brand [the Whip] makes no allowance for the moral force of a contest through the country for a great principle and a great cause. Besides there is something far worse than a defeat, namely, to carry on your Government with a party poisoned and enfeebled by the baseness of the 40 traitors.'

The fears of the great Whip of facing a dissolution with a divided party prevailed over Bright's more heroic advice. But at least the fatal snare of trying to carry on the Government without dissolution was avoided, and Earl Russell's Cabinet resigned. Another Derby-Disraeli Government was formed, but it was not joined by Lowe and his Adullamites. There was therefore still hope for Reform, since Benjamin Disraeli's mind was more plastic than Robert Lowe's. If outside pressure analogous to that of the Anti-Corn Law League could during the recess be brought to bear on the new Ministry, Disraeli and Derby might do that for doing which they had destroyed Peel—they might take the statesmanlike course and settle a great question by a great surrender.

It is here that we take leave of Earl Russell as an active politician. He never again took office. With the exception of Peel, Bright approved more of Russell, personally and politically, than of any other official 'statesman' prior to the neo-Gladstonian era now commencing. Russell had done almost as much to hasten the transition of old Whig to modern Liberal as Palmerston had done to retard it. His personal friendliness to Bright had been more unbroken than Bright's personal friendliness to him. For John Bright always tended towards the sterner view of familiarity between political opponents, namely, that it is difficult to attack in public a man with whom the orator consorts much in private. Their personal relations at the end were, however, most cordial, largely, no doubt, because Russell in June 1866 resigned rather than abandon Reform as he had abandoned it in 1861. A pleasant picture of these two great Liberals in the sunset of their lives is given in the following letter of Bright to his wife in the summer of 1875:

> 'Yesterday I went to Richmond and drove two miles to Pembroke Lodge, where I found the old Statesman [Russell]. He seemed really glad to see me; he said, "I have read your speeches with great pleasure"; I replied, "and I have read your book with much interest," to which he added, laughing, "and so we compliment each other." We talked a little on public matters. I told him the Palestine Explorers have discovered the "Cave of Adullam," which amused him very much.'

There was more than mere political agreement in John Bright's feeling towards him; two days after Russell's death he wrote to Lady Russell:

> 'What I particularly observed in the public life of Lord John—you once told me you liked his former name and title—was a moral tone, a conscientious feeling, something higher and better than is often found in the guiding principles of our most active statesmen; and for this I always admired and reverenced him.'

CHAPTER XVII

BRIGHT'S CAMPAIGN IN THE COUNTRY, 1866. THE CONSERVATIVE SURRENDER. DISRAELI'S REFORM BILL, 1867

'I speak not the language of party. I feel myself above the level of party. I speak, as I have endeavoured to speak, on behalf of the unenfranchised, the almost voiceless millions of my countrymen. Their claim is just, and it is constitutional. It will be heard. It cannot be rejected. To the outward eye, monarchs and Parliaments seem to rule with an absolute and unquestioned sway, but—and I quote the words which one of our old Puritan poets has left for us—

"There is on earth a yet auguster thing,
Veiled though it be, than Parliament or King."[1]

That auguster thing is the tribunal which God has set up in the consciences of men. It is before that tribunal that I am now permitted humbly to plead, and there is something in my heart—a small but an exultant voice—which tells me I shall not plead in vain.'—BRIGHT *at Birmingham*, Dec. 1865.

IN July 1866 Derby and Disraeli came into office because their party had, with the help of Lowe's 'Cave of Adullam,' defeated Gladstone's very moderate Reform Bill. In the spring and summer of 1867 they presided as Ministers over the enfranchisement of the working men in the towns on the basis of household suffrage, a scheme far more extensive than that which they had successfully opposed as revolutionary in the preceding year. The only events that occurred in the interim to account for so great a change of mood in the Conservative party, were half a dozen vast gatherings, amounting between them to a million people, of whom fractions commensurate with the powers of the human voice were addressed by John Bright.

Peaceful demonstrations that could persuade the Conservative party against its will that the working men were dangerously in earnest about Reform, must have been of a very remarkable kind. They were, in fact, the fitting culmination of Bright's career, and brought about the final triumph of the policy that he had advocated for twenty years, through those peaceable but forceful methods of agitation by which, ever since the

[1] This is the fine modernisation in Coleridge's *Table Talk* of two lines from the close of Wither's *Vox Pacifica*, 1645.

Chartist collapse, he had been slowly reconstructing the democratic movement in politics.[1]

An important prelude to Bright's own campaign occurred at Hyde Park in July 1866, a fortnight after the assumption of office by the Conservatives. The working classes had watched the progress of Gladstone's Bill without enthusiasm, because it was too meagre to satisfy their demands. But when even that Bill was defeated in the Commons as being too democratic, and a Ministry was formed out of the men who had destroyed it, the anger of the unenfranchised was kindled, and Members of Parliament were sharply reminded that there was a nation outside the walls of their House.

On July 2 the Reform League and its President, Mr. Edmund Beales,[2] 'an honorable man and very sincere,' as Bright calls him in his private journal, had asserted against the orders of the police the legal right of the public to hold meetings in Trafalgar Square. They now proposed to hold a monster meeting in Hyde Park. The new Cabinet, overriding the opinion of their liberal-minded Home Secretary, Mr. Walpole,[3] yielded to the clamour of those who regarded Hyde Park as an enclosure sacred to wealth and fashion; they determined to close the gates and to refuse entrance to the demonstrators. As soon as this unwise resolve was known, Bright, who was absent from London, wrote a public letter to the Secretary of the Reform League:

(Rochdale. July 19, 1866.)

'I thank your council for the invitation to the meeting intended to be held in Hyde Park on Monday next. I cannot leave home for some days to come, and therefore cannot be in London on the 23rd instant. I see that the chief of the metropolitan police force has announced his intention to prevent the holding of the meeting. It appears from this that the people may meet in the parks for every purpose but that which ought to be most important and most dear to them. To meet in the streets is inconvenient, and to meet in the parks is unlawful—this is the theory of the police authorities of the metropolis. You have

[1] 'Moderate but irresistible in our moderation' was a watchword of the Bright Reform movement.

[2] Few even then remembered that Edmund Beales had been one of the writers in Praed's *Etonian*, the most famous of schoolboy journals.

[3] The best existing account of the whole affair will be found in chapter ix. of *The History of Twenty-Five Years*, by Spencer Walpole, who was his father's private secretary at the time of the Hyde Park controversies.

asserted your right to meet on Primrose Hill and in Trafalgar Square. I hope after Monday next no one will doubt your right to meet in Hyde Park. If a public meeting in a public park is denied you, and if millions of intelligent and honest men are denied the franchise, on what foundation does our liberty rest ?—or is there in the country any liberty but the toleration of the ruling class ? This is a serious question, but it is necessary to ask it, and some answer must be given to it.'

On the appointed day (July 23) Mr. Beales, at the head of an orderly procession, presented himself at the Marble Arch and formally demanded entrance to the Park, which was refused by the authorities. Thereupon the leaders, having thus lodged their protest, carried off the organised procession to Trafalgar Square, where they held a Reform meeting and passed votes of confidence in Gladstone and Bright. But the mob which had come to the Park gates to see what would happen there, stayed behind, and in a spirit partly of political indignation and partly of good-humoured rowdyism, pulled down the ill-secured railings, and swarmed over the forbidden ground.[1] There was no further violence done, except the inevitable trampling down of the flower-beds and the occupation of the fenceless Park for some days to come by the idlers and unemployed of London.

These events aroused deep and varying emotions : in some, disgust at the conduct of the mob and anger with Beales for coming to the gates to demand admittance, which he knew would be refused ; in others, indignation with the Government for closing the Park. But all were agreed that a new and ugly temper was at work in the people. If the affair had been deliberately organised by Beales or Bright, a strong reaction would have set in against Reform. But the violence had been the accidental and unpremeditated outcome of the political unrest which it revealed. So its lesson went home. And although the Government surrender did not begin to take place for another six months, and was not consummated for another year, the violence was never repeated, but was followed up instead by a series of monster demonstrations in the provinces, each consisting of the adult male population of some great city, called out by John Bright to lodge their demand for the

[1] The Park railings, fixed into a narrow stone kerb, were unable to resist the weight of a crowd applied to their upper section : the leverage tore up railings and kerb together. I have seen the railing of the Cambridge Senate House give way for the same physical cause, but in that case the crowd did not intend to pull it down.

franchise in a manner equally peaceful and impressive. Without the sequel of these demonstrations the Hyde Park riot alone would not have won Household Suffrage, and the repetition of such scenes of violence would have been fatal to the cause. It was Bright's characteristic merit that he found for the feelings of the unenfranchised masses a more profitable vent than aimless rioting.

A political agitation in our own day takes the form of innumerable meetings up and down the country, in buildings of every size from the village school-room to the Albert Hall. But in those days meetings were rare. Half a dozen great outdoor demonstrations at the principal centres of population, and a dozen speeches in great halls by Bright, sufficed to awe the Conservative party into submission. But on no political question since this of the Household Franchise would it have been possible to organise demonstrations so universally and enthusiastically attended by the inhabitants of the great industrial centres, as those over which Bright presided at Birmingham in August, at Manchester in September, at Glasgow and Leeds in October. At all these places the order of the day was a mass meeting on some moor outside the town of 150,000 to 200,000 citizens, a march past of the Trades Unions and Trades Societies before Bright, and in the evening one of his orations delivered in the largest hall of the city to as many as could find room therein. On the next day all England would be reading admirable reports of his speech.[1] The campaign

[1] The following newspaper description of the Glasgow demonstration can be read, *mutatis mutandis*, for those of Birmingham, Manchester, and Leeds:

'During the Reform agitation of 1832, a large assemblage of Reformers, numbering about 70,000, met together on Glasgow Green; and this morning [1866] a similar meeting, only of twice the size, estimated at 150,000 persons, assembled on the same spot, under the auspices of the Reform League, to pass resolutions in favour of another Reform Bill. A large Trades procession, containing 30,000 persons, was formed on the Green at eleven o'clock, and marched thence through the principal streets of Glasgow and back again to the starting point, where from various platforms several meetings were held simultaneously, and resolutions in favour of Reform adopted. Mr. Bright, M.P., who had accepted an invitation to address the inhabitants of Glasgow at an evening meeting, witnessed the procession from the window of the Cobden Hotel in Argyll Street. As the procession and the immense crowd that accompanied it passed by the Hotel, repeated cheers were given for Mr. Bright, who bowed his acknowledgments. Flags and banners of the Glasgow colours floated from the windows on every side along the route of the procession. Business in the city was almost entirely suspended throughout the day and almost every shop was closed. Each trade carried numerous flags. The cabinet-makers of Glasgow marched under the inscription, "*The people should be the cabinet-makers.*" One of the flags bore a huge coloured portrait of Mr. Gladstone, and a companion picture representing Mr. Bright on another flag bore the inscription, "*Honour Bright.*"'

in the provinces culminated early in December with the march through the capital of the London Trades Societies, and Bright's speech to their representatives in St. James's Hall.

Bright on these occasions was accompanied only by local members and the local magnates. The absence of prominent statesmen was quoted by Bright's enemies to prove his isolation, but in fact this only served to make his figure stand out ominously against the sky-line of politics. In vain the *Saturday Review* redoubled its sneers at the demagogue and the *Times* its lamentations over his wasted talents; in vain were the country houses filled that Christmas with young and old abusing Bright. In their hearts they were afraid, with that wise old English fear of their fellow-countrymen when thoroughly aroused, which has done as much to save England as many more heroic virtues. How much they were afraid they hardly knew themselves till their representatives gathered together on the Government benches for the opening of the next session.

During this long and memorable recess few other meetings were held, except those addressed by Bright. Only at Tyneside, whither he had promised to come but could not, his supporters held a monster demonstration similar to those which he had attended elsewhere. Gladstone, so far from making a passionate pilgrimage through the country, as he would assuredly have done in similar circumstances in later life, was wintering in Rome, and complaining privately of Bright's proceedings. Yet he himself very shortly learnt to imitate them as an essential part of the functions of statesmen in a democratic age. Gladstone was still so far from foreseeing his own near future that he wrote to Brand from Rome on October 30: 'I do not like what I see of Bright's speeches.' 'The reform movement is by degrees complicating the question. It is separating Bright from us, and in one sense thus clearing the way.'[1] But it was not by separation from Bright that Gladstone's way was to be cleared.

What were Bright's inner feelings as he went about his task of agitation on this the decisive campaign of his life's warfare? His oratorical powers were still at their best, his personal influence with his fellow-countrymen was greater than ever before, and the occasion was one of supreme opportunity. Yet already there is a certain note of weariness, not indeed in his speeches, but in his letters to his wife on the days when he left his home at Rochdale, loaded with his undelivered speech. 'I

[1] Morley's *Gladstone*, book v. chap. xiv.

wish it were not necessary to leave home,' he writes on one of these occasions in October. 'I seem to long very much for quiet. I suppose it is my advancing age which causes this and my love for my family.' But a month later he writes to Villiers in a more cheerful strain about the prospects of the London Trades' march past and the St. James's Hall meeting :

'If the thing goes off well and in great force it will help the Derby Conspiracy in their deliberations, and Walpole's tears will be shed amid the sighs of his colleagues.[1] I do not think Bob Lowe can now do a government much good —and I suspect there will not be much cheering during next session if he repeats his venomous attacks on the unenfranchised. It will not need much more of his Statesmanship to drive the people to a new and dangerous policy. It would be easy to induce many scores of thousands of men to provide themselves with arms—to form something like a great national volunteer force, which, without breaking the law, would place the peace of the country on a soil hot with volcanic fire. It is impossible, after what has happened in America and in Germany—with a wide suffrage extending everywhere—that *84 out of 100* of our countrymen should be content to be excluded from the franchise, and with a system so scandalous and fraudulent as to create a Parliament, more than one half of whose members are returned by *3 per cent.* of the grown men in the kingdom. This cannot last, and if a remedy is not found and applied peaceably, by some accident it will come with violence and great calamity to the upholders of what now exists. I am not responsible for what may come, any more than I am for an outburst from the bowels of Etna or Vesuvius.[2] They are responsible who despise and insult five millions of their fellow-countrymen, and who rejoice in and applaud the Statesmanship of Bob Lowe.

'Our friend Gladstone is on his way home. His letter just published will offend the Protestant feeling of many. There is somewhat too much of "his holiness" in it. It is a term which I think it is rather shocking to apply to any living man. What is likely to come of Gladstone's

[1] A story was current, and very popular, to the effect that the Home Secretary, in receiving a deputation on the vexed Hyde Park meeting question, had been so much harassed that he had shed tears. But G. J. Holyoake, who was on the deputation, has demonstrated the untruth of the legend.

[2] He developed this figure in a famous passage in his St. James's Hall speech on December 4.

leadership in the Commons? Will the jealousy which some of the Whigs feel towards him give way to party necessity and the public good or not? . . .

'I think no one can foresee what is coming. The "shooting stars" were foreseen—and I sat up and saw many of them—but of the session no man knoweth anything.'

The chief characteristic that differentiated Bright's agitation of 1866 from the Chartist agitation of 1838 and 1848, was the close mutual alliance of the radical middle class and the wage earners. At Birmingham the Mayor took the chair at Bright's meeting and identified himself with his cause; at Glasgow 'it seemed as if almost the whole male population of the city' took part in the demonstration. Bright had succeeded in his life-long object of combining every one against the existing monopolists of power. The Reform Act of 1832 had left half the middle class unenfranchised and the rest insufficiently represented under the arbitrary system by which the seats were distributed in favour of the landed interest. The Whigs and Conservatives should, long before 1866, have given votes to all the middle classes if they wished to separate their interest in the matter from that of the working men. It was now too late to make such offers. 'They set class against class,' said Bright at Manchester,

'and ask you to join with the past and present monopolists of power in the miserable and perilous determination to exclude for ever the great body of your countrymen from the common rights of the glorious English constitution. There is no greater fallacy than this—that the middle classes are in possession of power. The real state of the case, if it were put in simple language, would be this—that the working men are almost universally excluded, roughly and insolently, from political power, and that the middle class, whilst they have the semblance of it, are defrauded of the reality.'

At Glasgow (October 16) he made his most complete statement of the theory of democracy as he understood it, arguing that the vote must be given to the poor in order that justice should be done to them by the State. So long as the State was in the control of the rich, justice could not be done, and the social evils would continue without remedy.

'Now, if the Clerk of the House of Commons were placed

at Temple Bar, and if he had orders to tap upon the shoulder every well-dressed and apparently cleanly-washed man who passed through that ancient bar, until he had numbered six hundred and fifty-eight; and if the Crown summoned these six hundred and fifty-eight to be the Parliament of the United Kingdom, my honest conviction is that you would have a better Parliament than now exists. This assertion will stagger some timid and some good men; but let me explain myself to you. It would be a Parliament, every member of which would have no direct constituency, but it would be a Parliament that would act as a jury that would take some heed of the facts and arguments laid before it. It would be free, at any rate, from the class prejudices which weigh upon the present House of Commons. It would be free from the overshadowing presence of what are called noble families. It would owe no allegiance to great landowners, and I hope it would have fewer men amongst it seeking their own gains by entering Parliament.

. . . .

'I maintain with the most perfect conviction that the House of Commons, representing as it now does counties and boroughs such as I have described, does not represent the intelligence and the justice of the nation, but the prejudices, the privileges, and the selfishness of a class.

'What are the results of this system of legislation? Some of them have been touched upon in that Address which has been so kindly presented to me. You refer to the laws affecting land. Are you aware that half the land of England is in the possession of fewer than one hundred and fifty men? Are you aware of the fact that half the land in Scotland is in the possession of not more than ten or twelve men? Are you aware of the fact that the monopoly in land in the United Kingdom is growing constantly more and more close? And the result of it is this—the gradual extirpation of the middle class as owners of land, and the constant degradation of the tillers of the soil.

. . . .

'Your Address refers to pauperism—the gulf of pauperism. In the United Kingdom at this moment there are more than 1,200,000 paupers. . . . Now look, I beg of you, to this mass of misery. It is so great a mass that benevolence cannot reach it. If benevolence could do it, there would be no pauperism in England, for in no country do I believe that there is more benevolence than there is in the United Kingdom. But benevolence can touch scarcely the fringe of this vast disorder. There is another virtue we could add, and that virtue and that quality is justice. It is not benevolence but justice that can deal with giant evils. It was not benevolence that gave the people bread twenty years ago, but it was justice embodied in the abolition of a cruel and a guilty law. But justice is impossible from a class. It is most certain and easy from a nation; and I believe we can only reach the depths of ignorance and misery and crime in this country by an appeal to the justice, the intelligence, and the virtues of the entire people.

. . . .

'I am of opinion that the rich people of a country, invested with power, and speaking generally for rich people alone, cannot sufficiently care for the multitude and the poor. They are personally kind enough, but they do not care for the people in the bulk. They have read a passage in Holy Writ that "The poor ye have always with you"—and therefore they imagine that it is a providential arrangement that a small section of the people should be rich and powerful, and that the great mass of the people should be hard-working and poor. It is a long distance from castles, and mansions, and great houses, and abounding luxuries, to the condition of the great mass of the people who have no property, and too many of whom are always on the verge of poverty. We know very well all of us how much we are influenced by the immediate circumstances by which we are surrounded. The rich find everything just as they like. The country needs no reform. There is no other country in the world so pleasant for rich people as this country. But I deny altogether that the rich alone are qualified to legislate for the poor, any more than that the poor alone would be qualified to legislate for the rich.'

If the Franchise were extended to the working men, it would alter the attitude of the wealthier classes:

'Probably what I call the Botany Bay view of their countrymen would be got rid of, and we should have a sense of greater justice and generosity in the feeling with which they regard the bulk of the nation. And if there was more knowledge of the people, there would assuredly be more sympathy with them; and I believe the legislation of the House, being more in accordance with the public sentiment, would be wiser and better in every respect. The nation would be changed. There would be amongst us a greater growth of everything that is good. . . . The class which has hitherto ruled in this country has failed miserably. It revels in power and wealth, whilst at its feet, a terrible peril for its future, lies the multitude which it has neglected. *If a class has failed, let us try the nation.*'

These passages from the most important speech of his whole career, ending on a sentence which summed up the political creed of his life, prove that although John Bright could by no means foresee all the methods by which the social problem was to be attacked, he well knew that it was the end and object of political life, and he more than any other man taught his countrymen that democratic institutions were the first step towards its solution.

During the interval between the close of Bright's campaign in the country and the opening of the session of 1867, a personal incident occurred that attracted the national attention, representing as it did the hatred with which Bright was now regarded by the upper classes, and his very potent abilities for self-defence. In December 1866 Mr. Richard Garth, Q.C., was elected Member for Guildford at a by-election. During the contest he said in a speech at the White Hart Hotel that Bright was unpopular in Rochdale, that he had been 'hooted away from his own premises—his own people distrust him,' and that he had not subscribed to the Lancashire distress funds during the cotton famine. The audience in the White Hart Hotel, Guildford, was delighted, but the working men of Rochdale were furious. Like their comrades throughout the rest of industrial England, they had taken 'Honour Bright' for their motto. In January 1867 two meetings were held in Rochdale about the Garth libels: first an indignation meeting of the work-people of Bright Bros., held in the Public Hall, to which they invited John Bright, who came to receive their address, while they excluded all strangers to the works except Goldwin Smith, who begged hard to be allowed to come.[1] Secondly, a meeting was held in the theatre at Rochdale, of Tories, Whigs, and Radicals, to protest no less emphatically that the libels against their fellow-townsman were 'curiously the reverse of the truth.' The last sentences of Bright's reply to Garth gave great satisfaction :

> 'On a review of your speech and your letter, I come to this conclusion—that you wished to get into Parliament, and were not particular as to the path which might lead to it. You threw dirt during your canvass, doubtless knowing that, if needful, you could eat it afterwards. There are many men who go "through dirt to dignities," and I suspect you have no objection to be one of them.' [2]

Bright was well able to defend his honour against definite false charges, but he was not of a disposition to rush into controversy with those who made personal attacks upon him. He was combative in the public interest, but not quarrelsome on his own behalf. On one occasion when a celebrated antagonist was reviling him with marked animosity, one of his family exhorted him to reply, but in vain : 'a man in a clean coat should never wrestle with a sweep,' he said.

In February 1867 Parliament assembled for the most chaotic yet productive session since that in which Peel had surrendered the principles of his party to the national interest and the national demand. Disraeli had then offered him up as a sacrifice to the outraged ghost of political consistency. That Disraeli would now make a *volte-face* as complete as that of Peel in 1846 was by no means certain when the House met. The Conservatives, indeed, were in a chastened mood, and every one knew that the state of public opinion made it necessary that a Reform Bill of some kind should be introduced. The Government began badly for its prestige, putting forward and withdrawing in rapid succession several outline schemes of Reform ; one of these, on account of the speed with which it was drawn up by a Cabinet in distress, has won posthumous notoriety as the 'Ten Minutes Bill.' There was division and threat of resignation in the Cabinet, and searchings of heart on the Government benches. But union and loyalty were as

[1] Mr. George Ingham, who was present at this meeting of his fellow-workmen, told me this about Goldwin Smith.

[2] The correspondence between Bright and Garth will be found in *Bright's Public Letters* (Leech), pp. 117-27.

far to seek among the Liberal Opposition. Except Disraeli's bargain with himself to conduct these high affairs to some possible issue, there was no firm understanding anywhere save that which now united Bright and Gladstone; their alliance was destined in the end to dominate the confused fortunes of the session. Gladstone had quickly forgiven Bright for having, as he thought, too crudely stated the democratic case on the platform, without those 'sub-intents and saving clauses' so dear to the nursling of Oxford and the friend of Peel. And John Bright, for his part, felt no mean jealousy of Gladstone. As soon as they were again under the parliamentary roof, he became Gladstone's most loyal supporter, for he recognised that here at last, after many years, was a 'statesman' whom he could trust not to betray the interests of the people. If we consider Bright's long career as an independent force in the House and country, and his immense popularity at that moment with the great majority of Englishmen, his ready consent to serve under Gladstone's banner will appear as creditable to him as it was certainly useful to his cause. The greatest guerilla warrior of our parliamentary history, he had contracted none of the indiscipline characteristic of irregular troops.

After the shipwreck of the Government's first abortive schemes of Reform in the early weeks of the session, a curious passage occurred between Disraeli and Bright, which may perhaps have had influence on the course shortly afterwards taken by the Minister. The relations of the two men had for fifteen years past been friendly and sometimes strangely intimate. It is not, therefore, surprising to find the following entry in Bright's journal for March 1, 1867:

> 'Position very curious. Tory party in chaos. Cabinet divided—party divided—its members speaking openly of the anarchy that prevails.
>
> 'Conversation with Disraeli in the lobby—asked him what was to be done, and could he do it: he said he "would do it if he could, was doing all he could"; I said, "You ought to have taken me into your counsels": he said, "I offered you that in 1852 you remember":[1] I said, "Yes, but I do not mean officially": he said, "The Whigs have only betrayed you, I told you they would do nothing for you": I replied, "I want nothing, I am satisfied with my position, and office would be intolerable to me." He said, "Well, I have had enough of it; I have had 30 years

[1] See chapter ix., p. 206 above.

of Parliament, and 20 years as leader of a party. I am sick of it, and if I can get this thing done, then I shall (or can) go away." I told him of a conversation with three of his party in the smoking-room, how far they were willing to go, and that at the pace they were moving, I should soon have to hold them back. He thought they were fair specimens of a considerable section of the party. I advised him to advance his offers so far in regard to the suffrage that he would not be driven to accept defeat on every proposition—that £5 rating franchise or household suffrage would save him in the boroughs, and that £10 or £12 would do for the counties. He said he did not care much for the counties. The working class question was the real question, and that was the thing that demanded to be settled. He had once proposed a £10 franchise for the counties. He said, "You will attack me whatever I propose." I said, "No, I will not, I will do all I can fairly to help a bill through, if you will do the right thing. I am against faction, and if our leaders do as you did last year I shall openly denounce them." I told him that people said he and I always fought with gloves on, but sometimes I had been tempted to take them off. He said, "There had always been something of sympathy between us," which I suppose is true, though our course and aims have seemed so different.

'As we were talking, Mr. Brand, the Opposition "Whip," went by, and Disraeli said, "He will think it is a coalition," that he and I should be seen in conversation at such a crisis as this. At parting he pressed my hand with an apparent earnestness of feeling, saying, "Well, whatever happens, you and I will always be friends."

'Disraeli has been possessed by a devouring ambition, not to preach and act the truth, but to distinguish himself. "We come here for fame!" he said to me many years ago, and he has distinguished himself, but on a low field, and with no results which can be looked back upon with satisfaction.' [1]

A few days later (March 9) Bright sent Disraeli a memorandum marked *Confidential*, entitled *Suggestions on the coming Reform Bill*. He there set out reasons why the Government

[1] It was Bright who had recently invented a name for Disraeli that long stuck to him. 'Now Mr. Disraeli is a man who does what may be called the conjuring for his party. He is what among a tribe of Red Indians, would be called *the mystery man.*' Birmingham, July 1865.

should terminate the agitation in the country by an Act establishing in the boroughs unconditional household franchise together with a moderate lodger vote, and in the counties a £10 or £12 occupation franchise—the very Bill which finally emerged from Committee that summer and passed into law.[1]

Already much more restricted proposals had caused important resignations in the Cabinet. On March 3 Bright notes in his journal:

> 'Government in a crisis. General Peel, Lords Cranborne[2] and Carnarvon resigned; they object to Reform as urged by Disraeli; excitement in political circles. I seem to feel it less than others, but am deeply concerned in the evident progress the Reform question is making.'
>
> [March 4.] 'House. Ministerial crisis. The three Secretaries of State resigned; their places easily filled up, and Government will attempt to go on. Derby and Disraeli intend to propose and carry a Reform Bill. Great interest excited. Wonderful conversions to Household Suffrage on every side. I begin to be an authority with the Tory party! What next?'

Thus at the initial cost of three Cabinet resignations, Disraeli introduced a Reform Bill, nominally on the basis of Household Suffrage for the boroughs. The phrase 'Household Suffrage' would, he hoped, prove a talisman to charm the democracy. But he hedged round this popular principle with so many safeguards and make-weights, that the Bill as first introduced was not democratic. For on the one hand it added to the upper class vote, and on the other it enfranchised only a portion of the working class householders. It proposed to exclude, in effect, from the franchise not only all 'lodgers,' but the large class of so-called 'compound householders' whose rates were paid by their landlord.

The first question before the Liberal party was whether to accept this bad Bill on second reading, in hope of altering its character in Committee, or whether to oppose it outright. Gladstone and Bright were in favour of the latter course, but they were overruled at a party meeting, and acquiesced readily enough in this decision, which proved in the event a fortu-

[1] This paper is printed at the end of the chapter. As a possible though inferior alternative to Household Franchise, he mentions £5 rating franchise, embodied in Mr. Gladstone's abortive 'instruction' a month later.

[2] Lord Robert Cecil (afterwards Lord Salisbury) had just become Lord Cranborne.

nate choice. For in Committee Disraeli's safeguards against democracy were swept away one after the other, and the Bill emerged on third reading a widely democratic measure—more democratic indeed than any which a Liberal Government, badly supported by its own Whig followers and opposed by the whole Conservative regiment, could have passed through the Lords' or even through the Commons' House.

The principal changes made in Committee, besides the all-important abolition of compounding for rates, were the creation of a lodger franchise in the boroughs; the reduction of the county franchise from £15 to £12; the rejection of Disraeli's 'fancy' franchises—educational and pecuniary—and his 'dual' vote for rich men; and the reduction of the qualifying period of residence from two years to one. Also the number of seats transferred from small to large boroughs was increased.

The Radical triumph in Committee is the more remarkable because of the painful position in which Gladstone and Bright were placed all through these critical weeks by the Whig revolt against their leadership. Bright's journal contains daily evidence that they were much more conscious of the anxiety and discomfort of the situation than of the success that they were actually achieving. After one of many rebuffs from their own supporter, the two walked home together across St. James's Park at midnight, Gladstone speaking to Bright 'of the reckless and unwise character of the House. Since the Russian War he thought the tone of the House changed for the worse. In Sir R. Peel's time a more just and even liberal spirit prevailed.' How under these circumstances the Radicals succeeded in dictating terms to the Conservative Ministers, remains one of the most complex problems of our parliamentary history. Perhaps the ultra-Conservative revolt of Cranborne and his friends against the Reform Bill at any price, compelled Disraeli to depend more on Radical support. Perhaps the quasi-democratic leanings of the author of *Sybil*, and the desire to lay the question at rest, influenced him in his surrender of the vital positions. Certain it is that in May he adopted, either voluntarily or by compulsion, the advice which Bright had given him in conversation and writing at the beginning of March.

Throughout the session Bright's speeches in Committee were very good and very useful. According to one who heard them day by day, they were better and more effective than his speeches in the House in subsequent years. Indeed, his private letters reveal that already he was beginning to be conscious of the approach of age and of physical weakness; but these as yet had no effect on his performance, except on occasions when his voice failed him.[1]

(Journal. March 19, 1867.)

'Called on Mr. Gladstone to discuss course to be taken on Government Bill. He is strong in condemnation of the Bill and wishful to oppose the second reading; there were 25 or 30 of the Tory party at least who would oppose the Bill. I agree with him as to the proper course, but doubt if our side will take it. There is much jealousy, some fear of dissolution, however absurd this may be, and much ignorance of Parliamentary tactics.'

[March 21.] 'Meeting at Mr. Gladstone's (Liberal Party). Agreed not to oppose second reading of Government Bill owing to differences of opinion in the party. I consented to the policy adopted, though expressing my entire dissent from it.'

[March 28.] 'Long conversation with Gladstone on course to be taken on the Reform Bill. He proposed to move resolutions on motion that "the Speaker do leave the chair" to fix the franchise in boroughs, which the House would agree to. Thought £5 rating the point which would meet the views of a large majority of the House, to which I assented as probably the best thing that could be carried, and as much better than the Bill of the Government as it stands [right] or as the House will accept it [proved wrong in the event]. Gladstone spoke of Disraeli and his severance from his party, and of his personal character and qualities, and said "I do not despair of meeting you some day at Hughenden Manor," Disraeli's house in Buckinghamshire.'

[April 8.] 'Expected debate abandoned. Some malcontents on our side met this afternoon—conspired to defeat measures of Mr. Gladstone—urged him to withdraw "Instruction" to the Committee, to which he consented; they have done their utmost to humiliate him and the Liberal party. The Bill went into Committee, and Disraeli in great spirits at the failure of the effort which was to have been made against him. The corruption of the House is something extraordinary—men fear a dissolution, and will descend to any meanness to escape it.

[1] At the end of June he writes to his wife: 'I seem as if I could not make up my mind about anything [*sic!*]. I suppose I am growing weaker as I know I am growing older.'

They are destroying the unity and power of the Liberal party, and are making its leader an object of commiseration. They are more willing to express want of confidence in Mr. Gladstone than in Disraeli.'

The group whose conduct is here censured by Bright was known as 'The Tea-room,' on account of the place where their plot was hatched. They prevented Gladstone from moving his 'Instruction' (£5 rating), which would have been more liberal than the Bill as then unamended; but the Bill as finally amended gave a yet broader franchise than Gladstone's 'Instruction' would have given. Unlike the 'Cave,' the 'Tea-room' consisted of Radicals, who differed from Gladstone and Bright only as to tactics.

At first things went very ill in Committee for those who hoped to amend Disraeli's measure in a democratic direction. By far the most important issue was whether, as the Bill originally proposed, the right to vote should be confined to those who paid their rates in person to the exclusion of the 'compound ratepayer.' On April 13 an amendment extending the vote to the 'compound ratepayer' was successfully resisted by Disraeli, by a majority of 21. Bright notes the catastrophe in his journal: 'We are destroyed by deserters from our party, some honest and misled, some far from honest.' It must be remembered that throughout this strange session those on the Opposition side of the House were in a majority, whenever they could be induced to vote together.

Yet in spite of this rebuff on the main issue on April 13, the question of the 'compound ratepayer' was, as we shall see, solved in the Radical sense a month later by another expedient—the abolition of compounding for rates.

During April little had been done to improve the Bill in Committee. But in May the tide turned.

(Journal. May 2.)

'Debate on "residence" clause in Reform Bill, two years or one year. Government defeated by large majority. Conversation with Mr. Gladstone. He is in good spirits and does not abandon the contest with the Government.'

At this stage the Reform League determined to hold a meeting in Hyde Park. Bright went to interview Home Secretary Walpole on the subject, and found him, as usual, 'kind and moderate'; his colleagues in the Cabinet would have liked, but did not dare, to stop the demonstration, which took place peacefully on May 6. The right of meeting in Hyde Park was thereby established. The surrender of the Government on this question, which they had disputed a year before, so much incensed the upper strata of society that Walpole found it necessary to resign.

Some changes for the good had now been effected in the Bill, but it was still far from democratic, for the 'compound ratepayer' was still excluded from the franchise. John Bright was still returning night after night from the House, disgusted with what he regarded as the treachery of many of the Liberals to the democratic cause, and comforting himself in his lodgings with writing his griefs to his wife and reading Milton, 'who seems always to raise me above the disappointments of the world and the meanness which I meet so often among men.' 'I am going,' he writes to his wife on May 11, 'with a large deputation to Gladstone this afternoon. I do not see what can be done unless a scheme I have devised and which I have written out for his consideration can be adopted.' This scheme was an amendment to prohibit in the borough areas the practice of 'compounding' for rates, to compel every householder to pay rates personally instead of through his landlord, and thereby honestly to bring every householder into the scope of the boasted 'Household Franchise' Bill. This all-important amendment was moved by Mr. Hodgkinson, with the support of Bright and Gladstone. Its mover expected that it would be easily defeated, since the analogous amendment enfranchising the compound householder had been defeated a month before. But Disraeli rose and accepted the new amendment, thereby establishing industrial democracy in England.[1]

This great surprise occurred at dinner-time on May 17, in a thin House. As Members trooped back, they were met by the news. When Gladstone was informed of Disraeli's move, he

[1] The precise words of Mr. Hodgkinson's famous amendment were: 'Provided always, that no person other than the occupier shall, after the passing of this Act, be rated to parochial rates in respect of premises occupied by him within the limits of a Parliamentary Borough, all Acts to the contrary now in force notwithstanding.' This was accepted by Mr. Disraeli, May 17th and 20th. After the franchise had been secured to all householders in Parliamentary Boroughs in this roundabout and thoroughly 'English' way, the affair was straightened out again in 1869, when compounding for rates was again permitted by law, but without disqualifying any one for the franchise. 32-3 Vict. 41. The legal and technical details of this very complicated Franchise Bill of 1867 and its amendments are unravelled in the *History of the Reform Bills of 1866 and 1867*, by Homersham Cox, 1868. *He calculates that the Hodgkinson amendment quadrupled the number of voters added by the Bill to the Borough Registers.*

could scarcely believe his ears. Another Liberal Member was asked by a friend: 'What has happened? I met Forster dancing down the Lobby.' 'It is very mortifying,' wrote Robert Lowe that evening, 'after so much success as I had last year, to find everything betrayed and lost.' Bright noted the victory of his cause very quietly:—'Government accepted our demands on Borough Franchise.'

> [May 28.] 'Reform Bill. Spoke against restrictions on Franchise and *showed that the Bill adopted is the precise franchise I recommended in 1858-9.*' [1]
>
> [July 15.] 'Third reading of Reform Bill. Spoke briefly. Amusing recriminations between Lowe and Disraeli. *Bill passed with cheers from our side.*'

Lord Derby's proverbial account of the matter was that he and his colleagues had 'dished the Whigs,' and had compelled the country to 'take a leap in the dark.' As in 1846, the Conservative chiefs had made their party the instrument of legislation more democratic than any which the Liberals could have passed against the opposition of the Conservatives and of the House of Lords. On this second occasion, since there was no one who could treat Disraeli as Disraeli had treated Peel, Conservative unity was not broken up as a consequence of the abandonment of Conservative principles. Disraeli was able to boast that he had 'educated his party.' Lowe, indeed, attacked him with the brilliancy and bitterness that the occasion demanded, but Lowe was not a Conservative, and his outcries against the betrayal did not evoke from the Government benches the cheers that had greeted the great philippics against Peel. One unfortunate Conservative Member who attempted to imitate those philippics was interrupted with extreme and exceptional violence while he spoke, and was made to feel in the lobbies the weight of social ostracism by which discipline was maintained in the Conservative ranks. But it was not possible to treat Lord Cranborne in this fashion, and on the third reading debate he made his party listen in uncomfortable silence as he compared the action of Peel in 1846 most favourably to the 'political morality on which the manœuvres of this year have been based.' 'I have heard,' said the future Lord Salisbury, 'that this Bill is a Conservative triumph. If it be a Conservative triumph to have adopted the principles of your most determined adversary, the hon. Member for Birmingham; if it be a Conservative triumph to have introduced a Bill guarded with

[1] See p. 271 above.

precautions and securities, and to have abandoned every one of those precautions and securities at the bidding of your opponents, then in the whole course of your annals I will venture to say the Conservative party has won no triumph so signal as this.'

At this period of his career John Bright was not only a great orator, but a parliamentary tactician and debater of no mean power. Throughout the all-important Committee stage, when the Reform Bill was turned inside out by the House of Commons, Bright was almost as important as Gladstone in the conduct of these nice operations. We have seen that it was he who devised and drew up the great amendment abolishing the compound householder, which was put into Mr. Hodgkinson's hands to propose and was so strangely accepted by Disraeli. Bright's speeches in Committee were frequent, to the point, and full of the kind of humour dear to the House of Commons. Motley describes his style—not indeed his only or his greatest style—as 'easy, conversational, slightly humorous, rather fluent.' He would lay traps for his enemies, baiting them with that apparent simplicity so thoroughly in keeping with his character, but sometimes not far removed from an innocent species of guile. For instance, on June 20 he was arguing, in Committee on the Reform Bill, against a clause which would have permitted electors to vote by voting papers instead of in person. There are many good reasons against this proposal, but Bright put forward among other reasons one which seemed far-fetched, and, as he argued it, a little ridiculous :

> 'If,' he said, 'a man had given his voting paper three days before an election, he would not be at liberty to change his mind. No doubt the elector might attempt to outwit his proxy, by being at the poll before it opened, and then it would be a scuffle between him and his proxy as to the vote to be given.'

Here the House began to laugh, and Bright's friends to shift uneasily. He did not seem to notice, but went on as if talking to himself in rather a feeble way :

> 'Generally speaking there are many persons who honestly change their minds between the time an election is proclaimed and the time that it takes place.'

Here a mocking laugh passed along the Government benches. Suddenly Bright seemed to wake up, and flashed out at them with extraordinary impetuosity :—'Hon. Members opposite do not appear to believe that there can be any honest change of opinion. If Members of the House of Commons in great numbers can change their opinions at once on a question——' Before he could finish, a roar of applause and laughter went up from the delighted Liberals, and the rows of Government converts to Household Suffrage sat looking foolish enough.

In August the Bill went through the Lords. They would never have accepted such a measure from Gladstone and Russell, but they accepted Disraeli's Reform Bill at Derby's bidding, just as they had accepted Peel's Corn Bill at the bidding of Wellington. The only important change on which they insisted was Lord Cairns' amendment, supported by Earl Russell and blessed by John Stuart Mill and the Liberal 'Philosophers,' but disliked by Gladstone and abominated by Bright. This amendment enacted that in half a dozen great cities like Birmingham and Leeds, which were to return three Members each under the new Act, the electors were to dispose of only two votes apiece. A very small minority could therefore elect one Member against the two Members chosen by the majority. Bright complained that in effect this reduced the greatest provincial cities to the same voting power in the House of Commons as the smallest single-Member constituency in the kingdom. The arrangement which he so much disliked lasted until 1885. In Birmingham, indeed, the Liberal majority was so great, and the organisation and discipline of the party so perfect, that by scientific distribution of votes among the three Liberal candidates the return of all three was actually secured.

Bright regarded the Ballot, for which he had contended all his life, as the necessary sequel of the Franchise Act. But he had to wait for the next Liberal Government before that security could be obtained for the working men, who exercised their newly acquired franchise at the General Election of 1868 under the old system of open voting.

Another question had been raised by John Stuart Mill in Committee on the Reform Bill. On May 26 he had moved an amendment extending the franchise to women, which secured the unexpected support of as many as 73 votes against 196. 'The surprise,' Mill writes in his *Autobiography*, 'was general and the encouragement great, the greater, too, because one of those who voted for the motion was Mr. Bright, a fact which could only be attributed to the impression made on him by the debate, as he had previously made no secret of his non-concurrence in the proposal.' But the following letter shows that, nine years before, Bright had been, academically, in favour of Women's Suffrage at some future date. The letter (dated

'Nov. 17, 1858, Llandudno. Private') is addressed to Mrs. Agnes Pochin, who had written to ask him to insert Women's Suffrage in the Franchise Bill which he was then drawing up:

'MADAM,—I know no valid argument against your proposal, but I do not think I should include it in any scheme I might bring before the public. In the present state of opinion I fear it would do harm to the cause of improved representation, without doing any good to the object you have in view. The time may come, and I think it will come, when opinion will be more correct on this question. There is, however, perhaps *one* argument against you. If women may vote, why should they not be eligible to sit in Parliament? and I fear Parliament would not be much better in the transaction of business if men and women equally had seats there.

'Your question is somewhat too far in advance I fear.'

But in 1871 he wrote to his friend, Miss Eliza Sturge of Birmingham:

'I voted with J. S. Mill three or four years ago. But I am never free from doubt as to whether my vote was a wise one. I do not think the bestowal of the Suffrage on Women will be of any advantage to *them*, and I fear at present, and perhaps always, it will tend to strengthen the Party which hitherto has opposed every good measure passed during the thirty years in which I have taken part in political affairs. I think it would add to the power of Priestcraft in every part of the Three Kingdoms. I hope this view of the question may be a mistaken one, because it does not seem to me very unlikely that the suffrage will be granted to women. Forgive my doubts.'

On April 26, 1876, he spoke and voted in the House against Women's Suffrage. It was one of the very few public questions on which he changed his mind. Whichever one of his two opinions on the subject was wrong, it was not formed for want of hearing the question discussed, for there were ardent female suffragists in his intimate circle who, headed by his sister, Mrs. McLaren, kept the question more to the front than was always altogether pleasant to him. They declared that their beliefs had been greatly strengthened by his fervent advocacy of the principle of national citizenship. But he would no more fashion his opinions to please his dearest relatives than they would conceal theirs to please him.

NOTE

The following is from a copy kept by Bright of his memorandum to Disraeli, referred to on pp. 371-72 above. It is headed :

'3rd month, 9, 1867.

'*Letter to Disraeli.* *Confidential.*

'Suggestions on the Coming Reform Bill

'What is wanted is (1) a Bill on which the Cabinet can be agreed, (2) one which the House will accept, and (3) one which will so far content the people as to extinguish the Associations now agitating the Question.

'If it fail on the points 2 and 3, the agreement of the Cabinet is useless, and if it meet only the points 1 and 2, it will be of no real value. It must meet the points 2 and 3, or it should not be attempted.

'I believe a Bill may be proposed which the House will accept, and which will put an end to Suffrage agitation. If the Government cannot propose such a Bill, it has no right to meddle with the Question. What should the Bill be ?

'The oldest and wisest basis for the Borough franchise is Household Suffrage. Probably only a minority of the House is in favor of it, though [if] proposed by the present Government, it would be carried. This would end the agitation.

'The next thing to the wisest is a rental franchise of £6, or a rating franchise of £5. For either of these there would be a large majority in the House. If proposed by the Government it would pass probably without a division—if proposed against the Government as an amendment on any higher qualification, it would be carried by a considerable majority. Either of these would terminate the agitation.

'The Household Suffrage would be better than the £6 or £5, but would be less acceptable than either if accompanied by any novel propositions, in themselves evil or undesirable, and proposed only as restrictions on or compensations for Household Suffrage. The proposal of such restrictions and compensations will be unfavorably viewed by the House, and by Reformers outside, and will tend to create the opinion that the Government is insincere.[1] If they should be rejected by the House, which is all but certain, then the question may be involved in fresh difficulty, and the Government

[1] It was solely because such 'restrictions and compensations' were inserted in the Bill as introduced by Disraeli, that Bright and Gladstone refused to support it and wanted to divide against it on second reading. Bright's course was consistent and straightforward in the whole affair.

may fail to carry any Bill. In the Counties the franchise most in favor is that proposed in 1859 and 1860—the £10 occupation. If the Borough franchise is fixed at £5 or £6, as above mentioned, then £10 or £12 in the Counties would probably be acceptable. Such a proposal made by the Government would pass by a large majority, and probably without a division.

'For London a lodger franchise is absolutely necessary, and the clause in the Bill of last year seemed to meet the views of the friends of Reform, and it would be wise to adopt it now.

'The Ratepaying clauses should be abolished to simplify the Borough franchise; but if the Government did not propose this, it might leave it to the decision of the House after a fresh discussion of it.

'A Bill framed as above sketched would pass without difficulty, and there would be an end of all agitation on the Suffrage Question for an indefinite, but, I believe, for a *very long period*. If the Government is in earnest about doing anything, it should do the right thing, with simplicity and courage. If the Conservative Party has determined to capitulate on this Question, it should act with the foresight and the breadth which are inseparable from a true Statesmanship. It will be more honorable to the Government to propose the right clauses than to have them forced upon it by the Opposition.

. . . .

'I am not a Minister, or a partisan of the present Government; but I have some responsibility in regard to this subject of Reform. If I were a Minister or a partisan of the present Government, I should say precisely what I say now.

'The Government may propose a Franchise Bill which will pass the House without difficulty, and will extinguish all the existing and growing agitation. If the Ministers cannot agree among themselves, or if their Party will not allow them to do what is right and needful to be done, then the Government should abandon the attempt, and leave Reform to be dealt with by the friends of Reform.

'These suggestions are made with an honest purpose; to assist in the settlement of a great question, and with no hostile feeling to the existing Administration.'

CHAPTER XVIII

BRIGHT'S ORATORY. THE LIBERAL HARVESTING. IRISH CHURCH. GLADSTONE'S REFORM MINISTRY. BRIGHT IN OFFICE. SECOND ILLNESS AND EDUCATION BILL, 1868-70

'He was the greatest master of English oratory that this generation has produced, or I may say several generations back. I have met men who have heard Pitt and Fox and in whose judgment their eloquence at its best was inferior to the finest efforts of John Bright.'—LORD SALISBURY *in the House of Lords*, April 1889.

LORD SALISBURY's opinion, which would place Bright as an orator above Gladstone, is not universally accepted; it would indeed be easy to draw up two lists—one in favour of Gladstone and the other in favour of Bright—from among statesmen who heard them both and were competent to judge. John Bright had the merits and defects of simplicity, Gladstone of complexity. Gladstone—even in the whirlwind of his own oratory, arms overhead and eyes flashing—was always a debater, meeting his opponent's every argument, instructing his audience, often exciting them over the details of some financial or legislative measure. Bright, on the other hand, for all that he never gave the rein to his passion, never swung his arm and scarcely raised his voice—was first and foremost a preacher of broad principles in their moral and poetic force, a speaker less instructive but even more moving than Gladstone. He has himself described the difference between them thus: 'When I speak, I strike across from headland to headland. Mr. Gladstone follows the coast-line; and when he comes to a navigable river he is unable to resist the temptation of tracing it to its source.'

Of the two, it is Bright whose speeches can be read with greatest pleasure, though that, perhaps, is no test of oratory. Gladstone's orations suffer in the reading from a quality which made them delightful to hear, their dependence on the skill of the speaker to effect his escape with grammar intact from the maze of parentheses—an operation safely sustained on that magnificent voice and by those dramatic gestures. Bright's voice, too, was a gift of heaven ; he had never to shout in order that it might thrill with its music the farthest corner of the largest hall. But he had no gesture except to raise his hand, and that not above the level of his breast.[1] Gladstone was everything at once—actor, missionary, debater, exponent of legislative detail—such an one as never before or since rose to address an audience ; Bright excelled in pure oratory in its stricter sense.

It is not to be wondered at that John Bright's speeches are still good to read. He took pains in preparing not only the subject-matter but the words, although it was only the peroration that he wrote out in full, and even that, as he delivered it, was not word for word the same as what he had written down. He often lay awake over his speech : 'I find when in bed that my ideas come easily and fix themselves on the mind,' he writes in 1866 ; 'I suppose the dim light and the silence are favorable to the imagination and the memory.' He worked 'at leisure perfectly,' for he had not the legislative and executive duties that burdened his great contemporaries or successors, and he gave a larger portion of his life than they to the mere perfection of his eloquence. He had more of what we should now call the 'artistic conscience.' Even the 'artistic temperament' was not wholly wanting, in his uneasy and preoccupied air for two or three days before a speech, and his traditional complaint that 'the day was cold,' when he came down to breakfast on the morning before a meeting.

His chief artistic inspiration lay in his sense for the value of words, and for the rhythm of words and sentences. In spite of what is sometimes said, he had not, any more than Milton, a special fondness for short words with Anglo-Saxon roots, but loved and understood all good, honest English words, whether their ancestors had come over from Germany or France, Rome or Norway, and whether they themselves were short or long, high or low, provided they did not come stale from Fleet Street, like the language of most politicians. His invariable quality is the choice of the right word or run of words. The volumes of his speeches are one long illustration of this : 'a small but *exultant* voice within me tells me that I shall not appeal in vain.' 'This *incapable and guilty administration.*' 'I should like to ask him whether this Irish question is *above the stature* of himself and his colleagues.' After his 'Angel of Death' speech,

[1] See the portrait of Bright speaking, frontispiece.

Cobden said to him: 'You went very near that time. If you had said "*flapping*" instead of "*beating* of his wings" the House would have laughed.' But Bright could no more have said "*flapping*" than Mr. Gladstone could have made a false quantity.

His greatest passages are those in which his sense of poetry and of grandeur come closest to his vision of homely, common life, which was to him, as it was to Wordsworth, the source of high thoughts and great imaginings. Thus, in his other Crimean speech, he leads up to the death of Colonel Boyle [1] by telling how he lately met the Colonel at 'Mr. Westerton's, the bookseller, near Hyde Park Corner,' a place well known to the Members whom he was addressing, and how their late colleague had there told him his fears as a husband and father at going to the war. Then comes the thunderous climax—'the stormy Euxine is his grave; his wife is a widow, his children fatherless'—which quite overpowered his hearers. If Bright had been in the habit of using adjectives freely, 'stormy' would have carried less weight, but it was one of his first principles to eschew adjectives unless they meant much. The Miltonic 'Euxine' for 'Black Sea' also marks a solemn occasion, and the words together have 'a sound like the sound of the sea.'

Since he did not deal in gesture, men all the more watched his face. He once said to a friend, 'An orator should be shaved,' and certainly the play of his lip was very fine. As he spoke, he used to drop the little slips of paper on which his notes were written, one by one into his tall hat, until when the peroration was finished, there they all lay in a heap.[2]

But the influence that John Bright exerted over his countrymen was due at least as much to his own moral weight as to the artistic perfection of his speeches. In November 1868, when he was presented with the Freedom of Edinburgh, he said in returning thanks:

> 'In the resolution of the Town Council there are phrases

[1] See p. 237 above.

[2] On the opposite page is a facsimile, very slightly reduced, of one of these little slips, which were always the same in size and shape. This one is from a speech in which he compares the recent Italian revolution of 1860, giving representative government to twenty-four million Italians—a revolution blessed by England through Lord John Russell's dispatch—to the deplorable state of English representation. It is a fair example of his notes; each idea in its order is represented by a few words or figures, while the 'key sentence' or 'island,' as he used to call it, is written out at full—'working men, whom bad laws most injure, whom good laws most speedily bless.' And the dispatch which he intends to quote is copied out for accuracy. (The peroration of this speech, as of all others, he has written out in full.)

which almost make me blush and to which I find it difficult to refer. I am there described as an orator and a statesman. Now more than thirty years ago, when I was very young indeed, only beginning to think about public affairs, in reading the prose writings of John Milton, I found a passage which fixed itself in my mind. This passage time has never been able to take from my memory. He says—"Yet true eloquence I find to be none but the serious and hearty love of truth." And I have endeavoured, as far as I have had the opportunities of speaking in public, to abide by that wise and weighty saying. So far as I am able to examine myself, during the thirty years that I have been permitted to speak at meetings of my countrymen, I am not conscious that I have ever used an argument which I did not believe to be sound, or have stated anything as a fact which I did not believe to be true. I have endeavoured, further, always to abstain from speaking on subjects which I had not examined and well considered, and perhaps it is because I have endeavoured to attend to these rules that what I have said has met with some acceptance, and perhaps in some quarters has been influential with the country.

'As to the title of statesman, I may say here what I said many years ago in the House of Commons, that I have seen so much intrigue and ambition, so much selfishness and inconsistency in the character of many so-called statesmen, that I have always been anxious to disclaim the title. I have been content to describe myself as a simple citizen, who honestly examines such public questions as affect the public weal and honestly offers his counsels to his countrymen.'

After the passage of the Reform Bill of 1867, John Bright stood for a little on the summit of happy hours, before illness and advancing years clouded his prospect. From the slippery path through the jungle of the Reform Bill Committee, Gladstone and Bright emerged into such sunlight as they had scarcely hoped for, with a straight road before them leading to sure success. For the appeal to the new electorate could not well be deferred more than a year, and its result was but little in doubt. Meanwhile in the old Parliament the Liberals were once more united in loyalty to their leaders, being encouraged or compelled thereto by the near prospect of an electoral victory on radical lines. The initiative in the country and the true leadership of the House during its last session (1868) belonged not to Disraeli and his Government minority, but to Gladstone and the reunited Opposition. A statute was passed abolishing compulsory Church-rates; and the principle of Irish Disestablishment, embodied in Gladstone's famous 'resolutions,' was carried in the Government's despite. The process of translating Bright's programme into law had fairly begun. Since the working men were in possession of the franchise and were about to be consulted, the whole political atmosphere had changed. Liberal legislation was felt to be inevitable in the new world created by the Reform Act, and now that the harvest was being gathered in, it was no longer seemly to revile the labourer who had followed the plough. Men began to reflect that John Bright had been right about Free Trade, right about the Crimea, right about the American Civil War, and right about the Franchise. And it was beginning to appear that he had been right about Ireland. No other statesman had such a record.

And so Bright came to be regarded, even in circles where he had fewest friends, at least as a national institution. It ceased to be customary in the West End to avow a readiness 'to go twenty miles to see John Bright hanged.' Lords no longer complained that their hosts had insulted them if they saw his massive form making its way through the throng in a London drawing-room. Society was no longer scandalised when Russell asked him to dinner. At the Royal Academy Banquet of 1868 he found himself the object of marked attentions in a gathering of 'Archbishops, Bishops, Lords and Dukes in abundance.' The Prince of Wales wished him to be called on to speak, but gave up the proposal when he showed reluctance. After dinner, he writes, the Prince 'spoke to me about his recent trip to Ireland, which has pleased him greatly. I told him there must be legislation as well as civilities, but that I thought his visit had been very wise.' 'The Bishop of Oxford remained late and we looked at some pictures together, Professor Huxley being also with us,'—Samuel Wilberforce, the smooth and supple champion of Barchester theology and politics, making the most of a truce with his two flint-hearted antagonists. 'I asked the Bishop,' continues Bright, 'why he wore a *violet*-colored coat; he said, that Bishops should be *inviolate*, at which we laughed.' Thus do great minds unbend.

A gentleman at whose house Bright often stayed during the last twenty years of his life, declares that the People's Tribune came to speak and think less severely of aristocrats and churchmen than had formerly been his wont. This may well be. But such softening was only gradual, and his vigilance was never of the sort to be disarmed by a little flattery. In 1868, at a public meeting in honour of our peaceful relations with America, Lord Stratford de Redcliffe, joint author with Palmerston of the Crimean War, found himself next to John Bright, and began telling him 'that a speech I made some years ago had given him great pain, but that he had not borne ill-will against me, that he had always been for peace and had been willing to surrender for peace everything except a principle. I told him I often heard these sentiments from platforms, but diplomats and statesmen in action did not adhere to such professions of regard for peace.'

In the winter of 1867-68 Gladstone made up his mind to disestablish the Irish Church.

(Bright's Journal. Nov. 30, 1867.)

> 'An hour and a half with Gladstone this morning on future politics, on Ireland in particular. He is willing wholly to suppress State Church in Ireland, but with a wish it had not been necessary. Conversation very free and interesting.'

But the Whigs they had still with them, though not for long. In December Gladstone wrote to Bright that 'it is well to ponder much on the Irish Church question, which may again lead the Liberal party to martyrdom.' In January 1868 Bright wrote to Villiers:

> 'I confess I am very unhappy when I survey the present condition of our home affairs. Mr. Gladstone is willing to go on [with the Irish Church question], but he hesitates, knowing the bad material of his forces.'

Certainly Gladstone did not attack the Irish Church in order to catch votes; he expected that it would lead to a Whig secession or a popular anti-Popery movement. But his fears proved groundless. The party in the House reunited on the proposal; and the cry, idealist and altruistic as it was, touched a chord in the new working-class electorate which Bright had for years trained up to take generous views, in particular of Ireland. The idea that the English and Irish democracies should join forces had been brought into practical politics by

Bright. In the middle of his Reform campaign in the autumn of 1866 he had gone over to a great meeting of the popular party in Dublin and exhorted the Irish to unite with the English democracy on the Franchise and other questions, in order to get their alien Church disestablished and their absentee aristocracy removed. And for years past he had kept the questions of Irish Church and Land honestly to the fore in addressing his own countrymen. Gladstone now reaped the benefit of this preparation.

> [Journal. March 12, 1868.] 'To Mr. Gladstone's at 12 o'clock at his request; met there Lord Granville, Mr. Cardwell, Mr. C. Fortescue with Mr. Brand and Mr. Glyn [the Whips], to discuss course on Irish question—agreed that a *specific* motion should be brought forward after present debate is over, in such form as to pledge the House to the abolition of the Irish Church. I was thus admitted to a sort of "opposition Cabinet Meeting," and feel myself somewhat embarrassed at the prospect of responsibilities which I do not wish to undertake.'

Meanwhile Disraeli had succeeded to the Premiership.

> [Journal. March 9.] 'Since the House opened Lord Derby has resigned and Benjamin Disraeli reigns in his stead! A great triumph of intellect and courage and patience and unscrupulousness employed in the service of a party full of prejudices and selfishness and wanting in brains. The Tories have hired Disraeli, and he has his reward from them.' [1]

Ever since that night in 1852 when Disraeli on the eve of his first fall from office had sent for Bright to propose an impossible political alliance, there had existed between the two men much personal friendliness and even a kind of sympathy. These pleasant relations now came to an end. What Bright thought of Disraeli has been often recorded in these pages in the words of his private journals. He had always admired his genius but had never believed in the sincerity of his principles. We have only to ask why he quarrelled with him in 1868 rather than on any of a dozen former occasions. One reason was that Disraeli's voice, when raised in defence of the Irish Church, rang more than usually false in Bright's ears,

[1] It was during this Parliament that a Conservative Member, a famous cricketer, speaking to a Liberal friend, described his own party as 'the gentlemen of England with a player given.'

because twenty-five years before they two had been almost the first politicians in England to denounce the 'alien Church' in Ireland, and Bright did not believe that Disraeli had since changed his real opinion.

Another cause of bitterness was that, when Gladstone's Resolutions for Irish disestablishment were passed by large majorities against the Government, Disraeli remained in office, to the great indignation of the Liberals. He could not well dissolve, because the registers under last year's Reform Bill had not yet come into operation. But meanwhile the Gladstonian majority was fully prepared to carry on the business of the House and Government. Disraeli preferred to continue in occupation of the Treasury Bench, and vaguely to threaten the majority with a dissolution on the old register if they pressed him too hard. The Liberal leaders also believed that he was using the interim to influence the Queen against the new Irish policy of those who must ere long be her advisers. Such were the causes of those angers of celestial minds that filled the first week of May 1868, which parliamentary veterans called 'Passion week.' On May 7 there was a crowded and shouting House, already stirred to that quality of mutual rage engendered when the Opposition thinks the Government is morally bound to resign. Bright poured oil on the flames in the following words :

> 'I have held consistently for twenty years the conviction which the right hon. gentleman at the head of the Government himself held then, and which, if it were possible now to put him under an accurate examination from which he could not flinch, he would be obliged to say that he holds now ; because, on a recent occasion, he admitted that the main sentiment of that speech which he delivered twenty-five years ago was right. But I am in a different position from the right hon. gentleman. I have not been endeavouring to climb the ladder of Parliamentary promotion and notoriety. No, Sir, I have only had the single object—so far as I have had anything to do with Irish questions—to promote what appeared to be just to that country, and which would tend to the advantage of the United Kingdom. The right hon. gentleman the other night, in a manner at once pompous and servile, talked at large of the interviews which he had had with his Sovereign. I venture to say that a Minister who deceives his Sovereign is as guilty as the conspirator who would dethrone her.

> I do not charge the right hon. gentleman with deceiving his Sovereign; but if he has not changed the opinion which he held twenty-five years ago, and which he has said in the main was right, then I fear that he has not stated all that it was his duty to state in the interviews which he had with his Sovereign. Let me tell hon. gentlemen opposite, and the right hon. gentleman in particular, that any man in this country who puts the Sovereign in the front of a great struggle like this into which it may be we are about to enter—who points to the Irish people, and says from the floor of this House, "Your Queen holds the flag under which we, the enemies of religious equality and justice to Ireland, are marshalled,"—I say that the Minister who does that is guilty of a very high crime and a great misdemeanour against his Sovereign and against his country.'

Then, after Gladstone had for five minutes added to the indictment of the Prime Minister, Disraeli rose, pale with anger, and the House for once had the privilege of seeing the great actor in deadly earnest. 'He spoke,' so one who heard him has written, 'as perhaps he had never spoken before, and as most certainly he never spoke afterwards—with no sparkling epigrams, or fanciful turns, or picked phrases; but with unwonted emphasis and abundance of natural gesture, and amazing vehemence of emotion':

> 'The hon. Member for Birmingham says that I was at once *pompous and servile.* Well, Sir, if it suits the heat of party acrimony to impute such qualities to me, any gentleman may do so. But I am in the memory and in the feeling of gentlemen on both sides of the House—and fortunately there are gentlemen on both sides of the House; they will judge of the accuracy of this representation of my conduct. The hon. gentleman says that he will make no charge against me—and then he makes insinuations which, if he believes, he ought to bring forth boldly as charges. I defy the hon. Member for Birmingham, notwithstanding his stale invective, to come down to this House and substantiate any charge of the kind which he has presumed only to insinuate. Let him prefer those charges; I will meet him; and I will appeal to the verdict only of gentlemen who sit on the same side of the House as himself.'

Bright was in no position to prove in public his 'insinuations' that Disraeli had been unduly influencing the Queen against Irish disestablishment. Therefore he had better have said nothing on that score. The following entry in his journal a few days earlier shows the origin of his suspicions :

> 'April 25th. Conversation with Lord Clarendon;[1] he is angry at the course of the Government, and thinks Disraeli is poisoning the mind of the Queen on Irish Church question.'

The day after the storm, Bright wrote to his wife: 'The night was rough in the House and it finished with a great explosion between me and Disraeli. I suspect our ancient alliance or understanding now exists no longer.' It was never renewed, and when in later years Disraeli revived Palmerston's Crimean War policy, Bright regarded him with whole-hearted dislike.[2]

Coming events already cast their shadows before. A few days after Gladstone's 'resolutions' were carried, Bright notes in his journal :

> 'A deputation from Presbyterians in Ireland to make "better terms" on Regium Donum in case of disestablishment of Irish Church. Mr. ——, a very unsatisfactory specimen of Christian minister, fierce against Catholics and full of greed for public money for his own sect. I rebuked their subservience to the Tory and Church party.'
>
> 'June 17th. The session has been arduous and wearying, but evidently every day is breaking up old parties and old prejudices, and I have had my share in the great changes which are in progress.'

During that summer John Bright was busy laying the foundations of the union between the democracy of England and the democracies of Ireland and of Wales, which has since played so great a part in the history of British politics. In Ireland, indeed, he had been preaching the same doctrine for twenty years past, but the time of fruition was now at hand. The phrases of his speech at Limerick on July 3 are remarkable :

> 'I am willing and anxious if possible to supplement

[1] Formerly, and afterwards, Liberal Foreign Minister.

[2] In Disraeli's *Vivian Gray* occurs the passage (bk. ii. p. 70): 'The Hon. Sidney Lorrain prospered in his political career. He was *servile and pompous*,' etc. When, after the altercation in the House, Bright's attention was drawn to this passage, he said he had not remembered it, and that it explained Disraeli's anger. Perhaps no such explanation was necessary.

> that fraudful—as I would call it—Act of Union by deeds of generosity and justice which shall really unite the three Kingdoms. What I would propose would be to undo, absolutely undo, the territorial and ecclesiastical arrangements of the last two or three hundred years with regard to Ireland. But I would do all this without inflicting upon any living man the smallest act of injustice in connection with his interest in the territorial and ecclesiastical arrangements of the country.'

He then again propounded his schemes of land purchase and disestablishment.

His appeal to Wales was more of a novelty. On June 3 he addressed the Welsh National Reform Association at Liverpool. The avowed object of the meeting was to call upon the Welsh people to 'arouse themselves from the political apathy which had hitherto characterised them.' And seldom, perhaps, has a meeting been more fruitful of results. 'If,' said Bright, after showing his audience that he knew something about the national and religious life of Wales, 'if you have all these great qualities, if you are capable of this remarkable organisation which you exhibit in religious matters, surely you may do something in another field in which it is hardly less your duty to work than in that religious field in which you are so preeminent. Our great poet has described the Welsh as

> "An old and haughty nation, proud in arms."

The arms that you wield now are not such as your forefathers wielded; but they are infinitely more effective and infinitely more irresistible. You could not in the times that are past contend with the power of England; but now you may unite your power with the power of all men who love freedom, whether in England or in Ireland.' The thousands of Welshmen who had come to Liverpool to hear him, accustomed as they were to the highly trained oratory of their own great preachers, were captivated by Bright's method of speaking as well as by the words he spoke. They went back to their homes declaring that there was no orator like John Bright; what impressed them most of all was the restraint of his voice and gestures, analogous to the best style in their own chapels, where shouting and thumping were little known and less liked. Mr. Lloyd George and other Welshmen well acquainted with their country's history, declare that this speech of Bright's did more than any other one event to make Wales active in the Liberal cause.

In November the General Election took place under the new Franchise Act. Bright's campaign was perforce confined to Birmingham, where he saw to it that, in spite of the 'minority clause' by which the 'dreamers and schemers' had sought to disenfranchise the great city,[1] all three Liberal candidates were returned. 'Since,' he said, 'if every part of the sea is salt, every district and every ward of the constituency of Birmingham is Liberal.'

Besides his advocacy of Irish disestablishment, on which mainly the General Election was fought, Bright devoted the whole of one speech to an earnest plea for a system of national education. This speech must to some extent modify the general proposition that Bright was an 'individualist' of the straitest school. 'Possibly some persons,' he said, 'may think that there are rates enough already, and to add a school rate to the other rates would only be to add burden to burden. But let me remind you that as the school rate would rise, the poor rate and the criminal rate would fall.' He proposed to establish School Boards—'Education Committees' he called them—elected by the ratepayers, not for the County, which he thought too large, nor for the Parish, which he thought often too small, but for the area of each Poor Law Union. He did not foresee the extent of the 'religious difficulty,' and appears, if his words are to bear their full meaning, to have favoured what we should now call the 'secular solution.'

> 'I may be told,' he said, 'that the great difficulty is what is called the religious difficulty. The difficulty has never been great in the minds of the great body of the people. It is a difficulty which has mainly been created by ministers of religion, not with any wrong intention, but because their eye was directed so much to one question, one great object of human endeavour, that they seemed to feel it necessary to tie it up with everything else. As to the religious difficulty, there are seven days in the week, and on one day we cease from our labours and the churches are open for religious worship and religious instruction, and the Sunday School would stand with open doors, and there would be thousands and scores of thousands of devoted men and women who, during one, two or three hours as the case may be, on that day would supplement the general education of the people in ordinary instruction

[1] P. 379 above.

by giving them that religious instruction which may be of value to them.'

The only place outside Birmingham at which he spoke during the General Election, was Edinburgh, where he advocated 'a free breakfast table,' a phrase which he had previously coined and now brought into general notice, to signify the 'untaxing of tea, coffee and sugar.'

The borough constituencies were swept for Gladstonianism and Irish Church Disestablishment. As soon as the result was clear Disraeli resigned without waiting for the new Parliament to meet. On November 27, a day or two before Mr. Gladstone's summons to the Queen's service, Bright wrote to him urging that National Education and the Ballot were two pressing duties of any new Government, and enclosing a copy of his speech on Education.

And now the Nemesis of Bright's success was upon him. Because his principles had triumphed, he must enter the prison-house of office—for to him it was a prison. Where most statesmen think that their careers begin, his true calling ended. He himself was under no deception. He knew that he was unfitted to preside in Whitehall, or to sit at the table in Downing Street; that his true 'office' was that of unofficial critic of ministers and educator of the people. 'I abhor the very idea of joining the Administration,' he wrote to Mrs. McLaren on November 23. '*I am in office now,* and who will take my place if I relinquish it?' Indeed, it has been vacant ever since.

But, against his wishes and his instincts, he decided that he could not honourably resist Gladstone's appeal. Gladstone had transformed the old Whig-Liberal party into a Liberal-Radical party on the basis of Bright's programme. He had started out upon this hazardous adventure, trusting to the support of his friend's popularity and influence. If Bright now refused to embark his fortunes in the ship that had been built after his own design, what might not happen? Division, mutiny, and Whig reaction. Would the public believe that Bright and Gladstone were truly in accord, if Bright supported him only from the back benches? Reasoning thus, Bright felt compelled to acknowledge the claim that Gladstone so insistently made upon him.

Yet, if he came into the Cabinet at all, he would probably have done well to have taken some office like the Duchy of Lancaster, that did not involve executive functions, for which he had no zeal or training. And he might well have insisted, as a condition of his own entry into the Government, that some of his own more Radical supporters should have come in with him. It was, indeed, characteristic of him to make no terms when he might have made any terms. As it was, his entry into office did very little good except the original service of uniting the progressive forces of the country behind the new Reform Ministry.

The process of mind which led up to the final decision can be traced in his journal and in his letters to his wife. On December 4, in his home at Rochdale, he received a telegram calling him up to London to see Mr. Gladstone.

> [Journal.] 'He wished me to join his Government. I objected strongly and would not consent, and left him at midnight. Did not sleep that night. Miserable at the thought of entering office, and yet his urgent entreaty seemed to make a refusal impossible. He "thought he had a claim upon me which I could not reject."'

That night, before he attempted in vain to sleep, he wrote the following letter to his wife:

> '*Very private.* EUSTON HOTEL. Half-past 12 night.
>
> 'I have spent two hours with Mr. G. and am in the greatest difficulty. He thinks I am bound honorably to stand by him whilst the Irish Church Question is being settled, and has pressed me in a manner far more earnest than I expected. He thinks his Government will go into the conflict crippled if I refuse. I have resisted all promise for to-night, but must decide in the morning, as other arrangements depend upon me. I am sorely pressed, and know not how to escape. The Queen spoke to him about me, and said "I had said kind things of her which she could never forget," and she is most willing that I should go in with him. I left him much against his will—for I thought I would have another night before saying more. The arguments are in favor of *Yes*, but my dislike of work, and of fetters, and of official position would say *no*. I shall go and see Hargreaves to-morrow morning, and perhaps Vaughan before I see G. again. The offices vacant still are India, Post Office, Poor Law, *Board of Trade*, and Duchy of Lancaster—the last but one is the one I should select if driven to take one of them.
>
> 'I wish thou wert here with me, and yet I don't know

what thou could say to lessen my difficulties, except to say that I had better go in with G. and not desert him in a great question. This will reach thee to-morrow afternoon, I hope: by then perhaps I shall have swallowed what I have so much dreaded and wished to escape. Farewell, dearest, and don't condemn me whatever turns up in this matter.

'In old days men had visions and dreams to guide them in difficult times. I am afraid I cannot expect them, but if I try to decide rightly, it may be accepted.'

'Reform Club, Dec. 5, 1868.

'My dear Mr. Gladstone,—Since I left you at midnight I have had no sleep, from which you may imagine the mental disturbance I have suffered from our long conversation of last night. Nevertheless, I am driven to the conclusion to take the step to which you invite me, surrendering my inclination and my judgment to your arguments and to the counsel of some whom I have a right to consider my friends. I shall do the best I can, but I fear I shall disappoint you. I must trust to your kindness in judging of what I do. I am deeply grateful to you for the confidence you are willing to place in me, and for the many kind words you spoke to me yesterday. If you can now make any arrangement that will set me at liberty I shall rejoice—if not, then you may consider me at your service.'

Next day he wrote to his wife:

'I think I resisted almost more than any other man ever did, but yesterday morning I consented to join the new Government. Mr. Gladstone offered me the Indian Secretaryship, which I could not take. I feared the labor, and I could not take part in the duties of the office which are connected with the military affairs of India. I think Mr. Gladstone and all his colleagues were very anxious for me to join them, and my friends in the country would have complained if I had longer refused.'

On accepting office he was re-elected for Birmingham without opposition. His speech on December 21, thanking his constituents for their renewed favour, is memorable for his application to himself of a Bible passage which touched the heart of the nation:

'I have not aspired at any time of my life to the rank of

> a Privy Councillor, nor to the dignity of a Cabinet office. I should have preferred much to have remained in that common rank of simple citizenship in which hitherto I have lived. There is a passage in the Old Testament which has often struck me as being one of great beauty. Many of you will recollect that the prophet, in journeying to and fro, was very hospitably entertained by what is termed in the Bible a Shunammite woman. In return for her hospitality, he wished to make her some amends, and he called her to him and asked her what there was he should do for her. "Shall I speak for thee to the king," he said, "or to the captain of the host?" Now it has always appeared to me that the Shunammite woman returned a natural answer. She replied, in declining the prophet's offer, "I dwell among mine own people." When the question was put to me whether I would step into the position in which I now find myself, the answer from my heart was the same—I wish to dwell among mine own people. Happily the time may have come—I trust it has come—when in this country an honest man may enter the service of the Crown, and at the same time not feel it in any degree necessary to dissociate himself from his own people.'

'My speech will please thee,' he writes to his wife. 'The Shunammite woman would not be left out, though I did not intend to introduce her till the moment I finished the preceding sentence. The story told well on the meeting, and I think will please many who read the speech who are friendly to me.' Their name was legion, and they were drawn now from all parties and sections of the community. Yet 'Bright in office' still seemed strange to some. 'I was satisfied with John having taken office,' wrote Mrs. McLaren, 'when those Tories set up a derisive laugh as he took his seat.'

One lady, who had thought ill of him before, shared very fully the softening of heart now going on towards John Bright. At the St. James's Hall Reform meeting, just a year before, a leading Radical had made an impertinent attack on the Queen because she had not come out of her Palace to smile on the Reform meeting in the Park hard by. Bright had risen and censured him before the audience, adding the following words:

> 'Mr. —— referred further to a supposed absorption of the sympathies of the Queen with her late husband to the exclusion of sympathy for and with the people. I am not

accustomed to stand up in defence of those who are possessors of crowns. But I could not sit and hear that observation without a sensation of wonder and of pain. I think there has been, by many persons, a great injustice done to the Queen in reference to her desolate and widowed position. And I venture to say this, that a woman—be she the Queen of a great realm, or the wife of one of your labouring men—who can keep alive in her heart a great sorrow for the lost object of her life and affection, is not at all likely to be wanting in a great and generous sympathy with you.'

These words laid the foundation of Bright's favour at Court, though they had certainly not been spoken with that intent. The story of Bright's first visit to Osborne has been told so delightfully by Lord Granville that the many who are already familiar with his letter to Gladstone in Lord Edmund Fitzmaurice's biography will pardon the reintroduction of a portion of it here:

'OSBORNE, December 31, 1868.

'MY DEAR GLADSTONE,—. . . We had a fine passage, during which Bright left us to ourselves, and was mean enough, I am much afraid, to pump the open-hearted captain on the extravagances connected with the royal yacht. He was much pleased with the royal footman who was waiting for us at Cowes, and asked whether they were really hired by the length. All went well till our entry at Osborne. He was really angry with the footman at the door for transferring his carpet bag to a man in an apron. In vain we pleaded the division of labour, the necessity of the former preserving his red coat and his white stockings from the dirt of luggage. "If I had known the fellow was too fine to take it, I would have carried it myself. . . ."

'The combined influences of Bright's connection with the press, the platform, and the House of Commons, together with the great simplicity in which this combative and able man was brought up, and which he has maintained in his social and family habits, give his conversation a singular flavour.

'He told us he only informed his wife two days ago of his visit here, and of her almost reproachful answer—"It seems strange you should be going where I cannot follow."

'I called for him at dinner time—his dress was irreproachable, after he had readily agreed to take off a pair of bridal white gloves. He was rather pleased, quoted his tailor's approval of tights, and acknowledged he had promised to rehearse the costume before his wife and daughter.

'The beginning of dinner was awful—the Queen with a sick headache and shy—Princess Louise whispering unintelligibly in my ear, and Lady Clifden shouting ineffectually into the still more impenetrable receptacle of sound belonging to Charles Grey. Bright like a war-horse champing his bit, and dying to be at them. At last an allusion to children enabled me to tell Bright to repeat to her Majesty his brother's observation, "Where, considering what charming things children were, all the queer old men came from." This amused the Queen, and all went on merrily.'

The Queen was always nervous before meeting a new Minister, especially one of those who were reputed to be Radicals and 'powerful personalities.' She had therefore sent a note before dinner to Lord Granville—'The Queen hopes Lord Granville will not draw out Mr. Bright too much.' But all went well beyond expectation.

Of the private interview next day, Bright left the following account in his journal:

'Soon after one o'clock a servant came for me, and I followed to an elegant room where I waited for the Queen. She came in immediately by another door, bowing to me, as I to her. I drew a chair from the table, and she sat down, I standing by the fire. She said she wished to say how much she had been touched by the kind manner in which I had spoken of her on more than one occasion—that I had said "kind words which she could not forget." I thanked her for this, and said what had happened on the occasion referred to was an unhappy accident, that I had only said what I had always felt and said in private, and that the people were just and sympathised with what I had said.[1] She replied that "some people pretended they did not care for sympathy and could do without it." She thought there was great good in sympathy, and "that it

[1] The St. James's Hall meeting had risen, when Bright sat down, and sung 'God save the Queen.'

was often a great alleviation in sorrow, and sorrow comes to persons of all classes." Something was said about my dear friend Mr. Cobden; she regretted she had not known him, but the Prince had a high regard for him; she asked after his family. Then something was said of the lovely prospect from the window. I said I had seen below an engraving of the old Osborne House, and it seemed a large house. "No," she said, "it was not a large house, but we were very comfortable in it whilst this was building," and this was said with a tone which indicated that she was dwelling for the moment upon days passed for ever. Some reference was made to political changes of late years, and I said I thought both the condition and the temper of the people was greatly improved since her accession to the throne. The Queen looked much better than last evening, and there was a kindness in her eye and in the tones of her voice. I am not a "courtier," but I can respect an ancient monarchy, and can admire and even reverence a monarch whom monarchy has not spoiled, and I have always felt a true sympathy with the Queen in her deep sorrow.'

The attitude of John Bright towards the monarchy at the period of his greatest influence over the working men was of some importance. For at that time the democratic movement had in it an element of Republicanism that has since disappeared, although the democratic movement itself has grown and flourished. About this time a gentleman wrote to Bright to tell him that he understood the English Republicans would select him as their first President and to inquire if he was prepared to accept the post. Bright replied as follows:

'Your Republican friend must not be a very desperate character if he proposes to make me his first President, though I doubt if he can be a friend of mine. As to *opinions* on the question of monarchy or republicanism, I hope and believe it will be a long time before we are asked to give our opinion: our ancestors decided the matter a good while since, and I would suggest that you and I should leave any further decision to our posterity. Now from your letter, I conclude you are willing to do this, and I can assure you I am not less willing.'

The Queen was in every way considerate to the scruples of her new Minister. She did not insist on his kneeling when he kissed her hand, and after some negotiation she humoured him in his refusal to wear the 'full' Court dress with gold lace and sword. His objection to the monstrous paraphernalia in which the great ones of our land are compelled to encase themselves, was not æsthetic, as it might well have been, but moral! It seems indeed to have been a question more of self-respect than of religious principle, but the two with Bright were closely connected. At the crisis of the question—and it came to a real 'crisis'— he wrote to Mr. Gladstone: 'I told you my difficulty on that unhappy evening, and it does not diminish. I have never put on *livery* and I think I never shall. I dare say you will think me childish and perhaps I am so, but the sentiment of a lifetime is not easily to be abandoned.' Finally the Queen was content that he should appear in a plain Court suit of black velvet, cut very like the coat and breeches of old-fashioned Friends. 'My dress,' he writes, 'was generally admired as plain, simple and rich,' and his sister Mrs. McLaren, when she came to see him try it on, laughingly declared that he looked like William Penn.

However that may have been, he was the first Nonconformist who ever sat in a British Cabinet. He was also the first nominee therein of the working men. His promotion had great symbolic value, for all men saw that the barriers of privilege had fallen. The enthusiasm with which Gladstone's Ministry was greeted at its formation, and the power that it consequently had to carry its programme into law, was not a little due to Bright's presence at its counsels.

The year 1869 saw the disestablishment of the Irish Church, thanks to the legislative genius and political energy of Gladstone, backed at last by a loyal majority. The House of Lords, after some hesitation, elected not to put itself into conflict with the people, and contented itself with driving a good bargain for the Church over the number of loaves and fishes to be left to her in her widowed state. When the Bill reached harbour at the end of July, Bright wrote to his friend, Lord Granville, who had conducted the Bill through the Upper House: 'So far as I can learn, all our Party are delighted with the settlement of the great question. For myself I am grateful to you for what you have done. The mingled force and gentleness and the wisdom you have displayed are, I believe, felt by all your colleagues. We may leave the session with the consciousness that we have done a great work.'

While the Lords were still hesitating, John Bright had written the following public letter (June 9):

> 'The Lords are not very wise, but there is sometimes profit to the people even in their unwisdom. If they should delay the passing of the Irish Church Bill for three months, they will stimulate discussion on important questions, which, but for their infatuation, might have slumbered for many years. It is possible that a good many people may ask what is the special value of a Constitution which gives a majority of 100 in one House for a given policy, and a majority of 100 in another House against it. It may be asked also why the Crown, through its Ministers in the House of Commons, should be found in harmony with the nation, whilst the Lords are generally in direct opposition to it. Instead of doing a little childish tinkering about life peerages, it would be well if the peers could bring themselves on a line with the opinions and necessities of our day. In harmony with the nation they may go on for a long time, but throwing themselves athwart its course, they may meet with accidents not pleasant for them to think of.'

These words, coming from a Member of the Government, provoked a storm in political circles and a debate in the House of Lords. *Punch* had a cartoon of Bright as the footman calling to the Lords' coach, 'Pull out o' the way there, with that "infatuated" old machine,' and Gladstone as butler touching him on the shoulder and saying, 'John, John, you 're forgetting your place—you mustn't use that sort of language now.' It was not till 1883-84 that Bright formulated his memorable scheme for dealing with conflicts between the two Houses.

On an earlier occasion, in April, he had indulged in a similar unministerial freedom of speech, though his remarks had then been less serious than his indictment of the lay Peers in June. The Fishmongers were entertaining the Ministry, and John Bright was for the first time called on to speak at a City dinner—without expectation on his part, but with immense expectation on the part of those present. He found a congenial theme in the Bishops, who had been feasting and making episcopal jokes in the same hall a few days before. 'The report of their proceedings,' said Bright, 'was of a very humorous description. In fact I might ask the Prime Warden and his predecessors whether they ever had in this hall before so jolly a company. Now if I had been a Bishop,' he said, whereat the imagination of the City magnates was stirred to gusts of post-prandial laughter ; 'if I had been a Bishop,' he went on, 'with an income of five to fifteen thousand a year, why it is very likely that I might have been as full of humour as those right reverend gentlemen. I might have been as merry as any of them, because I should have had an inexhaustible source of rejoicing and of merriment, in the generosity if not in the credulity of my countrymen.'

On one occasion during the parliamentary debates on the Irish Church Bill, Bright amused his audience with less conscious intent on his own part. On July 16, in reply to Disraeli's Cassandra prophecies of the danger to true religion if the Bill should become law, he was saying that he had often before heard such lamentations from the same quarter in connection with Free Trade, and yet the country had survived. 'I have seen the right hon. gentleman just as angry about many other great questions. I have seen him come down—as I might say if I were not afraid of being thought classical—*crinis disjectis*, with dishevelled hair. . . .' At those two terrible words, while the lighter spirits laughed, Gladstone bounded in his seat and was observed with bent brows hastily writing a note to inform his colleague of the lamentable error into which he had been betrayed. It was in vain that the leader-writer of the *Daily News* conjectured that Bright had intended to employ the more idiomatic *crines disjectus*; the emendation was voted more ingenious than convincing.[1]

Bright's belief that he was unfitted for office was mainly justified. Mr. Shaw Lefevre was Secretary to the Board of Trade under Bright as President, and in later years he wrote his recollections as follows:[2]

> 'Mr. Bright told me when we first met at the office that I must do most of the work, and only bring before him the more important questions. He had no experience of official work, and I gathered that he had not taken much part in the business of the manufacturing firm of which he was a partner.[3] At the age of fifty-seven it was rather

[1] I owe the story to Lord George Hamilton, who was present in the House. Hansard has Bowdlerised *crinis disjectis* into the more orthodox *crinibus disjectis*. But Lord John Manners' remark on the same page about the last speaker's 'eccentric Latin' gives the case away.

[2] Pp. 216-18, Mr. Barry O'Brien's *John Bright*.

[3] He always made up the private ledgers, until three or four years before his death.

late in life to begin work at the head of a great Government department. He had a great distaste, and almost an incapacity, for wading through a bundle of official papers. It was said in the office that he did not know how to untie the tape which held them together. I don't think he often did this. I don't recollect his ever writing a minute on them. He liked me to state the case to him, and he would then discuss it fully and with practical common sense. What he said was always of the greatest value, and his conclusions were sound and wise. Sometimes, however, before deciding, he would go down to the House of Commons and discuss the matter with some friend in the smoking-room there, and it was difficult then to meet the arguments or objections of this unknown person. In details of administration and in proposals for legislation Mr. Bright was distinctly conservative, far more so than I was. He objected to interference or to legislation if it could possibly be avoided. . . . He struck me as a very good judge of men.'

It must be remembered that Bright, when he took office, was already within twelve months of the second break-down of his health. Indeed, throughout the year 1869 there were clear premonitory symptoms. To this and his advancing age must be largely attributed his shrinking from 'labor,'—as he always spelt it; there had been no such shrinking in the old days, when he was arming himself with facts for the daily battle against the Corn and Game Laws. In his letters to Sir Louis Mallet at the Board of Trade, we find expressions like 'I am too old to do what is termed "departmental work" as it should be done.' [1]

Similarly it may be surmised that the John Bright of the 'fifties and early 'sixties would have proved an important and formidable personage at the Cabinet table. But when the first serious differences arose in the Gladstone Ministry, Bright was already a broken man. The Education Bill was the measure on which the representative of Birmingham and the champion of the Nonconformist world would have had most right and most will to influence Cabinet decisions, but his second illness had been long approaching, and in February 1870 it came to a

[1] The only important question of the day connected with his office during his brief tenure was that of the renewal of the Commercial Treaty with France, which was already beginning to be discussed. He held with Sir Louis Mallet, in opposition to Lowe, then Chancellor of the Exchequer, that Commercial Treaties were not opposed to Free Trade principles, and that the Treaty of 1860 should be renewed, even if such good terms could not be obtained as the Emperor had made with Cobden.

head, disabling him during the critical months. He had raised no protest in the Cabinet against the first draft of the Bill, though it is a fair conclusion, from the principles he avowed both before and after, that he would have found in it matter for objection had he not already been greatly incapacitated by ill-health in the winter of 1869-70. But the fatal decision to double the parliamentary grant to the Church schools was only taken in the following June. Bright had then ceased for four months past to attend Cabinet Councils or to follow the course of public affairs, although, owing to the delusive hope that he would soon recover, he did not resign until December. When at length he partially recovered and found out what had been done, he objected, but too late. The following letter to Mr. Forster, written in October 1873, gives his account of the affair:

> 'My recollection of what took place in regard to the Education Question just before I was withdrawn from the Cabinet is this.
>
> 'The only document which I can *recollect* to have received and read is the Draft Bill of the date Jan. 22, 1870, of which I think it is but fair to say that my impression at the time was rather favorable than otherwise.[1] I was at that period, I mean in the fortnight preceding the complete break-down of my health, not able to give much attention to it, being harassed with the Irish Land Bill, and especially with the Clauses I had proposed to facilitate the purchase of farms by the tenantry—and by the feebleness which I felt to be increasing upon me. What I recollect of the Cabinet discussions is only this, that it was a question whether the Education Bill should be announced or not. I was not in favor of proceeding with it, with the Irish Land Bill in hand—but Lord De Grey I think took a different view and referred to your strong wish to proceed. I do not think any definite result was arrived at on that occasion—but later, a result in accordance with your view was come to or assumed, and the intended measure was announced. I think it likely that I gave less attention to the whole question than it deserved; for I was burdened with much work and much weakness.

[1] Mr. Forster's letter, to which this is a reply, made the point that Bright, like other Members of the Cabinet, had received Mr. Forster's memorandum of November 5, 1869, in which the main principles of the coming Bill—'to supplement the present voluntary system, that is to fill up the gaps,' not to replace it—were fairly set out.

'But if the Bill had passed as it appeared in the original draft, or rather, if no change had been made in the annual grant, and none in the mode of Election, I should not have condemned it. I know something of the difficulties of the question, and I can make allowance for any one having to deal with it; and I think the Nonconformists would also have regarded the measure with forbearance, and probably with approval.

'The increase of the annual grant not only made the Church party the more cling to their schools, but induced them to make efforts far greater than before to give notice of new schools—that they might secure first the building grant, and then the increased annual grant, with which they can maintain many of their schools without any voluntary contributions, and the rest of them with small and unimportant voluntary aid. This great concession—unexpected, and as I think, wholly evil—has had the effect of fastening on the Country the old system, and it has thrown into School Board Elections an element most unfavorable to an honest and successful working of an education measure. The old question of Supremacy is raised and the money payments of the State are struggled for by Priest and Parson and their partisans—to the exclusion of the real interests of public Education.

'Then we have the cumulative vote with its aggravation of every other evil. The School Board is composed of delegates of Church or Chapel, and the miserable squabbles of these delegates, suspecting and thwarting each other, fill up many of the reports of the School Board discussions. . . .

'What I have mainly condemned in the policy of 1870 is the increased annual grant which has entirely changed the spirit and nature of the Bill, and the mode of Election which gives to the sects a power which was intended to be given to the public. . . .

'As to the changes and concessions made during the session, which alone I seriously condemn, I knew nothing of them for many months after they were settled, and of course cannot accept any responsibility in connexion with them.'

Since Bright was *hors de combat* throughout the summer months when the Bill was in Committee, there is no need to describe in detail the proceedings that proved so fatal to the hopes of emancipating national education from clerical control. Contrary to the general expectation of both parties, the Church schools were re-endowed in perpetuity by the State. 'The Bill of 1870,' wrote Bright to Lord Granville in 1873, 'was one which the Tories might have proposed but could not have passed. A Liberal Government only could pass a measure so far wide of the Liberal line of march.' Just as the Conservative Ministers in 1846 and 1867 had, with the aid of the Liberals, passed measures more democratic than any which a Liberal Government could have carried, so did Mr. Gladstone and Mr. Forster in 1870 give the Church better terms than she expected from them or could have obtained from their Conservative rivals. As in 1867, so in 1870 the mutiny in the House was easily put down. One Junior Member of the Government resigned. Mr. Miall and other private Members who protested on behalf of the Nonconformist and lay world were punished by Mr. Gladstone in the way that protesting supporters are punished by a great Minister who has half his own party and all his opponents to cheer him. If John Bright had that day been present in the House and in his old vigour, Mr. Gladstone would not with impunity have spoken as he did to Mr. Miall.

It was possible to crush Liberalism in the House, but it was not possible to crush it in the country. Mr. Gladstone soon found that he had alienated his real friends in order to satisfy implacable enemies. In November 1871, when Bright had sufficiently recovered to understand what had happened, he wrote to Mr. Gladstone:

> 'The whole misfortune—and the magnitude of it cannot yet be measured—has arisen from the error of making the new Act instrumental in preserving and extending indefinitely the system of "Denominational Schools"—a system bad from the beginning, and only adopted and tolerated under the difficulty of doing anything—instead of employing it to fill up the void which "Denominationalism" had left, in the hope that by and by all the schools of the Sects and Churches would merge into and become parts of the new system. I know not how the error is to be repaired, but if not repaired, it will breed continual turmoil—it will, I fear, break up the Government and destroy, for a time, the political party which has done so much, and from which so much is expected.
>
> 'The Reform Government of 1832 went to ruin by trying to please or placate its enemies; the Education Bill has

pleased the Church, but the Church will not maintain the Government.'

The feeling in Birmingham was intense, but it was not effectively represented on the floor of the House, because John Bright was no longer what he had been before his second illness, and Mr. Chamberlain only became Member in 1876.

(Bright to Gladstone. November 1871.)

'The Education Bill has done a tremendous mischief to the party, and I am not sure that the exasperation felt by earnest Dissenters will not bear evil fruit. There seems much force in some of the charges brought by Mr. Dale against the Education Department. He is a man of great influence in Birmingham and among the Independents, and speaks the sentiments of a considerable and growing section of the whole Dissenting Body.

'The Dissenters feel that somebody in London is working the Machine for the "Church" through the phrase of a "denominational system," for, owing to the great Nonconformist Body being divided into several sects, the power of building school-houses exists to any great extent only with the Church, and in a smaller degree with the Catholics. . . . I think there is a feeling that *you* are disposed to regard with fairness the grievance complained of, but that Mr. Forster not only does not seem to comprehend, but rather despises the sentiment which he has done so much to arouse and to irritate. I cannot suppose this is true as regards Mr. Forster, but he may be surrounded by an atmosphere which prevents a clear examination of the question.'

Bright used to say of the Education Bill that it 'passed a year too soon.' He had urged in the Cabinet that it should be postponed till 1871, on the ground that the Irish Land Bill would occupy Parliament fully during 1870. He objected to overcrowding the session, declaring that 'it is not easy to drive six omnibuses abreast through Temple Bar.' And indeed, it was because Mr. Gladstone was devoting his titanic energies to bearing up alone the vast burden of the Irish Land Bill, that he could not adequately attend to the Education Bill and to the grievances of his followers against Mr. Forster. Whether, if he had had more leisure, he would have attempted to apply a remedy, will always be open to conjecture.

'I suspect,' Bright wrote to Charles Villiers in January 1868,

'I suspect Mr. Gladstone has never considered the Irish Land Question.' In 1869-70 he 'considered' it with a vengeance, and by one of the memorable achievements of human wisdom, dexterity, and courage, persuaded a Parliament puzzled by the question and overawed by his authority, to accept a measure of far-reaching novelty in social and economic principles. Alone he did it. John Bright, the veteran of the cause, did not suggest the actual provisions of the First Irish Land Act. Bright's remedy, as he had so often proclaimed, was nothing less than Land Purchase. But opinion had not yet ripened for an operation on those lines, and Mr. Gladstone's embodiment of the custom of Ulster Tenant Right in a law for all Ireland was quite as far as the Cabinet or Parliament of 1870 could have been induced to go. Indeed Bright himself only ventured in the first instance to propose very gradual and partial schemes of purchase; and even these aroused in Mr. Gladstone's mind, ever frugal for the commonwealth, 'the question how the State, after buying out the landlord at a thumping price, is to get back its money?'[1]

Bright, though he had memorialised the Cabinet in favour of a Land Purchase Bill, finally recognised the great value of the scheme which Gladstone preferred, and offered it his loyal support. He would have helped his chief to fight the Land Bill through Parliament, had not his own illness left the Prime Minister to do battle alone on behalf of the Irish peasantry. On February 8, 1870, he wrote to Mr. Gladstone:

> 'I cannot tell you how much I am disappointed at being absent from the Meeting of Parliament—but I have distinct warnings of an attack something like that from which I suffered 14 years ago, and I dare not disregard them. I am quite unable to work and must leave London for a time. I regret deeply that I cannot be at your side to vote and plead for the Irish Land Bill. To some it will seem strong; others will think they detect a want of strength. For myself, I think it a just and comprehensive measure, and I hope the moderation and patriotism of Parliament will enable it soon to become law. And further, I trust all who are thoughtful and right-minded among the people of Ireland may accept it as a measure intended and calculated to allay much of the disquiet which has prevailed in their country. Forgive this poor note which I have written with much difficulty.'

[1] Gladstone to Bright, May 22, 1869.

CHAPTER XIX

IN AND OUT OF OFFICE. THE EASTERN QUESTION. DEATH OF MRS. BRIGHT. 1870-78

'I have had my part in some great questions, and other parts must be left for other men. The County Franchise and the Land Question are coming to the front. I could advise upon them, but cannot enter again into great conflicts.'—BRIGHT *to* CHAS. VILLIERS, Dec. 1872.

'The history of the last forty years of this country is mainly a history of the conquests of freedom. It will be a grand volume that tells the story, and your name and mine, if I mistake not, will be found in some of its pages. For me, the final chapter is now writing. It may be already written; but for you, this great constituency, you have a perpetual youth and a perpetual future. I pray Heaven that in the years to come, when my voice is hushed, you may be granted strength, and moderation and wisdom to influence the councils of your country by righteous means, for none other than noble and righteous ends.'—BRIGHT *to his Birmingham constituents,* Oct. 1873.

BRIGHT'S second long illness, which removed him from public life in February 1870, though he did not actually resign until December, was of the same nature as his illness of 1856, but it was even more severe. He was an older man, and in addition to the 'nervous break-down' there were grave threatenings of an apoplectic seizure. He remained in a critical condition of physical weakness all the summer. His second daughter, Mary, who was with him during the worst of his illness, wrote:

'He was hardly able to walk without assistance, unable to read or even to sign his name for a long time, although his brain remained perfectly clear and unharmed, sharing for the time in the general feebleness, but nothing more. He always enjoyed being read to, and during those weary months he became acquainted with many of the best novels for the first time.[1] Every fine day he was lifted on to a quiet Welsh pony, and with wife or daughter rode at a walking pace for more than two hours on the sands or

[1] Like every one else of his generation, he had grown up with Scott and Dickens. He had also read some of Disraeli and of other novelists, but he preferred poetry and history.

in the quiet lanes round Llandudno. In this way he used often to visit a lonely cottage under the Welsh hills where for twenty years a poor little woman had lain in a bed as small as a child's cot, too crippled by disease in her joints to move anything but her head; entirely dependent on a husband out all day and a neighbour who came in once or twice to move and feed her. Her one companion was "Robin," a devoted collie, who would sit in the lane listening for the horse's feet and then run in to tell his mistress who was coming. My father always carried a packet of bones for "Robin" and some little comfort for the invalid, and would sit on his pony at the open door talking to the occupant of the cot with the deformed and shrunken figure and the bright eager eyes. Her cheerfulness under the terrible conditions of her life, and above all, the look in her face, which is only given by an abiding and sustaining faith, were lessons not to be forgotten. My father often said he left that cottage "humbled yet uplifted." He never forgot her, and continued to care for her in various substantial ways till she died.'

In May 1871 he was well enough to go to Scotland, where he remained until the autumn. He caught a good many fish, as his letters testify, but he writes:

'. . . I do not really care much about the fishing; whether I get anything or nothing on any particular day is much the same; I get the exercise and am content, and if I get no fish, I have not killed any creature living in these Highland waters, which ought to be reckoned something in the whole question. . . .

'Scotland would be a much less interesting country without its dogs, the collies and terriers; they seem to have the virtues without the vices of the "superior animal," and I like them very much.'

Dogs played a large part in his home life. So did a grey parrot, who was taught by the rising generation to interrupt the master of the house by the disconcerting remark, 'John Bright, let it drop,'—a phrase which he himself often employed to put a term to discussion. One day the bird opened its cage, flew away, and was lost for a considerable time. Finally it was picked up in the town and restored to One Ash, because it plaintively explained to the crowd that it was 'John Bright's Polly.'

In April 1872 he resumed his seat in the House of Commons. But he dared not make the effort to address his Birmingham constituents until October 1873, upon his return to office in Gladstone's reconstructed Cabinet, now drifting fast to its doom. He became Chancellor of the Duchy of Lancaster. There were not the same strong reasons for rejoining the Government in 1873 as there had been for his original acceptance of office in 1868. But his better judgment was overcome by a chivalrous feeling for Gladstone in distress. It is difficult to believe that he would have accepted office again under any other chief. 'I never made a greater sacrifice,' he wrote to Mr. Thomasson of Bolton, 'but I could not desert Gladstone. Don't blame me; I am, perhaps, more deserving of pity.' It is doubtful whether a man who thinks he is to be 'pitied' for taking office is fit to discharge its duties.

The truth was that he felt deep gratitude to Gladstone for having passed his programme into law, and changed the party from Whig to Liberal. And he was further bound to him by the common element of idealism in their natures and the belief which they shared that religious or ethical principles should guide nations as well as men. So Bright readily forgave Gladstone for the faults of the Education Bill, or rather he continued to lay them to the account of others. His letters at this period contain severe expressions about Mr. Forster, but none about Mr. Gladstone. He made allowance for the fact that Mr. Gladstone had been born and bred a Churchman. He was now a frequent guest at Hawarden, sympathetic with all except the outward and visible signs of the inward and spiritual grace which he found there. In September 1873 he notes in his journal: 'Hawarden. To Church. Service *high*. Three parsons. Mr. Gladstone most earnest in the singing, etc. To me much of the service seemed only fitted for a very ignorant people.'

In these later years one of Bright's most famous speeches in the House was a very moving appeal for the rights of dissenters in public cemeteries, made in the debate on the Burials Bill. In the course of it he said: 'The Friends' burial-grounds have not been—what do they call it?—consecrated,' at which some Members laughed, and Bishop Magee in the Gallery was scandalised, and subsequently protested that Bright had sneered at consecration. Bright wrote him the following explanatory letter:

'Dear Bishop of Peterborough,—I have read your speech, and write to make one correction in it. You refer to my speech on the Burials Bill, to which you give too much praise, but you condemn what you term the " sneer " intended in my mention of the ceremony of " consecration." I assure you there was no sneer intended. The speech was entirely unpremeditated. I had no intention of saying anything on the question when I went down to the House, and what I said arose from feelings excited during the debate. When I came to the word " consecration," it entirely escaped me, and for the moment I could not recall it. In my difficulty I turned to my friends on the bench near me and said, " What is it called ? " or, " What do they call it ? " One or more of them answered " Consecration," and one or more laughed, I suppose, at my ignorance or forgetfulness, and this laugh, which was somewhat ill-timed, made that seem a sneer which was never so intended by me.

'You will not blame me if I do not believe in the virtue of " consecration." I cannot believe in what is called " holy ground " any more than you can believe in " holy water,"[1] and for the same reason, that there is nothing in it ; but it is not necessary to ridicule all that one cannot believe, although it is certain that ridicule has had its share in clearing the world of some portions of the superstitions which have misled and afflicted it.' (Nov. 1877.)

In London on Sunday he regularly throughout his life attended the Friends' Meeting in Westminster, and seldom omitted in writing to his wife later in the day to give the names of those who had offered prayer or spoken, often adding a brief summary of what had been said, with comments. He continued always to take a thoughtful interest in the doings of the Society both in the conduct of its business and in the position it took up on many public questions, with which as a rule he was in complete sympathy. He always remained a Friend both in his heart and in his life.

The words spoken to his Birmingham constituents on his return to office in 1873,[2] as well as his private letters, show that John Bright regarded his main work in life as finished. He had now become, and he remained until the end, the most revered and the most generally loved figure in politics ; but after 1869 he was no longer one of the three leading men in the country. Indeed, he altogether ceased to lead. 'I cannot,' he wrote,

[1] The Bishop was generally regarded as an Evangelical.
[2] Quoted at the head of the chapter.

'enter again into great conflicts.' In 1876, when a newspaper man attempted to fasten an 'interview' upon him, he would say nothing except, 'I am now on the shelf and am not before the public.' This attitude can be attributed partly to advancing years and the diminution of his physical and nervous energy after his second illness; and in part to the fact that the great causes to which he had devoted his life were accomplished. The Liberal Ministers, who had entered office with such reforming zeal at the end of 1868, were in 1872 nicknamed by Disraeli 'a range of exhausted volcanoes,' but meanwhile their lava had fairly covered the land below: they had disestablished the Irish Church, passed the Irish Land Act, set up—however imperfectly—national Education, abolished Purchase in the Army, opened the universities to dissenters, and established the ballot at elections. These changes, together with the earlier boons of Free Trade, Household Franchise in the towns, and the abolition of Church-rates, and above all, the withdrawal of England from European entanglements, constituted a nearly complete adoption of Bright's programme.

He was too old to launch a new programme, to investigate new principles more suited to the coming age, or even to fight with his old vigour for what still remained to be done on the principles of his youth. He never again took up a great cause and made it his own. Many of his later speeches—still beautiful in their literary form—are reminiscences, or rejoicings over battles won and progress registered. His position was that of veteran attached to the party, half retired and continually talking of retiring altogether, but never making up his mind to go. In a less unselfish man this state of things would soon have become intolerable to himself or to his colleagues. But his entire indifference to his own 'position' in the party made his presence there welcome to all the warring sections and rival personalities in the distracted Liberal fold. In Bright's letters of the 'seventies and 'eighties there is a remarkable absence of talk about intrigues, though these were plentiful enough among the Liberals of that era. One did not go to John Bright when one had an intrigue on hand.

At the General Election of 1874 the Liberals, divided and discontented, were defeated by Disraeli's hosts, united as good Conservatives should be on the programme of doing nothing. Gladstone abandoned public life, and Bright thought his retirement a very great catastrophe.

'As to your successor,' he wrote to him in January 1875,

'I do not see any way where to find him. Some newspapers speak of Forster, but I do not think the plan will answer. He has done much to make a Liberal Government or party impossible. If Lord Granville were in the House the difficulty would vanish. I intend to go to the House, with no fixed determination of any kind, beyond this, that if I find myself unable to give a reasonable attention to business, I shall finally withdraw from Parliament and from public life, comforting myself with the occasional survey of the many good measures, in the passing of which I have had some part.'

When Lord Hartington was chosen leader, Bright was most loyal to him, and would encourage no 'restoration' movement. He writes to Thomas Potter in August 1876:

'I do not know what you mean by Harcourt & Co. keeping "our Chief out in the cold." If he is in the cold he has chosen that position. Harcourt & Co. have not driven him to it and cannot keep him there. I see no way by which after such an abdication there can be a restoration. Mr. Gladstone cannot suggest it, and they who are parties to the succession cannot now turn round on the appointed leader. . . . I regret deeply the course that Mr. Gladstone has taken, but I hope no one will treat Lord Hartington with disrespect or will endeavour to remove him. He accepted the office most unwillingly. I was chairman of the meeting which chose him as leader, and I can take no part in any action of which he is not fully informed.'

The definite lead given by Mr. Butt to the Irish Members on the subject of Home Rule had made co-operation between them and the English Liberals more difficult than in the last Parliament. At the end of 1875 Bright wrote to Lord Granville:

'The Irish Question is, as usual, one of much present difficulty, for with the "Home Rule" question acting as a wedge to split our side of the House, I do not see anything possible for our Parliamentary minority. We may, however, be glad that forty years of Liberal Governments have made the country more worth living in than it ever was before—and that such a Tory administration as is possible must act as if it were quite as Liberal as some Liberal Governments we have known.'

This was true of Disraeli's administration in many respects, but there was soon to be a notable exception in the matter of Foreign Affairs. Disraeli revived the Crimean policy of Palmerston.

Ever since the House and country had refused to follow Palmerston into a war against the German powers on Denmark's behalf,[1] Bright's principles of non-interference in European questions had been observed by our Foreign Office in practice, whether or not they had been accepted in theory. It was not considered necessary for England to take sides in the Austro-Prussian War of 1866, and even the *Times*, in reviewing the events of that year, spoke of 'the recent English policy of withdrawing as much as possible from foreign complications' as being common ground to both parties. Lord Granville, who came to the Foreign Office in June 1870, proved a Minister after Bright's own heart. Gladstone and Granville did not embroil their country on either side in the Franco-Prussian War. In August 1870 John Bright, then at the worst of his illness, could just gather strength to send letters to Gladstone, protesting against our undertaking the defence of Belgium by war against either France or Germany; and in November warning him not to oppose the suddenly revived claim of Russia to have a fleet and arsenal in the Black Sea, which had been denied to her by the treaty ending the Crimean War.[2]

> 'November 17, 1870. This Russian business is awkward, but was to be expected. The clause in the Treaty was a stupidity at best—a great empire was not likely to consent to a permanent limitation of its sovereign rights. But what next? No more war I hope and believe. Any interference on our part would fail, and General Grant would come down on you for payment of *Alabama* claims and for an apology. Then the blackness of darkness. War would destroy your Government and ruin your own reputation. The ruffians of the *Times* will support you only to betray. . . . The Crimean War is the greatest blot on the reign of the Queen, and what is passing now only the more demonstrates the folly and uselessness of it. Don't be angry with me—you have no greater or more honest friend than I am. War is the ruin of dynasties—and I suspect you would meet a fate only less melancholy than Ollivier's, if under your Government we again are

[1] See p. 333 above. [2] See pp. 246-47 above.

involved in war for the impossible object of upholding the Turk and crushing Russia. I do not complain of Lord Granville's dispatch—but you should negotiate and *yield*—first because it is just, and *second* because you cannot avoid it. Forgive this, the last opinion I may have to give as a Minister. I should give it, if it were my last word as an Englishman and your friend. Be strong for peace—and show a good front against the "services" and all who would urge you to military preparations. Every man added to the forces and every ship put in Commission strengthens your opponents and weakens your own power.'

Gladstone and Granville not only avoided war with Russia on this issue, but won a great victory for the cause of peace and arbitration by settling the prolonged and dangerous *Alabama* dispute with the United States.

The question was one of damages for the depredations done by the *Alabama* to American shipping during the Civil War.[1] Bright was deeply anxious to see the case settled, and used his influence with Americans to moderate the claims with which they sought to avenge themselves on our original fault in letting the *Alabama* sail from an English port. In August 1869 he had written a long letter to a friend over there, which was shown to the President and to Mr. Fish, the Foreign Secretary, arguing in favour of arbitration on the disputed points. And when matters came to the final crisis at the Geneva arbitration court in 1872, owing to the 'indirect claims' for compensation advanced by the Americans, he wrote to Granville:

'It is a great misfortune that it seems hardly permitted to Governments to go back from any position they have taken up—or surely the U.S. Government would at once yield the point they have so unwisely raised. The whole "indirect claim" is absurd, because it is not capable of proof. I don't believe the pirate fleet prolonged the war a day.'

When finally the award was given in a manner equitable to both parties, and the nightmare of fratricidal war was laid to rest, Bright wrote thus to his friend who had won the real 'peace with honour':

[1] See pp. 319-20 above.

'Sept. 25, 1872.

'My dear Lord Granville,— . . . The great virtue of the Treaty, beyond the settlement of a dangerous dispute, is the exhibition and adoption by two great nations of a principle of fairness and reason in its settlement, and, as we may trust, in the adjustment of any future question that may arise between them. I believe if the English Government had shewn the same wise and just disposition in time past, almost all wars with European powers since the days of William III. might have been avoided.'

When the Conservatives came into power two years later, there was no reason to suppose that they would prove more warlike than their predecessors. Since Waterloo the Conservatives had been less inclined than the Whigs to stir up racial hatred and international strife. To this rule Disraeli had been no exception, for he had joined in sharp attacks on Palmerston's 'spirited' foreign policy, had been on the side of economy in what he called 'those d——d defences,' and had even undergone some unpopularity by advocating an early termination of the Crimean War.

Unfortunately it occurred to Lord Beaconsfield in his old age that what he called 'the sublime instinct of an ancient people' could be easily aroused by an appeal in the old Palmerston vein against Russian encroachment on Turkey. The revival of the Crimean policy was the less excusable because it no longer had, as in the time of the Czar Nicholas, a claim to be subserving the cause of freedom in any part of the world. For on this later occasion it was Alexander II., the reforming Czar, the liberator of the Russian serfs, who was engaged in driving the Turks out of Bulgaria and setting up that province as an independent State. This was achieved, and in March 1878 Macedonia and Thrace, also liberated by the Russian arms, were actually assigned by the Treaty of S. Stefano to the new Bulgaria. But in the following months, owing to the action of the English Government, they were thrown back under Turkish rule for another generation. And had it not been for Gladstone we should have had war with Russia, in order to thrust back Bulgaria also under the régime of atrocities.

John Bright spoke out straight on the old issue both in House and country. His speeches were good, but they were not like his Crimean speeches, and it was Gladstone who converted the majority of Englishmen to believe what Cobden and Bright had preached more than thirty years before, as to the nature of the Turkish rule in Europe. Bright's journal serves to remind us that the question was taken up by Gladstone—the retired leader of the party—and not by its official chiefs. It was his genius, kindled at the flame of his indignation, that, sweeping aside official indifference and timidity, put the terrible facts of Turkish rule before the British people, and aroused over here a movement compact of political and moral passion, that amazed Europe and has caused the oppressed Christians of Macedonia to forget that they owed the prolongation of their slavery to England.

In April 1877 the question had come to a head on Gladstone's 'resolutions' in the House:

> [April 26.] 'Gladstone, Lord Granville and I had a long talk on Eastern question, Granville not agreeing with Gladstone as to wisdom or necessity of proposing resolutions to the House. After Granville left I remained, and the conversation serious. Gladstone, burdened with sense of responsibility in connexion with his share in the Crimean War, and anxious to urge that sense of responsibility on the conscience of the nation, declared he must act alone if his former colleagues and friends declined to act.'
>
> [April 27.] 'To meeting at Lord Granville's; 15 or 16 present. Gladstone not well, and not present. Long discussion, but nearly all unwilling to submit any resolutions to the House, and much regret expressed that Gladstone was so resolved to act alone. I was requested to see him and to represent opinions of his friends. Went up to Harley Street [1] and found him in bed—an hour of earnest conversation with him—not surprised but grieved at the conclusions of his friends. His soul full of the great subject of sufferings of Christians in Turkish provinces—could not restrain himself—his conscience and sense of responsibility made it imperative upon him to speak, and he had decided to give notice of resolutions, and wished me to see that it was done in conjunction with Mr. Goschen, to whom he had spoken on the subject. How I wished at this moment that this remarkable man had been clear of the tremendous mistake of the Crimean War! How it would have enabled him to have proclaimed true principles and policy in our foreign affairs, and, especially, on this Eastern question.'
>
> [May 2.] 'Lord Granville's—meeting of late Govern-

[1] Mr. Gladstone had recently moved from Carlton House Terrace to Harley Street, where his windows were broken by the Jingo mob in February 1878.

ment on Gladstone's resolutions—much discussion and great difficulties, which threaten to break up the party and may drive Lord Hartington to resign his leadership.'

[May 7.] 'Found note from Lord Granville to say the Party difficulty removed by concession on the part of Mr. Gladstone, which was a great relief to me.'

He had consented to reduce his five resolutions to one. And so the fight went on for the rest of the year, Gladstone warring like Samson in the midst of the Philistines, far in front of the van of his own host.

At the beginning of 1878 the victorious Russians were nearing Constantinople, and the crisis grew acute. While an armistice was being agreed to between Turkey and Russia, Beaconsfield's Government sent our fleet through the Dardanelles and asked Parliament for a six million vote of credit. War between Russia and England was imminent.

[January 29, 1878.] 'At Lord Granville's at 12 o'clock—large meeting of late Government—discussion on "Vote of Credit"—difficulty in coming to conclusion as to amendment to be moved, Hartington doubting the wisdom of direct opposition to the vote. I left them before decision arrived.

'Evening, learned that Forster was to give notice of amendment, which I fear is a blunder—a leader should lead.'

[31st.] 'House. Forster's speech solid and good, but he is not gifted with special power of public speaking. I spoke after 10 o'clock for an hour. House received it well. Some Tory member called out "Poland" to remind me of past ill deeds of Russia—this stirred me to quote four lines from some verses I attempted in my young days which were received with great cheering from both sides. The Speaker has since asked me where I got the lines from, and I told him he would not find them in any of the books, leaving him to suspect that they were original.' [1]

[February 1.] 'The debate continued. A curious incident happened. Sir Robert Peel referred to my speeches on the Crimean War—1854-56, and said their

[1] They ran as follows:

> 'Where Poland sees her gallant sons,
> Her first, her best, her bravest ones
> On the cold earth all gory lie,
> For Poland breathe a prayer and die.'

effect on him had been such that he had then resolved that he would never do anything to support the Ottoman power in Europe.'

At this crisis in the House, Layard, the British Ambassador at Constantinople, telegraphed the false information that in spite of the armistice the Russians were moving on the Turkish capital. This caused Forster to hesitate in his opposition to the vote of credit, which was therefore passed next day by the abnormally large majority of 328-124. Bright, unlike Forster and Hartington, voted with Gladstone in the minority.

Layard's false telegram had divided the Liberal opposition. Fortunately, however, the Conservative Government was not at one with itself as to the expediency of war in such a cause.

> [March 28.] 'Resignation of Lord Derby, Foreign Secretary. "Reserve force" to be called out. Alarm that war is intended.'
>
> [April 3.] 'Great deputation from 120 towns to Lord Hartington on the question peace or war. Lord Granville present; his speech very good. I was made to introduce the deputation, and to act somewhat as chairman.'
>
> [5th.] 'At Lord Granville's at two o'clock—long discussion as to course in the House; no leaders—no followers. Agreed to have no amendment to the address on "reserve forces"—evidently some present have a policy so like that of Government as not to be easily distinguished from it. Mr. Gladstone always strong and earnest, but few up to his mark.'

At this supreme crisis John Bright stood firmly by Gladstone in the cause of peace, when too many of the Liberal leaders quailed before the systematic violence of the war party. Bright was now speaking with something of his old fire. On April 30 he addressed a large and enthusiastic meeting in the Free Trade Hall, Manchester. As he came out he was attacked, and his hat was smashed over his head by the Jingoes, who were being set on in all parts of the country to intimidate the advocates of peace. A fortnight later he was removed from the struggle by domestic calamity. But the corner was safely turned. War was avoided. Lord Beaconsfield accepted the compromise of Berlin, and contented himself with the arrangement that only Macedonia and Thrace should be re-enslaved to the Turk. This, the great achievement of Disraeli's life, is known in English history as 'peace with honour.'

On May 13, 1878, Mrs. Bright died at Rochdale—so suddenly that her husband could not be called back from his duties in London in time to see her alive. His letter to her on May 11 contains no word of alarm, and she wrote to him as usual on the following day, within twenty-four hours of her death. These were the last of many thousand letters exchanged between them; for a quarter of a century she had been obliged to live with their growing family at One Ash even when Parliament was sitting, so that he and she had shared half their life only through the written word. 'Thy daily notes,' he wrote to her once, 'are a sort of daily bread, and I am hungry, in a certain sense, all day when deprived of them.'

After his wife's death, he became visibly older, weaker and less attached to life. He was on most affectionate terms with his children; they loved to be with him in the house, and he gave to their affairs attention and counsel that was both sympathetic and wise. But as they were married one by one, they could not continue always to keep house for him. Yet even then they and his grandchildren were so often at One Ash that he was seldom left alone there.[1] The death of his wife, declining powers, and after the brief flush of victory in 1880, a long series of political disappointments and differences with old friends, rendered him sometimes sad in the evening of life. Four years after Mrs. Bright died he wrote in his journal, 'Time is not a remedy and there is no cure.' But he was still a cheerful talker in company or by the family hearth.

Among many hundreds of letters of condolence which he received on his wife's death was one from the saintly Bishop Fraser of Manchester, a man of whom he had said one day, 'Ah! the good Bishop! He cannot help straying from Churchism into Christianity.' There is certainly nothing 'denominational' about the following letter:

'My dear Sir,—May I, without being deemed an intruder upon the sanctities of sorrow, venture to offer you

[1] The names of Bright's children in order of age were:—

Helen Priestman [by his first wife], married William S. Clark of Street.
John Albert, married Edith Eckersley Shawcross.
Mary Harriot, married R. F. Curry, H.M. Inspector of Schools, who died 1907.
William Leatham, at one time M.P. for Stoke, died 1910, married (1) Isabella McIvor Tylor; (2) Mary Burton Durham, who died 1911.
Anna Elizabeth, married Bernard Roth, F.R.C.S.
Margaret Sophia, married John Theodore Cash, F.R.S., Professor at Aberdeen University.
Leonard, died 1864.
Philip, married Alice Houlder.

this simple, but heartfelt, expression of my sympathy and respect, under the heavy blow which has just befallen you.

'I have often heard your home life described not long ago by our common friend, E. J. Broadfield: and his picture of your household gathering together, and yourself reading the 103rd Psalm to them, is one that will not soon fade from my memory. I have rejoiced to think that it is only a type of many homes in England still uncontaminated by that fashion-service and world-worship, which seems to be almost eating out the old, honest heart of the nation.

'And she, whom you have lost, was part of this picture; and I can understand what the blank must be, now that she is gone. As a fellow Christian man, I pray that God may comfort you, and that you may still be able to say in those beautiful words which sank so deeply into Edward Broadfield's ears, as he heard you read them a few weeks ago, "Praise the Lord, O my soul; and *forget not all His benefits*."'

Lord Morley has said that the most impressive and pure piece of religion that he ever witnessed was John Bright reading a chapter of the Bible to his maid-servants shortly after his wife's death, in his beautiful and feeling voice, followed by the Quaker silence.

Bright's voice had magic qualities, and he loved best to use it in repeating or reading the poets.[1] It was fortunate when, as most often, Milton was on his lips. Nor did Byron ever fail him. But no words came amiss when once his voice was heard in the room. Like other men of strong emotions and scanted education, he could find his own deep feelings in lines of no great literary power, provided he agreed with their senti-

[1] The only marked oratorical gesture that I have read or heard of Bright using, either in public or private, is that recorded by Justin McCarthy in Mr. Barry O'Brien's *John Bright*:

'I heard him quote with exquisite feeling the line from Wordsworth's poem which asked whether the cuckoo is a bird "or but a wandering voice." I may say, too, that he delighted in Shelley's poem "To a Skylark," and Logan's lines "To the Cuckoo." Of the three poems—that of Wordsworth, that of Shelley, and that of Logan—he liked Logan's the best, as a whole; but the particular line from Wordsworth which I have mentioned held his fancy more than anything else in the three. I shall never forget the manner in which he quoted the words "or but a wandering voice," giving them additional expression and meaning by a quick gentle moving of his hand here and there, as if to indicate the places from which the wandering voice made itself successively heard.

ment. He was devoted to Whittier, the poet of humanity and democracy, and in a lesser degree to Lewis Morris.

Yet of the many who understand far more about literature than Bright understood, few can draw from books such deep, lifelong enjoyment of the very best as he drew from Milton and the Bible. 'What *poets* those old Hebrews were,' he used often to exclaim. And to Milton his mind was married. Compared to love like this, the wider and more shallow habits of latter-day readers who find the *Paradise Lost* tedious, are perhaps not in everything an improvement. John Bright's taste in *belles lettres* was sometimes to seek; but the orator whose speeches, when read by the fireside, are greater as literature than those of Macaulay or of Gladstone, must have got something more than most of us ever get from the perusal of the printed page.

CHAPTER XX

THE LIBERAL VICTORY AND DISILLUSIONMENT. EGYPT AND BRIGHT'S RESIGNATION. COUNTY FRANCHISE AND THE LORDS

'The House knows that for forty years at least I have endeavoured to teach my countrymen an opinion and doctrine which I hold, namely, that the moral law is intended not only for individual life but for the life and practice of States in their dealing with one another. I think that in the present case there has been a manifest violation both of International Law and of the moral law, and therefore it is impossible for me to give my support to it.'—BRIGHT *explains his resignation after the Bombardment of Alexandria. House of Commons*, July 17, 1882.

'What the view of Ministers may be I know not; but the view of the English people will be, that, if their forefathers had the power to curb a despotic monarchy, you have the power equally to curb an arrogant, and I think—speaking of the majority of the Peers—an unpatriotic oligarchy.'—BRIGHT *at Manchester*, July 1884.

EVEN after Gladstone's Midlothian campaign of 1879, it was by no means universally expected either that the Liberals would win the coming election, or that, if they did win it, Gladstone would resume the official leadership which he had vacated by his own act five years before. The following letter of John Bright's is addressed, in January 1880, to his friend and correspondent, Mr. Thomas Potter, M.P., who had evidently been writing in a gloomy strain on Liberal prospects, and urging Bright to work for Gladstone's return:

> 'I do not think the world is coming to an end or this country to ruin. There are "ups and downs" in political life. Lately we have had a gloomy period, but more good things have been said during the last year than at any former time, and I think what is moral in our political life has come more to the front. In past times the Liberal party has only been a little less foolish and wicked than the Tories. Now it has pronounced in favor of, to it, new principles, and a new policy. In this I rejoice.

'As to leadership, what can I do? When the time comes the necessities of the case will decide the question. I was chairman of the meeting which selected a new leader; it is impossible for me to move. Our friend at Hawarden is full of honorable feeling and he has no idea of playing false to his successor. I rely with perfect confidence on the honor of Granville, Hartington and Gladstone, and am content to leave the future to the future. Any attempt now to force Gladstone into the leadership would fail, as he could not accept it; and the very attempt might do far more damage to the party than the present state of things. I recommend to you that greatest of virtues, Patience. Watch the course of events which often clears up great confusions, and will do so, I do not doubt, in this instance.'

The General Election came, and was decided in the first days of April. Contrary to the prophecies of those who knew England through the London Clubs and newspaper offices, Beaconsfield, with his crude Jingo appeal, proved less popular than the idealist of Midlothian. Who then, among the Liberals, had the best claim to the power that victory gives? The ex-chief, who, fighting in the ranks, had chosen the ground, sounded the onslaught, and won the battle? Or the honourable men who, from no motives of ambition, had performed the thankless tasks of nominal leadership? On April 18 Bright wrote to Mr. Chamberlain: 'I think the power and success of the new Government will be greater in Mr. Gladstone's hands than in any other. I think the country will rejoice if he accepts his old place, although no one undervalues the services or the character of Lord Granville and Lord Hartington.'

The course of events led inevitably to Gladstone's Premiership, and he filled up his Cabinet with a goodly supply of Lords and Whigs, balanced by Mr. Chamberlain, and by John Bright, who was again Chancellor of the Duchy of Lancaster. Thus Birmingham gave two of its Members to the Cabinet, the one representing the spirit of the new age, the other the victories of the past. Bright wrote in his journal:

'My colleague Chamberlain to be in the Cabinet: will be good for advice and for administration. Shows how by degrees the old exclusive system is breaking down. I wish his coming in would let me out. My head will not stand much excitement, and last night have slept badly. But

I do not like to disappoint Mr. Gladstone, and to appear changeable on a matter of importance.'

It is difficult in the face of many such entries in his journal, not to feel that he had better have refused office.

In these lonely years after his wife's death he was often at Hawarden or at the mansion of some other Liberal grandee. In the winter of 1880 he was at Mentmore with Lord Rosebery, where he witnessed the meet of a stag hunt. 'The stag,' he writes, 'let out of the van near the house, went off lightly over the fields. The stag is not to be killed—this is understood, and I hope the stag understands it.'

There has seldom been a more inspiriting victory than that of 1880, and seldom have the fruits of victory, through combined misfortune and mishandling, tasted so like the fruits of defeat. Bradlaugh, Ireland, Transvaal, Egypt—in these four deep bogs the victorious Liberals floundered for four years, then half extracted themselves by the Act enfranchising the agricultural labourer, only to plunge and disappear in the chasm of Home Rule.

The first disenchantment was a split in the party on the question whether Bradlaugh should be allowed to take his seat. The illiberal section of the Liberals joined with the Conservatives to humiliate and out-vote Mr. Gladstone, in order to keep an atheist out of the House. The movement for Bradlaugh's exclusion originated with and was engineered by the Fourth Party. It will be readily admitted that Mr. Gladstone and John Bright knew as much about religion as that jovial pair of crusaders, Lord Randolph Churchill and Sir Drummond Wolff. The two great men who had done most to exalt public life above the material level stood together to resist the imposition of religious tests. To Gladstone the performance of his duty in the Bradlaugh case was more painful than it was to Bright, and therefore even more honourable; for Gladstone wholly disliked everything about Bradlaugh, whereas Bright said one day to his son: 'It is not Bradlaugh's atheism which they hate, but his unconscious Christianity.' In one of his speeches on the question John Bright shocked the conventionalities by stating that 'to a large extent the working people of the country do not care any more for the dogmas of Christianity than the upper classes care for the practice of that religion.' [1]

[1] Bradlaugh had his admirers even among old ladies. One of them came to the House to see him, and asked for 'the Member for Northampton.' She

Meanwhile Ireland's ancient wounds were bleeding afresh. England's attention was again secured to her, by the Land League, agrarian crime, and Parnellite obstruction in the House. Coercion Bills were easy and were forthcoming, but, while Forster thought he could checkmate the Land League by locking up certain 'village ruffians,' Bright told his constituents in November 1880 that 'Force is not a remedy.' Fortunately Gladstone was there to apply the true 'remedy,' which, after being disastrously delayed by the Lords, took shape as the Land Act of 1881. Bright supported both coercive and remedial measures in the House, though he sorely groaned over the former in the Cabinet and in his private journal. 'Cabinet Council. Long discussion on Habeas Corpus Suspension. Most unpleasant matter for discussion. I wish I could escape from official responsibilities.'

But while he disliked coercion as an evil sometimes necessary, his pacific instincts were even more outraged by the Land League, which he denounced as criminal in its methods though right in its objects. 'If your League were conducted as our League was,' he told the Irish across the floor of the House, 'I should not have opposed you. I should have sent you a subscription and become one of your members.' Certainly there were differences between the Anti-Corn Law League and the Land League; neither was Parnell exactly Cobden. The obstructive and noisy tactics of the Parnellites in the House alienated John Bright almost as much as the methods of the agrarian agitation, for he was a great respecter of Parliament. As early as 1881 he was writing to Gladstone of the Parnellites as 'the rebel faction,' and he shortly afterwards began to use the word 'rebel' in his public speeches.

But he supported the Land Act none the less warmly. The most telling passage of his speech was that which gave rise to the phrase 'prairie value of land':

> 'To the complaint that the Bill gives so much to the tenants and takes it all from the landlords, I should make this answer: if at this moment all that has been done by the tenant in Ireland were gone, imagine that!—if all that the tenants have done were gone, and all that the owners have done left—that is the picture, the sort of map I should very much like to see; it would be charming; it would

was promptly introduced to Bradlaugh's colleague in the representation of that city, Mr. Labouchere. 'Are you Mr. Bradlaugh?' she eagerly asked, 'No, ma'am,' was the reply, 'I'm the *Christian* Member for Northampton!'

finish this debate in five minutes—if this map were drawn; then, over nine-tenths of Ireland the land would be as bare of houses, of barns, of fences, and of cultivation, as it was in prehistoric times. It would be as bare as an American prairie where the Indian now roams, and where the foot of the white man has never yet trodden.'

The Irish trouble sprang inexorably from 'old, unhappy far-off things.' But the South African trouble was due to the folly and carelessness of the British Cabinet of the day. Disraeli had annexed the Transvaal and Gladstone had criticised him for that act, but given no definite undertaking on his own part to reverse it if he came into office. After the electoral victory he pledged his Government, not indeed to repeal the annexation of the Transvaal, but to give the Boers full self-government under the British flag. He then delayed to fulfil this pledge. The new Liberal Ministers trusted to 'men on the spot' who could not understand the temper of a liberty-loving people, and allowed themselves to be misled by some mirage of securing the Confederation of South Africa before instead of after the grant of self-government to the people of the Transvaal. In breach of our plighted word and in disregard of the Republican traditions of a proud and warlike race, our Ministers allowed the Transvaal to continue under the arbitrary rule of permanent officials. The Boers had conceived high hopes from the result of the General Election of 1880; and when they found themselves thrown over by the English party on whose sympathy they had relied, they conceived that no course was left them but to assert in arms the title of white men to freedom.

Culpable negligence is perhaps the most just and is certainly the lightest verdict that can be brought against the Liberal Cabinet in this matter. The indignation heaped upon them for ending the war after the defeat of Majuba has often made people forget their fault in allowing the war to begin. The failure of an English Government to fulfil its pledges and of a Liberal Government to act on Liberal principles, brought on the first Boer War, the parent of the second. The very different conduct pursued in our own time, after another Liberal victory at the polls, has done all that might so easily have been done in 1880 by the Ministry of the day.

Bright paid no attention to the question, and failed to warn his colleagues of their negligence until it was too late. The first mention of the Transvaal in his papers occurs in his journal of February 15, 1881:

> 'Cabinet. Transvaal War. Agreed to propose armistice, and to send commissioners to propose terms of Settlement. All most anxious to prevent further conflict and bloodshed.'

A little more anxiety to prevent the beginning of 'conflict and bloodshed' would have been still more to the point. A fortnight later came the news of Majuba.

> 'March 1st. Bad news from the Transvaal. Sir George Colley and many men of his force killed. Prospect of peace much further off.'
>
> '3rd. At 1 o'clock called on Mr. Gladstone for an hour, discussed the unhappy Transvaal question. I argued that the recent disaster should not interfere with measures for Peace—that negotiations should go on as if it had not happened—that no operations for the sake of vengeance should be adopted. Mr. Gladstone agreed with me. I said it would be impossible for me to consent to any measures of a vindictive character, or to the shedding of blood to restore the credit of British arms. Mr. Chamberlain holds the same view. Mr. Gladstone spoke on this subject as I hoped and expected.'
>
> '5th. Cabinet at 2 o'clock. . . . On Transvaal affair, no member of the Government urging war for sake of recovering reputation of English arms—terms of pacification the same as before conflict on Majuba Hill.'

In purely English affairs one good thing at least was done after Bright's own heart. A legislative step of great importance in the reform of the Game Laws was taken, more than a generation after he had agitated the question in Parliament and country.[1] Sir William Harcourt's Hares and Rabbits Bill enabled the tenant farmer, within certain restrictions, to retaliate on those destroyers of his produce. Harcourt had for many years been Bright's personal friend. He was now Home Secretary, and Bright said of him that he was the most humane Home Secretary with whom he had ever had to deal. He said this after long experience, for during forty years of public life Bright had kept a watchful eye on death sentences in particular and on criminal justice in general, making private appeals to successive Home Secretaries on behalf of those convicted persons

[1] See pp. 124-28 above.

who seemed more unfortunate than criminal. Again and again in his journal we find such entries as this of March 1864: 'Letter from Sir George Grey, saying he had reprieved the convict at Warwick; great relief to me, for his fate has been a burden on my mind for some days,' though the man was an entire stranger to him, with no private or public claim upon his benevolence.

One day in February 1882 John Bright visited Mr. Gladstone and found him

> 'resting on a sofa reading one of the reviews. He spoke very freely about his prospects—he seems much resolved to quit office during this year. I showed him the difficulty of it, and what should be done before he doffs his harness—the question of the Land, the County Suffrage, and the Distribution of Seats. He did not think he was especially bound to continue through these great questions, though his zeal in regard to them had not slackened.'

But instead of retiring, or proceeding at once with County Franchise, the Prime Minister allowed himself to be drawn on the tide of destiny into nothing less than the founding of the Anglo-Egyptian State.

John Bright stood alone in the Cabinet in decided opposition to measures that led inevitably to the occupation of Egypt. He was surprised that his colleagues, who had been unanimous in favour of making peace after Majuba, were equally unanimous in favour of taking up the Khedive's quarrel against Arabi and occupying Egypt with British troops. Bright had observed with keen pleasure that his views of peace and non-intervention had been acted on by the Foreign Office, during the ten years between the death of Palmerston and the revival of the Crimean policy by Beaconsfield. The circumstances of the Gladstonian victory of 1880 seemed to warrant the belief that the new 'Jingoism' had been a failure, and was dead. As regards the Balkan question this was true. But Bright now realised to his grief that the modern 'statesmen' of both parties were more or less under the influence of a certain atmosphere pervading the new age; they were by no means entirely pacific, and they desired further to extend the boundaries of the Empire. In the Egyptian question Gladstone himself could not resist the pressure brought upon him in a thousand ways by old Whigs and new Radicals who were bent on pushing England into Egypt. Bright was unaffected by the change of atmosphere, but although he could still say 'No' when it came to the crisis, he had not the health or energy to fight the case from the first, point after point, nor had he the resolution to tackle Mr. Gladstone in time. He allowed himself to be put off from day to day by his old friend's profuse and sympathetic assurances that they were not going as far as Bright feared and that all would yet be well. But when he heard that our fleet had actually bombarded Alexandria, he resigned, and never again took office.

> 'I think,' he wrote to Mr. Gladstone on July 12, 1882, 'in reviewing the doctrines connected with our Foreign policy which I have preached and defended during 40 years of my public life, you will not be surprised at the decision I am now compelled to take. I cannot accept any share of the responsibility for the acts of war which have taken place at Alexandria. I cannot see to what they may lead, and I know not to what greater wrong and mischief they may force the Government. I feel therefore compelled to withdraw from the Administration, and to ask you to place my resignation of the office I hold in the hands of the Queen. I bitterly lament the disappointment of many hopes as I separate myself from your Government. My feelings towards yourself are those of profound esteem and regard, and an overpowering sense of duty has alone forced me to the only course which seems now open to me. To add to your difficulties and to give you trouble is a cause of much unhappiness to me. I can only hope you will be able to judge me rightly and to forgive me.'

Bright did not speak at all in the country on the Egyptian question, nor in the House except to announce the fact of his resignation and its cause. He felt too old to fight his countrymen as he had fought them over the Crimean War, and he was much more tenderly attached to his Liberal colleagues, from whom he was now forced to part, than he had ever been to the Palmerston Whigs. It does not appear from his letters that he studied the Egyptian question as he had studied the Russo-Turkish question. He contents himself with the broad view that the internal affairs of Egypt were not our business, that the war against Arabi was therefore unjustifiable, and that it would lead to obligations and difficulties of which no man could foresee the end. He was not so foolish as to suppose that we could come out of Egypt as easily as we could go in. He disliked the 'city influences' at work, and he did not think that we ought to involve ourselves in a series of wars in order to collect the debts of bondholders or find new lands for company exploitation. He agreed with his friend, Mr. Goldwin Smith, who wrote to him : 'It is a Stock Jobbers' war. We shall very likely have more of this sort of thing. One set of causes of war departs, but another crops up in its place.' The occupation of Egypt has proved to the material advantage of the Egyptian peasant, but in Bright's opinion it was undertaken in the yet more material interest of the bondholders.

Bright had an interview with Mr. Wilfrid Blunt, and without committing himself to complete adoption of his view of Arabi as a national hero, he wrote that 'Mr. Blunt has been wiser than the Government or than those who seek to discredit him.' When, after Tel-el-Kebir, the question of Arabi's punishment arose, Bright wrote to Gladstone :

> 'As to Arabi—I should contest much of your letter. . . . For myself, I consider the case very plain. He gave himself up to *English* authority, and not to the puppet Khedive, from whom he may expect, not mercy or justice, but rather vengeance. Are we to be the "thief catcher" for the creature we call the ruler of Egypt, and are we to hand over to him the rebellious subject whom we have overthrown ? I think it a great mistake that Arabi has been given up—to have banished him from the country would have been the judgment that History will approve, or would have approved. As to the "Flag of Truce" surely the authors of the bombardment cannot complain seriously of this—it would be an instance of straining at a gnat and swallowing something much larger than a camel, such as we have no other example of. Is to transgress in some minute or inferior matter what are called the laws of war a greater crime than war itself ? Is deception worse than slaughter ? As to permitting the Khedive and his sham Government to put Arabi to death, I venture to assert that such a course would cover the English Administration, not with discredit only, but with something even worse, but which in writing to you, I will not name. Pray forgive me if I write strongly. I am outside, and can judge, I hope, with something like impartiality. I value your reputation almost as my own, and hope it may have no stain upon it in connexion with the fate of Arabi and his supporters in the attempted Egyptian revolution.'

It was on the Egyptian question that the long latent difference of opinion on foreign policy between himself and Mr. Chamberlain became fully apparent to Bright. It had long ago been evident to Mr. Chamberlain.[1] In December 1882 Bright wrote to Mr. George Dixon about a proposed meeting in Birmingham :

'I do not see how I can with advantage take part in a meeting at which it will be impossible to avoid a discussion of the Egyptian question, on which Mr. Chamberlain and I are far as the poles asunder. In his recent speech at Ashton he speaks of the "ignoble doctrine of non-intervention" and the whole tone and argument of his speech in defence of the Government are exactly of the stuff on which the foreign policy of Lord Palmerston, and I may almost say of Lord Beaconsfield, was defended. I can have no part in it and shall denounce it when I am forced to speak upon it. But I do not want to assail the Government or to get into open conflict with my colleague, still less to create any difficulty with my friends in Birmingham ; and yet how to escape it I cannot see if I stand on the same platform with Mr. Chamberlain at this moment.

Early in 1884, when the Soudan difficulty had grown out of the Egyptian, Bright wrote to Mr. Chamberlain :

'As to the Egyptian hole into which my late colleagues plunged with "so light a heart," I may say that the fleets went to Alexandria to protect English and French subjects and not to make war. The Admiral made the war by his excited telegram, and Childers and Northbrook, hot from their departments, fell into the snare. You suggest that I should have pressed my views more strongly, but I may reply that, as you will remember, I was alone. Up to a certain point Gladstone and Harcourt were, in a sense, peace-men. You were not free from excitement, and when Granville joined the fever, you said no word in aid of my view. I told the Cabinet that they had lost their heads. If the reins had not been handed over to the ruffians of the fleet, who were eager for war, the worst would have been that Tewfik would have come on board an English ship, there would have been for the moment a bloodless revolution, and England, France and Turkey would have discussed the future of Egypt. But there would have been no war, no bombardment, no city in flames, no thousands of men

[1] See p. 280 above.

slaughtered, and furthe: we should not have had an Admiral hoisted into the House of Lords, who, if he had his due, would have been court-martialled! The past is past, but it leaves an ugly future and for "Radical" members of the Cabinet an awkward one to discuss. Let us hope the clouds will lift.'

In March 1885, after the tragedy of Khartoum, Gladstone one day talked confidentially to Bright, saying that 'he had suffered torture' over the whole question. He told Bright that he 'never saw Gordon, he was appointed by Ministers in town, and Gladstone concurred but had never seen him. He was totally unsuited for the work he undertook,' that is, for the *evacuation* of the Soudan. 'Mr. Gladstone very friendly to me—tells me how much he wishes I was with him in the Cabinet. I am very sorry for his troubles. I did not make them, and would have saved him from them if he had been strong enough to have taken my advice.' Bright had no responsibility for the mission of Gordon or for his fate. He did not share the enthusiasm for Gordon's career and character that swept over a proud nation indignant at their hero's death. The idea of a 'Christian warrior,' which attracts so many, appeared to the Friend as a contradiction in terms, except when the warrior is fighting in a just quarrel that immediately concerns him. In March 1885 he wrote to a correspondent, who had praised Gordon:

> 'Gordon cared little for his own life and apparently less for the lives of others, or he would not have devoted himself to the savagery of war in China and the Soudan. No Chinese and no Soudanese had injured him, and yet he accepted the business of war and slaughter in countries many thousands of miles from his own country, and I suppose thus imagined he was serving God and his country. This seems to me a sort of madness, which I cannot understand. Would the merciful Saviour have deemed this a service rendered to him? The war spirit which reigned supreme in Gordon seems to me wholly at variance with the spirit inculcated in the New Testament.'

The question how far the occupation of the Soudan by England has checked the slave-trade in Africa, does not appear to have been raised in Bright's mind. His view of Gordon's interference in China gains renewed interest from words which the

Japanese statesman, Prince Ito, in 1909 said to Sir Valentine Chirol:

> 'There can be very little doubt that the Manchu Dynasty had reached the end of its proper tether when the Taiping Rebellion occurred; and, by preventing its overthrow Gordon and his "ever-victorious army" arrested a normal and healthy process of nature. Nothing that the Manchus have done since then affords the slightest evidence that they deserved to be saved. Rather the contrary. And when they fall, as fall they must and will before very long, the upheaval will be all the more violent and all the more protracted for having been so long and unduly postponed.' [1]

During the years 1882-85 Bright was very conscious of his growing isolation. 'There seems not a single friend of mine with whom I can consult,' he wrote in his journal on the day he determined to resign. 'My dear friend Cobden! How often have I wished him here for his counsel and help.' The popular festivities held in his honour at Birmingham in June 1883, to celebrate 'the completion of his twenty-fifth year of service' as Member for the city, gratified him, but did not remove his sense of loneliness. He writes to a friend in 1885, when war with Russia again seemed likely: 'Be the Government Liberal or Tory, much the same thing happens—war with all its horrors and miseries and crimes and cost. Talkers and writers being mostly in favor of it, and the multitude approving or consenting to the wickedness in high places.' Nevertheless he believed that since the Crimean War there had on the whole been progress towards the ideals to which he had devoted his life. 'Thirty years ago,' he wrote, 'the Church and Tory classes were scarcely more warlike than the Nonconformists and their ministers. Now, I believe, the latter are generally in favor of peace, and I have letters from Church clergymen anxious that war may be avoided.'

There was for John Bright one gleam of the old glory before the strength of Liberalism was broken by the catastrophe of the Home Rule split. The enfranchisement of the working men in the towns by the Act of 1867 rendered it, in the eyes of many, only a matter of time when the agricultural labourer also should obtain the vote. The question had been kept alive in the House by a private Member with his annual motion on the

[1] *Quarterly Review*, April 1912.

subject, and the heart of official Liberalism was seriously inclined thereto by the result of the General Election of 1874, when, under the restricted Franchise, only four Liberal County Members were returned for England south of Trent and north of Cornwall. The movement among the agricultural labourers themselves was stirred up by Joseph Arch. On July 6, 1875, Bright notes in his journal:

> 'Call from Joseph Arch of the Agricultural Laborers' Union—a sensible and I think an honest man. Long talk on Union and the condition of farm laborers and the question of giving them votes. He wished me to present a petition from them with 60,000 signatures, which I promised to do.'

He presented the petition next day, and in the following year spoke in the House in favour of the motion for County Franchise. But still Lord Hartington and what may be called the official wing of the Liberal party did not give their full support to the proposal. On May 16, 1877, a great meeting of delegates from the associations of agricultural labourers was held in Exeter Hall. At least forty Members of Parliament attended. John Bright took the chair, and made a most interesting and earnest speech. There was something pathetic about it. The form was perfect, and the tone singularly noble; but there were few of the old points, and epigrammatic turns of phrase by which his speaking had been enlivened in the past. The sympathy he showed to the unrepresented rustics was warmly appreciated; and the moral effect upon the action of the Liberal party was instant and complete. The minority which hitherto had supported the extension of the County Franchise had never exceeded 173. After the meeting in Exeter Hall Lord Hartington, in June 1877, spoke and voted for Household Suffrage in the Counties; his personal adherents followed suit, and the minority rose to 220 votes, which practically was the entire Liberal strength in that Parliament. After the electoral oratory of 1880, it was regarded as one of the duties of the Gladstonian Government to enfranchise the rural labourer before the end of the Parliament.

In 1883 there was a strong movement among the rank and file to repair the party fortunes, sinking in Egyptian sands, by the too-long-postponed measure of County Franchise. A Liberal Conference was held with this object in Leeds in October 1883, at which Bright attended and spoke. It was already foreseen that the House of Lords would, if it dared, place its veto on the enfranchisement of the rural democracy. The discussion turned much on this prospect, and Bright delighted the Conference by bringing forward his famous proposal, that has become still more famous owing to its partial adoption more than twenty years after his death :

> 'The Crown,' he said, 'cannot now reject any Bill sent up for its acceptance. If the Crown may be limited in this way, why may not the Peers ? Why not enact that if the Peers have rejected a Bill once and it has been considered in a subsequent session by the Commons, and, after due deliberation, has been again sent up to the Peers, then the Peers must pass it on and it will receive the Royal assent and will become law ? '

In January 1836 James Mill, father of John Stuart Mill, published an article in the *London Review* which he signed by the initials 'P. Q.,' advocating the precise measure passed in the year 1911. Whether John Bright or any one else remembered this in 1883-84 it is impossible to say. But it is certain that Bright's speech first brought the proposal to the serious notice of the political world, though in a somewhat more stringent form.

In 1884 the County Franchise Bill was duly brought in, passed and sent up to the Lords. As had been foretold, its passage was there barred ; but in cautious mood the Peers left their retreat open in case they found the country against them. They shelved the Bill, and demanded that before it was further pressed, a Redistribution Bill should be produced. In the crisis that followed John Bright remembered his ancient valour. *Punch* had a cartoon of 'The Old Lion' coming out of his lair to crush the lordly coronet beneath his paw.

The game began at a party meeting of the Liberal Members summoned to the Foreign Office to consider the situation. Mr. Goschen made a speech, not well received, deprecating an agitation against the Lords. The moment he sat down John Bright was seen to have risen at the other end of the room :

> 'I hope,' he said amid much cheering and laughter, 'that everybody that can be calm during the next three months, like my Rt. Hon. friend, will be as calm as they can, and will not unduly judge those who may show by their expressions a little warmth for the great question which is before the country. I recollect the crisis of 1846, and the crisis of 1866 and 1867, but looking back on these

periods I do not take the advice of Mr. Goschen. I do not know whether it was given then; I dare say it was, but it was not followed. . . . A hereditary House of Parliament is not and cannot be perpetual in a free country. The Crown, so popular throughout the country, and so important in our system, has long ago given up its absolute veto. It would be to the great advantage, in my opinion, of the House of Lords, if some limit were put upon their power of veto.'

While the crisis lasted John Bright used to the full the liberty of exceedingly free speech to popular audiences which he enjoyed as being no longer a member of the Government. But he noted with pleasure in his journal that his Birmingham colleague, when they two addressed their constituents from the same platform on August 4, 'spoke well—very strongly against the Lords for a member of the Government.' At this meeting Bright again put forward his scheme for limiting the veto of the second chamber, after dismissing the alternative proposals of total abolition and reduction of numbers, the former as too strong to meet with general acceptance, the latter as inadequate to secure fair treatment for Liberal measures.

'The proposition that I should make would be this: that they should have, unimpaired, all the power they have now with regard to any Bill that has passed the House of Commons during the session in which the Lords are called upon to deal with it. That is, in the case of this Bill they would be at liberty to amend it, and send it back to the Commons. If the Commons did not like the amendments, and would not accept them, the Bill would go back to the Lords, and if the Lords chose they might reject it. But, in the second session, if practically the same Bill was sent up to the Lords, they would then also have a right to debate and to amend; but when the Bill came down to the House of Commons in this second session, and the Commons would not agree to the amendments of the Lords, then the Lords should be bound to accept the Bill.'

Before the autumn was over, further agitation proved to be unnecessary. Negotiations were opened between the two parties, which ended in the passage into law of the County Franchise Bill and of a Redistribution Bill drawn up on lines agreed between the Liberal and Conservative chiefs.

For several years past there had been a revived Protectionist movement, based on the two facts that agricultural depression had set in in the late 'seventies, and that foreign countries had not adopted Free Trade. Bright wrote a number of public letters from time to time combating the new arguments.

In answer to the cry raised in 1881 for the re-establishment of Corn Laws to save agriculture in years of bad English harvest, John Bright pointed out that in those very years Corn Laws must have caused dear bread for all.

> 'Between the harvests of 1879 and 1880, that is in the year after the bad harvest of 1879, out of every four loaves of bread eaten by the people of the United Kingdom three loaves came from abroad, and in no other year in my lifetime have our people been fed so cheaply or on bread of such excellent quality.'

In the same year he wrote another public letter on the subject of Foreign Tariffs as an argument for Protection over here:

> 'We all regret that France, the United States of America, and other countries continue to maintain their high tariffs; it is, we believe, a misfortune to them and injurious to us; but we can only legislate for our own country and not for them. If you think that, *not being able to sell freely*, we should mend ourselves by *giving up the power to buy freely*, I must leave you to that opinion, only expressing my wonder at it. But you will perhaps say that we can force other nations to reduce their tariffs if we impose a tariff against them. You forget probably that we have tried this in past times, and that it has wholly failed. Sir Robert Peel taught this nearly forty years ago, and he believed, as I believe, that the best defence we can have against the evils of foreign tariffs is to have no tariff of our own.
>
> 'If you doubt what Free Trade has done for England, go back to your histories, and read what was the condition of our working men and their families for the first forty years of this century, when everything was supposed to be protected, and compare it with what it is now.'

And in November 1884, when a 'bad winter' was stimulating the 'Fair Trade' movement, he wrote:

> 'To sell freely would be a great advantage, as to buy freely is a great advantage; but neither to buy freely nor

to sell freely as the Fair Traders recommend, would, in my view, enormously increase the injury to our trade arising from foreign tariffs.

'I have known the depression in trade to be much greater than it is now, and the sufferings of traders and workmen during our time of Protection, previous to 1842, when the reform of our tariff began, were beyond all comparison greater than they are now. In foreign countries where high tariffs exist, say in Russia, in France, and in the United States, the disturbance and depression of manufacturing industries are far greater at this moment than with us. Their tariffs make it impossible for them to have a larger foreign trade; we have a wider field for our exports, which they cannot enter. . . . The field for our manufacturing industry is far wider than that for any other manufacturing nation in the world, and I cannot doubt that we shall gradually rise from the existing depression, and shall reap even greater gain from our policy of Free Trade in the future than we have reaped in the past.'

Those who read the trade returns of the last few years will find reason to think that this cheerful prophecy has been most abundantly fulfilled.

CHAPTER XXI

HOME RULE

'Mr. Gladstone stops the way. He insists on an impossible legislation for Ireland, and insists upon it to the exclusion of legislation for the whole Kingdom, and his followers still have faith in him and are anxious to return him to power. They are furious because the Conservatives are in office, and blame me and others for keeping them there. They seem blind to the fact that Mr. Gladstone put them in office. He would appeal to the Electors on the merits of his Irish Bills, and the Electors of Great Britain by a majority of nearly two to one condemned his Bills and destroyed his Administration. We cannot allow Mr. Gladstone to come back to office with his Irish policy, and are willing to support a Government which the Constituencies have, by a great majority, placed in power. I prefer to join hands with Lord Salisbury and his colleagues than with Mr. Parnell and his friends, the leaders of the Irish rebellion.'—BRIGHT *to a correspondent,* November 1887.

THE passage of the County Franchise and Redistribution Bills into law was regarded by many Conservative Members as the doom of their party. In March 1885 one of them said to Bright: 'The Conservative party is almost destroyed. The next Parliament will be fatal to us.' And so it might have been, but for Egypt and Ireland. In June Gladstone was defeated, nominally on the Budget, really on account of the discredit arising from the Khartoum tragedy. An interim Conservative Cabinet carried on affairs until the General Election in November 1885. After negotiations between Parnell and the Conservative Lord-Lieutenant of Ireland on the subject of Home Rule, Parnell tells us that he left Lord Carnarvon 'believing that I was in complete accord with him regarding the main outlines of a settlement conferring a legislature upon Ireland.' At the General Election Parnell cast the Irish vote in England on the Conservative side. The election was, in fact, fought with great bitterness as between Irish and Liberals in the English boroughs, particularly in Lancashire, and these feelings had not wholly died away when a few months later Mr. Gladstone asked the Liberals to take the Irishmen to their hearts.

The Soudan catastrophe also greatly helped the Conservatives, who won many seats in the boroughs. But the newly enfranchised agricultural labourers voted with unexpected courage for the party which had enfranchised them, and from which they hoped great things, not destined to be fulfilled. An even more remarkable result of the new Franchise Act was the solid phalanx of 85 Home Rulers from Ireland, most of them elected by majorities grotesquely large, and all ready to march and wheel and fight for the Home Rule cause under the generalship of Parnell. In the last Parliament he had only counted 35 regular followers ; there had then been 26 moderate Home Rulers not under Parnell, and 26 Irish Liberals, but these two classes disappeared in the election of 1885. Parnell's 85 were a 'great fact,' whether regarded as a proof of what Catholic Ireland wished, or as a voting power now holding the balance of English parties. Exclusive of the Irish, the Parliament contained 333 Liberals and 233 Conservatives. Parnell could not, therefore, hope to obtain anything by continuing the alliance with the Conservatives which had held good during the election. But neither could Gladstone carry on the Government without coming to terms with Parnell.

Such were the events that led up to the adoption of a Home Rule and Land Purchase policy by Mr. Gladstone, when he was called on to assume office in the early months of 1886. The events that followed, so far as Bright's part in them is concerned, appear very clearly in his journal and letters, which can be left to tell their own story. Bright's views on Home Rule prior to 1886 and his previous impressions of Irish Nationalist leaders, which largely determined his attitude at the crisis, can also be set down in his own words.

'ROCHDALE, January 20, 1872.

'MY DEAR O'DONOGHUE,—It is said that some persons engaged in the canvass of the county of Kerry have spoken of me as an advocate of Home Rule for Ireland. I hope no one has ventured to say anything so absurd and untrue. If it has been said by any one of any authority in the country, I shall be glad if you will contradict it. To have two Legislative Assemblies in the United Kingdom would, in my opinion, be an intolerable mischief ; and I think no sensible man can wish for two within the limits of the present United Kingdom who does not wish the United Kingdom to become two or more nations, entirely separate from each other.'

'INVERGARRY, March 15, 1874.

'Tell the merchant that he must not rely for one moment on the Home Rulers for any one thing that is wise and good, nor indeed on any political combination of Irishmen. They have never yet done anything for themselves or their country and have never yet as a party shown what ought to be done. The absence of political and economical knowledge in Ireland is remarkable, and what there is of a sensible middle class is apparently crushed or smothered by the extreme men, who are always in pursuit of some phantom and who seem not to know the substance even when they see it.'

With the arrival on the scene of Parnell, of the Land League, and of the obstructionists in the English Parliament, Bright's dislike of Irish politicians, as we have already seen, was greatly increased. He used to write and speak of these new influences collectively as 'the rebel party.' Indeed it would almost appear that his distrust of the Parnellites in the flesh was greater than his objection to Irish self-government in the abstract, for in his journal of March 22, 1885, we read:

'Long talk with Dalhousie on Egypt and on Ireland. I suggested a mode of dealing with the Irish question: Ireland—32 counties—32 County Boards—64 representatives to a Central Council in Dublin, for internal affairs, excluding army, navy, import duties, Church, perhaps police, but leaving to it education, local taxation and control. The question a great difficulty, but some solution must be found.'

His comment on the General Election appears in a letter to Lord Granville, dated November 30, 1885:

'I would not have been a candidate at this election if I could have offered to my friends an honest and good excuse. I could not desert my friends in Birmingham or run away before the opponent who presented himself [Lord Randolph Churchill].[1] Lancashire Boroughs are very bad. The Irish have done much temporary mischief—the Church and the Catholics have helped them. There must come an

[1] Bright only defeated this opponent by 800 votes, and the Liberal majority over Conservatives in Birmingham fell from 'two to one' in 1880 to 'three to two' in 1885.

Irish crisis, but in what precise form is not yet to be seen. The two parties may form a policy and adhere to it, and something may be granted—and the main thing demanded sternly refused. The future is clouded—but I wait in patience. The people can trade, and work and live—past reforms have saved our working millions and we may wait for sentimental reforms awhile longer.'

On December 15, 1885, he wrote to Mr. Chamberlain:

As to Ireland—there are two lines—to refuse what is described as Home Rule in the shape of an Irish Parliament or to yield everything. It would be a blessed thing to get rid of Ireland in the English Parliament, and if England is not to meddle with internal Irish business, how can Irish members be permitted to deal with English and Scottish matters? The more I consider the whole question the more do difficulties start up, and yet I try to judge it without prejudice or, if I have any prejudice, it tends to favor something very like what the rebel party say they want. I have some ideas which are better spoken than written, so I may leave them till we have a spare hour or more in your library.'

On January 4, 1886, he was visited at Rochdale by two gentlemen of importance in the Dublin commercial world—Mr. Jonathan Hogg and Mr. Pim, both well-known Liberals and Friends—who pleaded against Home Rule from the Irish Protestant point of view in a manner that had its effect upon John Bright.

He remained at Rochdale during the first weeks of the Parliament, while the Conservative Government was defeated and the new Cabinet formed. On February 4 he wrote to Mr. Chamberlain, who was then entering Gladstone's ill-fated Cabinet:

'If the *rebel* party were not *rebels* an arrangement would not be difficult, but with *rebels* how can you negotiate with or trust them? If you propose anything less than a Parliament, fear of the Fenians and of the American Irish and contributors may compel the rebel leader to turn upon you. I suspect that anything they can accept will be rejected by the constituencies.'

At length, at the beginning of March, he went up to London.

'March 10. Called on Lord Hartington. An hour's talk with him on the great Irish question. He is very reasonable and his course greatly to his credit.

'March 12. After dinner much private talk with Mr. Gladstone on Ireland. His object is to settle the Land question which I rather think ought *now* to be considered as settled. On the question of a Parliament in Dublin, he wishes to get rid of Irish representation at Westminster, in which I entirely agree with him if it be possible.

'March 17. Long talk with Mr. Chamberlain on his difficulties and resignation. I think his view is in the main correct and that it is not wise in him to support the intended measures.

'March 20. Downing Street—long interview for two hours with Mr. Gladstone at his request. He gave me a long memorandum, historical in character, on the past Irish story, which seemed to be somewhat one-sided, leaving out of view the important minority and the views and feelings of the Protestant and loyal portion of the people. He explained much of his policy as to a Dublin Parliament, and as to Land purchase. I objected to the Land policy as unnecessary—the Act of 1881 had done all that was reasonable for the tenants—why adopt the policy of the rebel party, and get rid of landholders, and thus evict the English garrison as the rebels call them? I denied the value of the security for repayment. Mr. G. argued that his finance arrangements would be better than present system of purchase, and that we were bound in honor to succour the landlords, which I contested. Why not go to the help of other interests in Belfast and Dublin?'

It will be observed that Gladstone and Bright had since the year 1869 reversed their respective attitudes towards the policy of land purchase. It was then Bright who wished to 'undo, absolutely undo, the territorial arrangements of the last two or three hundred years with regard to Ireland,' and who thought every remedial measure short of land purchase insufficient. It was then Gladstone who 'denied the value of the security for repayment.' [1]

The conversation between them continued on Home Rule:

'As to Dublin Parliament, I argued that he was making a surrender all along the line—a Dublin Parliament would

[1] See p. 410 above.

work with constant friction, and would press against any barrier he might create to keep up the unity of the three Kingdoms. What of a volunteer force, and what of import duties and protection as against British goods? He would not object, but any armed force must be under officers appointed by the Crown, and he did not think duties as against England would be imposed. Mr. G. is in favor of excluding all Irish representatives from Imperial Parliament—thinks Irish members in Dublin and at Westminster not possible. Irish members think they could not supply representatives for both Houses. I told him I thought to get rid of the Irishmen from Westminster, such as we have known them for 5 or 6 years past, would do something to make his propositions less offensive and distasteful in Great Britain, though it tends to more complete separation. I told him how anxious and alarmed many of his friends were, and quoted what Mr. Paget, Agnew, Rathbone, and others said—many would vote out of regard for him—many fearing a dissolution of Parliament possible, but few would like his great schemes. I said I was as much against his Land purchase as against the Dublin Parliament, and suggested that he should lessen the amount to be advanced by showing that only voluntary sale was contemplated, and that if the offer made by the Government was at a moderate or low figure, the landlord's demand would not be so great as rumour had imagined.

'I thought he placed far too much confidence in the leaders of the rebel party. I could place none in them, and the general feeling was and is that any terms made with them would not be kept, and that through them I could not hope for reconciliation with discontented and disloyal Ireland.

'Our interview lasted for two hours—the conversation very free and open. Mr. Gladstone was cheerful and earnest; he has given incessant attention to this great question for two months past. He spoke of the authority of Lord Bessborough, Lord Monck, and Lord Spencer, and Sir Robert Hamilton, and is resolved to go on. He does not understand the course and object of Mr. Chamberlain, and hinted at correspondence with him which would show how much he had changed his ground. He said this question should not be made a great party question involving a struggle in the constituencies, and that if he failed he should retire and leave others who thought themselves capable of doing it to undertake the settlement of the Irish difficulty. He was very friendly, and said how much he relied on such assistance as I could render him.

'I came away not wholly without some sense of relief, but still burdened with a feeling that so great a question has not in my time been before us.

'April 3. Conversation with Mr. Childers on Irish question and Government. He is miserable, and the Government in a very unpleasant and unsafe condition. He urged me to call on Mr. Gladstone, which I did on leaving him. Only a short time with Mr. G.—he seems weary, and not so brisk and eager as when I saw him a fortnight since. He insisted upon it that there was no Cabinet difficulty, only the ordinary differences as to details —this I know not to be accurate. I know that two of his chief colleagues are entirely against his Irish policy, but he seems obstinately determined to go on with it. He suggested I should see him at the House on Monday evening. . . .

'A note from Mrs. Gladstone asks me to dine on Tuesday. In my present position as to the Irish question, would rather not. It is difficult to oppose a Minister on a critical question, and to associate with him and frequent his table.

'This morning I told him I thought he could not carry his Bill, but I do not see how he is to escape the danger he has placed himself in. I am grieved to see the peril to himself, and to the party, and to Ireland. There is a certain wilfulness in all this not usual with him, and it does not promise any good.'

On April 8 Mr. Gladstone introduced the Home Rule Bill, which was read a first time without a division, but not without the disclosure of ominous divisions in Liberal opinion. Bright did not take part in the debates in the House. At the end of the month his old friend and brother-in-law, Duncan McLaren, died, at the age of eighty-six, and he went up to Edinburgh to attend the funeral and to comfort his sister Priscilla. Thence he did not return to the crucible of parties at Westminster, but to the quiet of his home at Rochdale. On the 13th of May, the anniversary of his wife's death eight years before, he received a note from Mr. Gladstone asking him to come up to London to see him. He replied in a letter which has been printed in full in Lord Morley's *Life of Gladstone*. The following are its most important passages :

'One Ash, Rochdale, May 13, '86.

'My dear Gladstone,—Your note just received has put me in a great difficulty. To-day is the anniversary of the greatest sorrow of my life, and I feel pressed to spend it at home. I sent a message to Mr. Arnold Morley last evening to say that I did not intend to return to town before Monday next—but I shall now arrange to go to-morrow—although I do not see how I can be of service in the great trouble which has arisen.

'I feel outside all the contending sections of the Liberal Party—for I am not in favor of Home Rule, or the creation of a Dublin Parliament—nor can I believe in any scheme of Federation as shadowed forth by Mr. Chamberlain.

'I do not believe that, with regard to the Irish question, "the resources of Civilisation are exhausted," and I think the plan of your Bill is full of complexity and gives no hope of successful working in Ireland or of harmony between Westminster and Dublin. I may say that my regard for you and my sympathy with you has made me silent in the discussion on the Bills before the House. I cannot consent to a measure which is so offensive to the whole Protestant population of Ireland, and to the whole sentiment of the province of Ulster so far as its loyal and Protestant people are concerned. I cannot agree to exclude them from the protection of the Imperial Parliament. I would do much to clear the rebel party from Westminster, and do not sympathise with those who wish to retain them—but admit there is much force in the arguments on this point which are opposed to my views upon it.

'Up to this time I have not been able to bring myself to the point of giving a vote in favor of your Bills. I am grieved to have to say this. As to the Land Bill, if it comes to a second reading, I fear I must vote against it. It may be that my hostility to the rebel party, looking at their conduct since your Government was formed six years ago, disables me from taking an impartial view of this great question. If I could believe them loyal—if they were honorable and truthful men, I could yield much—but I suspect that your policy of surrender to them will only place more power in their hands to war with greater effect against the unity of the 3 Kingdoms with no increase of good to the Irish people.

'How then can I be of service to you or to the real interests of Ireland if I come up to Town? I cannot venture to advise you, so superior to me in Party tactics and in experienced statesmanship, and I am not so much in accord with Mr. Chamberlain as to make it likely that I can say anything that will affect his course. One thing I may remark, that it appears to me that measures of the gravity of those now before Parliament cannot and ought not to be thrust through the House by force of a *small* majority. The various Reform Bills, the Irish Church Bills, the two great Land Bills were passed by very large majorities. In the present case, not only the whole Tory Party oppose, but a very important section of the Liberal Party, and although numerous meetings of Clubs and Associations have passed resolutions of confidence in you, yet generally they have accepted your Irish Government Bill as a "Basis" only, and have admitted the need of important changes in the Bill—changes which in reality would destroy the Bill. Under these circumstances it seems to me that more time should be given for the consideration of the Irish question. Parliament is not ready for it, and the intelligence of the country is not ready for it. If it be possible, I should wish that no Division should be taken upon the Bill. . . .

'Still, if you think I can be of any service a note to the Reform Club will, I hope, find me there to-morrow evening.'

And so on May 14, in consequence of Mr. Gladstone's request to hasten his arrival, he came up to London for the crisis of the Home Rule Bill. At the Reform Club he found the following letter awaiting him in reply to his own of the day before:

'*Private.*

'10 DOWNING STREET, WHITEHALL,
'May 14, '86.

'MY DEAR BRIGHT,—

'1. I am concerned to find that the demand on your patience and patriotism was so untimely; and I am, in the same proportion, sensible of and thankful for the self-sacrificing effort you have made.

'2. I should not have ventured to press you in obedience to a desire of my own, or a desire of any ordinary man.

'But I look upon Whitbread, relatively to the present circumstances, as not an ordinary man. I think he will probably communicate with you on the very question you have started, that of time.

'3. You have no doubt asked yourself the question, how is all this to end? Can it end in any way but one?

'4. The offences of Nationalists have been great: the worst of them, I frankly say, was committed against *you*, by Sexton, in a well-known speech.[1] *He* has given you a splendid opportunity: and I am confident you will turn it to account.

'5. Are you not struck with the warm emotion, and strong conviction, of the great British race throughout the world: that race which already tops 100 millions, and which increases by several millions a year.

'We shall, I hope, meet soon.—Most sincerely yours,

'W. E. GLADSTONE.'

That evening at the Reform Club Mr. Whitbread came to him 'to urge him to support a proposal to read the Bill a second time and then to hang it up for six months.'[2] The letter quoted above shows that Gladstone himself had commissioned Whitbread to discuss with Bright 'the question of time,' in other words the postponement of the Bill provided it were allowed a second reading. Bright describes the interview in his journal:

'Evening, Reform Club. Mr. Whitbread came up—long conversation with him—he supports Mr. Gladstone, but is anxious to get him out of his trouble with his Irish Bills. Could the Bill be read a second time and then withdrawn? Difficulty great—no solution possible at the moment.'

Four days later Bright gave Mr. Whitbread a definite answer in the following letter, in which he urged that Mr. Gladstone should withdraw the Bill before the division on second reading:

'EUSTON HOTEL, May 17 '86.

'MY DEAR MR. WHITBREAD,—I have not seen Lord Hartington since our conversation—it seemed useless to go to him, as the meeting at Devonshire House had decided unanimously that they would not under any circumstances vote for the 2nd reading.

[1] Sexton's angry speech in the House, July 28, 1885, in answer to Bright's charge against the Irish Members of being 'disloyal to the Crown.'

[2] *Life of Gladstone*, bk. ix. chap. vii. Mr. Whitbread was 'the old Parliamentary friend, of great weight and authority,' there spoken of by Lord Morley.

'I met Mr. Caine later in the evening—he is active in the case, and he confirmed what I had before heard. I think, with their views, they are quite right in refusing. To read the Bill a 2nd time would add great strength to the demands of the rebel party—they would say, "Your most eminent minister has made this proposition, and your Imperial Parliament has in effect and in principle accepted it. Who shall now deny it to us?" The 2nd reading would be recorded on the journals of the House, and the effect and result would be important.

'I think there is only one thing which Mr. Gladstone can do wisely, and with any good result—that is to withdraw the Bill before the 2nd reading Division.

'If it is carried, which is now thought impossible, it can only be by a majority so small that the Bill cannot go on. It must be withdrawn, and its author and the House and the public can only regard this as a defeat. Would it not be better to withdraw now, in terms of explanation which Mr. G. could so well use, which would add something of dignity to defeat; expressing a hope that further consideration on both sides of the Channel would enable Parliament to deal more successfully with the question at an early period?

'If Government is beaten, there is talk of dissolution. I cannot believe Mr. G. will dissolve—it would only make the Liberal split the more serious, and make it beyond the power of healing. He would be responsible for the greatest wound the Party has received since it was a Party. What a dissolution would bring, no one knows—greater strength to the Tories I cannot doubt—some, perhaps great weakness to the Liberals—a feeling of great bitterness between the two sections of Liberals, and, in my opinion, no power in the new House to deal with the great question before us. If the Bill were now withdrawn, the whole present difficulty in our Party would be gone. In the further business of the session something useful would be done. The rebels friendly to our Leader would for a time not be in an unfriendly mood to him, and the present growing bitterness would be healed.

'Mr. G. can do all this if he has courage and strength—no one else can do it, and he can do it with the unanimous approval of all his friends. *He* has a multitude of friends—but the Bill, himself disconnected from it, has no friends unless in the Irish Party in the House.

'I am urged by several men in the House to say in the House what I now am writing. I fear to speak—lest I should say too much. So I write to you, as I rely on your Parliamentary wisdom, and if there is anything in this letter which meets your view, I hope you will speak your mind to Mr. G.—perhaps he may take the course of wisdom and dignity. Yours very sincerely,

'JOHN BRIGHT.'

In his journal for that day he notes:

'May 17. Gave letter to Mr. Whitbread. Spoke to Mr. Chamberlain, whose anxiety is very apparent; showed him the letter to Whitbread. Talk with Harcourt in his room; he says a dissolution of Parliament will follow the defeat of the Irish Bill. I condemned it [viz. a dissolution] as a wicked policy leading probably to greater confusion and difficulty.'

Then came the famous meeting in Committee Room 15—a place of evil omen for the unity of parties. The invitations to this conference were issued, not to Lord Hartington and the unequivocal opponents of Home Rule in any and every form, but only to those Liberal Members 'who being in favour of some sort of autonomy for Ireland, disapproved of the Government Bills in their present shape.' Whether John Bright should have been held to belong to this group rather than to Lord Hartington's the readers of this chapter can judge for themselves. In any case he wrote to Mr. Chamberlain the following letter, which materially influenced the decision come to at this meeting; and the meeting was thought to hold in its hands the event of the coming division on the Bill:

'May 31, 1886.

'MY DEAR CHAMBERLAIN,—My present intention is to vote against the Second Reading, not having spoken in the debate. I am not willing to have my view of the Bill or Bills in any doubt. But I am not willing to take the responsibility of advising others as to their course. If they can content themselves with abstaining from the division, I shall be glad. They will render a greater service by preventing the threatened dissolution than by compelling it, if Mr. Gladstone is unwise enough to venture upon it. You will see from this exactly where I am. A small majority for the Bill may be almost as good as its defeat and may save the country from the heavy sacrifice of a General Election. I wish I could join you, but I cannot now change the path I have taken from the beginning of this unhappy discussion. Believe me always, Sincerely yours, JOHN BRIGHT.

'*P.S.*—If you think it of any use you may read this note to your friends.'

For what happened in the Committee Room we have the narrative of Mr. Chamberlain, who presided at it, supplied in the following letter to Mr. John Albert Bright, dated January 16, 1899:

'MY DEAR BRIGHT,—I now send you in two small packets all the letters I have from your father which are of any interest. . . .

'The smaller packet contains the celebrated letter read in Committee Room 15, and two letters immediately following on the same subject.

'Mr Caine appears to me to be very loose in the statements which have been attributed to him. As far as I know he received no letter from your father. Certainly he never read one. The only letter read at the meeting was the one I now send you, and it was read in full from beginning to end. The real point before the meeting was whether they should vote against the Second Reading and so destroy the Bill and bring about a dissolution, or should abstain from voting, thereby allowing the Bill to be carried by a small majority and reserving further opposition to a subsequent stage.

'Your father's announcement that he intended to vote against the Second Reading undoubtedly affected the decision, which I have no doubt now was the correct one.

'I opened the meeting in a speech which I endeavoured to make absolutely impartial, putting the respective advantages of the two courses of action without giving any opinion of my own. I concluded by reading your father's letter.

'Caine, Trevelyan and some others strongly supported opposition to the Second Reading, and a minority preferred to abstain ; but after the vote had been taken, on a second vote there was, I believe, a unanimous resolution to oppose the Second Reading.

'After the first vote was taken I stated my entire concurrence with it. . . . Believe me, Yours very truly,

'J. CHAMBERLAIN.'

On the day after this meeting, John Bright wrote the following letter:

'EUSTON HOTEL, June 1, '86.

'MY DEAR CHAMBERLAIN,—I was surprised when Mr. Caine told me last night of your decision and that my proposed vote had much influenced it—for my note was intended to make it more easy for you and your friends to abstain from voting in the coming division. If I had thought I should do harm I should have said something *more* or *less*. Even now if it is not too late I could join you in abstaining if we could save the House and the country from a dissolution which may for the Liberal Party turn out a catastrophe the magnitude of which cannot be measured. For myself I have no anxiety, for to leave Parliament now would be an immense relief, but I care for the Party and for its objects and for the country.

'To dissolve will be an act of grievous wrong on the part of the Minister, the question does not require it, the country does not demand it, and only the pride of the chief who is disappointed at his failure can make it in any way necessary.

'I am very much grieved at the crisis at which we have arrived and wish I could discover any way of escape. If there is no way we must submit, but the prospect is very gloomy for the Party and for the two countries.

'Lord Hartington meets his friends this afternoon. Having moved the amendment, to withdraw is almost, perhaps quite, impossible with him and them.

'You are to speak this evening and will have to declare your course. So that I fear there is not time for any reconsideration of the position unless you make some reservation which will enable you to change front before Thursday. I will do anything I can to meet your views. Yours sincerely, JOHN BRIGHT.

'I shall be at the Reform Club if you have anything to write.'

'EUSTON HOTEL, June 5, '86.

'MY DEAR CHAMBERLAIN,—I see nothing more that can be done. Mr. G. is very obstinate and I suspect cannot now yield. I see some of the Government party ask for my letter to you. I am unwilling to put any weapon into their hands, although in that letter I see nothing that can be of use to them. I am not sure we shall have a dissolution if the Bill is rejected, for I suspect the Government people are less confident as to the future Parliament. Courtney told me yesterday that John Morley was in low spirits at their prospects. I should think so, whether they get a small majority or are beaten. I seem unable to speak, but I should not fear an hour in your Town Hall. The [National Liberal] Federation seems gone or nearly so, perhaps it is not so great a misfortune as some have imagined. Jealousy is the great enemy of union, and Birmingham has been too large and too earnest to please those affected with envy. I am not sure that the fear of dissolution will not after all carry the second reading. I shall regret it, but the discussions between now and October or February will I hope more effectually kill the Bill. But I believe no [Irish] Parliament is needed and I shall not support one. Always yours very sincerely,

'JOHN BRIGHT.

'I thought your speech admirable.'

On June 7 the Home Rule Bill was defeated on second reading by 341 votes to 311, John Bright voting in the majority. Two days later he wrote to Mr. Chamberlain about the draft of an address on the Irish question, which was passing about between the three Liberal Unionist leaders:

'I have received your address from Lord Hartington. It is perhaps rather long, but it is in the main very good. I think it better not to have it signed by the three names, as we do not really quite agree as to the Irish question. I am against anything in the shape of taking the name of a Parliament in Dublin, and I will not go to the Colonies for an example for us. The Canadian Confederation is even now showing symptoms of breaking down, and I wish to maintain the unity of our Government. Our business seems to me to be to show that the Bills are bad, rather than to suggest something better, although if I go down to Birmingham I may try to prove that "the resources of civilisation are not yet exhausted."

'I have just had a long talk with Harcourt, he is for dissolution and professes to be strong for the Dublin

Parliament as the only possible thing after Gladstone's concessions to the Irish. He expects violence, outrages, and no rent and no remedy except coercion of the worst quality, if even that be a remedy. The strife seems even now beginning in Ireland, and it may spread and the future is dark. It is sad that this has been promoted by the unwise action of our great Minister. Harcourt says there will be no contests in Birmingham. I hope this is true, though I should think it rather doubtful. For myself, I waver from day to day as to the wisdom or the duty of remaining in Parliament. I see no prospect of further usefulness. And quiet, after long years of work, is both needful and pleasant.

'Perhaps the storm may blow over, but some wrecks may strew the shore.'

Gladstone dissolved Parliament and went to the country on the Home Rule issue. Bright thought the dissolution very wrong indeed, because it made the split in the Liberal party definitive. At the General Election he was, for the last time, returned by his Birmingham constituents. The speech that he made to them in the Town Hall on July 1 was of great importance in guiding the votes of Liberals all over the country who disliked Home Rule, but disliked also to break with their party. An exhortation from John Bright to put the Union above the Liberal party could not fail to have an immense effect. The combination of Lord Hartington, John Bright, and Mr. Chamberlain, each appealing to three different sections and spirits in the Liberal party—the Whig, the old traditional Radicalism, and the new Radicalism—was ruinous to the least prospect of Gladstonian success. Bright's great Birmingham speech was widely circulated, and produced a profound impression because it was his. And it was, in itself, a powerful marshalling of the arguments against Home Rule. Lord Morley writes of it: 'The heaviest and most telling attack came from Mr. Bright, who had up to now in public been studiously silent. Every word, as they said of Daniel Webster, seemed to weigh a pound. His arguments were delivered with a gravity and force that told powerfully upon the large phalanx of doubters all over the kingdom.' At the end of this speech he put forward an alternative proposal for an Irish Committee for Irish Bills in the House of Commons.

In his last Parliament, sitting as a Liberal ally of a Conservative Government, Bright said little, and his most important action was a silent one. Lord George Hamilton, who watched it as an interested spectator from the Treasury Bench, thus describes the occasion :

> 'On March 22nd, 1887, Mr. W. H. Smith made the following motion : "That the introduction and second stage of the Criminal Law Amendment (Ireland) Bill have precedence of all Orders of the Day and Notices of Motions," etc.
>
> 'On that an amendment was moved by Mr. John Morley : "That the House declines to set aside the business of the Nation in favour of a measure for increasing the stringency of the Criminal Law in Ireland whilst no effectual security has been taken against the abuse of the Law by the exactions of excessive rents."
>
> 'The Debate commenced on the 22nd, and lasted until the 25th March. Mr. John Bright took no part in the discussion, but a great deal depended upon the action which he personally took. If he abstained from voting or voted against the Government, the Unionist Coalition would have been practically broken up. On the other hand if he, in order to avert Home Rule, voted for a procedure which was so contrary to his previous professions, the Coalition would receive fresh source of strength and cohesion.
>
> 'When the Division Bell rang, Mr. Bright, who was sitting close by Gladstone, without a moment's hesitation walked straight into the Government lobby.'

In these last two years he saw nothing of Mr. Gladstone, but he was often thinking and talking of him. Two such men who have been so close to each other for so long and done such great things together, cannot part and think no more about it. It was much better that he should speak as severely of Gladstone as he did than that he should have been indifferent. When he heard news of Mr. Gladstone he used to put it down in his journal :

> 'Conversation with M. Waddington, the French Ambassador, who had visited Mr. Gladstone at Dollis Hill a month ago. In talk with Mr. Gladstone found him absorbed in the Irish question—on former occasions they could discuss other subjects—he would always rise to Homer or some other literary topic, but now Homer failed, and only Ireland

now, always Ireland. He thought, while as brilliant as ever in point of language, that his judgment was impaired —one idea had got full possession of him.'

At length chance brought Bright and Gladstone together in a London street. The careful entry in the journal, with the hour and the spot noted as he was not accustomed to note the details of casual meetings, shows that to Bright the occasion was full of emotions which he does not attempt to define.

'February 17, 1887. Walking along Piccadilly, I met Mr. Gladstone—had not seen him since the defeat of his Irish Bill last year. We stopped and shook hands. I remarked we had been far apart for some time. He said: "I hope we may before long be nearer together again," which I doubted or feared we might not be. I asked after his family: his son Herbert is in India, but is soon expected home. Herbert told him how good in India had been the influence of Lord Ripon's Government. Mr. Gladstone took his glove off to shake hands with me as indicating more cordiality of feeling. We met at 1.30 just opposite the house where one of the Rothschilds lived—I think the house where Lady Rosebery's mother lived.'

Four months later an exchange of letters took place; Gladstone wrote to correct a statement of Bright, and Bright replied as follows:

'June 14, 1887.

'My remark as to your speech was not strictly accurate. I wrote from memory, and the sentence about Ulster was not sufficiently definite to have fixed itself in my memory. I regret the apparent want of accuracy. But on reading over the report of your speech I may observe that you deal with the Ulster question in a way not calculated to give any comfort or any hope to the loyal population of that Province. In dealing with this question, even in a speech to Welshmen, I think Ulster has a claim upon you for a definite expression of opinion as to your plan for the future Government of the Province. Your plan a year ago was to place Ulster under the rule of a Parliament in Dublin, and the people know and dread that their fortunes would be subject to the control of a body of men about whose character and aims you and I differ very seriously—you deem them patriots, I hold them to be not patriots, but conspirators against the Crown and Government of the

United Kingdom. It is not long since we agreed, or, I thought we agreed, on this point. You have changed your opinion, I can only regret that I have not been able to change mine.

'The recent astounding revelations in the *Times* newspaper must have confirmed the fears and anxieties of the people of Ulster, and have increased their dread of being subjected to the rule of Mr. Parnell and of his agents and followers in Ireland and in the House of Commons. I grieve that I cannot act with you as in years past, but my judgment and my conscience forbid it.

'If I have said a word that seems harsh or unfriendly, I will ask you to forgive it.'

CHAPTER XXII

THE DEATH OF JOHN BRIGHT

'Nothing is here for tears, nothing to wail
Or knock the breast, no weakness, no contempt,
Dispraise, or blame, nothing but well and fair,
And what may quiet us in a death so noble.'
MILTON, *Samson Agonistes.*

JOHN BRIGHT'S last illness and death took place at One Ash, the house where he had lived for half a century, during so many happy and so many lonely years. Just across the common lay the factories where his workpeople were employed, and Greenbank where the home of his birth and childhood used once to stand, and where his brother Thomas still lived, although in a new house. John Bright was taken seriously ill in May 1888, recovered to some extent in August and September, and became worse again in October. In the last week of November, knowing that he was in extreme danger, he sent for his children, told them his wishes, and finally arranged his affairs. His calmness and fortitude, and his kindness in thinking of every one, touched all around him. On November 27 his son Albert, who saw eye to eye with him in politics, and had been much in his confidence, wrote the following letter to Mr. Gladstone:

'My Father is sinking, and the end cannot be far off. He sent for me last night when he became aware of his condition in order to tell me of some things which he wished me to attend to after his death, and he wished me to write to you and tell you that "he could not forget your unvarying kindness to him and the many services you have rendered to the country." He was very weak and did not seem able to say any more, and I saw the tears running down his cheeks. He is quite conscious and calm, and suffers no pain. He is just slipping away from us.'

To this letter Mr. Gladstone replied from Hawarden on the same day:

'I thank you very much for your kindness in writing to me, and I am deeply touched and moved by hearing that I have been even for a moment in your Father's thoughts at this solemn hour.

'I can assure you that he has been little absent of late from mine, that my feelings towards him are entirely unaltered by any of the occurrences of the last three years, and that I have never felt separated from him in spirit. I heartily pray that he may enjoy the peace of God on this side the grave and on the other.

'His many noble acts and words will live in the memory of his countrymen, and in my own they will always be associated with a thankful sense of the singularly harmonious relations which during many years it was permitted me to hold with him as friend and as colleague.

'With the terms of your letter before me I dare not send him a message; but, if there should be when you receive this letter a time of favourable reaction, I should much prize his knowing that all his kindly sentiments are returned now when his hour draws near and mine can hardly be far distant.'

Letters and telegrams of sympathy came in from all manner of people, from the Queen downwards. Among others came the following:

'DEAR SIR,—I trust I may be permitted notwithstanding temporary political differences, to express my profound sympathy with you in your illness and my best hopes for a speedy and secure recovery. Your great services to our people can never be forgotten, for it was when Ireland had fewest friends that your voice was loudest on her side. I hope you may still be spared to raise it on her behalf according to your conceptions of what is best, for while we go on struggling for our own views, there can be nothing but regrets on our part for the sharpness of division in the past.

'Again wishing you strength and comfort, I remain.
Your obedient servant, TIM HEALY.'

The latter part of his illness was protracted for four months, without acute suffering, but with ever increasing weakness, patiently borne. During this long watch he was nursed by his daughters in turn, aided by his friend and housekeeper, Mrs. E. Rowntree, who afterwards wrote as follows :

> 'I should like to add my own testimony to the beauty of Mr. Bright's home life, where I best knew him. His unfailing courtesy and consideration for all about him were very striking. He shrank from giving trouble and always acknowledged any little attention most kindly. His generous heart was ever open to any appeal for help, and full of sympathy for any one in trouble. To me he was the best and kindest of friends, and during his long illness, so patiently and cheerfully borne, it was the greatest privilege I have ever known to be near him and wait upon him.'

His faithful little dog 'Fly' was his constant companion. A devoted nurse cared for him during the long restless nights. During these months his little granddaughters came to One Ash, and when he was well enough sat quietly in his room ; even when very ill he liked to have them. His love for children was great, and the gentleness of his manner always drew them to him ; more than once he was heard to say, 'There is nothing in the world that gives as much pleasure as poetry—except little children.'

At length, when spring was returning, the end came. On March 27, 1889, a beautiful clear morning, after some hours of unconsciousness, he sank peacefully to his rest.

> 'He was placed in the coffin on Thursday evening,' wrote one of his daughters, 'and they carried him down to the drawing-room, where he was laid in the middle of the room, just where Helen's young mother lay 48 years before. His little shaded lamp was placed on a table at the head of the coffin. He looked exquisite—his face refined and pure, with a look of majesty on it and perfect peace.
>
> 'On Friday the workpeople from the Mill came to see him. It was a strange and touching sight ; they came straight from the Mill in their working clothes—the women with their shawls over their heads, and many brought their children. It was curious to watch their faces as they came, a constant stream, walking gently in single file round that coffin and out again, in perfect silence, many quietly weeping, especially the older people who had been at the Mill all their lives.

'Aunt Tilla's (Mrs. McLaren's) little bunch of flowers lay beside him, giving one touch of colour to the surrounding whiteness. He looked so beautiful, it was hard to close the coffin—we all returned to see the beloved face over and over again.

'The funeral day was like a long terrible dream, and I remember little of it clearly. The vast crowds, the perfect order, the impressive silence and evident sorrow and sympathy of all, were very touching—I think everything was done as he himself would have liked it.'

And so he lies, 'as he himself would have liked it,' not under Gothic arches hung with conquered flags and echoing back the organ's peal, not among warriors and princes, and the statesmen who played for fame and power; but under the northern sky, in front of the humble house of peace where he had worshipped as a child, in silence sometimes broken by the sound of workmen's footsteps up the steep flagged street, he dwells among his own people.

INDEX